Microfoundations of Economic Growth

The International Schumpeter Society, founded in 1986, is a group of economists who share the aim to promote the scientific study of the problems of economic development and innovation along the lines suggested by Joseph Alois Schumpeter. The series includes the volumes that come from the biennial meetings of the Schumpeter Society.

Microfoundations of Economic Growth

A Schumpeterian Perspective

Gunnar Eliasson and Christopher Green, Editors

Charles R. McCann, Jr., Associate Editor

Ann Arbor

THE UNIVERSITY OF MICHIGAN PRESS

A CIP catalog record for this book is available from the British Library.

Library of Congress Cataloging-in-Publication Data

Microfoundations of economic growth : a Schumpeterian perspective
      p.   cm.
   "International Schumpeter Society series."
   Selected papers from the sixth biennial conference of the
International Schumpeter Society, held in Stockholm, June 3–5,
1996.
   Includes bibliographical references and index.
   ISBN 0-472-10904-9 (alk. paper)
   1. Technological innovations — Economic aspects — Congresses.
2. Economic development — Congresses.   3. Evolutionary economics —
Congresses.   4. Schumpeter, Joseph Alois, 1883–1950 — Congresses.
I. Eliasson, Gunnar.   II. Green, Christopher.   III. McCann, Charles
R. (Charles Robert), 1956–   .   IV. International Schumpeter
Society.   Meeting (6th : 1996 : Stockholm, Sweden)
HC79.T4M52   1998
338'.064 — dc21   98-5012
                                                                          CIP

Contents

Acknowledgments

The Sixth Biennial Conference of the International Schumpeter Society was held in Stockholm, June 3–5, 1996. The conference drew a record number of submissions and participants. This volume, entitled *Microfoundations of Economic Growth: A Schumpeterian Perspective,* is a set of 22 essays drawn from the nearly 100 presented. The title of the volume aptly describes the main theme of the conference.

At the Stockholm meeting, the 1996 Schumpeter Prize was awarded to Maureen McKelvey for her book *Evolutionary Innovation: The Business of Bio-Technology,* Oxford University Press, 1996. The Schumpeter Prize was donated and the award dinner underwritten by the German economic weekly magazine *Wirtschaftswoche.* We express our appreciation to *Wirtschaftswoche* for its continuing support of the Schumpeter Society. The conference was made possible by a generous grant from the Marcus Wallenberg Foundation for International Scientific Cooperation and from several Swedish corporations. Because of the generosity of the Swedish State Railways (Statens Järnvägar), some sessions were conducted on a conference train between Falun and Stora. Stora, the world's oldest corporation, a mining and forestry firm founded in 1288, hosted the society's General Assembly. We are grateful to the City of Stockholm for the magnificent reception in the City Hall on the opening day. To the members of the Scientific Committee and to the persons who handled local organizing, notably Monica Hamrén, Christina Carlsson, Staffan Laestadius, and Per Storm, we wish to say thanks for a job well done. Finally, we wish to thank Edith Breiner and Wera Nyren for secretarial services in the preparation of the volume.

The following firms and institutions contributed to the Sixth International Conference of the Schumpeter Society.

ALMI Företagspartner	OM-Börsen	SCANIA
ASTRA	PERSTORP	STORA
ABB	The SAAB Group	TELIA
ERICSSON	Statens Järnvägar	

Other contributors include:

The Marcus Wallenberg Foundation for International Scientific Cooperation
The City of Stockholm
The Industrial Institute for Economic and Social Research (IUI)

Introduction

Gunnar Eliasson and Christopher Green

The theme of the Sixth Biennial Conference of the International Schumpeter Society held in Stockholm, Sweden, was the microfoundations of economic growth. The microfoundations theme of this volume stands in some contrast to earlier Schumpeter Society conference volumes. Previous volumes reflected such Schumpeterian themes as evolutionary economics (1986), technology and market structure (1988), the role of technological innovation and technological change in economic growth (1990), innovation and institutional change at the industry level (1992), and technological progress and economic dynamics (1994). This volume brings several of these themes together, linking the institutions that support market processes and firm behavior to the performance of the macroeconomy.

The collection of essays included in this volume, therefore, provides the reader with a different perspective on the "microfoundations of economic growth" — one that the editors would broadly describe as Schumpeterian. Our use of the term *microfoundations* is broader, more dynamic, and less *formally* rigorous than the meaning given that term in traditional, neoclassical, or neo-Walrasian — to use Clower's term — static aggregation. We strongly believe that the study of microinstitutions such as firms, and the evolving nature of markets, are necessary ingredients to understanding macro-oriented phenomena such as economic growth. It is in this sense, then, that this collection is concerned with microfoundations.

Realigning the Microfoundations

Standard neoclassical theorizing combines the analysis of agent behavior (utility maximization) with the analysis of the agents' technical constraints (production function). At the time it was propounded in the late nineteenth century, the utility maximization hypothesis raised eyebrows. However, for the most part, economists have effectively blunted attacks on the neoclassical foundations of individual agent (consumer) behavior and have done so in a more or less convincing fashion since the concepts of expected utility and bounded rationality were added to the vocabulary.

In contrast to the microfoundations of consumer behavior, the neoclassical production function version of the firm has come under increasing attack. Criticism of the bare-bones, neoclassical version of the firm has had two mainsprings of inspiration. The first, transaction cost theorizing, dates from the early 1970s when Alchian and Demsetz and Williamson attempted to reinvigorate, operationalize, and extend the insights of Coase's seminal paper "The Nature of the Firm" (1937).

The second strand is the renewed interest in the work of Joseph Schumpeter, especially on the role of innovation and institutional/technical change. The rekindling of interest in Schumpeter's theories came at a time (early 1980s) when the post–oil crisis world economy was in disorder, economic growth had seemingly disappeared, and what had served as mainstream economic theory (static neo-Walrasian and Keynesian) gave little intellectual insight and no, or the wrong, guidance to policymakers. As a result, there was a renewed interest in growth theory, a development that was abetted by the establishment of the International Schumpeter Society in 1986.

The indications are that the transaction cost–Schumpeterian attack on the neo-Walrasian foundations of general equilibrium theory will not be as easy for neoclassical orthodoxy to blunt as were the critiques of marginal utility analysis. The growing evidence that coordination, communication, and transaction costs account for a large, perhaps dominant, share of resource use in an advanced economy, not a negligible or small part, makes it necessary to model explicitly economic organization and information processing in markets and hierarchies, using expanded versions of neoclassical theorizing. To accommodate this extension, the assumptional structure of neo-Walrasian, general equilibrium theory must be pried open to make room for live actors who behave in dynamic markets. To understand economic growth, one needs innovators, entrepreneurs, and firms as an explicit part of the theory.

The 22 papers that comprise this volume are all in one way or another concerned with firms; they attempt to say something about how economic theory should treat its production agent, the firm, in light of what is known about technical change and evolving institutions. As might be expected of essays initially presented at a Schumpeter Society conference, almost all have something to do with, or say about, innovation. But, although innovation is a common thread, only the essays in part 3 of the volume make it the center of attention. The remainder are either concerned with how innovation influences the way in which we should view the firm and entrepreneurship or how innovating behavior, in the aggregate, feeds through labor markets and investment decisions to influence an economy's employment, investment, or growth rate. Taken as a whole, the essays in this book carry the reader beyond the realm of the firm and industry to the economy as a whole. It is in this sense that the essays contribute to the microfoundations of growth.

The Context: Institutions, Markets, and Entrepreneurs

The essays that comprise parts 1 and 2 of the volume tackle institutional-organizational-historical issues that are preliminary to a study of the firm and support viable market processes.

In "Institutions, Organizations, and Market Competition," Douglass C. North provides a setting for much that follows. He makes a fundamental point: one cannot introduce Schumpeterian ideas (innovation) into the standard theory of firms and markets without considering transaction costs and other elements of the new institutional economics. Technological change involves knowledge, and the protection and use of proprietary knowledge involves (transactions) costs. Moreover, technological change, through the process of creative destruction, can produce a degree of social upheaval, which, in turn, involves costs. For the benefits to exceed the costs, the productive force of technological change must be large — as indeed it is.

In "Paradigm Lost," Frank M. Machovec shows how the static, equilibrium-centered version of the market adopted by neoclassical economists sterilized the evolutionary and dynamic conception of the market that was inherited from the classicals. Machovec views Schumpeter's theme of "creative destruction" as an attempt to breathe new life into the concept of the market. He also argues that in all but name "creative destruction" is a classical concept, one that was lost after the Walrasian version of the market became firmly implanted.

Richard N. Langlois reopens an old debate: the role of entrepreneurs — a debate made important by Schumpeter's apparent change of mind between 1911, when the *Theory of Economic Development* (TED) first appeared, and 1942, when *Capitalism, Socialism, and Democracy* (CSD) appeared. The entrepreneur of TED is the "hero" of the piece (almost Wagnerian in stature). He is the innovator in a world (very modern in tone) in which innovation includes finding new markets and introducing new organizational forms as well as the development of new products and production processes. This is "personal capitalism." By the time CSD appears, Schumpeter has relegated innovation to the R&D laboratory of corporations — firms large enough to afford a formal search for new products and processes. Personal capitalism gives way to "managerial capitalism" and its logical extension, "organizational capabilities." Langlois argues, however, that "some essential part of capitalism must always remain personal," and illustrates his point with the example of the Swiss watch industry.

The institutions and infrastructures that contribute to the evolution of industry are partly collective, but mostly private, and develop endogenously as part of industrial evolution. Such evolution can best be understood historically. Jan Glete recounts how the extremely successful industrialization of Sweden included the development of a management competence structure that is perhaps best illustrated by the now-successful giant engineering firms founded around the turn of the century. These firms have provided generous career opportunities for talented young managers for several generations, luring them away from the bolder and more demanding tasks of entrepreneurship and the establishment of new firms. But this closely knit and increasingly narrow competence infrastructure may now be locking Sweden into an industrial-technological regime of the past, in a manner similar to that demonstrated analytically in the Ballot and Taymaz essay. The consequence has been an increasing concentration of Swedish manufacturing output in a small number of large, international, and so far successful firms. However, this structure is increasingly exposed and vulnerable to the new innovative and competitive forces in the world. The disappearance of "personal capitalism" (discussed by Langlois) in Sweden is one possible explanation for this vulnerability.

In contrast to Langlois and Glete, S. Y. Wu approaches the role of the entrepreneur from a theoretical perspective. As with Machovec, Wu argues that the neoclassical model cannot explain the boundary between firms and markets, and only with the greatest of difficulty can it incorporate growth and technological change. (This is a theme that Clower picks up in the final essay in the volume). According to Wu, what is needed is a model of an entrepreneur-centered economy. Wu goes on to sketch the nature of such an economy and its temporary equilibrium methodology, and he then compares his model's treatment of firms, equilibrium, growth, and development with that of the neoclassical model.

In Machovec's and Wu's essays, legal institutions are given and/or not specified. In Clas Wihlborg's essay, legal institutions are central to market processes and develop endogenously. Wihlborg introduces the concept of *enabling law,* as opposed to *mandatory* law, under which contractual arrangements are specified in detail and cannot be changed without a change in the law. Enabling law is a legal framework that facilitates the creation of flexible and customized contracts, ones that contribute to dynamic market processes and efficiency. There are two dimensions to enabling law: the first is flexible and customized contracts, and the second is the development of flexible interpretations and enforcement of desirable voluntary contracts.

While enabling law may increase visible contractual and litigation costs, mandatory law, by supporting inflexible and thereby dynamically inefficient contracts, leads to larger real (if not explicitly accounted for) costs in the form of lost output and slower economic growth. In contrast, enabling law is conducive to dynamic efficiency. By extending competition to contractual, institutional, and organizational arrangements, Wihlborg's enabling law provides at least a partial response to the transactions-cost-increasing nature of technological change that is the main concern of Douglass North's essay.

The Firm as Innovator

The nine essays that comprise part 3 focus on the firm as an innovator in addition to its standard role as a producer. In "Bounded Rationality and Firm Performance in the Experimental Economy," Richard H. Day makes a central point. If "bounded rationality" is taken as given, as it must be, then organizational decision making should be viewed as experimental, and tacit knowledge becomes important, as Eliasson (1992) has argued. The experimental nature of decision making shows up in the way economic agents economize, manage, communicate, perform, and coordinate. Such experimentation necessarily requires institutional arrangements that make real markets and real economic agents markedly different from the neo-Walrasian characterization of the rational actor in a pure market economy.

To deal with the uncertainty of the experimentally organized economy, Day defines five means of what he calls *economizing behavior,* namely, experimentation, imitation, more or less undirected search, habitual repetition, and creative visualization. All these notions of behavior more or less contradict explicit optimization. Much of the underlying rationale for this behavior is not communicable. Thus, tacit knowledge becomes the foundation of firm behavior and characterizes firm management and the nature of the market process.

In their essay "Routinized Innovations," Uwe Cantner, Horst Hanusch, and Andreas Pyka address the ways in which firms make R&D decisions and allocations. Instead of formulating the decision-making process in standard optimization terms, the authors ask what set of rules shape the innovative strategies of firms. Various strategies are explored using the technique of simulation. Cantner et al. find that an "absorptive" strategy (one that focuses on the firm's ability to explore and exploit technological spillovers) dominates a conservative strategy (reliance on one's own research) or an imitative one. This finding lends support to Day's experimental view of decision making and to Carlsson's technological systems approach to firm dynamics, with its emphasis on the role of spillovers. The finding is supported by empirical evidence (see, e.g., the Arvanitis and Hollenstein paper) on the importance of spillovers.

The dynamic aggregation effects of systems formation is studied by Bo Carlsson. He views the firm in terms of a *technological system* that leverages up the effects of generic technologies such as robotics and the microprocessor. The main function of a technological system, according to Carlsson, is to capture and enhance spillovers and exploit the existing knowledge base more efficiently than can the market. To look at spillovers as externalities, Carlsson argues, is to underestimate seriously their systems effects. Rather, he emphasizes the synergetic effects of the *competence* of agents to exploit the knowledge available. As we shall see, empirical work reported in this volume also indicates that spillovers and competencies are important influences on firm productivity.

The next three essays focus on knowledge formation in specific industries: biotechnology, information technology, and the paper industry. In "Knowledge Sources in Biotechnology through the Schumpeterian Lens," David B. Audretsch and Paula E. Stephan explore the knowledge production function in one of the most dynamic, innovation-intensive industries: biotechnology. The authors provide theoretical and empirical support for the proposition that an important input to the innovating firm is "tacit," as distinct from "scientific," knowledge. Supporting evidence is found in the geographical concentration of biotechnology firms relative to the network of scientists on whom they depend. Audretsch and Stephan conjecture that in biotechnology it is the firm that is *endogenous,* and scientific knowledge that is *exogenous,* rather than what is usually supposed: *exogenously* existing firms *endogenously* seeking out and applying knowledge inputs.

As Audretsch and Stephan acknowledge, their view of the creation of (many) firms in the biotechnology sector is traceable to an observation by Frank Knight (1921). Knight suggested that an agent who is deciding how best to appropriate the value of his endowment must choose between hiring out to a firm at the going wage or setting up his or her own firm. Audretsch and Stephan theorize that when the endowment is new scientific knowledge, the commercial possibilities of which are often difficult for outsiders to assess, agents who wish to maximize the return to their knowledge will often find it necessary, or desirable, to create a new firm. More than incidentally, this view of the entry decision has implications for the treatment of entry barriers in highly innovative industries.

Maureen McKelvey investigates R&D investment as a premarket selection process in which genuine uncertainty (as distinct from computable risks) rules, but firms nevertheless have to reach a decision as to how to proceed. She applies her reasoning to two genuinely uncertain R&D projects: Genentech's genetically engineered and produced growth hormone (a winner) and Ericsson's ATM project, which the firm discontinued.

According to McKelvey, R&D fulfills three functions: (1) the generation of novelty, (2) the development and maintenance of competencies, and (3) the development of project selection criteria. McKelvey focuses on the last of these, the role of internal selection criteria, and thereby complements Day's view that organizational decision making in the presence of bounded rationality is experimental.

Staffan Laestadius's study of the Swedish paper industry questions the closeness of the link between technology level and knowledge formation, on the one hand, the R&D expenditure (investments) on the other. Laestadius shows that the success of the Swedish paper industry depended heavily on (1) large-scale standardization, in order to capture increasing returns, and (2) traditional on-the-job learning of technologies. The main focus of both management and investment decisions in the industry has been on the exploitation of economies of scale in the production of a single output line. But, in failing to develop new products, is the industry preparing itself, as Glete's essay suggests, for a less successful future?

The next four essays use national data sets (Canadian, Finnish, Swiss, and Italian) to assess the impact of knowledge inputs and outputs on firm performance. In the first of these essays, "Innovator Typologies, Competencies, and Performance," John R. Baldwin and Joanne Johnson evaluate the relationship between innovation and the success of small and medium-sized businesses. Using responses to a survey of Canadian firms, Baldwin and Johnson categorize the firms as process, product, or comprehensive (both product and process) innovators. They find that innovation, especially process innovation, and finance are related to firm success. However, none of the measures relating to investment, human resources, or management were (statistically) significantly related to success. The authors also find that comprehensive innovators are the most successful over the life cycle of the firm.

Aija Leiponen uses a panel data set of Finnish manufacturing firms to investigate the impact of firm competencies and knowledge capital on the economic performance of firms. Leiponen uses formal education and innovation as proxies for competencies and the *process* of accumulating internal capabilities and knowledge, respectively. Profits are used to measure firm performance. Leiponen finds that educational competencies are an important determinant of the profitability of manufacturing firms, that innovative firms tend to be more profitable than noninnovative ones, and that there is an interaction between innovativeness and competency.

Spyros Arvanitis and Heinz Hollenstein use Swiss firm data to explore the impact of knowledge capital spillovers on firm output and productivity. Using patent counts and R&D expenditures as proxies for knowledge capital and material input flows to account for spillovers, the authors confirm the existence of substantial spillovers from the innovative activities of other domestic firms and industries and foreign trade partners.

Rinaldo Evangelista, Guilio Perani, Fabio Rapiti, and Daniele Archibugi use survey data from Italian manufacturing industries to explore the characteristics and determinants of innovative activities in Italy. The authors find that: the main characteristic of innovative activity is its gradual, and cumulative, nature; the main determinant of innovative activity is firm size, with R&D highly concentrated in a small group of large firms; and the main outcome of innovative activity is its tendency to concentrate in certain industries.

The four empirical essays in part 3 help confirm the importance of innovation, knowledge, spillovers, and competency for firm performance. Despite the difficulties of properly measuring innovation, and the possibility that measured R&D spending may not be the most important input into innovation (as Laestadius observes), these essays, taken together, are important because they speak with a similar voice. Moreover, they do so based on the analysis of four different national data sets. The four essays not only provide crucial empirical support for the importance of R&D and other measured skill factors in explaining firm success, but they also indirectly provide confirmation of the importance of factors that are conducive to innovation: entrepreneurs, experimentation, acquired competence, and organizational modes capable of minimizing transaction costs.

Firm Dynamics, the Macroeconomy, and Economic Growth

The six essays in parts 4 and 5 move the analysis from the level of the firm to the economy as a whole. Gérard Ballot and Erol Taymaz use the MOSES model (a macroeconomic model with microfoundational elements on the production side that was developed by Eliasson) to investigate endogenous changes in technologies chosen by firms. The Ballot and Taymaz essay formally addresses the micro (interior firm) to macro problem. The authors use a firm-based evolutionary macromodel to investigate how boundedly rational firms choose among radically new technologies using a neural net learning pattern. There is an explicit representation of human capital as a platform from which to acquire competence and make successful technological choices. This is, in a way, an explicit modeling of McKelvey's problem of premarket selection. Ballot and Taymaz show that (under increasing returns) competition leads firms to cluster around a limited number of technologies. Locking in and locking out occur endogenously.

The novel and important finding of the Ballot and Taymaz essay is that minor events can tilt the economy into different evolutionary patterns and lock firms, or groups of firms, into more or less successful technologies for a long time. The macroeconomic effects of this nonlinear property are significant. In fact, the Ballot and Taymaz essay may help explain the macroeconomic consequences (observed by Glete) of the long-term historical lock-in of Swedish technology to long-established firms and manufacturing industries.

Countries as well as firms specialize. Thus, it is not surprising that we observe differences in the patterns of technological specialization across countries. Valentina Meliciani and Roberto Simonetti explore whether these differential patterns contribute to uneven growth among nations. Using patent data as a proxy for technological competencies, Meliciani and Simonetti find a positive association between the "quality" (measured in terms of technological opportunity and emerging technologies) of technological specialization and rates of growth for a sample of highly developed and medium-income countries for the period 1970–94.

How does skill-biased technical change affect the distribution of wages? In "Technology Regimes and the Distribution of Real Wages," George Johnson and Frank Stafford investigate the impact of a technical shift in favor of more skilled workers in sectors that previously were the domain of less skilled workers, such as the automobile industry. The authors employ a simple, closed-economy, macroeconomic model with a Cobb-Douglas production function. Within this framework, the shift in demand for skilled and unskilled labor affects not only wages but the availability of subsidized forms of compensation in kind, such as health benefits. The Johnson and Stafford essay suggests how and why the distribution of income is shifting away from the type of employment created by the post–World War II expansion of the U.S. manufacturing sector.

One of the factors affecting the distribution of labor income between skilled and unskilled workers is "corporate restructuring." Dagobert L. Brito, Michael D. Intriligator, and Erica R. Worth argue that corporate restructuring in the past decade substantially lagged technological changes that began a quarter century ago and made some workers unproductive or less productive. The authors argue that at first, as technological change occurred, implicit contracts contributed to the continued employment of workers now made unproductive. But eventually the deadweight of unproductiveness, and the added liabilities created by the elimination of mandatory retirement, induced corporate restructuring that eliminated many jobs and downsized the work forces of firms. The authors suggest that the driving force behind this breach of implicit contracts was the disappearance of the quasi rents initially produced by technological change. The essay nicely complements the Johnson and Stafford explanation of the impact of technological change on the distribution of real wages.

How important is human capital? Gunnar Eliasson and Pontus Braunerhjelm argue that human-embodied capital is the dominant input in production. It constitutes what can broadly be defined as "competence," the allocation of which is a driving force behind economic growth. The authors provide a broad measure of this form of capital, of which R&D is only a part, and estimate its impact on firm performance. A novel feature of the Eliasson-Braunerhjelm procedure is the use of valuations from the merger and acquisition market to bracket measures of intangible capital. Their estimates suggest that intangible (human-competence) capital was overwhelmingly important, creating increasing returns in labor and capital that were only limited by decreasing returns in learning or competence accumulation. The essay illustrates how standard econometric estimates can be interpreted in dynamic terms.

In the final essay in the volume, Robert W. Clower brings together some of the pieces in the puzzle of the microfoundations of economic growth. Clower makes clear that he is more sympathetic to the historical, institutional, and dynamic approach taken by Schumpeterians than he is to axiomatically based, neoclassical, general equilibrium analysis.

Clower begins by outlining the stylized microfacts necessary for an explanation of growth and contrasts these with the microfacts of neo-Walrasian theory. He then sets out an institutional and technical framework for economic growth, two fundamental components of which are an economy's wealth-consumption and wealth-income loci. One outcome of the interaction between these loci is the limited role of savings, alone, in generating growth. Thus, to account for rapid growth of productive capital, Clower argues, we are forced to look to the forces of invention and innovation and to institutions and policies that contribute to autonomous increases in per capita income. In this way, saving is viewed as a *lagged* adjustment to changes in consumption and real income.

Clower concludes that, while in developed countries continued growth depends on innovation, in developing economies growth depends on the willingness of a society not to consume all of its increases in productive wealth. Hence, faster growth in an underdeveloped economy implies that a substantial share of resources is kept from nonsavers and allocated to innovators-entrepreneurs. In an analogous fashion, the Eliasson and Braunerhjelm essay suggests that growth is abetted by an allocation that keeps resource flows away from government accounts and allocates them through private capitalists (cf. Langlois), who attach innovation and entrepreneurial competence to the resource flow.

As one reads through the essays in this volume, a number of themes are evident. One is that successful innovative performance of firms is crucial to sustained economic growth. Another is the possibility that its institutional structure could lock an economy into what eventually becomes an inferior technology or industrial structure (see Ballot and Taymaz, Glete, and Laestadius). A third is that bounded rationality gives rise to an experimental organization of the economy (see Day, Carlsson, Audretsch and Stephan, and Cantner et al.). Finally, several of the authors tend to orient their work toward the Schumpeter of the TED (1911) rather than the Schumpeter of the CSD (1942) (Langlois, Glete, Wu, Audretsch and Stephan and McKelvey). But, whatever the specific theme, the essays that follow make a convincing case for Schumpeterian underpinnings to economic growth.

REFERENCES

Alchian, Armen, and Harold Demsetz. 1972. "Production, Information Costs, and Economic Organization." *American Economic Review* 62 (December): 777–95.
Coase, Ronald H. 1937. "The Nature of the Firm." *Economica* (New Series), 4, no. 16 (November): 386–405.

Eliasson, Gunnar. 1992. "Business Competence, Organizational Learning, and Economic Growth: Establishing the Smith-Schumpeter-Wicksell (SSW) Connection." In *Entrepreneurship, Technological Innovation, and Economic Growth: Studies in the Schumpeterian Tradition,* edited by F. M. Scherer and M. Perlman. Ann Arbor: University of Michigan Press.

Knight, Frank H. 1921. *Risk, Uncertainty, and Profit.* New York: Houghton Mifflin Co.

Schumpeter, J. A. 1911. *Theorie der wirtschaftlichen Entwicklung.* Berlin: Humbolt und Duncker. (Translated in 1934 as *Theory of Economic Development.* Cambridge, MA: Harvard University Press.)

———. 1942. *Capitalism, Socialism, and Democracy.* Cambridge, MA: Harvard University Press.

Williamson, Oliver. 1975. *Markets and Hierarchies: Analysis and Antitrust Implications.* New York: Free Press.

PART 1

The Setting

Institutions, Organizations, and Market Competition
Douglass C. North

In this essay, I would like to apply the new institutional economics to suggest modifications of the theory we employ in economics to make that theory useful for the study of the performance of economies through time. The modifications I shall suggest are in the spirit of Joseph Schumpeter.

Formal economic theory has become increasingly mathematical, elegant, and precise. It also increasingly has failed to confront the economic problems of societies. Economics, in consequence, is slowly and painfully moving away from the formal mathematical models built around a frictionless, static, conceptual structure. Frank Hahn, one of the pioneers of general equilibrium theory, expressed it succinctly when he wrote that "there will be an increasing realization by theorists that radical changes in questions and methods are required if we are to deliver, not practical, but theoretically useful results" (1991, 47).

It is not as clear where economics is going. But the direction is suggested by two glaring shortcomings of neoclassical theory: it is a frictionless theory in a world in which the frictions are where the action is, and it is static in a world in which dynamic change is occurring at an unprecedented rate. Remedying these defects requires that economics builds on its strengths, modifies the unrealistic assumptions that made it frictionless, and incorporates time into the analysis to confront the issues of economic change.

The strength of neoclassical theory has been its uncompromising focus on scarcity and hence competition as the key to economics and its power as an economic way of reasoning, evinced in microeconomic theory. Its most unrealistic assumption, which underlies its frictionless character, has been the rationality assumption. Finally, time is the dimension in which human learning, the most important source of long-run economic change, occurs.

I shall briefly elaborate on the rationality assumption and the role of time in economic change (sec. I), set the scene for dynamic economic growth by describing the historical source of modern economic development (sec. II), suggest the direction that theoretical reconstruction must take to make the theory applicable to solving economic problems (sec. III), and conclude by raising some issues resulting from market competition (sec. IV).

I

The rational choice framework assumes that individuals know what is in their self-interest and act accordingly. That may be correct for individuals making choices in the highly developed markets of modern economies, but it is patently false in making choices under conditions of uncertainty — the conditions that characterize most of the crucial economic and political decisions that have shaped (and continue to shape) economic change.

Herbert Simon has stated the issue clearly.

> If . . . we accept the proposition that both the knowledge and the computational power of the decisionmaker are severely limited, then we must distinguish between the real world and the actor's perception of it and reasoning about it. That is to say we must construct a theory (and test it empirically) of the process of decision. Our theory must include not only the reasoning processes but also the processes that generated the actor's subjective representation of the decision problem, his or her frame. (1986, 210–11)

But just what determines the actor's perception of the world and reasoning about it? That they vary as between, say, a Communist Party official in the former Soviet Union, a Papuan tribesman, and a businesswoman in the United States is obvious; more important for us is that, faced with identical problems, these actors would frequently make different choices. The key to their differential perceptions is the kind of learning that the individuals in a society acquire through time. Here I do not refer simply to the learning and experiences of an individual over his or her lifetime but the cumulative experiences of past generations that are embodied in culture. Collective learning (Hayek's term) consists of those "kinds of learning" that have passed the slow test of time and in consequence have become embedded in our language, institutions, technology, and ways of doing things. It is culture that provides the key to path dependence — the powerful influence of the past on the present and future. The current learning of any generation takes place within the context of the perceptions derived from collective learning. That is, the learning process appears to be a function of the way in which a given belief structure filters the information derived from experience and the different experiences confronting individuals and societies at different times.

How do the modification of the rationality assumption and the incorporation of time into our framework alter economics? Modification of the rationality assumption means that ideas, dogmas, prejudices, and ideologies matter. It means that the actors making decisions in the face of the uncertainty that characterizes major political and economic choices frequently are doing so with results that are widely at variance with intentions. And specifically it means that we must incorporate into our analysis the belief systems the actors hold that determine the choices they make. And that brings us to time and human learning.

Time in this context consists of both the past experiences embodied in collective learning and the current learning experiences of individuals. Learning, then, is a cumulative process of cultural conditioning in which the experiences of each generation are filtered through the existing belief system and result in its incremental modification.

II

The source of dynamic economic change is the second economic revolution — a revolution that we are still attempting to assimilate. That revolution is the wedding of science and technology, which is the underlying determinant of modern productivity. It is a revolution because it is a fundamental change in the stock (and flow) of knowledge, which entails an equally fundamental change in the organization of human beings and the structure of societies.

The development of the disciplines of physics, chemistry, biology, and genetics is the source of the growth in the stock of scientific knowledge. The systematic application of these disciplines to the basic economic problem of scarcity has not only purged the Malthusian specter of diminishing returns from our purview but has created the vision of a potential world of plenty. To achieve that potential, however, entails a restructuring of economic, social, and political institutions and organizations in order to realize the increasing-returns attribute of the technology in which this scientific knowledge is embodied.[1]

The technology requires occupational and territorial specialization on an unprecedented scale, and in consequence the number of exchanges grows exponentially. In order to realize the gains from the productive potential associated with a technology of increasing returns, one has to invest enormous resources in transacting. In the United States, for example, the labor force grew from 29 to 80 million between 1900 and 1970; during that period, the number of production workers grew from 10 to 29 million, while white-collar workers (the great majority of whom are engaged in transacting) increased from 5 to 38 million. The transaction sector (that part of transaction costs that goes through the market and therefore can be measured) in the United States in 1970 made up 45 percent of GNP (Wallis and North 1986).

The transaction sector has been (and still is) growing because of the increasing costs of coordination and enforcement. Necessary to be able to realize the gains of a world of specialization are control over quality in the lengthening production chain and a solution to the problems of increasingly costly principal-agent relationships. Much technology, indeed, is designed to reduce transaction costs by substituting capital for labor or by reducing the degrees of freedom of the worker in the production process and automatically measuring the quality of intermediate goods. An underlying problem is that of measuring inputs and outputs so that one can ascertain the contribution of individual factors and the output at successive stages of production. For inputs, there is no agreed upon measure of the contribution of an individual input. Equally, there is room for conflict over the consequent payment to factors of production. For output, not only is there residual unpriced output, that is, waste and pollutants, but also there are complicated costs of specifying the desired properties of the goods and services produced at each stage in the production process.

Another characteristic of this new technology is that firms have large fixed capital investments with a long life and (frequently) low alternative scrap value. As a result, the exchange process embodied in contracts has to be extended over long periods of time, which entails uncertainty about prices and costs and the possibility of opportunistic behavior on the part of one of the parties to the exchange. A number of organizational problems emerge from these characteristics associated with technology.

First, increased resources are necessary to measure the quality of output or the performance of agents. Sorting, grading, labeling, trademarks, warranties, licensing, time and motion studies, and a variety of other techniques employed to measure the performance of agents are all, albeit costly and imperfect, devices used to measure the characteristics of goods and services and the performance of agents. Despite the existence of such devices, the dissipation of income is evident all around us in the difficulty of measuring the quality of automobile repairs, in evaluating the safety characteristics of products and the quality of medical services, or in measuring educational output. The problems of evaluating performance are even more acute in hierarchies because of the difficulties of achieving low-cost measurement of the multiple dimensions of an agent's performance.

Second, while team production permits economies of scale to be realized, it does so at the cost of worker alienation and shirking. The "discipline" of the factory is a response to the control problem of shirking in team production. From the perspective of the employer, the discipline consists of rules, regulations, incentives, and punishments essential to effective performance. From the viewpoint of the worker, they are frequently viewed as inhuman devices to foster speedups and exploitation. Since there is no agreed upon measure of output that constitutes contract performance, both are right.

Third, the potential gains from opportunistic behavior increase and lead to strategic behavior both within the firm (labor-employer relations, for example) and in contractual behavior between firms. Everywhere in factor and product markets the benefits of withholding services or altering the terms of agreement at strategic points offer large potential gains.

Fourth, the development of large-scale hierarchies produces the familiar problems of bureaucracy. The multiplication of rules and regulations inside large organizations to control shirking and principal-agent problems results in rigidities, income dissipation, and the loss of flexibility essential to adaptive efficiency.

Finally, there are external effects: the unpriced costs reflected in the modern environmental crisis. The interdependence of a world of specialization and division of labor increases exponentially the imposition of costs on third parties.

The institutional and organizational restructuring necessary to take advantage of this technology are much more fundamental than restructuring economic organization — although that task, the creation of efficient markets, is complicated enough. The entire structure of society must be transformed. This technology and accompanying scale economies entail specialization, minute division of labor, impersonal exchange, and urban societies. Uprooted are all the old informal constraints built around the family, personal relationships, and repetitive individual exchanges. Indeed, the basic traditional functions of the family — education, employment (the family enterprise), and insurance — are either eliminated or severely circumscribed. New formal rules and organizations and an increased role of government replace them.

The contention of Marxists was that these problems were a consequence of capitalism and that the inherent contradictions between the new technology and the consequent organization of capitalism would lead to its demise. The Marxists were wrong in thinking that the problems were a consequence of capitalism; they are ubiquitous to any society that attempts to adopt the technology of the second economic revolution. However, Marxists were right — and the foregoing paragraphs have attempted to make it clear — in concluding that the tension arising between the new technology and organization is a fundamental dilemma.[2] These tensions have only partially been resolved in the market economies of the Western world. The growth of government, the ever increasing resources that must be devoted to transacting, the disintegration of the family, and the incentive incompatibility problems in many modern political and economic hierarchical organizations are all symptoms of the consequent problems besetting Western economies. These issues will be the subject of the concluding section of this essay.

However, it is the relative flexibility of the institutions of the Western world — both economic and political — that has been the mitigating factor in dealing with these problems. Adaptive efficiency, while far from perfect in the Western world, accounts for the degree of success that such institutions have experienced. The basic institutional framework has encouraged the development of political and economic organizations that have replaced (however imperfectly) the traditional functions of the family, mitigated the insecurity associated with a world of specialization, evolved flexible economic organization that has induced low-cost transacting, resolved some of the incentive incompatibilities of hierarchies and encouraged creative entrepreneurial talent, and tackled (again, very imperfectly) the external effects that are not only environmental but also social in an urban world.

III

The second economic revolution is transforming the economies, polities, and indeed the entire structure of human societies. Understanding the nature of that transformation is a prerequisite to confronting effectively the policy issues of both the developed and the third world. The place to begin is to understand the nature of efficient markets — economic and political — and the way they evolve.

The key to efficient markets is institutions that result in low costs of transacting. Transaction costs are the costs involved in protecting property rights, measuring what is being exchanged, and enforcing agreements. Goods and services or the performance of agents have multiple valuable attributes, and the ability to measure those attributes at low cost is a necessary condition for capturing the gains from trade that were the keys to Adam Smith's *Wealth of Nations*. But a sufficient condition requires in addition that the contracts embodying the exchange process can be enforced at low cost. As noted, these conditions have been only partially met in the developed economies. They are not met in third world countries, and in consequence markets either do not exist or are beset by very high costs of transacting. Because transaction costs will influence the technology employed, both transaction and transformation costs will be higher in the factor and product markets of such economies.

The inability to have low-cost specification of the attributes being exchanged and enforcement of agreements in economic markets is ultimately a function of the political markets of economies because it is the polity that specifies the property rights and provides the instruments and resources to enforce contracts. But political markets are inherently less efficient than are economic markets. Not only are the measurement and enforcement of agreements more difficult and the incentive of the voter to be informed less than that of the buyer in economic markets, but also the complexity of the issues (together with the lack of incentive of the voter to be informed) leads to ideological stereotypes dominating political discourse and decision making. It is the economic and political institutions in a society (together with the technology employed) that determine the efficiency of markets.

It is one thing to define the characteristics of efficient markets at a moment in time; it is quite another to model the way markets evolve through time. To do so, we must explore the interaction between institutions and organizations over time. But first it is essential to distinguish clearly institutions from organizations. Institutions are the rules of the game of a society or more formally the human-devised constraints that structure human interaction. They are composed of formal rules (statute law, common law, and regulations), informal constraints (conventions, norms of behavior, and self-imposed codes of conduct), and the enforcement characteristics of both.

Organizations, too, specify the constraints that structure human interaction *inside* the organization, but in addition they are action groups. They are composed of groups of individuals bound by a common purpose to achieve objectives. They include political bodies (political parties, a legislature, a city council, a regulatory agency), economic bodies (firms, trade unions, family farms, cooperatives), social bodies (churches, clubs, athletic associations), and educational bodies (schools, colleges, vocational training centers). Organizations in pursuit of their objectives are the primary source of institutional change. These definitions undergird five propositions that define the essential characteristics of institutional change.

1. The continuous interaction of institutions and organizations in the economic setting of scarcity, and hence competition, is the key to institutional change.

2. Competition forces organizations continually to invest in skills and knowledge to survive. The kinds of skills and knowledge individuals and their organizations acquire will shape evolving perceptions about opportunities, and hence choices, that will incrementally alter institutions.

3. The institutional framework dictates the kinds of skills and knowledge perceived to have the maximum payoff.

4. Perceptions are derived from the mental constructs of the players.

5. The economies of scope, complementarities, and network externalities of an institutional matrix make institutional change overwhelmingly incremental and path dependent.

Let me elaborate on these propositions. Economic change is a ubiquitous, ongoing, incremental process that is a consequence of the choices individuals and entrepreneurs of organizations are making every day. While the vast majority of these decisions are routine (Nelson and Winter 1982), some involve altering existing "contracts" between individuals and organizations. Sometimes that recontracting can be accomplished within the existing structure of property rights and political rules, but sometimes new contracting forms require alteration of the rules. Usually, existing informal norms of behavior will guide exchanges, but sometimes such norms will gradually be modified or will wither away. In both instances, institutions are gradually being modified. Modifications occur because individuals perceive that they could do better by restructuring exchanges (political or economic). The source of the changed perceptions may be exogenous to the economy — for instance, a change in the price or quality of a competitive product in another economy that alters the perceptions of entrepreneurs in the given economy about profitable opportunities. But the fundamental source of change is learning by the entrepreneurs of organizations.

While some learning is a result of idle curiosity, the rate of learning will reflect the intensity of competition among organizations. Competition is a ubiquitous consequence of scarcity, and hence organizations in an economy will engage in learning to survive. But the degree can and does vary. If competition is muted as a result of monopoly power, the incentive to learn will be reduced.

The rate of learning determines the speed of economic change; the kind of learning determines the direction of economic change. The kind of learning is a function of the expected payoffs of different kinds of knowledge and therefore will reflect the mental models of the players and, most immediately at the margin, the incentive structure embodied in the institutional matrix (which consists of the framework of interconnected institutions that together make up the formal rules of an economy). If the institutional matrix rewards piracy (or more generally redistributive activities) more than productive activity, then learning will take the form of learning to be better pirates.

Change is typically incremental, reflecting ongoing, ubiquitous, evolving perceptions of the entrepreneurs of organizations in the context of an institutional matrix that is characterized by network externalities, complementarities, and economies of scope among the existing organizations. Moreover, since the organizations owe their existence to the institutional matrix, they will be an ongoing interest group working to assure the perpetuation of that institutional structure — and thus assuring path dependence. Revolutions do occur, however, when organizations with different interests emerge (typically as a result of dissatisfaction with the performance of existing organizations) and the fundamental conflict between organizations over institutional change cannot be mediated within the existing institutional framework.

Path dependence means that history matters, that the choices we make today and tomorrow are constrained by the past evolution of the belief systems and institutions of the society.

IV

There is no implication in the foregoing propositions about institutional change of progress or growth, only of change. A much more difficult question is, where are we going? Even when humans do structure economic and political institutions to be efficient in the sense of efficient markets, what are the long-run consequences? The question is akin to those that Schumpeter raised in *Capitalism, Socialism and Democracy.*

A long enough time horizon might incline one to conclude that increasing economic efficiency, as reflected in rising world per capita income, is evolving, but over the past 10 millennia — the period in which I am interested — the result is surely a mixed bag. Not only has growth (even as it is narrowly defined in quantitative terms) been episodic, but even after 10 millennia material well-being still eludes almost half of the world's population. And, indeed, sustained growth is a modern phenomenon still confined to parts of the world.

Sustaining such growth into the future depends on successfully dealing with two fundamental issues: (1) that the stock of (useful) knowledge continues to grow at something like constant returns and (2) that the costs of transacting (reflecting the costs arising from human interaction) do not grow more rapidly than the productivity gains from improvements arising from the increments to the stock of knowledge. I don't regard either of these issues as having necessarily positive outcomes.

The growth of the stock of knowledge at something like constant cost is not exclusively a scientific issue since it also involves the kind of belief systems that evolve as well. I feel less than qualified to say anything about the scientific issues inherent in the question of whether diminishing returns may set in with regard to the growth of scientific knowledge. And it would appear on the surface that the obvious and demonstrated utility of science would forever banish the institutional and belief constraints that have shackled scientific advance in the past. But the widespread existence of religious fundamentalism and deep distrust of much modern scientific development makes the issue a live one, indeed.

The second issue can be put quite simply. Can human beings construct viable political, social, and economic organizations in the evolving global economy of worldwide interdependence? The developed economies of the modern world offer some heartening evidence that the essential social capital (to use Jim Coleman's felicitous term) has been created to make possible productive economic organization, and the historical study of the growth of the transaction sector of the American economy by Wallis and North (1986) offers support.

But:

Since 1960 the U.S. population has increased 41%; the gross domestic product has nearly tripled; and total social spending by all levels of government (measured in constant 1990 dollars) has risen from $143.73 billion to 787 billion — more than a fivefold increase. Inflation adjusted spending on welfare has increased by 630%, spending on education by 225%.

But during the same 30 year period there has been a 560% increase in violent crime; a 419% increase in illegitimate births; a quadrupling in divorce rates; a tripling in the percentage of children living in single parent homes; more than a 200% increase in the teenage suicide rate; and a drop of more than 80 points in SAT scores. (*Wall Street Journal,* March 15, 1993)

Are these rising social costs a temporary phenomenon and irrelevant for economic efficiency? They suggest that modern economies are paying a substantial price for economic development. The growth of government is both a consequence and a cause of the price. And there are clear implications for the cost of transacting (which is really a surrogate measure for social capital). The clear implication is that the social glue that underlies informal institutional constraints is dissolving. And ultimately it is the strength of the complementary informal constraints that reduces the costs of contracting — that provides the trust, honesty, and integrity that makes possible complex low-cost exchange. When these informal constraints decline in effectiveness, we can expect an increase in formal rules and increasing costs of enforcement, which will be reflected in increasing litigation and the growth of government, resulting in rising costs of transacting per exchange. Is this development a temporary phenomenon of Western economies?

NOTES

This essay is partly drawn from the Adam Smith lecture given at the annual meeting of the National Association of Business Economists in 1994 entitled "Economic Theory in a Dynamic Economic World."

1. See my *Structure and Change in Economic History* (1981), chapter 13, "The Second Economic Revolution," for an elaboration of this argument.

2. It is surely one of the great ironies of history that Karl Marx, who first pointed out the necessity of restructuring economic and political organizations in order to be able to realize the potential of new technologies, should have been responsible for the creation of societies that foundered on precisely this issue.

REFERENCES

Hahn, F. 1991. "The Next Hundred Years." *Economic Journal* 101, no. 404 (January): 47–50.

Nelson, R., and S. Winter. 1982. *An Evolutionary Theory of Economic Change.* Cambridge: Harvard University Press.

North, D. 1981. *Structure and Change in Economic History.* New York: Norton.

Simon, H. 1986. "Rationality in Psychology and Economics." In *The Behavioral Foundations of Economic Theory,* edited by R. Hogarth and M. Reder. Supplement to the *Journal of Business* 59:S209–24.

Wallis, J., and D. North. 1986. "Measuring the Transaction Sector in the American Economy." In *Long Term Factors in American Economic Growth,* edited by S. Engerman and R. Gallman. Chicago: University of Chicago Press.

PART 2

The Context
Institutions and Markets

Paradigm Lost: The Walrasian Destruction of the Classical Conception of the Market
Frank M. Machovec

[I]t is the models that lead people to view
the economic system as they do.
—*Frank Hahn*

The history of economic thought provides surprising insights on how and why mainstream economists have come to see the world as they do. My unconventional thesis is that the judgment criteria implanted through the equilibrium vision of Walras created a new mode of thinking—and seeing the world—that would have been alien to our forefathers. The Walrasian system inspired a paradigm that not only discarded the entrepreneurial heart of the market's discovery process but also came to misrepresent (as "wasteful") the trials and errors through which firms improve their knowledge on what to produce and how to produce. This essay challenges the broadly accepted belief that the British classical vision of the market was shaped primarily by a latent equilibrium perspective that was essentially entrepreneurless. Toward this end, I describe the distinctly *classical* roots of Schumpeter's creative-destruction theme, which gave a renaissance to insights that had been lost under the regime of modern economics. I will also describe the real-world process of efficiency enhancement; trace the intellectual rise and embrace of the Walrasian vision, which deflected attention away from the process of competition; and reflect briefly on how the change in our perception of the market affected the fields of antitrust, economic development, and international trade.

Except for those practitioners who labor in the side streams of the discipline, there had been little concern (until recently) with the heart of the market process: learning, entrepreneurship, and the dynamics of the firm. But it was not always this way. The classical economists saw entrepreneurial learning as the source of progress. They portrayed the market as a process through which firms were lured, in lottery fashion (Smith 1937, 106–11; Mill 1864 1:475–76), by the potential of so-called obscene profit—the ineradicable social cost of discovery—to test new products and to engineer hoped-for reductions in the cost of manufacture.

The establishment . . . of any new branch of commerce . . . is always a speculation, from which the projector promises himself extraordinary profits. Those profits sometimes are very great, and . . . more frequently . . . they are quite otherwise. (Smith 1937, 115)

This understanding, though carried over to the twentieth century by the old guard, was soon destroyed by the Walrasian model, which portrayed the market merely as a computer (Solow 1956, 8) whose algorithms determine equilibrium allocations of *existing* resources, using *known* preferences and *given* production functions.[1] These two portraits yield conflicting visions of the role of the state in a real world characterized by asymmetric information; that is, contrary to the claims of mathematical economists, the neoclassical model is *not* politically neutral, for it tacitly embodies the assumption that knowledge should be a public good, which thereby draws the technician toward a proplanning disposition to correct for the market's failure to maximize social welfare as seen through the unsuitable and misleading prism of an all-knowing mind.

An examination of the history of the influence of the Walrasian system on how we perceive firms—as passive reactors that promote allocative efficiency or as searching actors that create inefficiency—complements our understanding of entrepreneurship and the dynamics of the firm. In pursuit of improved methods, for instance, firms in some industries evolve to become more highly specialized, while in others they integrate vertically to capture economies of scale via widened sales and in still others they integrate horizontally to capture economies of scope. Although many of the technical terms we employ today to describe these phenomena were coined by twentieth-century mathematical model builders, the phenomena themselves were familiar to our late-nineteenth-century forefathers, who did not see them as necessarily harmful. Nor did they see as harmful the entrepreneur's search for knowledge about product, manufacturing techniques, transaction costs, and price, because classical economists, both on the Continent *and* in Britain, portrayed society's welfare as being *increased* by the knowledge-discovery activities of firms, despite the existence of pure profit derived therefrom. Since they focused on the motion-picture nature of a market economy, a model's stop-action ability to analyze a single frame against an ideal endstate would have been of little interest to them. In today's histories of thought, "the shadow" of classical economics (the "limiting . . . elements" of equilibrium) has been misinterpreted as "the substance"; hence, the process of the market (its "motor mechanism")—the protection of which motivated our forefathers' analyses—has not been placed in proper perspective (Beach 1990, 17). Marshall (1920, 540), perhaps sensing the tendency to see the past in terms of the new present that was overtaking the discipline, made it a point "to insist" that both he and "the older economists" did *not* assume perfect competition, which requires "perfect knowledge" (also see Eatwell 1987, 537; and Marshall 1920, xiv–xv, 347, 366 [n. 2], 368–69, 461, 852, 855, 856).

In a letter written in 1885, Walras himself set the tone of the new paradigm by asserting that an ideal system of social justice must "preclude . . . the presence of any income that is not a functional return" (as summarized by Jaffé 1980, 537). Given the judgment of Walras, two points should be noted. First, the entrepreneur's contributory function under classical economics was eliminated by the general equilibrium system's assumption of informational symmetry. Second, and more significant, entrepreneurial initiatives did not thereby come to be seen merely as benign appendages, for in the static, fully informed world of the neoclassical model, the systemic existence of profit is explicable only in terms of *im*perfectly competitive actions that are *harmful* to consumer welfare (Jaffé 1980, 530–36). Hence, the Walrasian vision, which cannot be reconciled with the role of ineradicable pure profit (in the aggregate), became thoroughly uncongenial with the process through which entrepreneurs discover what and how to produce. Moreover, the static notion of efficiency created by the concept of the perfect competitor—which was rooted in Cournot and resurrected by Walras (see Machovec 1995, 161, 175)—ultimately led twentieth-century mainstream economists to portray any deviation from a perfectly competitive equilibrium as welfare inhibiting and thus invited the idea of remediation through state action.

My goal is not to bash the use of mathematical models. I employ them myself, regularly, as indispensable analytical tools. Nevertheless, I am deeply concerned about how the models have led us to become fixated on the zero-profit equilibrium—to the exclusion of the method and cost to society of acquiring all the information that is presumed present in order to attain this particular endpoint. I demonstrate that economists' habits of thought were altered by the neoclassical paradigm—in a Kuhnian, revolutionary sense—and that the result proved damaging to the discipline because it transformed the beneficial actions of entrepreneurs into targets of punitive public policy. Three topics in support of my thesis are addressed.

1. I examine the classicals' thinking on what to produce, how to produce, and the nature of speculation. Convincing passages are provided to demonstrate that the very idea of creative destruction—and the semantic construction of the term itself—were solidly rooted in the writings of early economists.

2. I explain Adam Smith's perspective on dynamic economies of scale, as well as his understanding of the transaction-cost issue, all of which solidify my argument that successive particular stages in the entrepreneurial-learning process (which fuel changes in corporate structures over time) would not have been seen as harmful by the founders of the discipline.

3. Since it is important for scholars to know the origin of their thinking, I trace the intellectual genealogy of the triumph of the

Walrasian model and describe how the resultant expurgation of the entrepreneur caused a proplanning perspective to permeate the literature of economics, most pronouncedly in the approach to development, but elsewhere as well. In a nutshell: the classicals' aversion to governmental vetoes of private action was replaced with a belief that the visible hand of the state is needed to correct the "imperfections" and "failures" created by asymmetric information.

In short, this essay provides a concise yet comprehensive survey, from Adam Smith to the present, of the turning points in the shifting sands of theory on entrepreneurial learning, the dynamics of the firm, and social welfare.

Creative Destruction: An Old Concept

[I]n the pursuit of wealth, . . . projectors aim at any
thing that can be called an *improvement,* whether it
consists in the production of any new article adapted
to man's use, or in meliorating the quality . . . of
those which are already known to us.
        —*Jeremy Bentham, Economic Writings*

In describing the market, the classical economists did not think only in terms of the state of affairs that exists after the competitive process is completely spent, at which point all agents have perfect information. They also emphasized the nature of the process itself, especially the sociopolitical institutions that promote specialization and trade (N. Rosenberg 1960, 557, 560, 570; Robbins, 56–57).[2] Of course, the classicals were very interested in equilibrium (and distribution), but their "more comprehensive purpose" was to demonstrate that "a powerful normative argument for [a promarket] constitutional structure exists," a purpose from which the profession "was diverted" under neoclassical economics (Buchanan 1987, 585). This diversion caused economists to direct nearly all their energy to showing "how the system would behave in the *absence* of its most distinctive feature—innovation" (N. Rosenberg 1994, 44; italics added).

In the classical texts, the preferred panoply of consumer goods and the most efficient methods of production were identified through the profit-making activities of entrepreneurs. This information was not "given" to the system, as in neoclassical theory. Instead, it was ascertained through a trial and error process of discovery, with pure profit as the bait, enticing firms to offer various menus. Schumpeter's description of "creative destruction" appeared novel in 1942 because the profession's leaders had been divorced for two decades from the classical notion of the market, namely, the rivalrous nexus of advantage-seeking (yet socially beneficial) behaviors that came to be condemned as inimical to welfare maximization under the equilibrium paradigm. In the classical writings (including those of the British), knowledge of what and how was uncertain, and a special class of bold agents garnered pure profit from bearing this uncertainty. The search for profit led the entrepreneur (not the capitalist) to undertake four tasks for society: speculative intertemporal transfers of resources to relieve suspected future shortages, introductions of new products, the development of increasingly productive machinery, and the discovery and eradication of imperfect markets through the quasi-arbitrage antennae of retailers. (For a specific example of each of these activities, see, respectively, Longfield 1834, 55, 58–62; McCulloch 1832, 4; Bentham 1843, 76, 226, 277; and Smith 1937, 494–99.)[3]

In other words, the classical economists saw the market not as Walras had seen it (simply as an equilibrium calculating machine) but rather as Schumpeter had described it. This is not to say that our forefathers were unconcerned with the notion of equilibrium, for they certainly devoted much space to the endstate conditions to which the market converged; however, their overriding concern was with the maintenance of an institutional framework conducive to free entry, so that the market's competitive process could be protected. Adam Smith's oft-repeated and unifying point—his metaphor of the invisible hand (1937, 231–34, 423)—had nothing to do with the market's consummating state of affairs but rather was expressly targeted at our understanding of the nature and benefits of entrepreneurial behavior. "Smith was more interested . . . in the process of contracting than in its actual outcome" (West 1976, 587; also see the same conclusion in Coase 1977, 318; and Skinner 1990, 162).

Strangely, with the exception of the contributions of Bentham,[4] Schumpeter was apparently unaware of our forefathers' less celebrated yet very similar treatment of the entrepreneur that was reborn in *Capitalism, Socialism, and Democracy*. Perhaps Schumpeter's historical blind spot on this issue was a product of his admiration of Walras, who had mistakenly inferred that the British economists did not understand the separate functions of the capitalist and the entrepreneur (Walras 1954, 423; quoted in Walker 1984, 2). Schumpeter (1954, 1006) was justifiably impressed with the "immortal merit" of Walras's system, but he erroneously compared its static nature to the thinking of the classical writers, whom, he believed, had seen the market economy as Walras had seen it—as a more or less stationary system, largely devoid of endogenous entrepreneurial forces that create new equilibria through the introduction of fresh products and better ways of doing things (Schumpeter 1991, 166). It appears that neither he nor Hoselitz had recognized that the idea of creative destruction, as well as its semantic construction, were fruits of several classical minds (see Hoselitz 1960, 254). This is not to say that Schumpeter's work lacked inventiveness, for "Schumpeter *was* highly original." However, the originality of his contribution on entrepreneurship lies jointly in "the novel twists he gave" to long-neglected themes "and the new insistence [he placed] on these themes" (Streissler 1994, 14). Schumpeter's purpose was to challenge the preeminent role the profession was giving to static analysis; he believed that the Walrasian system had preoccupied the mainstream with a perfectly informed allocational framework that was "almost, though not quite, irrelevant" (Schumpeter 1976, 77; N. Rosenberg 1994, 44, 46). Schumpeter simply failed to recognize that the neoclassical paradigm had radically altered the profession's interpretive-evaluative criteria, which, in turn, had created a new generation of analysts whose training was devoid of the experience-based insights of the classicals and who, therefore, had become receptive to the idea of achieving efficiency through the visible hand of the state.

In tracing the genealogy of Schumpeter's main idea, the best starting point is *The Communist Manifesto*. Marx and Engels employed the classical vision of creative destruction quite effectively to describe the "[c]onstant revolutionizing of production" through which the capital and "specialized skill[s]" of "dislodged" businessmen and craftsmen ("swamped [by] competition") were "rendered worthless" by the introduction of "new wants" and "new methods of production." In short, "old-established national industries . . . are daily being destroyed . . . by new industries . . ." When socialism replaces capitalism, stability and foresight would presumably replace the "uninterrupted disturbance" and "everlasting uncertainty" that characterize the modern market process (quoted in Tucker 1978, 476, 480). Schumpeter certainly acknowledged Marx's contribution to his own thinking on creative destruction; in fact, Schumpeter's sociopolitical "crumbling walls" hypothesis (1976, 61, 139) was an evolutionary response to the politically revolutionary forecast of Marx. However, Schumpeter seemed not to notice any of the other classicals who had described the market's engine of creative destruction, probably because he shared the mainstream's unfounded conviction of a common static heritage; that is, most leading neoclassical writers, past and present, including Schumpeter, have genuinely believed that our British predecessors viewed the market through an essentially Walrasian prism (Schumpeter 1934, xi). Samuelson best expressed the mainstream's perception: "Inside every classical economist is a modern economist trying to get out" (1977, 42). But an ardent belief in something does not make it true. A professor who received his doctorate in the 1920s explained in 1957 that "the oft-repeated view" that the classical perception of the market was shaped by a qualitative version of the same equilibrium lenses employed by modern economists was "mildly shocking"; he asserted that "Marshall, [John Bates] Clark, and other theorists . . . from Adam Smith on, quite surely would have rejected . . . [the] *reconstruction* of their thought . . ." (Peterson 1957, 61–63; italics added).

The classicals' high level of interest in equilibrium is not being challenged here; however, neoclassical historians have virtually ignored the significance of the classicals' implicit yet parallel concern with promoting the *en*dogenous disturbances that prompt equilibrating reactions—an interest that was unambiguously signaled by their advocacy of the sociopolitical institutions that generate these creative yet destructive disturbances, which they saw as the heart of human progress. Convergence toward equilibrium was certainly the key scientific part of the market process addressed in the classical texts, but the raison d'être of their writings was to foster an appreciation for the beneficial essence of the spontaneous process itself, not to provide a technical description of the equalization of price and long-run average cost.

Conventional wisdom notwithstanding, the social-learning function of the entrepreneur *was* addressed, not only by Continental writers (whose contributions in this area have long been recognized) but also by writers in the United Kingdom (albeit less forcefully). Two nineteenth-century German economists, K. H. Rau and A. F. Riedel, whose ideas were standard fare for German and Austrian students at the turn of the century, were especially Schumpeterian in their descriptions of the entrepreneur's key role in pioneering "new combinations" (Streissler 1994, 16–20). Rau and Riedel did not mention the destructive aspect of the new combinations (14); however, some of their British contemporaries addressed not only the market's innovative impulse but also the damage wrought to those displaced by entrepreneurial change. The British appreciation of the entrepreneur's contribution has not yet been acknowledged by historians of economic thought. Adam Smith, for instance, described "the competition of producers, who in order to undersell one another, have recourse to new divisions of labor, which might never otherwise have been thought of." As a result of these competitive initiatives, firms "jostle one another *out of employment*" (1937, 706, and 717; italics added). J. S. Mill likewise noted that it was the existence of active rivalry that prompted innovations by those who "*fear being thrust back* by the efforts of others to push themselves forward" (1864, 2:337, 547–48; italics added). He also highlighted the pivotal error-correction role played by the "diversity of modes of action" among firms within a large, healthy, private sector. Mill warned that the ponderous uniformity that follows state expansion would prevent experimental learning by smothering the invisible hand's ability "to originate and . . . adopt improvements" (1987, 176–77, 181–83, 185; 1967, 366, 410, 617).

Nassau Senior, around 1860, mentioned the rise of oligopolists and the "extinction of the smaller capitalists" by a manufacturer who takes an "initiative" because he "thinks that he possesses . . . peculiar advantages of skill or situation" (1928, 11–12). He also said that innovative production techniques "must terminate ruinously" for those who continue using the old method (240). Sismondi's 1819 text described the costs of bankruptcy more starkly: "their . . . circulating capital will be lost; [and] their workers will [be] laid off and will lose their livelihood. . . . Each improvement . . . has killed . . . old producers no one saw, and which have disappeared unsung . . ." (1991, 264, 265). Although Sismondi's text was in French, his ideas were appreciated by the British, as evidenced by the invitation extended to him by *The Edinburgh Encyclopedia* to contribute a lengthy piece, in layman's English, on Smithian political economy (xxiii).

Even Ricardo, a truly equilibrium theorist for whom the entrepreneur was always invisible,[5] included a concise yet precise description of the paradoxical forces through which the market promotes progress: "All improvements in agriculture and manufacture . . . never fail, at the moment of their introduction, to deteriorate or annihilate the value of a part of the existing capital of farmers and manufacturers" (1957, 181). And, finally, writing at the dawn of the new era, Sidgwick echoed the classical perspective in his 1901 observation that the market's competitive forces produce an inescapable "destruction of the existing value" of physical *and* human capital, for the salability of a manual skill will be "diminished or annihilated" in the same manner as one's "material instruments" (1901, 364–66).

Consequently, Bentham's entrepreneurially oriented insights were not unique. The classical focus was bilateral, not unilateral as in neoclassical theory. Modern theorists became virtually obsessed with mathematically describing the state of affairs at equilibrium—at the expense of transmitting an understanding of the entrepreneurial forces and facilitative public policies that spur new equilibria. In Ricardo, creative destruction simply happens. And in Marx business life is portrayed as in Walras's mechanical system, where it "runs substantially by itself" (Schumpeter 1954, 556). But this was not how the market was seen by most of their British contemporaries. Perhaps Malthus said it best, for he, like Bentham, made an explicit distinction between the roles of the capitalist and the entrepreneur.[6] The task of innovation fell to the latter, on whose shoulders rested the burden of discovering new combinations "calculated" to generate "an increase in value owing to a better adaptation . . . to the tastes, wants and consumption of society."[7] He characterized the luring of consumers through the introduction of utility-enhancing products as "the grand difficulty"—whose accomplishment "certainly [does] *not* naturally and necessarily follow an accumulation of capital . . ." (Malthus 1968, 318). Furthermore, Malthus was not a solitary voice on the British Isles. His sentiments can be found, in various explicit or implicit forms, in the works of Bentham, Smith, Steuart, Senior, and McCulloch (see n. 3). Therefore, the classical economists were not rigidly focused on the idea of equilibrium; they also saw *and appreciated* a dynamic process based on entrepreneurial learning. After the paradigmatic absorption of the Walrasian model, the policy-making influence of the pro-entrepreneur perspective of the classicals was lost. The nearly single-minded focus of mainstream economics became the calculation of the interactive string of new equilibrium parameters caused by an *exoge-*

nous shock. Endogenous change—sparked either by learning from disequilibrium transactions (see Wicksteed [1910] 1946, 1:224–26) or from other sources of discovery—was eliminated, for it produced mathematically intractable equilibria. The only equilibria in which the profession was interested were those that could be calculated in advance, based on perfect knowledge of all factors by all agents (Kaldor 1934, 122, 125 [n. 4]).

Before proceeding, I must reassert that I am not saying that the concept of equilibrium was slighted by the classical economists. Quite the contrary. The early texts described at length the state of affairs brought about by the "competition of capitals," namely, uniform returns and price equal to natural value (average cost). Consequently, the founders' scientific interest in the nature of the final constellation of factors was manifest—*but their overarching concern was with the discovery nature of the process,* for their goal was to diminish the spheres of exclusivity that were routinely purchased at court by special interests, and to enlarge, thereby, the competitive forces of the postmercantilist era (Smith 1937, 61, 71–72, 95, 438, 577; West 1978, 830–33, including n. 4; and Koebner 1959, 389–91). This order of priority was reversed in neoclassical economics, so much so that attention to the market process practically disappeared from the mainstream literature, which devoted itself almost single-mindedly to describing the conditions prevailing at equilibrium. This turn of events had policy-making consequences that were not benign.

Changing Perspectives on Entrepreneurial Learning and the Firm's Dynamics

Within the static assumptions of the neoclassical model, deviations from perfect-knowledge outcomes cause suboptimal levels of social welfare that merit corrective state action. Two areas of the discipline that were perversely influenced by this new outlook were industrial organization and economic development. The impact on each is examined in turn.

The ultimate by-product of Walras's use of the perfect competitor[8] was the contribution of Robinson and Chamberlin (the model of monopolistic competition), which demonstrates the inferior *and hence antisocial* welfare outcomes of all imperfectly competitive forms. Since the behavior of real firms that introduce new product variants fits more readily within the Robinson-Chamberlin than the perfect-competition model, a "world of monopolies" view[9] was injected that soon transformed American antitrust policy. In addition, profit creation via cost-reducing initiatives became impossible in a perfect-information modeling environment; consequently, any new production arrangement that garnered excess returns came to be seen as a manifestation of "market power." With regard to the latter point, it will prove helpful to review how our early predecessors viewed the entrepreneurial exploitation of efficiency concepts later known as scale economies and transaction costs.

The heart of Book I of Smith's *Wealth of Nations* was his description of the causes of *dynamic* scale economies, namely, reductions in cost achieved by expanding output along a given average-cost curve in ceteris paribus fashion. Smith also described cost reductions attributable to the entrepreneur's deliberate violation of ceteris paribus. In other words, Smith addressed downward shifts in the average cost curve due to intrafirm or interfirm changes undertaken for that purpose. Specifically, Smith discussed cost savings from two sources: first, specialization per se; and, second, the integration of the tasks of related yet distinct specialists.

Specialization itself, the first source of savings, increased output per man hour through two learning-curve phenomena, one directly (the traditional static case), the other indirectly (by lowering the average cost curve). Specialization's direct channel is the "increase in dexterity" that causes downward movement along the given average cost curve. Specialization's indirect channel is the *en*dogenous "application of proper machinery" that is spurred by insights that arise within the workman as a result of his specialized routine (Smith 1937, 7, 9–10). The addition of better-adapted tools causes all average costs to fall. The second source of cost savings is achieved by dynamically integrating the tasks of related specialists. These savings are tied to the most micro, primitive category of transaction costs, namely, "the time commonly lost in passing from one sort of work to another," which is magnified by a spatially separated division of labor and is reduced through integration of the same under one roof, after which "the loss of time is no doubt much less" (Smith 1937, 8).

Another, more significant source of transaction cost savings in Smith is available through the institutional milieu. As the leading modern theorist in this field has explained, "contracts that pose hazards that are not mitigated by safeguards will be priced differently than contracts where those same hazards are mitigated" (Williamson 1993, 105). Smith clearly recognized this very point (as did J. S. Mill): "A very considerable degree of inequality . . . is not so great an evil as a very small degree of uncertainty" (Smith 1937, 778; see also Mill 1864, 2:491–92; Mill 1967, 746, 749). As institutions are introduced to reduce the costs of exchange, production can spread from agriculture to manufacturing, and then to foreign trade, each of which is progressively more uncertain, particularly the latter, which requires "giving great credits in distant countries to men, with whose character and situation [the merchant] can seldom be thoroughly acquainted" (Smith 1937, 357–58). Since the sociopolitical framework is the key to ensuring that transaction costs do not suffocate commerce, the "promises of others" must be guaranteed by civil penalties that "admit of no exceptions" (Smith 1976, 84, 175). "When the law does not enforce the performance of contracts, it puts all borrowers nearly upon the same footing with . . . people of doubtful credit . . ." (Smith 1937, 95). Fortunately, the neoinstitutionalists have resurrected an interest in the classical problem of transaction costs.

More on Dynamic Cost Reductions by Firms

In the middle of the nineteenth-century, Senior and Mill described the emergence of oligopoly, presumably linked to sales growth tied to scale economies engineered over time, but they never alluded in any way to the modern notion of vertical integration as a cost-reducing technique. (See Mill 1977, 136; and Senior 1928, 11–12.) Some early industrialists, however, did record how they were forced to integrate vertically to capture the Chandlerian "thoughtput" required to reap the scale economies and sales growth that *they* could envision but that their suppliers and retailers could not see as worth the risks of changing their operational scales. He who possessed an unshared vision, therefore, found himself with no other choice than to despecialize to make his dream a reality—to integrate, sometimes both upstream and downstream—a process that, along the way, reorganized the structure and volume of his industry, lowered costs, and thereby boosted the standard of living. (See the writings of steelmaker Henry Bessemer, as well as other illustrations, in Silver 1984, 12–17, 30–32, 64, 107–14, 122–29.)

Over time, disintegration will occur in some of the industries that rose to prominence via integration. As the original vision proves itself and is replicated with economic growth, new specialist firms will emerge to serve a particular decreasing-cost task common to *all* the larger, integrated corporations, thereby enabling further cost savings that were unavailable during the unshared vision era. Hence, specialization will again deepen to capture the external economies of scale created by the evolutionary path that was initially sparked by an entrepreneur's reluctant decision to despecialize. Of course, if the transaction and agency costs of using an outside specialist exceed the production cost savings from subcontracting, then no vertical disintegration will occur. (See Stigler 1951, 185–93; Marshall 1920, 271, 284–85, 318, 615, 809; and Becker and Murphy 1992, 1138, 1142–45, 1149.)

After the intellectual triumph of the Walrasian vision, the mathematical requirements for a determinate equilibrium[10] caused us to rule out the scale economies achieved over time through learning curves, vertical integrations, transaction cost reductions, and so on. What's worse, under neoclassical economics these dynamic phenomena came to be seen as entry-barrier manifestations of monopoly power. In fact, any deviation from perfect competition came to be viewed, in pure theory, as antisocial, correctable, and sometimes deserving of punitive action. And this prescription was rooted directly in the words of Walras: "[S]ince the factors which interfere with [perfect competition] are obstacles to the attainment of [utility maximization], they should, without exception, be eliminated as completely as possible" (1954, 355–56).

Of course, as Donald A. Walker pointed out to me at the 1996 conference of the History of Economics Society, Walras's admonition was originally aimed (in the 1870s) at the widespread governmental practice in Europe of granting exclusive corporate franchises. Nonetheless, the spirit of the message became highly useful to those who began to portray the real world market as suboptimal due to the entrepreneurial introduction of product differentiations (Robinson 1965, 5, 85, 129, 307; and see Knight 1964, 185–86, 189). In fact, the model of monopolistic competition—which led to the adoption of the perfectly competitive firm at equilibrium as the profession's efficiency benchmark (Stigler 1937, 717)—had a decisive impact on U.S. antitrust policy from the late 1930s onward. In short, from a static-modeling perspective, learning activity constituted proof of monopoly power, and hence many manifestations of the firm's search for knowledge (on product, method, and marketing) came to be condemned under the Sherman Act. This antientrepreneurial outlook moderated in the late 1970s, but under the Clinton administration the pendulum has begun to swing back (see Machovec 1995, 181–235).

Allyn Abbot Young, Frank Knight's mentor at Cornell University, worried aloud that the equilibrium paradigm that was steamrolling the discipline in the 1920s would lead to a complete loss of the classical and Marshallian understanding of the long-term evolution of more efficient forms of industrial organization. Young was distressed because he feared that the new, technical leaders of the discipline were embracing a model whose static-allocational mathematics was going to create a mode of reasoning that would extinguish a key classical insight, namely, that "progress . . . [is] dependent in part on a process of trial and error" (Young 1928, 534). He witnessed how economists' habits of thought were being altered by "the apparatus" of the Walrasian system, which "stand[s] in the way of a clear view of the more general or elementary aspects of the phenomena of increasing returns . . ." (527, 531). Frustrated and alarmed, he wrote to Knight that "I have yet to see that the method of general equilibrium gives us anything that *gets us anywhere*. . . . We have to depart from it somehow" (quoted in Blitch 1983, 363–64).

Edgeworth, himself one of the pioneers of mathematical economics, shared Young's concern over the inadvertent obliteration from our repertoire of how improvements occur in a market economy. He apparently appreciated that pure profit was the unavoidable transaction cost of the process of search, for his complaint about Walras's emphasis on the long-run, zero-profit nature of perfect competition was explained by pointing out that men and women discover the best course of action in any activity through "a series of tentatives" (1925, 311), not through manna from heaven omniscience. Despite the usefulness, said Edgeworth, of the advanced calculus of variations for handling several simultaneous optimization decisions, we are unable to describe the equilibrium path of a highly complex, ignorance-constrained economy; Walras's system masks the ineradicability of entrepreneurial profit and loss in the market process by "divert[ing] attention from a sort of higgling which may be regarded as more fundamental than his conception" (311; see also the conclusion of Newman 1990, 129).

Young and Edgeworth (and Marshall) correctly sensed the rapid shift in thinking that was under way in the 1920s. As Kuhn has explained, the general problem that was facing the old guard was that "paradigm changes do cause scientists to see the world differently" (1970, 111, 113). The impact of these retinal transplants was not confined to the field of industrial organization; the theory of international trade was also affected, though not adulterated. (See Machovec 1995, 110–12, 181–235, 261–64, 284–87, 307–9.) In the newly emerging field of economic development, however, the equilibrium vision yielded perverse notions that spawned harmful consequences. The growth of far too many nations has been inhibited by the proplanning attitudes introduced and nourished by the neoclassical paradigm; consequently, the next section chronicles the intellectual embrace of the Walrasian model by leading-edge theorists early in this century and concomitantly explains how this embrace led directly to the greatest irony of twentieth-century economics: the pronouncedly anti-Smithian perspective in the literature of development.

The Ascent of the Walrasian Vision

[I]n classical writing . . . the central normative concern is with the efficacy of market institutions. In contrast, the development of modern welfare economics can best be understood as an attempt to sort out . . . allocative efficiency from particular modes of social organization.
    —Frank Bator, "Simple Analytics"

Under Marshall's magisterial (and majesterial) influence, most old guard economists had ignored the general equilibrium model, a situation that understandably agitated Walras. (See Homan 1928, 274–75; Jaffé 1983, 115; Robinson 1966, vii; and Stigler 1990, 12.) But Walras was a patient man who eschewed "a quick harvest" in favor of "plant[ing] oak trees" to provide shade for his grandchildren (Walras, quoted in Jaffé 1965, 225).[11] And he was sufficiently long lived to enjoy his own acorns. In 1892, for example, he was elected an honorary member of the American Economics Association (AEA) in recognition of his "eminent services to the Science of Political Economy," a tribute that elated him (Walras 1954, 11). Many of the elder statesmen of the early AEA were devotees of the German Historical School and hence were probably more enamored with Walras's *social* economics than with the mathematical nature of his general equilibrium model; however, a small but growing group of technical economists was praising the nonpolemical nature of Walras's approach. The discipline's younger members were poised at the turn of the century for a more scientific paradigm, so the Walrasian system, on the shelf since 1874, probably appeared to have been sent from heaven. Most significantly, its methodological adoption paved the way for the mainstream's endorsement of the Lange model, which, in turn, led the field of development economics into an anti-entrepreneurial abyss that hindered economic growth where it was most needed. The acceptability of Oskar Lange's vision abetted collectivist approaches and thereby resulted in "agricultural misery" and "falling standards of living for people who were already poor . . ." (Krueger 1992, 12, 23–25, including nn. 29 and 58; also see Myint 1987, 108).

It must be noted that not every economist of high stature was enamored with applying the Walrasian model to promote the idea of the workability of socialism. Immediately after World War I, in isolated Stockholm, Gustav Cassel began to write about the problems of the marginal pricing mechanics of a theoretically efficient socialist system (Carlson 1994, 51, 57–58), and at the same time Eli Heckscher noted that only under ideal conditions would the state possess the resolve to follow the optimizing signals later proposed by Lange. Since the required degree of political will was not likely to be forthcoming (due to special interest pressures), the socialized economy would lack the "self-acting corrective" (price adjustments) that regulate the market economy (quoted in Carlson 1994, 43–44). But neither Cassel nor Heckscher anticipated the essence of the critique of Ludwig von Mises, namely, that without widespread *private* enterprise, *factual marginal-cost guidelines will cease to exist* because price-embodied knowledge on scarcity and the consumer's opportunity cost—as customarily recorded in ex post accounting data—"is what you get as a *result* of the [competition between entrepreneurs for capital], not something you can assume at the outset" (Prowse 1997, 31).

Lange's celebrated reply to Mises was a culmination of the ideas of several early leaders, all of whom were inspired by the apolitical, ahistorical nature of Walras's mathematical model and by his implicit embrace of the ownership-indifference proposition. Especially influential were Pareto, Barone, and Taylor, whose articles in 1897, 1908, and 1929 (respectively) paved the way for the acceptance of the Walrasian paradigm, in which we were to be freely supplied with what heretofore had to be discovered through the quest for pure profit, namely, answers to the questions of what to produce and how to produce it via the competitive value calculus of entrepreneurs (see Machovec 1995, 52–58, 72–76). In effect, to acquire modeling precision, we elected to eliminate the indeterminate nature of the opportunity cost calculation problem by accepting the convenience of the perfect knowledge postulate (see Machovec 1995, 104–5, 173–74; and Klein 1996, 11–17).

Frank Knight's prestige was added to the growing chorus when he published an article, slightly ahead of Lange, which explained that the theory of efficient (marginal cost) decision making stands independent of the sociopolitical institutions governing ownership: "Anything that can happen under one organization[al] form *could* happen under [the] other, without violating any known law of . . . human nature . . . [or] logic" (1936, 257; italics added). Knight strenuously objected to Mises's political arguments against socialism. Knight readily admitted that socialist systems were likely to lead people on "some romantic . . . 'crusade' "; nevertheless, he wanted economists to focus exclusively on efficiency evaluations within their framework of perfectly competitive markets, consumer freedom, and labor freedom, and hence not to venture into political "prophecy" about the ultimate goals and directions of real world socialist economies (1938a, 268). It should be noted, however, that *Knight also drew a sharp, unambiguously Hayekian distinction between what was theoretically possible in an abstract model blessed with perfect information versus the inappropriate use of Lange's conception to theorize about a real economy saddled with the division of knowledge problem* (1938b, 242, 243, 247, 249, 250). Unfortunately, this particular aspect of Knight's contribution to the debate was not incorporated by the profession at large, because the pro-Lange, perfect knowledge die had already been cast—in stainless steel. Even Schumpeter (1954, 968, 1006; 1991, 165) was sufficiently mesmerized by the "genius" of Walras's formulation (the "Magna Charta of exact economics") that he endorsed the theoretical basis of the model of his former student, Lange.

> Can Socialism work? Of course it can. . . . [F]uture generations of economists will look upon arguments about the inferiority of the socialist plan as we look upon Adam Smith's arguments about the joint-stock companies. (Schumpeter [1942] 1976: 167, 196)

Schumpeter's scientific acceptance of Lange's model did not mean that he advocated socialism. He remained a great admirer of the free market, so much so that in his final presentation to his peers he rebuked American economists for failing to attack the unabated expansion of intrusive government activities in the United States after World War II. The apparent acquiescence by those who should have been most alarmed at "the growing list of [statist] anathemata" was inexplicable to Schumpeter (1950, 449); he never understood that the entrepreneurless blueprint of the Walrasian system had eliminated from an entire generation the skepticism toward central planning that would have been acquired if the market had been taught from a classical, division of knowledge perspective. To repeat Hahn: "[I]t is the models that lead people to view the economic system as they do" (1970, 1).

Armed with 44 additional years of experience and introspection, Mark Blaug asked himself how he could have been convinced at one time that government bureaucrats could satisfactorily replace private entrepreneurs: "Only those drunk on perfectly competitive . . . equilibrium theory could have swallowed such nonsense. I was one of those who swallowed it as a student in the 1950s and I can only marvel now at my own dim-wittedness" (1993, 1571). Blaug, like most other economists, had been lured by the purity of the social welfare function, which "is antiseptically independent of institutional context, notably of competitive market institutions" (Bator 1957, 31). The profession's admiration of the Lange construct reached its zenith in 1975 with the award of a Nobel Prize to Koopmans and Kantorovich, whose model had demonstrated that "the basic economic problems are the same in all societies." Therefore, said the Swedish Academy in their citation, the study of the optimal allocation of resources "can be treated in a scientific manner that is independent of the political organization of the society under consideration" (quoted in Wasson 1987, 569). Although the Swedish Academy's allusion to a value-free treatment normally brings to mind the mainstream's application of the general equilibrium perspective to the communist systems of the post-war era, this particular Walrasian feature (of being apolitical) is likewise applicable to the fascist economies of prewar Europe. "[T]he creation and regulation of compulsory cartels . . . by a strong state," argued Heinrich von Stackelberg in the 1930s, could, "in principle," have "the same [efficiency] result as perfect competition." Hence, he echoed the accepted view of modern theory: "The actual deviations of the corporate-state equilibrium from its ideal should not . . . be assessed any differently from the actual deviations in the past of the . . . free capitalist economy from [its] theoretical ideal" (quoted in Konow 1994, 159).

The Nobel Committee's recognition of the work of Koopmans and Kantorovich in 1975 was not surprising. Just two years earlier, it had awarded the economics prize to Wassily Leontief for his three decades of empirical research on the Walrasian interrelations between the labor and intermediate goods required to satisfy every industry's production target. Leontief's aggregated, intersectoral data matrices were heralded, in large part, because they enabled "general equilibrium analysis [to become] a practical tool for planning purposes" (Wasson 1987, 624). So, putting ideological considerations aside,[12] the Nobel Prizes of 1973 and 1975 reflected the confidence felt by mainstream economists since the 1960s over the prospect that advanced mathematics and computing technology would eventually enable governmental bureaus to employ the Walrasian model to solve real world planning problems: "[W]e *knew* that . . . input-output analysis and linear programming would soon make [our theoretical vision] not just elegant but operational . . . ." (Blaug 1994, 17; also see Wiles 1977, 278; Jaffé 1983, 222, 281; Arrow 1974, 5; and Walras 1954, 225, 255).

A writer recently reminded us that 70 years ago "it was uncertain whether market supporters or critics would be more apt to make use of the neoclassical structure to better articulate their ideas" (George 1992, 96). The intriguing yet dangerously misleading idea of improving allocative performance by replacing private entrepreneurs (who were characterized as ill informed and shortsighted) with a cadre of centrally informed planners—who could identify all consumer wants, select the best methods of production, and adjust for all the market's failures—was commonplace among the new technical leadership by the mid-1930s. Harold Hotelling had employed this concept in his study of spatial monopoly in 1929 (52–56), and in 1935 Joan Robinson endorsed Walras's solitary robot-entrepreneur idea (1966, 50). The impact of this thinking on the virginal field of economic development was tragic yet predictable. The visible hand of the state was imagined as being capable of rescuing society from the suboptimal decisions of the private sector by becoming the overseer of investment, relative prices, and so on. Except for a few heretics such as P. T. Bauer, development writers have been hostile to entrepreneurially based analyses (see Machovec 1995, 59–69). The takeover of the field of development by this genre of thinking is the most regrettable (and damaging) by-product of the Walrasian revolution.

The promarket reforms of the second and third worlds have begun to draw the attention of academic development theorists but not their excitement. Furthermore, the textbooks in this field were *not* moving toward a modification of their proplanning views before the eruption of promarket thinking among the public officials of poor nations. This is best evidenced by the surprising decision to delete Hayek's seminal 1945 knowledge article from the sixth edition of *Comparative Economic Systems: Models and Cases* (1989). In fact, a full explication of the division of knowledge perspective of the market (with liberal quotes from Smith, Hayek, etc.), including the pro-entrepreneur policy implications of same—juxtaposed against an analogous treatment of the Walrasian perspective—is nowhere to be found in any pre-1996 English-language textbook on economic development or comparative systems. (If an example does exist, it has escaped my notice, and I offer a sincere apology to its author for my oversight.)

Summary

[The neoclassical assumption of perfect knowledge is]
the most important and pervasive single simplification,
bearing more logical weight than any other, in the
whole range of economic . . . analysis . . .
                    —*Hutchison (in Katzner, 20)*

This essay has demonstrated that creative destruction is a classical concept that was lost after the Walrasian vision became firmly implanted. Alfred

Marshall and his disciples resisted the changing tide, but they were unsuccessful. The new wave contributed valuable tools for conducting analyses of welfare in perfectly informed endstates, but it also swept out a plethora of equally valuable insights on entrepreneurial learning and the dynamics of the firm. The economics profession narrowed its focus by expurgating from its domain welfare enlargements obtainable by detecting profit opportunities created by asymmetric information. This was a major change that inflicted three serious wounds. First, it totally misrepresented the nature of the calculation problem and thereby reinforced the spurious idea that the basis of ownership doesn't matter. Second, it eliminated the classical concern with the role of promarket sociopolitical institutions, which, in turn, hastened the implantation of a proplanning theory of development. And, third, the loss of the entrepreneurial process perspective encouraged misguided antitrust policies that continue to weaken U.S. competitiveness. (See Baumol 1992, 135–36; Baumol and Ordover 1992, 82, 88, 94–95; Jorde and Teece 1992, 47–50, 53–54, 59–63; Schmalensee 1987, 43–47; Schmalensee 1992, 113; and Teece 1993, 208–9, 213–17, 219–20, including n. 40.)

The cardinal objective of this essay has been to convey the deleterious policy consequences of the Walrasian vision, which depicts the market as a black box that combines known equilibrium prices, known preferences, and known production functions to compute the most efficient vector of output allocations. (See Arrow 1974, 3; Jaffé 1983, 222–26, 231–35, 277–78, 353; Kaldor 1934, 127; and Walras 1954, 242.) A quite different (antiplanning) set of policies flows from describing the market as a stream of static-inefficient yet pardonable inconveniences, without which mass misery would be the norm because imagination and experience could not be harnessed to devise improved means of producing and transacting, nor to reveal preferences through competing menus of product variations.

Two important caveats must be added. First, the purpose of this essay is not to imply that all planning is somehow evil. Firms arise to plan and coordinate. But a billion miles separate private, imperfect-foresight planning and the chimerical idea of successful central planning that was begat by the perfect knowledge postulate. Nor should this essay be interpreted as an attack on equilibrium analysis, per se, for without concrete models of perfectly informed agents we would be unable to describe precisely the theoretical consummation of the market's discovery process. As Schumpeter explained, "we have here a proposition that can hardly apply to reality under any conceivable circumstances, [but] which is nevertheless of the utmost importance in order to understand this reality" (1954, 1050, n. 59). Thus, as Baumol had concluded, the perfect competition model "does what it was designed to do and does it well" (1968, 67). Static models have indeed provided a host of valuable insights, and without these irreplaceable instruments the profession would be analytically impoverished.

However, using static tools in a classroom environment that is largely devoid of the notion of dynamic market processes has also incurred a heavy toll: it gave birth, unwittingly, to an anti-entrepreneurial outlook by implicitly redefining as socially harmful a panoply of behaviors that are indispensable to human progress, such as the introduction of new products[13] and the deliberate creation of scale economies by vertically integrating and extending the market via lower prices.

As a postscript, it is worth noting that pathbreaking activity need not be seen only in a disruptive, disequilibrium context. Alternatively, it can be understood as an "equilibrating *response* to preexisting tensions"—tensions in the form of "opportunities that exist *already*" but lie unseized until they are recognized by an alert agent. This, I believe, is the essence of entrepreneurship, as best described in Kirzner 1973, 66–74, 77–81, 129–31. As explained over 60 years ago: "New knowledge and wider understanding may dislocate, but they are essential conditions for final equilibrium" (Radford 1936, 344). New knowledge, however, comes at a price: the unexpungible existence of pure profit (see Eliasson 1992, 252–54).

Conclusion

[The] model of perfect competition . . . is indeed a
wonderful model . . . because it helps us think [meta-
phorically yet] more clearly about . . . achieving efficiency under a market system.
          —*Paul Krugman, "How I Work"*

The mainstream values of an academic discipline are imperceptibly yet effectively transmitted through its analytical toolbox, which defines the terms of discourse and thereby shapes the interpretation of events, as exemplified in the preceding epigraph. The typical practitioner of any scientific culture, therefore, "absorbs a way of thinking and expressing his thoughts that is predetermined by [its] language . . ." (Mises [1919] 1983, 13). With the semiexception of the field of international trade, the pedagogical monopoly of the general equilibrium model has resulted in a "semantic infiltration" that, in turn, exerted "a powerful and baneful . . . influence on our minds" (Moynihan 1985, 30; and Richardson 1960, 138–39, respectively; see also Pipes 1990, 33). An interventionist proclivity was introduced: the perfect competitor would remain forever elusive, but the efficiency results of perfect competition could be artificially secured—through central planning! As a result, the entrepreneurial activities enumerated in this essay—through which we learn of higher utility uses of current resources—came to be seen, ironically, as welfare-reducing phenomena. The fields of antitrust and economic development were particularly susceptible to policies that were unfriendly to entrepreneurs. The post-1980 deregulatory environment has certainly improved matters, but the cognitive impact of the Walrasian model remains potent and dominant, as evidenced by the harsh criticisms of the new antitrust learning that have been flowing from President Clinton's Justice Department (Labaton 1993, F8; McGinley 1994, A1, A10; Davis and Davidson 1993, A1, A14; Novak 1994, A1, A14).

As mentioned previously, my purpose here is not to denigrate equilibrium thinking. One cannot talk about the market process without being ready to rigorously describe its hypothetical endpoint. Therefore, economics requires both modes of analysis simultaneously. They should be seen pedagogically as inseparably supplemental concepts. From the notion of equilibrium, we derive the scientific (i.e., predictive) basis of our discipline, and from the concept of process we derive our understanding of how the equilibrium condition is established; that is, we learn precisely how marginal costs are ultimately equated with marginal benefits, namely, through the competitive behavior of warring entrepreneurs who hold differing expectations of postreallocation values. Their imperfectly informed assessments are reappraised and reconciled through counterbidding, which ceases when marginal cost is driven up to expected price, yielding thereby our most cherished theorem: welfare maximization. The economics profession, therefore, is indeed fortunate, because it can avoid the unappetizing prospect of having "to choose between seeking improvement in prediction and making human action more intelligible" (A. Rosenberg 1995, 213). We possess the tools at hand, and the heritage, to easily accomplish both goals. And we should do so, because our divorce of market outcomes from execution caused us to lose the classical appreciation for the irreplaceability of the entrepreneurial essence of "the process of becoming" (Hegel's generic phrase, quoted in Krugovoy, 1992–93, 105). This led us to see invisible hand results as something untied to the nature of ownership, and hence we came to believe that equilibrium conditions could be mechanically replicated, Lange style (see Machovec 1995, 78–94).

The history of thought of the early decades of the neoclassical era needs to be reappraised. The profession had thus far been unwilling to acknowledge the damage that is directly traceable to its misleading intellectual framework, which implicitly recast the entrepreneur of the classical texts from angel to devil by, in effect, *redefining,* within the thinking engendered by the modern calculus of static welfare,[14] the social impact of entrepreneurially enlarged consumer choice and entrepreneurially reduced opportunity costs. These perceptions have been modified in recent years; nonetheless, the influence of five decades of training is not easily offset. So we remain, for the most part, prisoners of congenital tunnel vision, which largely confines our focus to endstates of perfect knowledge adaptation and thus gives rise to interventionist public-policy goals derived from a totally unachievable and misleading "nirvana" exemplar. (See the conclusions of

Demsetz and of Dahlman described in Langlois 1986, 14.) As the side-stream critics continue their assault on the unintentional yet harmful consequences of mainstream theory, the profession at large hopefully will acquire a better appreciation for, first, the learning cost (pure profit) that *must* be incurred by society to ameliorate ignorance and, second, the public policies that are appropriate to the task of broadening and coordinating knowledge in a world of decentralized specialists.

NOTES

I gratefully acknowledge the Earhart Foundation's generous assistance, which enabled me to write this essay and the 1995 book upon which it is based. Unless noted, all italics in quotes are those of the original authors. A more comprehensive version of this essay is scheduled to appear in the 1998 issue of *Review of Austrian Economics*. It includes separate sections on the impact of the Walrasian vision on the theory of international trade and on the classical view of the effect of redistribution on output incentives. In addition, its discussion of the profession's misunderstanding of the calculation debate of the 1930s is more detailed than that contained herein.

1. Solow's analysis was brought to my attention by Dieter Schneider of Ruhr-Universität Bochum.

2. For a detailed accounting of the various institutions emphasized by Smith and J. S. Mill, see Machovec 1995, 17, 25, 27–33, 80, 90–93, 115–16, 137–38, 144–58, 239, 340.

3. Many additional classical-text illustrations of the four entrepreneurial tasks are contained in Machovec 1995, 22, 96–98, 105–10, 112–18, 121–37, 139–44.

4. See Schumpeter 1991, 254.

5. For more on the equilibrium style—and hence distinctly *un*classical nature—of Ricardo's analysis, see Machovec 1995, 48, 96–97.

6. J. S. Mill also appreciated the different functions of the entrepreneur versus the capitalist (1864, 2:540–41, 544–45; 1967, 422–23). Schumpeter did not recognize that Mill possessed this insight (Schumpeter 1991, 255–56).

7. Malthus's theme reappeared in more fully developed form in the work of Say and Mangoldt (described in Machovec 1995, 127–29, 157). Schumpeter described the latter as one of the nineteenth century's "most significant" economists (1954, 503). A novel modern-day aspect of the discovery of the "better adaptations" of Malthus is described in Green 1996, 315–30.

8. The perfect competitor is the cornerstone of Walras' model. See Jaffé 1983, 222–26; Walras in D. Walker 1984, 461; and Walras 37, 40, 83–85, 106, 117, 164, 167–72, 196–97, 224–25, 242, 247–48, 289–90, 380.

9. Joan Robinson and Piero Sraffa spearheaded this perspective (Machovec 1995, 181–84, 270–73). Eli Heckscher, at the same time, had also begun to frame the issue in these terms (Carlson 1994, 42).

10. The general equilibrium vector is mathematically indeterminate if scale economies have not been exhausted; that is, a firm's profit-maximizing level of output cannot be calculated unless the second derivative of total cost is positive (upward-sloping marginal cost). See either Blaug 1983, 398–400; or Arrow 1971, 68.

11. The quoted phrases are from a reprinted 1903 letter that was supplied to me by Donald A. Walker (of Indiana University in Pennsylvania) and translated by Caroline Cunningham of the Wofford College Foreign Language Department.

12. Even a scrupulously nonpartisan analyst could not claim that the nomination and selection process that resulted in the two Nobel Prizes at issue here was largely unaffected by the proplanning atmosphere that heavily dominated Western intellectual circles throughout the middle half of this century. World War I had brought the tentacles of state direction to the European economies 25 years ahead of the U.S. experience with wartime measures. But, as Cassel explained in the mid-1930s, the Versailles Treaty did not bring a retrenchment of the "unparalleled expansion of the state's functions in the economic field"; instead, this pattern "showed a . . . tendency to continue of its own volition" (quoted in Carlson 1994, 36). Cassel and Heckscher had seen the writing on the wall early. They debated the socialists in Stockholm in 1907, and in 1919 Cassel warned against the worldwide "tidal wave of strivings to bring every possible activity under state control . . ." (quoted in Carlson 1994, 35). Furthermore, Heckscher used a 1934 address to complain about the growing influence of socialist thought and to forthrightly confront those who were preaching it, including two of his younger colleagues who were influential stars in the profession, Gunnar Myrdal and Bertil Ohlin, whom he criticized for being "apostles of the planned economy": "Their nostrils are filled with the new air to the point where they seem in no condition to breath any other" (quoted in Carlson 1994, 100–101). The general populace of Sweden had also been won over. According to the Swedish Oil Committee report of 1947, the prosperity inherited from the old Liberal order had ironically created the chimerical notion that a modern industrial economy is a perpetual production machine, and it was "in this psychological situation that the idea of a 'planned economy' found sustenance and grew to a dominant force in . . . revolutionary circles [as well as] in [the] bourgeois world" (quoted in Carlson 1994, 98).

13. The entrepreneurial widening of choice became a welfare-reducing act in neoclassical theory because, in a static resource world, "unnecessary" variety causes idle capacity in plants—capacity that would be put to use in a world of homogeneous goods produced under perfect competition. This phenomenon is better known as "the waste theorem." See Bishop 1967, 254–56, and Samuelson 1980, 486–87; also see the helpful diagram and related discussion on Mill's neoclassical perspective on this subject in Machovec 1995, 132–36.

14. In the general equilibrium model, the perfect knowledge postulate precludes the existence of profit-making opportunities through its total elimination of the entrepreneur's comparative advantage, namely, his superior ability to detect and exploit *a*symmetric information. Since new information is immediately transmitted to everyone in a Walrasian system, a frictionless jump to a new equilibrium occurs through the simultaneous, fully coordinated (i.e., perfectly informed) adjustments of all agents. But the perpetual equilibrium condition does not mean that per capita income must be stagnant. If scientific advancement is allowed (presumably through state-funded R&D), *and* if the ultimate effects of each new technology are predictable, then, at the moment of introduction, every firm will react to a revised optimization calculus and supply curves will shift outward, causing an instantaneous movement to a new, higher income equilibrium (Stigler 1957, 11–12). Allyn Young's

previously cited complaint to Knight—that the general equilibrium system, standing alone, cannot "get us anywhere"—was therefore prescient. Without *exogenous* (governmental) infusions of innovation, the Walrasian model can describe only a steady-state economy. This limitation is in no way sinful, but the inappropriate application of such a system to make unwarranted efficiency judgments about a real world economy *is* sinful. Ironically, the instrumental role of the genuine entrepreneur—who earns economic profit from recognizing and seizing opportunities created by asymmetric information—was correctly described by Walras (see Walker 1986, 4–6); however, Walras chose to abstract away from this conception in his model by giving the same set of information to all agents via his "auctioneer" (see Machovec 1995, 45–46, 122, 161–79, 302). That is, the perfect information postulate precludes any *en*dogenous behavior that enhances welfare through profit creation; moreover, all such initiatives came to be portrayed in our baseline general equilibrium model as welfare-reducing phenomena amenable to improvement through the corrective actions of a better informed overseer.

REFERENCES

Arrow, Kenneth. 1971. "The Firm in General Equilibrium." In *The Corporate Economy,* edited by R. Morris and A. Wood. Cambridge: Harvard University Press.
———. 1974. "Limited Knowledge and Economic Analysis." *American Economic Review* 64, no. 1 (Mar.): 1–10.
Bator, Francis M. 1957. "The Simple Analytics of Welfare Maximization." *American Economic Review* 47, no. 1 (Mar.): 22–59.
Baumol, William J. 1968. "Entrepreneurship in Economic Theory." *American Economic Review, Papers and Proceedings* 58, no. 2 (May): 64–92.
———. 1992. "Horizontal Collusion and Innovation." *Economic Journal* 102, no. 410 (Jan.): 129–37.
Baumol, William J., and Janusz A. Ordover. 1992. "Antitrust: Source of Dynamic *and* Static Inefficiencies?" In *Antitrust, Innovation, and Competitiveness,* edited by T. M. Jorde and D. J. Teece. New York: Oxford University Press.
Beach, E. F. 1990. "Marshall on Statical Assumptions." *Indian Economic Journal* 37, no. 4 (April–June): 7–22.
Becker, Gary S., and Kevin M. Murphy. 1992. "The Division of Labor, Coordination Costs, and Knowledge." *Quarterly Journal of Economics* 107, no. 4 (Nov.): 1137–60.
Bentham, Jeremy. 1843. *The Works of Jeremy Bentham.* Edited by J. Bowring. Vol. 3. Edinburgh: Wm. Tait.
———. 1952. *Jeremy Bentham's Economic Writings,* edited by W. Stark. New York: Burt Franklin.
Bishop, Robert L. 1967. "Monopolistic Competition and Welfare Economics." In *Monopoly Competition Theory: Studies in Impact,* edited by R. E. Kuenne. New York: Wiley.
Blaug, Mark. 1983. *Economic Theory in Retrospect.* 3d ed. Cambridge: Cambridge University Press.

———. 1993. Review of *From Marx to Mises: Post-Capitalist Society and the Challenge of Economic Calculation,* in *Economic Journal* 103, no. 421 (Nov.): 1570–71.

———. 1994. "Not Only an Economist: Autobiographical Reflections of a Historian of Economic Thought." *American Economist* (Fall): vol. xxxviii, no. 2. pp. 12–27.

Blitch, Charles P. 1983. "Allyn Young on Increasing Returns." *Journal of Post Keynesian Economics* 5, no. 3 (Spring): 359–72.

Boornstein, Morris, ed. 1989. *Comparative Economic Systems: Models and Cases.* Homewood, IL: Irwin.

Buchanan, James M. 1987. "Constitutional Economics." In *The New Palgrave: A Dictionary of Economics,* edited by J. Eatwell et al. vol. 1. London: Macmillan.

Carlson, Benny. 1994. *The State as Monster: Gustav Cassel and Eli Hecksher on the Role and Growth of the State.* Lanham: University Press of America.

Chamberlin, E. R. 1933. *Theory of Monopolistic Competition.* Cambridge: MA: Harvard University Press.

Coase, Ronald H. 1977. "The Wealth of Nations." *Economic Inquiry* 15, no. 3 (July): 309–25.

Davis, B., and J. Davidson. 1993. "Clinton Team Is Split about Antitrust Policy as Big Mergers Wait." *Wall Street Journal,* October 28.

Eatwell, John. 1987. "Competition: Classical Conceptions." In *The New Palgrave: A Dictionary of Economics,* edited by J. Eatwell et al. London: Macmillan.

Edgeworth, Francis Y. 1925. *Papers Relating to Political Economy.* Vol. 2. London: Macmillan.

Eliasson, Gunnar. 1992. "Business Competence, Organizational Learning, and Economic Growth: Establishing the Smith-Schumpeter-Wicksell Connection." In *Entrepreneurship, Technological Innovation, and Economic Growth,* edited by F. M. Scherer and Mark Perlman. Ann Arbor: University of Michigan Press.

George, David. 1992. "Obscuring the Normative: How the Texts Evaluate Monopolisitic Competition." *Methodus* 4, no. 2 (Dec.): 96–104.

Green, Christopher. 1996. "Economic Dynamism: Durability, Learning, and Time-Differentiated Demand." In *Behavioral Norms, Technological Progress, and Economic Dynamics: Studies in Schumpeterian Economics,* edited by Ernst Helmstädter and Mark Perlman. Ann Arbor: University of Michigan Press.

Hahn, Frank. 1970. "Some Adjustment Problems." *Econometrica* 38, no. 1 (Jan.): 1–17.

Hartwell, Robert M. 1978. "Adam Smith and the Industrial Revolution." In *Adam Smith and the Wealth of Nations, 1776–1976: Bicentennial Essays,* edited by F. R. Ghade. Boulder: Colorado Associated University Press.

Homan, Paul T. 1928. *Contemporary Economic Thought.* New York: Harper.

Hoselitz, Bert F. 1960. "The Early History of Entrepreneurial Theory." In *Essays in Economic Thought: Aristotle to Marshall,* edited by J. Spengler and W. Allen. Chicago: Rand McNally.

Hotelling, Harold. 1929. "Stability in Competition." *Economic Journal* 39, no. 153 (March): 41–57.

Hughes, Jonathan. 1990. Review of C. Walker and M. Bloomfield, eds., *Intellectual Property Rights and Capital Formation in the Next Decade. Journal of Economic Literature* 28, no. 3 (Sept.): 1235–36.

Jaffé, William, ed. 1965. *Correspondence of Léon Walras and Related Papers.* Vol. 3. Amsterdam: North-Holland.

———. 1980. "Walras's Economics as Others See It." *Journal of Economic Literature* 18, no. 2 (June): 528–49.

———. 1983. *William Jaffé's Essays on Walras.* Edited by D. Walker. Cambridge: Cambridge University Press.

Jorde, T. M., and D. J. Teece. 1992. "Innovation, Cooperation, and Antitrust." In *Antitrust, Innovation, and Competitiveness,* edited by T. M. Jorde and D. J. Teece. New York: Oxford University Press.

Kaldor, Nicholas. 1934. "A Classificatory Note on the Determinativeness of Equilibrium." *Review of Economic Studies* 1 (Feb.): 122–36.

Katzner, Donald W. 1991. "In Defense of Formalization in Economics." *Methodus* 3, no. 1 (June).

Kirzner, Israel M. 1973. *Competition and Entrepreneurship.* Chicago: University of Chicago Press.

Klein, Peter G. 1996. "Economic Calculation and the Limits of Organization." *Review of Austrian Economics* 9, no. 1: 3–28.

Knight, Frank. 1936. "The Place of Marginal Economics in a Collectivist System." *American Economic Review* supplement, xxvi, no. 1 (Mar.): 255–66.

———. 1938a. Review of L. von Mises' *Socialism. Journal of Political Economy* 46, no. 2 (Apr.): 267–69.

———. 1938b. "Two Economists on Socialism [R. L. Hall and A. C. Pigou]." *Journal of Political Economy* 46, no. 2 (Apr.): 241–50.

———. 1964. *Risk, Uncertainty, and Profit.* New York: Augustus Kelley.

Koebner, Richard. 1959. "Adam Smith and the Industrial Revolution." *Economic History Review* Second series, 11, no. 3 (Apr.): 381–91.

Konow, James. 1994. "The Political Economy of Heinrich von Stackelberg." *Economic Inquiry* 32, no. 1 (Jan.): 146–65.

Krueger, Anne O. 1992. *Economic Policy Reform in Developing Countries.* Oxford: Blackwell.

Krugman, Paul. 1993. "How I Work." *American Economist* 37, no. 2 (Fall): 25–31.

Krugovoy, George. 1992–93. "Kant's *Critiques* and Dostoevsky's *Notes from Underground.*" Translated by the Association of Russian-American Scholars. Zapiski Russko Akademicheske, no. 25. Richmond Hill, NJ.

Kuhn, Thomas. 1970. *The Structure of Scientific Revolutions.* Chicago: University of Chicago Press.

Labaton, Stephen. 1993. "Rousing Antitrust Law from Its 12-Year Nap." *New York Times,* July 25.

Langlois, Richard. 1986. "The New Institutional Economics." In *Economics as a Process: Essays in the New Institutional Economics,* edited by Richard Langlois. Cambridge: Cambridge University Press.

Longfield, M. 1834. *Lectures on Political Economy.* Dublin: Richard Milliken & Son.

Machovec, Frank M. 1995. *Perfect Competition and the Transformation of Economics.* London: Routledge. For those who purchase this volume, please write the author for the errata list: Wofford College, Box 51, 429 N. Church St., Spartanburg, SC 29303.

Malthus, Thomas. 1968. *Principles of Political Economy.* 2d ed. New York: Augustus Kelley.

Marshall, Alfred. 1920. *Principles of Economics.* 8th ed. New York: Macmillan.

McCulloch, J. R. 1832. "A Treatise on the Principles, Practice, and History of Commerce." In *The Library of Useful Knowledge.* Misc. vol. London: Society for the Diffusion of Knowledge. Each entry was paginated separately. This was a commissioned essay. See W. D. Sockwell, "Contributions of Henry Brougham to Classical Political Economy." *History of Political Economy* (Winter 1991): 666–68.

McGinley, L. 1994. "Clinton's Regulators Zero in on Companies with Renewed Fervor." *Wall Street Journal,* October 19.

Mill, J. S. 1864. *Principles of Political Economy.* 5th ed. New York: Appleton.

——. 1967. *The Collected Works of John Stuart Mill,* edited by J. Robson. Vol. 5. Toronto: University of Toronto Press.

——. 1977. *The Collected Works of John Stuart Mill,* edited by J. Robson. Vol. 18. Toronto: University of Toronto Press.

——. 1987. *On Liberty,* edited by G. Himmelfarb. New York: Penguin.

Mises, Ludwig von. [1919] 1983. *Nation, State, and Economy.* Translated by Leland Yeager. New York: New York University Press.

Moynihan, Daniel. 1985. "Notable and Quotable." *Wall Street Journal,* April 18.

Myint, Hla. 1987. "Neoclassical Development Analysis: Its Strengths and Limitations." In *Pioneers in Development,* edited by Gerald Meier. 2d ser. New York: Oxford University Press.

Myrdal, Gunnar. 1957. *Rich Lands and Poor Lands.* New York: Harper & Row.

Newman, Peter. 1990. "Reviews by Edgeworth." In *A Century of Economics: 100 Years of the Royal Economic Society and the Economic Journal,* edited by J. D. Hey and D. Winch. Oxford: Basil Blackwell.

Novak, Viveca. 1994. "Nasdaq Investigation Showcases New Moxie at Justice Department." *Wall Street Journal,* October 20.

Peterson, Shorey. 1957. "Antitrust Policy and the Classic Model." *American Economic Review* 48, no. 1 (Mar.): 60–78.

Pipes, Richard. 1992. "Russia's Chance." *Commentary* 89, no. 3 (Mar.): 28–33.

Prowse, Richard. 1997. "The Road to Hayek: To Liberty via America." *National Review* 49, no. 3 (Feb. 24): 30–34.

Radford, Arthur. 1936. *Patterns of Economic Activity.* London: Routledge.

Rae, John. 1895. *Life of Adam Smith.* London: Macmillan.

Ricardo, David. 1957. *Principles of Political Economy and Taxation.* 3d ed. London: Dent.

Richardson, G. B. 1960. *Information and Investment.* London: Oxford University Press.

Robinson, Joan. [1933] 1965. *Economics of Imperfect Competition.* London: Macmillan.

Rosenberg, Alexander. 1995. *Philosophy of Social Science.* 2d ed. New York: Westview Press of HarperCollins.

Rosenberg, Nathan. 1960. "Some Institutional Aspects of *Wealth of Nations.*" *Journal of Political Economy* 68, no. 6 (Dec.): 557–70.

——. 1994. "Joseph Schumpeter: Radical Economist." In *Schumpeter in the His-*

tory of Ideas, edited by Yuichi Shionoya and Mark Perlman. Ann Arbor: University of Michigan Press.

Samuelson, Paul. 1977. "A Modern Theorist's Vindication of Adam Smith." *American Economic Review* 67, no. 1 (Feb.): 42–49.

———. 1980. *Economics.* 11th ed. New York: McGraw Hill.

Schmalensee, Richard. 1987. "Horizontal Merger Policy: Problems and Changes." *Journal of Economic Perspectives* 1, no. 2 (Fall): 41–54.

———. 1992. "Agreements between Competitors." In *Antitrust, Innovation, and Competitiveness,* edited by T. M. Jorde and D. J. Teece. New York: Oxford University Press.

Schumpeter, Joseph. 1934. *The Theory of Economic Development.* Trans. R. Opie. Cambridge: Harvard University Press.

———. [1942] 1976. *Capitalism, Socialism, and Democracy.* Edited by Thomas Bottomore. 3d ed. New York: Harper Colophon.

———. 1950. "March into Socialism." *American Economic Review, Papers and Proceedings* 50, no. 2 (May): 446–56.

———. 1954. *History of Economic Analysis.* New York: Oxford University Press.

———. 1991. *Essays on Entrepreneurs, Innovations, Business Cycles, and the Evolution of Capitalism.* Edited by R. Clemence. New Brunswick, NJ: Transaction.

Senior, Nassau. 1928. *Industrial Efficiency and Social Economy.* Edited by S. L. Levy. Vol. 2. New York: Henry Holt.

Sidgwick, Henry. 1901. *Principles of Political Economy.* 3d ed. London: Macmillan.

Silver, Morris. 1984. *Enterprise and the Scope of the Form: The Role of Vertical Integration.* Oxford: Martin Robertson.

Sismondi, J. C. L. Sismonde de. 1991. *New Principles of Political Economy.* Edited and translated by R. Hyse. New Brunswick, NJ: Transaction.

Skinner, A. S. 1990. "The Shaping of Political Economy in the Enlightenment." *Scottish Journal of Political Economy* 37, no. 2 (May): 145–65.

Smith, Adam. 1937. *Wealth of Nations.* Edited by E. Cannan. New York: Modern Library.

———. 1976. *Theory of Moral Sentiments.* Edited by D. D. Raphael and A. L. Macfie. Indianapolis: Liberty.

Solow, Robert. 1956. Review of Jaffé's translation of Walras's *Elements of Pure Economics. Econometrica* 24, no. 1 (Jan): 87–89.

Stigler, George. 1937. "A Generalization of the Theory of Imperfect Competition." *Journal of Farm Economics* 19, no. 3 (Aug.): 707–17.

———. 1951. "The Division of Labor Is Limited by the Extent of the Market." *Journal of Political Economy* 59, no. 3 (June): 185–93.

———. 1957. "Perfect Competition, Historically Contemplated." *Journal of Political Economy* 65, no. 1 (Feb.): 1–17.

———. 1990. "The Place of Marshall's *Principles* in the Development of Economics." In *Centenary Essays on Alfred Marshall,* edited by J. Whitaker. Cambridge: Cambridge University Press.

Streissler, Erich W. 1994. "The Influence of German and Austrian Economics on Joseph A. Schumpeter." In *Schumpeter in the History of Ideas,* edited by Yuichi Shionoya and Mark Perlman. Ann Arbor: University of Michigan Press.

Teece, David J. 1993. "The Dynamics of Industrial Capitalism: Perspectives on

Alfred Chandler's *Scale and Scope.*" *Journal of Economic Literature* 31, no. 1 (Mar.): 199–225.

Tucker, Robert C., ed. 1978. *The Marx-Engels Reader.* 2d ed. New York: Norton.

Walker, Donald A. 1984. "Is Walras' Theory of General Equilibrium a Normative Scheme?" *History of Political Economy* 16, no. 3 (Fall): 445–69.

———. 1986. "Walras's Theory of the Entrepreneur." *De Economist* 134:1.

Walras, Léon. 1954. *Elements of Pure Economics.* Edited and translated by William Jaffé. London: George Allen and Unwin.

Wasson, Tyler, ed. 1987. *Nobel Prize Winners.* New York: H. W. Wilson.

West, E. G. 1976. "Adam Smith's Economics of Politics." *History of Political Economy* 8, no. 4 (Winter): 515–39.

———. 1978. "The Burdens of Monopoly: Classical versus Neoclassical." *Southern Economic Journal* 44, no. 4 (Apr.): 829–45.

Wicksteed, Philip H. [1910] 1946. *The Common Sense of Political Economy.* Edited by Lionel Robbins. London: Routledge.

Wiles, Peter D. J. 1977. *Economic Institutions Compared.* New York: Halsted Press of Wiley.

Young, Allyn A. 1928. "Increasing Returns and Economic Progress." *Economic Journal* 38, no. 152 (Dec.): 527–42.

Schumpeter and Personal Capitalism

Richard N. Langlois

What kind of capitalism creates rapid and sustained economic growth? One perspective on this question, going back at least to Adam Smith, has focused on those background institutions of civil society that are able to channel the rent-seeking proclivities of individuals into the production of new wealth rather than into the redistribution of existing wealth. Somewhat more recently, however, a perspective has arisen that stresses the role in economic growth not of abstract institutional structures but of the concrete institutions of business organization, notably the modern business firm. Preeminent among living proponents of this latter view is Alfred Chandler (1977, 1990), who retells the story of recent (nineteenth- and twentieth-century) economic growth in the now-developed countries as a history of the rise of managerial capitalism. In at least some understandings of Chandler, this managerial capitalism, in which trained professional managers run large multidivisional organizations, is to be contrasted with the more backward structures of "personal" capitalism, in which firms are controlled by individual owner-managers.

Before there was Chandler, of course, there was Schumpeter, whose work is a source not only of an important view similar to that of Chandler but also—perhaps astonishingly—of the opposite view, namely, that the source of economic growth is indeed to be found in the behavior of individuals—of entrepreneurs—who create new wealth, often at the expense of old wealth, within the constraints of a particular kind of civil society. In an earlier essay (Langlois 1987), I presented an argument (not yet well absorbed by members of the Schumpeter Society[1] let alone by the profession at large) that, contrary to conventional wisdom, these two visions of capitalism and economic growth do not track the difference between an earlier (or "Mark I") and a later (or "Mark II") Schumpeter; rather, these two views coexist in a way that is remarkably consistent over time in Schumpeter's work. Like Chandler (McCraw 1988), Schumpeter was heavily influenced by Max Weber's theory of bureaucracy and social progress (Csontos 1991). In both his early (1934) and his later (1950) work, Schumpeter consistently espoused the view that "progressive rationalization" in Weber's sense would make innovation a matter of routine, thus rendering obsolete the personal capitalism of the entrepreneur and bringing to dominance in economic growth the role of the large bureaucratic organization.

In that earlier essay, I criticized Schumpeter's account of the obsolescence of the entrepreneur on the grounds that it reflects an illegitimate shift of underlying epistemology or, to put it another way, that it rests on a confusion about the nature of scientific knowledge and its role in what we would nowadays call the competences of the firm. In this essay, I take up this argument again, moving it away from the realm of the doctrine-historical and the epistemological into the provinces of the economics of organization. Using a detailed historical account of the Swiss watch industry as a focusing device, I will suggest that the notion of personal capitalism is a far more subtle and complex one than its detractors have recognized. Moreover, far from being a primitive holdover from precorporate times, personal capitalism—properly understood—is in fact an important engine of economic change and growth.

Schumpeter and Weber

The broad outlines of Schumpeter's theory of entrepreneurship are of Weberian provenance.[2] Indeed, one might say that Schumpeter's schema is an application of Weber's social theory to the problem of economic growth. Schumpeter's innovation is to associate Weber's category of charismatic leadership with the concept of entrepreneurship.

As it is for Weber, capitalist development is for Schumpeter a march from traditional to rational behavior. In "the circular flow of economic life," Schumpeter's version of equilibrium in early capitalism, behavior is rational only within the bounds of traditional or habitual behavior.

> The assumption that conduct is prompt and rational is in all cases a fiction. But it proves to be sufficiently near to reality, if things have time to hammer logic into men. Where this has happened, and within the limits in which it has happened, one may rest content with this fiction and build theories upon it. It is then not true that habit or custom or non-economic ways of thinking cause a hopeless difference between the individuals of different classes, times, or cultures, and that, for example, the "economics of the stock exchange" would be inapplicable say to the peasants of to-day or the craftsmen of the Middle Ages. On the contrary the same theoretical picture in its broadest contour lines fits the individuals of quite different cultures, whatever their degree of intelligence and of economic rationality, and we can depend upon it that the peasant sells his calf as cunningly and egotistically as the stock exchange member his portfolio of shares. But this holds good only where precedents without number have formed conduct through decades and, in fundamentals, through hundreds of thousands of years, and have eliminated unadapted behavior. (1934, 80)

This picture of economic behavior as guided by routines—indeed, by routines that seem to be the result of some kind of selection process—is the inspiration for much of the association of Schumpeter with modern evolutionary economics (Nelson and Winter 1982), an association that, pace Hodgson (1993), is not at all unwarranted despite Schumpeter's negative remarks about evolutionary biology (Langlois and Everett 1994).

Economic growth can take place only when the circular flow is upset, which requires the entrepreneur. Since—in early capitalism, at least—rational action can occur only within the bounds of evolved habit, the behavior of the entrepreneur must be non- or extrarational; it must be a matter of intuition.

> What has been done already has the sharp-edged reality of all things which we have seen and experienced; the new is only the figment of our imagination. Carrying out a new plan and acting according to a customary one are things as different as making a road and walking along it.
>
> How different a thing this is becomes clearer if one bears in mind the impossibility of surveying exhaustively all the effects and counter-effects of the projected enterprise. Even as many of them as could in theory be ascertained if one had unlimited time and means must practically remain in the dark. As military action must be taken in a given strategic position even if all the data potentially procurable are not available, so also in economic life action must be taken without working out all the details of what must be done. Here the success of everything depends on intuition, the capacity of seeing things in a way which afterwards proves to be true, even though it cannot be established at the moment, and of grasping the essential fact, discarding the unessential, even though one can give no account of the principles by which this is done. Thorough preparatory work, and special knowledge, breadth of intellectual understanding, talent for logical analysis, may under certain circumstances be sources of failure. (Schumpeter 1934, 85)

I will return to the cognitive implications of this view presently. For the moment, however, the important point is that entrepreneurial action is an instance of charismatic leadership, which, for Weber as for Schumpeter, is central to the theory of social change (Parsons 1949, 663).

Weber is principally concerned with the religious leader or prophet, and to a lesser extent with military and political leadership; Schumpeter borrows heavily from that analysis in his characterization of the entrepreneur. Here we begin to see the outlines of Schumpeterian "personal capitalism," which in its pure form is the antithesis of bureaucratic organization. Consider Weber's account of the organization of charisma.

The corporate group which is subject to charismatic authority is based on an emotional form of communal relationship. The administrative staff of the charismatic leader does not consist of "officials"; at least its members are not technically trained. . . . There is no hierarchy; the leader merely intervenes in general or in individual cases when he considers the members of his staff inadequate to a task to which they have been entrusted. There is no such thing as a definite sphere of authority and of competence. . . . There are no established administrative organs. . . . There is no system of formal rules, of abstract legal principles, and hence no process of judicial decision oriented to them. But equally there is no legal wisdom oriented to judicial precedent. Formally concrete judgments are newly created from case to case and are originally regarded as divine judgments and revelations. . . . The genuine prophet, like the genuine military leader and every true leader in this sense, preaches, creates, or demands *new* obligations. In the pure type of charisma, these are imposed on the authority of revolution [*sic*] by oracles, or of the leader's own will, and are recognized by the members of the religious, military, or party group because they come from such a source. (1947, 360–61)

But the charismatic organization is perhaps best understood in contrast to what it is *not.*

Charismatic authority is thus outside the realm of everyday routine and the profane sphere. In this respect it is sharply opposed both to rational, and particularly bureaucratic, authority, and to traditional authority, whether in its patriarchal, patrimonial, or any other form. Both rational and traditional authority are specifically forms of everyday routine control of action; while the charismatic type is the direct antithesis of this. Bureaucratic authority is specifically rational in the sense of being bound to intellectually analysable rules; while charismatic authority is specifically irrational in the sense of being foreign to all rules. Traditional authority is bound to the precedents handed down from the past and to this extent is also oriented to rules. Within the sphere of its claims, charismatic authority repudiates the past, and is in this sense a specifically revolutionary force. (361–62)

It is the charismatic, and therefore revolutionary, quality of entrepreneurship that makes it a source of economic growth, that allows it to play the role of "industrial mutation—if I may use that biological term—that incessantly revolutionizes the industrial structure *from within,* incessantly destroying the old one, incessantly creating a new one" (Schumpeter 1950, 83; emphasis original).

Recast in these explicitly Weberian terms, Schumpeter's theory of entrepreneurship looks something like this. In its undeveloped state, an economy is based largely on traditional behavior, which bounds the possibilities for conscious economic activity. In the right institutional setting—bourgeois capitalism—charismatic leadership arises, in the form of the entrepreneur, to break the crust of convention and to create new wealth by " 'lead[ing]' the means of production into new channels" (Schumpeter 1934, 89). Charisma is personal and revolutionary; "in its pure form charismatic authority may be said to exist only in the process of originating. It cannot remain stable, but becomes either traditionalized or rationalized, or a combination of both" (Weber 1947, 364). In the economic sphere, of course, the tendency is toward rationalization. Not only do imitators rush in once the entrepreneur has blazed the trail, but also the problem of succession within the entrepreneurial organization leads (if the organization is to continue) to bureaucratization, that is, to the substitution of rules for personal authority, to the creation of abstract offices divorced from their individual holders, and to the increasing preeminence of specialized knowledge and spheres of competence (Weber 1947, 330–34).

Progressive Rationalization

The transformation from the traditional to the rational takes place at two levels. At the level of each entrepreneurial organization, charismatic authority, having destroyed the traditional, must eventually give way to bureaucracy as the problem of succession arises. It is here that we can locate Chandler's notions of personal and managerial capitalism. What he finds wanting in personal capitalism is precisely the extent of rationalization in the Weberian sense. Compared with the foremost examples of managerial capitalism (e.g., in the United States), the British, Chandler argues, failed adequately to extend hierarchical control and create management based on abstract rules and spheres of competence.

> In most British enterprises senior executives worked closely in the same office building, locate in or near the largest plant, having almost daily personal contact with, and thus directly supervising, middle and often lower-level managers. Such enterprises had no need for the detailed organization charts and manuals that had come into common use in large American and German firms before 1914. In these British companies, selection to senior positions and to the board depended as much on personal ties as on managerial competence. The founders and their heirs continued to have a significant influence on top-level decision-making even after their holdings in the enterprise were diminished. (1990, 242)

British personal capitalism thus represented a kind of half-way house be-tween the charismatic founders and full rationalization on the American model. I will return to this strand of thought later.

At another level, however, resides the claim that progressive rational-ization affects the entire economic society, eventually displacing traditional-ism completely. The entrepreneur is both the agent and the victim of this transformation. In uprooting deeply planted traditional ways of life, the entrepreneur prepares the field for rational authority.[3] But—and this is the heart of Schumpeter's thesis—once the hard work of crust breaking has been done, charismatic leadership is no longer necessary, and the entrepre-neur must ride into the sunset. The entrepreneurial role is then taken up by large bureaucratic firms, organized along rational lines, which can engineer change without the need for charisma. The final result of process of progres-sive rationalization, indeed, is a kind of bureaucratic socialism, since, with-out any substantive function or source of legitimacy, entrepreneurial capi-talism as a system must ultimately follow the entrepreneur westward.

At first glance, Schumpeter's brief in favor of large organizations seems consistent with Weber, who praised the efficiency of rational bureau-cracy in the most lavish terms.[4]

> Experience tends universally to show that the purely bureaucratic type of administrative organization—that is, the monocratic variety of bureaucracy—is, from a purely technical point of view, capable of attaining the highest degree of efficiency and is in this sense formally the most rational known means of carrying out imperative control over human beings. It is superior to any other form in precision, in stability, in the stringency of its discipline, and in its reliability. It thus makes possible a particularly high degree of calculability of results for the heads of the organization and for those acting in relation to it. It is finally superior both in intensive efficiency and in the scope of its operations, and is formally capable of application to all kinds of admin-istrative tasks. (1947, 337)

Notice, however, that this paean does not portray bureaucracy as innova-tive. It is precise and reliable but not necessarily dynamic. "Both rational and traditional authority," as we saw, "are specifically forms of everyday routine control of action" (361). Bureaucracy is designed for "imperative control over human beings," that is, making people do what the boss wants, but not necessarily for performing the multifold tasks of an entire economy. And it produces results that are "calculable" because it reduces internal variance, not necessarily because it (or rationalization more generally) ex-tends the scope of human ability to "calculate" or predict the future.

Indeed, one could argue that Schumpeter goes well beyond Weber—into what, in my view, is illegitimate territory. Recall that, for Schumpeter, progressive rationalization seems to mean more than the Weberian idea of demystification; it seems also to mean that the growth of scientific knowledge will extend the bounds of rationality in the sense of Herbert Simon: with progressive rationalization, our "control of facts" becomes more perfect, and we become able "quickly and reliably" to calculate what had previously required intuition and a "flash of genius." Schumpeter is thus making a claim about the cognitive, not merely the command and control, possibilities of bureaucracy.

I doubt that we live in a wiser age; but I do think that we are perhaps more accustomed today than in Schumpeter's time to question the cognition-expanding character of conscious, scientific knowledge. The best and the brightest have too often failed to live up to their billing. As F. A. Hayek (1948) argued in the context of the socialist calculation debate, such stout claims for conscious scientific knowledge (on which the possibility of socialist calculation depends) are an insupportable hubris that ignores the large and ineradicable role of rules, routine, and tacit knowledge. Rationality—or, more correctly, cognitive ability—is perhaps even more bounded today, in the avalanche of information that "progressive rationalization" has generated, than it was in more traditional times.

Interestingly, it is far from clear that Weber would have been on Schumpeter's side in this matter. For one thing, Weber, as we saw, stressed the static character of bureaucracy. Bureaucracy is about imposing rules, not about changing them. It is a way to marshal well-defined means in service of a well-defined end; but, like the ideal type of traditional authority, rational authority is not dynamic. On the matter of bureaucracy replacing entrepreneurial capitalism, we can note that Weber came down explicitly *against* the possibility of socialist calculation, effectively endorsing the views of Mises.[5]

Schumpeterianism: Mark I and Mark II

We learn the most from writers like Weber and Schumpeter not when we approach them from the perspective of the antiquarian or the adoring disciple but when we treat them as capable of engaging our own research programs. How, then, can we apply their ideas to the present-day discussion of capitalism, organizational form, and economic growth?

Much of the modern literature has focused on the idea of *organizational capabilities,* which provides a language large enough to encompass the ideas of Weber and Schumpeter. Broadly speaking, organizational capabilities are what organizations can do well; and Weber was arguably talking about organizational capabilities when he described the efficiency of rational bureaucracy.

The term *capabilities* was first used by G. B. Richardson (1972, 888) to refer to "the knowledge, experience, and skills" of the organization. In

Richardson, however, the import of the concept was not to emphasize the *extent* of organizational capabilities but rather to stress their *limitations*. Because of what are effectively cognitive constraints, all organizations must specialize; and, since the chain of production in an advanced economy requires a diversity of very different capabilities, the costs of integrating across many links in that chain are necessarily high, and firms must rely on various kinds of market arrangements to coordinate their activities even in the face of the "contractual hazards" emphasized in transaction cost economics.

This point has also been made in a slightly different way by Nelson and Winter (1982) and to some extent by the "dynamic capabilities" literature they helped to inspire (Teece and Pisano 1994; Langlois and Robertson 1995). In Nelson and Winter, economic action, even within large organizations, is a matter of rule-following behavior. Agents possess repertoires of routines, which are habitual patterns of behavior that consist in tacit, skill-like knowledge. These agents are "boundedly rational" and do not consciously survey their environments and choose a substantively rational course of action except within the bounds of what routine behavior has made possible.[6] The parallels here with Schumpeter's account of traditional behavior in the circular flow should be obvious. The crucial difference, however, is that Nelson and Winter see such behavior not as limited to earlier society but as an inescapable implication of the mechanics of human cognition. Agents in advanced capitalism also follow rules and abide by habits. By implication, economic change to Nelson and Winter is a nonrational or entrepreneurial activity: it is taking a leap into the unknown, not a matter of conscious planning.

There are, however, some present-day writers who are inclined to take the notion of organizational capabilities in a different direction and to extract from it some very large claims for the efficacy of large organizations and for their superiority to individual action and smaller, more personal enterprises. For example, William Lazonick (1991), who likes his Schumpeter with a large dollop of Marx, presents what is arguably a historicist account of the progressive development of capitalism, which reaches its apex in "collective capitalism."[7] As in Schumpeter's account of later capitalism, large organizations in Lazonick's collective capitalism are not only effective at managing existing structures but are also prime engines of innovation. And, as in Schumpeter, the basis for the innovativeness and the wealth-creating character of large organizations resides in their ability effectively to break cognitive boundaries and consciously to reinvent the division of labor.

> The more technologically complex the innovation, the greater the need for innovative skills and the more extensive the specialized division of labor required to develop and utilize these skills. The organization must not only develop these specialized skills so that they can

contribute to the innovation, but also coordinate them so that they constitute a collective productive power. *Organizational capability permits the enterprise to plan* and coordinate the development of these innovative skills, integrating them into an enterprise-specific collective force. As far as the innovation process is concerned, therefore, *organizational capability permits the planned coordination* of the horizontal and vertical division of labor required to generate an innovation. (203; emphasis altered)

It is not clear what are the details of how this planning and coordination takes place, but we are left with the strong impression that it is decidedly not the handiwork of some charismatic central individual, or of the firm's owners in any sense, but is instead the product of professional managers.

At the risk of parody, let me denote these two visions of organizational capabilities as "Schumpeterianism Mark I" and "Schumpeterianism Mark II." Which of these is closer to right? History may shed some light on the issue, even if it may never be decisive. Consider, for example, a case with some clear Weberian resonances: the development, over more than four centuries, of the watchmaking industry in John Calvin's Geneva and the nearby Jura mountains.[8]

From Friedrich Hayek to Nicolas Hayek

Calvinism was in one sense responsible for the birth of the Swiss watch industry. Noted jewelry makers and goldsmiths in the Middle Ages, Genevans found it necessary to apply their capabilities in new directions in the austere climate of Calvinism. Fortunately, "the same puritanical regime that condemned jewelry was willing to make an exception for watches: if Calvinists were not interested in time and its measurement, who was?" (Landes 1983, 232). The reconversion was accomplished under the tutelage of immigrant Huguenots who were fleeing persecution elsewhere in Europe.

In the sixteenth century, watchmaking was a skilled craft carried out in individual workshops. Despite the medieval ideal of the "compleat" craftsman, there was in fact considerable division of labor within the workshop, with various apprentices and journeymen carrying on relatively specialized activities under the supervision of the master (Landes 1983, 206–7). The watch industry was already well established by the time Geneva, a most bourgeois and therefore mercantilist city, got around to forming a guild in 1601. Apart from normal restrictions on entry, the Genevan *fabrique* also sought to keep out immigrants and even their native-born children. In the face of success and growing demand, these restrictions generated an unintended incentive for evasion along with the intended economic rents. The result was the birth of the *établissage* system, in which a master watchmaker put out component fabrication to non-guild (and therefore cheaper) subcontractors outside the city gates. Soon the more routine tasks—like the production of the *ébauche,* the basic watch movement lacking finish and adjustment—were sent "offshore" to nearby France and Savoy, with the fine assembly reserved for Geneva (Landes 1983, 240–43).

The division of labor under *établissage* thus proceeded within a trajectory of vertical fragmentation and heavy reliance on arm's length coordination. Already by 1660, some craftsmen had begun specializing in the production of springs (Jequier 1991, 324), and by the end of the eighteenth century the industry could boast some 30 specialized trades (Enright 1995, 128). As Adam Smith would have predicted, the system of *fabrication en parties brisées*—separate-parts manufacture—was particularly conducive to the invention of specialized tools[9] (Jequier 1991).

This pattern was reinforced when, in the late eighteenth century, the industry took its next leap, from Geneva to the Jura. Following the lead of one Frédéric Japy, who had learned to mass produce relatively uniform *ébauches* in nearby France, the Jura began producing watches using techniques of standardization and mechanization. Like the Genevans, the Jurassians relied on specialized tools. "But the Jura makers went their predecessors one better. They bought their tools and improved them; invented their own; and went on from individual tool making (each watchmaker his own) to production by specialist toolmakers for general sale. In so doing, they created for the first time on the continent an equipment branch to match that of Lancashire and generate new devices and techniques" (Landes 1983, 261). In short, the Jura had blossomed into a true Marshallian industrial district.

With its center of gravity displaced to the countryside, the Swiss industry bettered the already significant success and reputation that Geneva had earned. By 1790, the Jura had produced some 50,000 units, a figure that would double by 1817 (Enright 1995, 129). The source of this dynamism was arguably the industry's structure. "That was really one of the great strengths of the Swiss industry: it was really a congeries of subbranches, of local *fabriques* specializing in watches of one or another variety or in one or another stage of manufacture. Whatever you wanted, someone somewhere could make. No run was too small, no order too special. As a result, the industry was able to cater to all markets, to experiment with novelty, to copy and exploit the inventions of others" (Landes 1983, 267).

Like the other great Marshallian districts of history, including Lancashire and Silicon Valley, the Swiss watch industry relied on those benefits of decentralization praised by F. A. Hayek (1948). Its diversity permitted the effective use of a far greater amount of dispersed and tacit knowledge than could be contained within the boundaries of even a large organization, and its porousness permitted experiment, adaptation, and innovation. To most minds, moreover, the Swiss watch industry in the eighteenth and nineteenth centuries would represent a classic example of economic progress along the line of Schumpeterian "early" capitalism. There was certainly plenty of (individual) entrepreneurship, which creatively destroyed older structures (as in the rise of the Jura over Geneva), without, however, altering the fundamental paradigm of industry evolution. The extent to which the early history of this industry best fits Schumpeter's account of the entrepreneur is a matter to which I will return. Notice here that, although not at all "rationalized" in the sense of Schumpeter or Chandler—that is, organized along the lines of large, vertically integrated firms—the Swiss watchmakers of this era were certainly already rationalized in Weber's sense. They were definitely oriented toward the mundane and rational ends. As a group, they were hardly tradition bound, welcoming new ideas so long as they promised a profit.

To the extent that traditionalism played a role in the industry, it was traditionalism in the sense of Nelson and Winter, not of Weber, that is, the traditionalism of habit and routine oriented toward a particular pattern of productive skill. As is clear in Jequier's (1991, 324–25) account of one typical firm, that of the Le Coultre family, successive generations were often forced to fight the conservatism of their fathers in introducing new methods and technology, sometime to the point of open secession. But within the larger system, old techniques could disappear and new ones replace them without fundamentally changing the structure of the industry. In the language of Tushman and Anderson (1986), innovation, including mechanization, was competence enhancing for the district as a whole, and usually even for the family firms it comprised. As Jequier (1991, 325) tells us, up until the mid–nineteenth century, the "division of labor and the introduction of the first machines, operated by the worker's hand or foot, constituted no threat to the work communities of the Jura."[10]

The transition from hand-operated machines to machine tools to automatic machines, which necessitated the separation of the workshop from the home and eventually the erection of factories, was somewhat more disruptive (Jequier 1991, 326), but in the end the changes were absorbed with considerable success. In part, the transformation was propelled by external competitive forces, notably the rise of American firms employing the so-called American system of mass production and wielding innovations in marketing. At the same time, however, mechanization already lay along the trajectory the Swiss were following, and the Marshallian character of their industry allowed them in the end to outdo the Americans on their own ground.

The story of the American challenge in watchmaking introduces some bright Chandlerian threads into the tapestry. For the rise of the American watch industry followed the pattern of many others discussed in Chandler's *The Visible Hand* (1977) albeit on a somewhat smaller scale. Lacking the pools of skilled workers and the webs of existing organization available in many European industries (like Swiss watchmaking), America had to create new capabilities administratively within vertically and laterally integrated organizations. Moreover, because of the lack of existing skills, American firms substituted physical for human capital or, to put it more instructively, shifted the locus of skill on the margin away from the workers and into the machines and the organization of production. This, indeed, is the task that the American system was intended to accomplish: to reduce the need for skilled adjustment by making the parts (relatively more) interchangeable and by using "skilled" machines that could turn out these more standardized parts in large numbers (Hounshell 1984). We now know that these parts were far less interchangeable than advertised (Clarke 1985; Hoke 1989). But the approach placed American firms on a technological trajectory that spurred mechanization and produced a high rate of productivity improvement. American firms were thus able eventually to overtake and surpass competitors (like the British in some industries) who were not on such a trajectory. As we will see, however, this approach worked less well on the Swiss.

The principal exemplar of the American system in watchmaking was the Waltham Watch Company. In production, the firm moved beyond the relatively versatile machine tools then in use in the industry toward more special purpose, high-volume devices. This often required Waltham to invent its own machines, as outside toolmakers were hard pressed to meet the tolerances necessary (Landes 1983, 315). The results were phenomenal. By 1877, Waltham was producing some 600,000 watches per year, with a cumulative output on the order of 10 million. Moreover, quality equaled or surpassed that of Switzerland, as Swiss representative discovered to their great shock at the 1876 centennial exhibition in Philadelphia, where American watches and watchmaking were on display (Landes 1983, 319; Jequier 1991, 326).

Waltham operated with a highly integrated structure that contrasted sharply with the Swiss industry. In one reading, this is rationalization à la Chandler (if not necessarily à la Weber) into large, formally articulated organizations. In this reading, Waltham, like so many other American firms in the late nineteenth and early twentieth centuries, succeeded because it represented an organizational structure inherently superior to the market it had replaced. In another reading, however, Waltham's structure reflected the inadequacies of existing American capabilities rather than the inherent superiority of its form. Because of the need systemically to reinvent the production process, and because of the lack of a ready web of outside suppliers, the Americans were forced to rely on integration as the best of actually available alternatives.[11]

In the specific case of watchmaking, the fragmented Swiss industry responded quickly to the American threat. "In spite of some inevitable resistance," Jequier (1991, 326) tells us, "the spirit of enterprise asserted itself"; assemblers began building new factories and introducing the same kind of machinery the Americans had. In 1870, three-quarters of the 35,000 employed in Swiss watchmaking worked at home; by 1905, only a quarter of the more than 50,000 workers did so (326). Nonetheless, when Switzerland regained the technological and market lead toward the end of the nineteenth century, it remained far less vertically integrated than the American industry, relied far more on outwork, and comprised thousands of firms to the dozen or so in America (Landes 1983, 323). Meanwhile, Waltham's highly integrated structure proved far less conducive to the routine administration of its operation than it had been to bringing that operation into being, and the firm virtually collapsed under the weight of principal-agent problems (329–34). Even its better-run competitors lost ground to the Swiss. Indeed, both Waltham and Elgin, Waltham's long-time domestic rival, are now Swiss owned.

By 1910, the Swiss industry dominated the world.

> The Swiss controlled the micromechanical export industry by cost competitiveness, superior manufacturing competency, high levels of precision, and extraordinary attention to details and style. The vertically integrated parts manufacturers achieved economies of scale through volume production. This benefit was passed on to assemblers in the form of low-cost movements. In the most labor-intensive aspects of the industry, the vertically disintegrated system of assembly and case manufacture kept overhead charges low. (Glasmeier 1991, 471)

This happy situation was not, however, to last long. In the years after World War I, incomes declined, protectionist barriers went up, and the large Russian market disappeared; as a result, demand for Swiss watches fell sharply (Glasmeier 1991, 471; Landes 1983, 326–27). Like many other industries around the world, the Swiss watchmakers responded with cartelization, in an attempt to stabilize revenues and—importantly in this case—halt the practice of *chablonnage,* the exportation of components to countries trying to create their own watch industries behind protectionist walls. The assemblers created the Fédération Horlogère in 1924 to safeguard their interests; the 17 makers of *ebauches* combined into the Trust Ebauches, S.A., in 1926; and the component makers grouped into the Union des branches annexes de l'horlogerie (UBAH) in the same year. By 1928, these associations had crafted cartel arrangements to set production, pricing, and export policies, especially, in the last case, with respect to *chablonnage* (Landes 1983, 327; Enright 1995, 130).

As is normally the case with private cartels, however, these arrangements proved unstable, especially once the Depression hit. The government of the confederation was called in, and, with the help of the banking industry, formed a huge holding company, called ASUAG after the acronym of its German name. The company bought up the majority of shares in Ebauches,

S.A., along with a number of component makers (Landes 1983, 328; Glasmeier 1991, 472; Enright 1995, 130). The trust immediately put a halt to *chablonnage*. In 1934, the government obliged further with a statute that put the finishing touches on a cartel that Landes (1983, 328) rates as one of the strongest in history. In addition to setting up detailed regulation of output, the statute essentially forbade component import and export and even prohibited the export of watchmaking machinery. Moreover, ASUAG got in the habit of buying up and subsidizing failing component makers.

By the late 1930s, the industry was in recovery. But, as even cartels cannot create rents where none are to be had, this resurgence surely had less to do with cartelization than with the quickening of watch demand upon the end of the Depression and the arrival of World War II, during which the neutral Swiss were able to supply both sides. After the war, Switzerland found itself in a position very like that of the United States: standing almost alone as an unscathed competitor amid the devastation of war. And, like the United States, Switzerland lived well on the resulting rents until the reemergence of German and (especially) Japanese industries by the early 1970s.

America had one threat to offer in the postwar years. In the 1940s, a Norwegian immigrant named Lehmkuhl had taken over the near-defunct Waterbury Clock Company with an eye to making fuses for the war effort. At war's end, he refitted the company to make cheap mechanical watches on an updated American system, using newly developed metals in production and following a mass-marketing plan that bypassed the jeweler's shop for the five-and-dime (Landes 1983, 339). Timex—as the brand was called—swept the American market and made inroads in Europe. But this was the sort of challenge the Swiss had seen before, and, despite their sluggish cartel structure, it was one to which they could eventually respond.[12] The real challenge to the industry in the late 1960s and early 1970s came from a much less familiar source: electronics.

A watch, even a mechanical one, is basically an oscillator: it divides time into pulses in order to calibrate the movement of the hands. By midcentury, solid-state electronics was beginning to make possible a different kind of oscillator, one based on piezoelectric crystals that can be made to vibrate precisely and dependably under alternating current. By the late 1960s, microelectronics had proceeded to a point at which the vibration of a crystal (like quartz) could be used to calibrate microcontroller circuitry driving tiny electric stepping motors. Indeed, it became possible to hook the circuits to light-emitting diodes and then liquid crystal displays, thus eliminating mechanical parts entirely. The quartz watch was born. This change, which took the better part of a decade to work itself out, proved far more competence destroying for the Swiss industry than anything that had come before. Although the Swiss retained many capabilities relevant

to analog quartz watches, the mechanical *ébauche,* a core Swiss competence, had been replaced by crystal, circuit, and motor.

The inability of the Swiss watch industry to respond to the electronic
challenge represents a clear instance of industrial inertia.[13] The Swiss industry was a well-tuned system of capabilities for producing precise and reliable mechanical watches in all price ranges. But it is the inevitable corollary
of having capabilities well adapted for one purpose that those capabilities
are not well adapted to other purposes. As a result, as Schumpeter remarks, "new combinations are, as a rule, embodied, as it were, in new
firms which generally do not arise out of the old ones but start producing
beside them; . . . in general it is not the owner of stage-coaches who builds
railways" (1934, 66). In this case, it was firms—in America and, especially,
Japan—with relevant capabilities in electronics and electromechanical assembly that took up the banner of quartz. Initially, at least, the Swiss
played down the threat, which, like most such threats, was far clearer in
retrospect than in prospect. When the pressure began to mount, the Swiss
industry responded with a burst of improvement in the productivity of
mechanical watchmaking. "That," notes Landes, "is a universal characteristic of once-dominant technologies: they make some of their greatest improvements under sentence of obsolescence; the finest days of the sailing
ship came after the advent of steam" (1983, 351). But these improvements
were too little too late. With quartz technology, firms like Citizen and
Seiko could make watches that were just as cheap—and far more accurate.

Although the decentralized character of the Swiss industry and its
reliance on Marshallian external economies may have been sufficient cause
for some inertia in the face of competence-destroying change (Glasmeier
1991), the rigid cartel structure must also take a good part of the blame for
the extent of that inertia (Maurer 1985). By restricting imports and exports,
and by tightly controlling what and how much could be produced, the cartel
stifled incentives for innovation and closed off the once porous structure
from new ideas. "The result," as Enright notes, "is that the industry had
neither the efficiency of a vibrant decentralized structure, nor the coordination advantages of hierarchy" (1995, 133). Swiss watch exports fell from a
peak of 84 million units in 1974 to 51 million in 1980; in that year, Japanese
exports, which had been less than 19 million units in 1974, surged past at 68
million units (Landes 1983, 388–89). At the same time, employment in the
Swiss watch industry fell almost by half, and the number of Swiss watchmaking establishments declined by more than half (Landes 1983, 353; Enright 1995, 133).

The story does not end here, however. In the early 1980s, when the
industry had hit rock bottom, a major, and perhaps even startling, reorganization took place. By that time, the equity of the major family firms—the
"watch barons"—had declined to the point that they could not or would

not oppose change, and the banks, which had written off hundreds of millions of francs, wanted out (Enright 1995, 133–34). In 1981, the banks engaged Nicolas Hayek, an engineer and management consultant, to find a solution to the industry's problems (Taylor 1993, 99; Zehnder 1994, 4). His proposal was to consolidate and radically restructure the industry. At Hayek's suggestion, the banks, with the help of the confederation and cantonal governments, engineered in 1983 the merger of ASUAG with SSIH, another major holding company that had been founded in the 1930s. The new company was called the Société suisse de microélectronique et d'horlogerie (SMH). The banks toyed with the idea of selling Omega, one of SMH's major brands, to the Japanese, who had offered a considerable sum. Hayek argued against the move and insisted that the reorganized firm not only could become successful but actually could produce a full range of watches competitively from a manufacturing base in Switzerland. The banks insisted in turn that Hayek put his money where his mouth was, which he and a consortium of backers promptly did. SMH is owned 51 percent by Hayek's group, and the banks no longer have an important interest (Taylor 1993; Zehnder 1994).

Once in charge, Hayek set about reorganizing the firm, which now comprised a significant fraction of the Swiss industry.[14] He centralized manufacturing into a division called ETA, and marshaled existing and developed new capabilities in microelectronics, notably in the specialized 1.5 volt integrated circuits used in watches. He also reorganized and decentralized marketing according to brand, giving each a separate identity and "message." But the most visible result of the strategy was the creation of the low-end Swatch brand, which married creative marketing to high-tech fabrication. A design shop in Milan generates as many as 500 models a year. The 70 of these chosen for production are turned out at the rate of one every 67 seconds, some 35,000 a day (Taylor 1993, 104; Zehnder 1994, 8). By 1991, more than 100 million Swatches had been sold (Enright 1995, 135).

The result of this reorganization was a startling turnaround, transforming a 1983 loss of $124 million on $1.1 billion in revenues into a 1993 profit of $286 million on $2.1 billion in revenues (Taylor 1993, 99). In 1992, SMH held 10 percent of the world market (Zehnder 1994, 3).

Plausible Personal Capitalism

What can this story teach us about entrepreneurship and rationalization? Certainly much of the story has a familiar Chandlerian ring. From the first *établisseurs* to mechanized production in a Marshallian industrial district, business was a personal and family activity. Beginning with trustification and cartelization in the 1920s, however, this began to change, and the industry set off—perhaps too slowly—on a path of rationalization that led ultimately to a fully articulated and vertically integrated modern corporation. As Enright puts it in describing the emergence of SMH, "[c]oordination through much of the Swiss watch industry had passed from markets, to cartels, to modern corporate management" (1995, 137). This sequence is indeed in keeping with the general pattern Chandler observed in large segments of American industry.

> Nearly all enterprises that grew by merger followed the same path. They had their beginnings as trade associations that managed cartels formed by many small manufacturing enterprises. The federations then consolidated legally into a single enterprise, taking the form of a trust or a holding company. Administrative centralization followed legal consolidation. The governing board of the merger rationalized the manufacturing facilities of the constituent companies and administered the enlarged plants from a single central office. The final step was to integrate forward into marketing and backward into purchasing and the control of raw or semifinished materials. By the time it completed the last move, the consolidated enterprise was employing a set of lower, middle, and top managers to administer, monitor, coordinate, and plan for the activities of its many operating units and for the enterprise as a whole. By then the visible hand of management replaced the invisible hand of market forces in coordinating the flow from the suppliers of raw materials to the ultimate consumer. (1977, 315)

In this account, the rise of SMH represents the final act in a familiar Chandlerian drama.

One interpretation, then, would run along the following lines. The history of the Swiss watchmaking industry reflects precisely the sort of "progressive rationalization" that Schumpeter described. The early history of the industry tells of Schumpeterian "early" capitalism, in which individual entrepreneurs provided the impetus for growth. The Chandlerian sequence, however, tracks an eventual transformation to Schumpeterian "later" capitalism, in which the collective enterprise takes preeminence over the personal element.

As the reader may suspect, I consider such an interpretation not merely wrong but close to backward. Having taken Schumpeter back to his Weberian roots, we are in a position to see why.

Despite their similar Weberian influences, the Schumpeterian story of the obsolescence of the entrepreneur is not identical to the Chandlerian account of the rise of the visible hand. In Chandler, as in Weber, the emphasis is not on the innovative character of the large bureaucratic organization but on its ability to deliver the goods. The managers "administer, monitor, coordinate, and plan." They do not carry out new combinations. For Chandler, economic growth is underpinned by an imperative to high volume throughput; the personal element in organization stands in the way of fully realizing this imperative, for which an abstract and professional structure is required.

As we saw, however, Schumpeter's claims are much different. He associates "personal" capitalism with charismatic leadership. It is the entrepreneur who makes dramatic, and often creatively destructive, changes. In Schumpeter, those who come along and fill in the details are important, but it is the changes that really matter. The obsolescence thesis is a claim not that large, fully articulated enterprises may be necessary to realize the vision of an individual entrepreneur; rather, it is a claim that those enterprises will be the sources of change. Let us put it succinctly. In Chandler, large organizations are the result of economic change; in Schumpeterian later capitalism, economic change is the result of large organizations.

My contention is that, whereas the story of Swiss watchmaking may (with some reservations to be noted) fit the Chandlerian pattern, it does not at all fit the Schumpeterian one. To put it another way, the transformation of the Swiss watch industry in the 1980s is precisely a story of charismatic individual entrepreneurship.

The first, and most obvious, point is that it was an outside individual, not an organization, who was responsible for the reorganization of the industry. Lazonick is right in saying that genuine innovation involves reorganizing or planning (which may not be the same thing) the horizontal and vertical division of labor.[15] But it was not in this case "organizational capabilities" that brought the reorganization about. It was an individual and not at all a "collective" vision, one that, however carefully thought out, was a cognitive leap beyond the existing paradigm. If SMH now possesses organizational capabilities, as it surely does, those capabilities were the result, not the cause, of the innovation.

Moreover, the formation and organization of SMH reflects many more elements of genuinely personal capitalism than the Chanderlian account would suggest. First of all, Hayek is the owner, not a manager. "I put my money on the line," says Hayek, "along with money from our investors. The fact that our group controls a majority of the equity means we could make decisions that other people were scared to make" (Taylor 1993, 110). But the enterprise is personal in other ways as well. Even discounting the usual rhetoric of entrepreneurship, Hayek is clearly charismatic in the ordinary sense of the term—the *Harvard Business Review* (Taylor 1993, 99) called him "a genuine business celebrity"—and probably in the Weberian sense as well. Consider Hayek's own words.

> It is extremely important to lead by example, while at the same time provide young managers with human and emotional support. You can only really motivate and reward someone by showing that you really are his or her friend. You have to establish an emotional connection.

You have to show your employees that you really care for them and that they can count on you. When somebody is in difficulties, I don't fire him or her, on the contrary I immediately jump at his or her side, provide support, and push him or her to do better. In that sense, I am a leader, one whose leadership extends beyond the usual. (quoted in Zehnder 1994, 9)

The visible hand of management here seems to be relying on "an emotional form of communal relationship" (Weber 1947, 360).

But is not SMH, however created, now a vertically integrated bureaucratic organization along Chandlerlian lines, and is that not the source of its superiority over the Marshallian industrial district it replaced? As I have argued elsewhere (Langlois 1992; Langlois and Robertson 1995, chap. 3), the benefit of centralization lies in the ability to bring about change, not in the ability to administer existing structures.[16] A centralized structure may remain centralized for reasons of path dependency or even of static transaction costs of the familiar sort. But, very often, an imperative of decentralization soon becomes clear even within the centralized organization once it has become well established. This is certainly true of SMH, which has 211 profit centers.[17] "Organizational structure," in Hayek's view,

> is the most inhuman thing ever invented. It goes against our nature as people. So we have clear boundaries and targets. Our brands work independently of one another. The people at Omega and Rado and Tissot have their own buildings. They have their own managements. They are responsible for their own design, marketing, communications and distribution. They are emotionally connected to their brands, not just to SMH as an entity. I want people at Rado to love Rado. And I want people at Longines to love their brand. (Taylor 1993, 110)

In fact, much of the integration at SMH is what Chandler would call "defensive," that is, ownership integration[18] aimed at controlling portions of the production process in a world in which there are only two other producers of movements, Seiko and Citizen (Taylor 1993, 109).

But does this case prove that entrepreneurship must always arise from *outside* the firm or that organizations cannot be sources of innovation? Surely no one case can be decisive. But this story reinforces what is arguably the theoretical conclusion of both organizational sociology and management theory.

In a very insightful gloss on Weber, the late sociologist James Coleman (1990) suggested that charisma of the sort Nicolas Hayek wields may actually be thought of as a "rational" form of authority, one that is especially important in times of crisis and radical change.[19] In his well-known study of bureaucracy, Michel Crozier also stresses the importance of crisis for organizational change. For Crozier, change in a bureaucratic organization must come from the top down and must be universalistic, i.e., encompass the whole organization *en bloc*. Change will not come gradually on a piecemeal basis. It will wait until a serious question pertaining to an important dysfunction can be raised. Then it will be argued about and decided upon at the higher level and applied to the whole organization, even to the areas where dysfunctions are not seriously felt. . . . Crises are important in another way. They exemplify other patterns of action, other types of group relationships—temporary, but of decisive importance. During crises, individual initiative prevails and people eventually come to depend on some strategic individual's arbitrary whim. (1964, 196)

In other words, bureaucracies always respond to crisis with what is in effect a temporary departure from the following of rules and a return to an arbitrary type of authority.[20] Thus, even to the extent that (more or less) radical change does take place within an articulated Weberian bureaucracy, it does so by emulating the cognitive and authority structure of Schumpeterian entrepreneurship.[21]

We find a similar story in the management literature. Consider, for example, the writings of Hamel and Prahalad (1994), who are not only among the more influential gurus of the times but also among the strongest proponents of an organizational capabilities view of management. As students of management and corporate consultants, of course, they are primarily interested in the question of how to make firms innovative rather than the question of whether innovation does or should take place within the bounds of firms. So they are in search of the innovative organization. And surely organizations can be innovative at some level. Even in Nelson and Winter (1982), for example, firms may be bound by routines, but some of those routines can be "higher-level" ones that govern the search for new lower-level routines. Nonetheless, innovativeness requires more than mechanistically searching for new routines. In Hamel and Prahalad, it essentially involves forcing the firm to take on more of the characteristics of a market: it must develop the kind of genetic diversity Friedrich Hayek praised. "In nature," they write, "genetic variety comes from unexpected mutations. The corporate corollary is skunk works, intrapreneurship, spinoffs, and other forms of bottom-up innovation" (1994, 61).

In the end, however, they, like Crozier, realize that the most radical kind of change must come from the top down: it requires a Schumpeterian entrepreneurial vision. "Top management cannot abdicate its responsibility for developing, articulating, and sharing a point of view about the future. What is needed are not just skunk works and intrapreneurs, but senior managers who can escape the orthodoxies of the corporation's current 'concept of self' " (Hamel and Prahalad 1994, 87). Example? Nicolas

Hayek's "crazy" vision that the Swiss could manufacture cheap watches competitively with the Japanese (98–99).

Economists, of course, must take a slightly different perspective, as they must remain open to the possibility that change might take place not within an existing organization but in new firms, groups of firms, or "markets" broadly understood.[22] And there is no reason to think that all innovation must come from "reengineering" existing organizations, even if some surely does.

Indeed, one might argue that the farther an innovation is from the ken of existing firms the more likely it is that the innovation will be instantiated in new organizations. We can think about this in the imagery of the economics of rugged landscapes[23] (Levinthal 1992). If we think of innovative opportunities as "peaks" in some suitably defined space, then we might expect those who inhabit known peaks to be able perhaps to discover nearby opportunities through relatively myopic search. But "peaks" that are far away—radical innovations—are likely to be discovered and exploited by quite different individuals and organizations.

Whether Schumpeterian entrepreneurship operates from the top of an existing organization or in the creation of new ones, the same conclusion seems unavoidable. The charismatic authority and coherent vision of such entrepreneurship remains an inevitable part of capitalism, however modern. For reasons that have to do with the nature of cognition and the structure of knowledge in organized society, some essential part of capitalism must always remain personal.

NOTES

The author would like to thank Fred Carstensen, László Csontos, and Karl Heinrich Oppenländer for helpful comments.

1. On the first page of his interesting new book, our esteemed president, Gunnar Eliasson (1996), tells us that, in "his dismal (1942) analysis of the capacity of large firms to routinize innovative behavior," Schumpeter gave up his "Austrian" account "of the innovator and the unpredictable entrepreneur." In fairness, Eliasson associates the "Austrian" Schumpeter with the 1911 first German edition of the *Theory of Economic Development*, and the obsolescence thesis did not appear in its full form until the second German edition (Csontos 1991). Nonetheless, I resist the idea that Schumpeter "gave up" anything in his 1942 book that he hadn't given up essentially from the beginning.

2. The influence of Weber is explicit in the second German edition, but the references were largely expunged from the English translation, probably because Schumpeter saw methodological fashions, and his intended audience, as having changed in the interim (Csontos 1991).

3. "A high degree of traditionalism in habits of life, such as characterized the

labouring classes in early modern times, has not sufficed to prevent a great increase in the rationalization of economic enterprise under capitalist direction. . . . Nevertheless, this traditionalistic attitude had to be at least partly overcome in the Western world before the further development of the specifically modern type of rational capitalist economy could take place" (Weber 1947, 167).

4. Weber did not, however, see bureaucracy as generally good, and he worried about its stultifying effect on humanity.

5. This was not an intellectually fashionable view in the 1930s and 1940s, when Weber's ideas began filtering into the English-speaking academic world. In a fit of early political correctness, indeed, Talcott Parsons found it necessary to insert into his translation of Weber a footnote apologizing for his author's failure to hold views in accord with "the principal weight of technical opinion" on the subject (Weber 1947, 194n). That weight must not have been tied down very tightly, however, as it has lately shifted decidedly to Weber's side.

6. To put it another way, substantive or "optimizing" rationality of the neoclassical sort is itself a learned routine or set of routines.

7. More recently, Lazonick has made clear that he includes in collective capitalism—or "organizational integration," as he now terms it—the activities of "individuals and groups who are employed by legally distinct firms that pursue common goals" (Lazonick and West 1995, 231). Taken seriously, however, this idea renders unhelpful if not tautological the notion of "collective capitalism," since it embraces activities that economists have viewed, and ought rightly to view, as reflecting the capabilities of markets (properly understood) rather than firms, and thereby calls into question any implications in the analysis for the advantages of large firms per se. On this point, see Loasby (1993) and Langlois (1994).

8. This is a case that has attracted significant scholarly attention, which makes the facts relatively easy to assemble. However, most of the best interpretive histories, notably David Landes's brilliant *Revolution in Time* (1983), stop before certain recent events that will be of considerable interest to the theme of this essay.

9. In fact, Smith did comment very briefly on watchmaking, in the context of the effect on real prices of the productivity improvements that arise in "consequence of better machinery, of greater dexterity, and of a more proper division and distribution of work" (1976, I.xi.o.1, 260). Real price reductions, Smith says, have been "most remarkable" in industries using the "coarser metals" as materials. "A better movement of a watch, than about the middle of the last century could have been bought for twenty pounds, may now perhaps be had for twenty shillings" (I.ix.o.4).

10. By contrast, artisans in Geneva were more organized, and the Association of Watchcase Workers, founded in 1842, stood in the way of changes in the division of labor. But the result was the establishment of separate factories using the new machines. "Here," says Jequier (1991, 325), "we may note another characteristic of Swiss watchmaking: the appearance of new manufacturing processes did not eliminate old practices, and usually the two systems operated side by side, which explains the extraordinary heterogeneity of this sector, first as a craft and then as an industry."

11. For an elaboration of this idea, see Langlois and Robertson (1995), especially chapter 3.

12. In fact, however, the Swiss never really needed to respond. Although their

market share had fallen from a postwar high of 80 to 40 percent by 1970, total demand was growing fast enough to keep capacity utilization and profits high (Enright 1995, 133).

13. On this, see Langlois and Robertson (1995), chapter 6.

14. In 1991, SMH was the largest watch company in the world, controlling some third of the Swiss watch industry by sales and a quarter of its employment (Enright 1995, 135).

15. On the notion of "planning" within the firm, see Langlois (1995).

16. Since Weber, there has developed a good deal more skepticism about the efficacy of bureaucracy even to administer existing structures. For example, Coleman (1990) criticizes Weber for conflating the idea of bureaucracy as an impersonal hierarchy of positions with the idea that bureaucracy is always the most efficient structure for allocating resources. Drawing on the modern literature of agency theory, he points out that positions can often be used to attain personal goals rather than the functional goals of the organization. (Remember the case of Waltham Watch Company.)

17. Moreover, even a highly integrated structure such as SMH remains embedded in the market. And some of the success of Swatch is arguably attributable to external capabilities in the region, notably injection molding (for the plastic case) and automated assembly technology that was unique to Switzerland (Taylor 1993, 107). Indeed, the Jura remains a Marshallian industrial district today, one that has diversified beyond watchmaking into microtechnologies more generally (Maillat et al. 1995).

18. This is distinct from genuine coordination integration. On this terminology see Langlois and Robertson (1995), chapters 2 and 7.

19. Similarly, Peter Temin (1980) makes a tripartite distinction—among rational, traditional, and command behavior—that is similar to that of Weber. Temin argues that people will behave according to different modes in different times and places. My argument is that entrepreneurship is an instance of command behavior, which is effective in times of radical economic change or opportunity.

20. Such authority is "personal" in the sense that it reflects the will of an individual at the top of the hierarchy, even if, in Crozier's account, it is not personal in the sense of being face to face or strictly charismatic in Weber's meaning.

21. And, as Joseph Berliner (1976) points out in his study of Soviet industry, a bureaucracy that makes individual initiative impossible makes innovation impossible.

22. These various alternatives are what Langlois and Robertson (1995) refer to as business institutions.

23. I am indebted to Massimo Egidi for this idea.

REFERENCES

Berliner, Joseph S. 1976. *The Innovation Decision in Soviet Industry.* Cambridge: MIT Press.
Chandler, Alfred D., Jr. 1977. *The Visible Hand: The Managerial Revolution in American Business.* Cambridge: Belknap Press of Harvard University Press.

————. 1990. *Scale and Scope: The Dynamics of Industrial Capitalism.* Cambridge: Belknap Press of Harvard University Press.

Clarke, Benjamin Neil. 1985. *Early American Technology: A Reexamination of Some Aspects of Connecticut's Industrial Development.* M.A. thesis, University of Connecticut.

Coleman, James S. 1990. "Rational Organization." *Rationality and Society* 2, no. 1: 94–105.

Crozier, Michel. 1964. *The Bureaucratic Phenomenon.* Chicago: University of Chicago Press.

Csontos, László. 1991. "Wieser's Influence on Schumpeter." Appendix to R. N. Langlois, "Schumpeter and the Obsolescence of the Entrepreneur." Working Papers, no. 91–1503, Department of Economics, University of Connecticut. Mimeo.

————. 1993. *Inside the Black Box of the Firm: The Economics of Internal Organization.* Ph.D. diss., University of Connecticut.

Eliasson, Gunnar, 1996. *Firm Objectives, Controls, and Organization: The Use of Information and the Transfer of Knowledge within the Firm.* Dordrecht: Kluwer Academic.

Enright, Michael J. 1995. "Organization and Coordination in Geographically Concentrated Industries." In *Coordination and Information: Historical Perspectives on the Organization of Enterprise,* edited by Naomi R. Lamoreaux and Daniel M. G. Raff. Chicago: University of Chicago Press.

Glasmeier, Amy. 1991. "Technological Discontinuities and Flexible Production Networks: The Case of Switzerland and the World Watch Industry." *Research Policy* 20:469–85.

Hamel, Gary, and C. K. Prahalad. 1994. *Competing for the Future.* Cambridge: Harvard Business School Press.

Hayek, F. A. 1948. *Individualism and Economic Order.* Chicago: University of Chicago Press.

Hodgson, Geoffrey. 1993. *Economics and Biology.* Ann Arbor: University of Michigan Press.

Hoke, Donald. 1989. "Product Design and Cost Considerations: Clock, Watch, and Typewriter Manufacturing in the 19th Century." *Business and Economic History* 18:119–28.

Hounshell, David A. 1984. *From the American System to Mass Production, 1800–1932: The Development of Manufacturing Technology in the United States.* Baltimore: Johns Hopkins University Press.

Jequier, François. 1991. "Employment Strategies and Production Structures in the Swiss Watchmaking Industry." In *Favorites of Fortune,* edited by Patrice Higonnet, David Landes, and Henry Rosovsky. Cambridge: Harvard University Press.

Landes, David S. 1983. *Revolution in Time.* Cambridge: Belknap Press of Harvard University Press.

Langlois, Richard N. 1987. "Schumpeter and the Obsolescence of the Entrepreneur." Paper presented at the annual meeting of the History of Economics Society, June 21, 1987, Boston. Circulated as Working Paper 91–1503, Department of Economics, University of Connecticut, November 1991.

———. 1992. "Transaction-Cost Economics in Real Time." *Industrial and Corporate Change* 1, no. 1: 99–127.

———. 1994. Review of *Business Organization and the Myth of the Market Economy,* by William Lazonick. *Journal of Economic Behavior and Organization* 23, no. 2: 244–50.

———. 1995. "Do Firms Plan?" *Constitutional Political Economy* 6, no. 3: 247–61.

———, and Michael J. Everett. 1994. "What Is Evolutionary Economics?" In *Evolutionary and Neo-Schumpeterian Approaches to Economics,* edited by Lars Magnusson. Dordrecht: Kluwer Academic.

———, and Paul L. Robertson. 1995. *Firms, Markets, and Economic Change: A Dynamic Theory of Business Institutions.* London: Routledge.

Lazonick, William. 1991. *Business Organization and the Myth of the Market Economy.* New York: Cambridge University Press.

———, and Jonathan West. 1995. "Organizational Integration and Competitive Advantage: Explaining Strategy and Performance in American Industry." *Industrial and Corporate Change* 4, no. 1: 229–70.

Levinthal, Daniel A. 1992. "Surviving Schumpeterian Environments." *Industrial and Corporate Change* 1, no. 3: 427–43.

Loasby, Brian J. 1993. Review of *Business Organization and the Myth of the Market Economy,* by William Lazonick. *Economic Journal* 103 (Jan.): 247–49.

McCraw, Thomas K. 1988. "Introduction: The Intellectual Odyssey of Alfred D. Chandler, Jr." In *The Essential Alfred Chandler: Essays toward a Historical Theory of Big Business,* edited by Thomas K. McCraw. Boston: Harvard Business School Press.

Maillat, Denis, Bruno Lecoq, Florian Nemeti, and Marc Pfister. 1995. "Technology District and Innovation: The Case of the Swiss Jura Arc." *Regional Studies* 29, no. 3: 251–63.

Maurer, Martin. 1985. "Technological Retardation: The Decline of the Swiss Watch Industry." *Zeitschrift für Wirtschafts und Sozialwissenschaften* 105, no. 6: 661–82.

Nelson, Richard R., and Sidney G. Winter. 1982. *An Evolutionary Theory of Economic Change.* Cambridge: Harvard University Press.

Parsons, Talcott. 1949. *The Structure of Social Action.* 2d ed. Glencoe: Free Press.

Richardson, G. B. 1972. "The Organisation of Industry." *Economic Journal* 82: 883–96.

Schumpeter, Joseph A. 1934. *The Theory of Economic Development.* Cambridge: Harvard University Press.

Schumpeter, Joseph A. 1950. *Capitalism, Socialism, and Democracy.* 2d ed. New York: Harper and Brothers.

Smith, Adam. 1976. *An Inquiry into the Nature and Causes of the Wealth of Nations.* Glasgow ed. Oxford: Clarendon.

Taylor, William. 1993. "Message and Muscle: An Interview with Swatch Titan Nicolas Hayek." *Harvard Business Review* 71 (Mar.–Apr.): 98–103.

Teece, David J., and Gary Pisano. 1994. "The Dynamic Capabilities of Firms: an Introduction." *Industrial and Corporate Change* 3, no. 3: 537–56.

Temin, Peter. 1980. "Modes of Behavior." *Journal of Economic Behavior and Organization* 1, no. 2: 175–95.

Tushman, Michael L., and Philip Anderson. 1986. "Technological Discontinuities and Organizational Environments." *Administrative Science Quarterly* 31:439–65.

Weber, Max. 1947. *The Theory of Social and Economic Organization.* Trans. A. M. Henderson and Talcott Parsons. Ed. Talcott Persons. New York: Oxford University Press.

Zehnder, Dominik E. D. 1994. "Nicolas G. Hayek." Harvard Business School Case 9-495-05.

Entrepreneurs and Social Elites: Some Reflections on the Case of Sweden
Jan Glete

> Thus, though entrepreneurs do not *per se* form a social class, the bourgeois class absorbs them and their families and connections, thereby recruiting and revitalizing itself. . . . [T]he bourgeoisie therefore depends on the entrepreneur and, as a class, lives and will die with him . . .
>
> —*Joseph Schumpeter, in Capitalism, Socialism,*
> *and Democracy*

Entrepreneurial and innovative abilities without entry into the powerful elite groups—those in control of capital and networks in the established society—have only limited capacity to change the society. On the other hand, elite groups unable to absorb entrepreneurs with radically new ideas will in the long run lose control over society. This essay[1] confronts this hypothesis of Joseph Schumpeter with recorded industrial change in Sweden from 1850 to 1990. I find:

1. Swedish industrialization (late nineteenth to early twentieth centuries) created a number of large, successful, and often international companies, which have remained the backbone of Swedish industry. It also created owner groups, bank groups, and networks between industry, owners, and banks with very long lives.

2. For most of the twentieth century, the vast majority of Swedes with entrepreneurial and innovative capacity has been attracted to and absorbed into the elite groups represented by the large industrial companies and their owners. Many smaller family companies have been acquired by these groups.

3. The few innovators and entrepreneurs who have created successful companies outside the network of established companies, owner groups, and large banks have remained isolated, often preferring to expand outside Sweden rather to taking a leading position within the Swedish business elite.

4. Managers of capital and banks have for several decades shown a limited ability to find and promote entrepreneurs and innovators with radically new ideas and stimulate them to an expansionist business policy. This is a total contrast to the situation that prevailed when

the present big industrial companies were formed. The very successful entrepreneurial and industrial past of Sweden appears to have had a negative influence on postwar entrepreneurship and future industrial growth.

My approach and method are historical: a systematical case study on the interaction and evolution of institutions and manufacturing business in Sweden up to the present. The hypothesis of Joseph Schumpeter in the epigraph would, however, suggest that my results are not restricted to Sweden but rather apply much more widely to the mature industrial world. This wider possibility is beyond the scope of this essay, but similar research in Europe, in my opinion, would probably be rewarding.

The Symptoms

For about a century (1870–1970), Sweden enjoyed rapid economic growth based on the industrial transformation of the society. After 1970, the performance of manufacturing industry as well as its owners has notably declined. The well-established industrial companies are still profitable, but their investments have increasingly been made outside Sweden and they are closely connected with technology and business ideas that were created in an earlier period. The creation of very large new companies has practically ceased. Today, Sweden is a country where a limited number of big international companies account for a large part of industrial production and new investments in industry. These companies are important buyers from small and medium-sized Swedish companies, and their influence over Swedish industry is larger than their own number of employees indicates. Several Swedish companies have shown considerable ability in restructuring mature firms in Europe and even in the United States (paper, heavy electrical engineering, household appliances, trucks and buses, welding equipment, etc.). There is, however, hardly an *individual* left who has created a big company. Swedish managers of big companies are usually rated high in international comparisons, but their ability to create such a new company out of a pathbreaking entrepreneurial idea is entirely unproven.

This may look like a case of a closed elite group unwilling to give new talent its chance. The realities, however, are more complicated. The established groups have been open to new talents who are prepared to develop and contribute to the survival of *existing structures.* Apparently, a genuine gulf exists between potential innovative entrepreneurs (who destroy established structures), on the one side, and managers and owners with easy access to the existing network and elite on the other. Innovators in entirely new fields have enjoyed insufficient stimuli to establish new and growing firms and have shown little interest in joining *and revitalizing* the elite. The deep attachment of the existing elite to existing structures may make it difficult to understand the potential of new ideas.

The number of individuals in late twentieth-century Sweden who actually have *created* a large company from its inception or from an inconspicuous small company is amazingly small. Ingvar Kamprad, the founder of IKEA, born in 1926, is still an active entrepreneur, while the brothers Gad and Hans Rausing, the second-generation entrepreneurs of their family, who did much to develop their father's ideas into the present Tetra Pak Company, have retired. IKEA and Tetra Pak are, however, no longer Swedish companies since their owners have transferred their domiciles abroad. In Sweden, you may find a few retired owners of large companies, such as Sten A. Olsson of Stena Line, the world's largest ferry company, and Erling Persson, founder of the international clothing chain H&M. Both were born in 1917, and their sons are running the companies. There are also a few owners of rather large companies who made their fortunes in finance and real estate in the 1970s and 1980s and managed to survive the crisis of the early 1990s. But none of these *created* a large-scale industrial or trading company. They bought existing companies.

Among Swedish-domiciled, active owners and managers, hardly anyone has experience in making a small company grow into a company of 5,000 employees or more through organic growth based on an innovation or through mergers and acquisitions centered around innovative ideas. There are many managers who have made an already large company into a very large organization—from, say, 10,000 or 40,000 to 25,000 or 200,000—but only through expansion in their old technologies and markets, or through acquisitions, not through radical change of the original idea of the company.

Why this paradoxical situation, of a country with an unusually large number of very large companies and no owner or manager under 70 years of age who has any experience of actually creating a big company? A look at the age of the existing large companies (counted from the period when they were founded or radically changed their core business idea) gives the beginning of the explanation. Of the 40 largest Swedish companies in 1990, at least three out of four were started in the period of rapid industrial transformation in Sweden (1890–1920) or in the period of early industrialization (1850–90). Of the remaining, nearly all were founded in the 1920s and 1930s. Only Stena Line and the medical equipment company Gambro, both founded in the 1960s, are of comparatively recent origin, and of these only Gambro was built around advanced innovative technology.[2] Several of the most promising new companies from recent decades have in fact already been acquired by larger companies.

Is this a problem? Nearly all of the large and usually old Swedish companies are profitable, internationally competitive, and regarded as technical or commercial leaders in their markets. The Swedish stock market is obviously attractive for foreign investors, who, since the liberalization of the stock market legislation in 1990, have become major buyers of shares in Swedish companies.

But this is not the whole picture. First, most large Swedish companies are concentrated in the mature technologies on which the first and second Industrial Revolutions were once based—the machine tools, mechanical engineering, and electrical industries. They are strong in middle technology but weak in frontline R&D.[3] Even companies that are strong in such R&D have been markedly path dependent. Second, as they often have reached a leading position in the mature branches they have been able to expand abroad through acquisitions of less vigorous companies in the same branches. Their growth in size increasingly reflects internationalization, not increased Swedish production. This concentration on mature branches, international ventures in restructuring, and the lack of new companies centered around frontline technology and new business ideas can be connected with the recent deterioration in Sweden's position in GNP per capita and real wages compared with other advanced industrial countries.

From Dynamic Transformation to Path Dependence

The industrial transformation of Sweden around 1900 created a new and dynamic structure in Swedish business. At the time, industrial companies, banks, and owners were to a large extent connected with recent experiences in entrepreneurship and creative performance. Most companies were founded on Swedish inventions or successful adaptations of foreign inventions, and the managers, owners, and bankers were entrepreneurs in the true Schumpeterian sense of this word. To fulfill their strategic visions, the young managers were trained in the same basic attitudes to become the second generation of decision makers in the large Swedish companies. The creative entrepreneurs of the early generation were transformed into increasingly efficient managers.

The successful *long-term* evolution of large-scale Swedish manufacturing, however, can only be understood in terms of the elaborate interaction between managers, owners, and banks, with the stock market as a potential but largely passive final arbiter. Large manager-led companies, entrepreneurial owner-families,[4] and a few large banks became the power centers for Swedish business life. When one type of power center developed signs of inertia, another more dynamic power center often took control of the industrial company. These changes were sometimes dramatic but more often gradual and only visible in a long-term perspective. However, most of the power centers—owners, banks, and industrial hierarchies—had had their formative periods during the great industrial transformation (around 1890–1920) and were based on the same fundamental business ideas.

Managerial Hierarchies

Sweden's transformation to an industrial society was largely achieved by the end of World War I, by which time most of the large companies of today were already in place. For a long time, the role of the large owners was limited. Several of the largest companies were dominated by highly independent managers and sometimes even by managerial dynasties. Their power base was the early successes of their companies. As long as a large number of small investors were willing to place their capital (often also their votes) in the trust of these managers and their boards of directors, industrial managers remained a strong independent force.

One result of the development of the managerial hierarchies and internationally oriented Swedish companies was that emerging new potential entrepreneurs had strong incentives to join these hierarchies rather than develop their own companies. The large companies offered a stimulating and well-paid environment for technical research, they had close contacts with international markets, and they offered successful managers access to the social elite. In the long term, however, this "taming" of potential entrepreneurs reduced attempts to create alternative innovative structures of development. Competitive capitalism was to a large extent replaced with organized capitalism.[5]

Entrepreneurial Owners

Several of the best-known Swedish entrepreneurial owners created their fortunes during the industrial transformation around the turn of the century, most of them through the promotion of new technology or business ideas. Their power continued to grow and culminated in the latter half of the twentieth century, thus creating an alternative power structure to the managerial hierarchies even in the largest industrial companies. Since 1920, very few new entrepreneurial families have reached the same level of power as those that created their fortunes before that year.

The most prominent industrial group was the Wallenbergs, who gradually specialized in active ownership in large international high-technology companies. The Wallenberg group also mirrors the development of Swedish industry. Until the late 1920s, medium-sized companies dominated the group and the Wallenbergs were focusing on the founding and development of new companies. The R&D-oriented drug manufacturer Astra and the aircraft and car manufacturer Saab were developed within this group.

Since the 1960s, however, the Wallenbergs have mainly been involved in large-scale structural change of mature industries. Their ability to recruit dynamic presidents to such industries and create long-term loyalty among entrepreneurially minded managers has been a major contribution to the continued efficiency of several old Swedish companies. Earlier the Wallenbergs were able to combine such activities with the maintenance of a network of contacts with entrepreneurs and small companies. Since the 1960s, and especially since the 1980s, however, their contacts have increasingly become identified with their large companies' networks. This has diminished the groups' ability to act as a transformer of industry. Most other old owner groups have, due to the retirement or extinction of the owner families, changed into funds or industrial hierarchies that for decades have had a vested interest in keeping the old structures as efficient as possible.

New Entrepreneurs

Why has there been so little industrial transformation since 1920 and especially since the mid–twentieth century? The number of new companies and owner families that grew up in the 1920s, 1930s, and 1940s was considerable by present-day standards, but only a few of them became large.[6] The most successful post-1920 Swedish entrepreneurs have created typical niche companies with a considerable potential for international growth. These companies have successively upgraded their products and created international companies around unique or unusual business ideas. Well-known examples were mentioned earlier: Tetra Pak, IKEA, and H&M, all based on innovative ways of combining production and distribution in order to make profits out of the modern markets for mass consumption.

The "new" companies and their owners for a long time acted as outsiders to the Swedish networks in business. The owners and managers seldom joined the boards of banks and other large companies, and they seldom acted as leading spokesmen for the business community. It has been suggested that the "new" owners may have been deliberately excluded by the established groups, but this explanation is hardly sustainable as a general explanation. Instead, it seems as if some of the most successful entrepreneurs have consciously or unconsciously decided to *avoid* being co-opted to the older groups in order to keep their companies dynamic and retain the original entrepreneurial idea that created them.

False Starts: The Rational Developers and the New Financial Capitalists

By the early 1960s, Sweden had had several decades of fairly straightforward industrial development along the lines established 50 to 100 years earlier. Few recent innovative ideas had matured into new companies. During the early 1960s, most banks started "development companies" to promote new companies. These development companies, however, soon became investment companies specializing in buying medium-sized family companies within their banks' sphere of customers. They illustrate the difficulties of *planning* transformation from the competence base of established structures.

The next group to make the same mistake was the Social Democrats, who in the late 1960s launched an ambitious program for reinvigorating Swedish business life through state-owned companies, an investment bank, and more active use of state-controlled pension funds. In the 1970s, this had to be changed into crisis management of several large, privately owned companies in the steel, shipbuilding, and forest industries. Ironically, it was during the time of nonsocialist governments, from 1976 to 1982, that the state-owned sector of Swedish industry really expanded, a result of the industrial crisis.

During the 1970s, and even more so during the 1980s, a new type of capitalist became prominent in Swedish business life, this being the pure financial capitalist. Pure financial capitalists, without long-term ambitions to own and develop a nonfinancial company, had been rare since the early twentieth century. Now they appeared and began buying undervalued companies, cleverly using the new financial instruments on the stock market as well as property speculation. But they did not attempt to make profits on new companies and nonfinancial innovations. The banks gave them large loans. Enormous fortunes were gained and most of them lost after 1990. Their appearance made the old owners and managers—who in the 1960s and early 1970s were often criticized as reactionary—look like socially responsible industrialists with long-term goals.

Illusions of Transformation: The 1980s

After the rather severe industrial crisis of the 1970s (primarily in steel and shipbuilding), the lack of new entrepreneurs again became apparent. In the early 1980s, the stock market experienced a boom. Many new small and medium-sized companies were launched on this market, saving in shares through funds and insurance companies increased dramatically, and new venture capital companies appeared. It looked as if the preconditions for a considerable transformation of the established structures of Swedish business life finally had appeared. However, hardly any of the many new companies quoted on the stock exchange showed interest in growth. In many cases, the owners had gone public in order to get a favorable price on their shares before they sold out to a large company. The venture capital companies failed to develop more than a small number of new companies, their patience with emerging companies being limited and the members of their boards usually being closely connected to established groups. Their network of contacts was probably not very different from that of the established owners, banks, and managers and hardly suitable for discovering and stimulating entrepreneurs outside that network.

Similarly, the banks showed little ability in promoting innovators and new companies with expansionistic ambitions. Instead, their money went to the traditionally safe real estate market. In the early 1990s, the Swedish banking system was struck by its worst crisis in almost 200 years. The losses were caused by loans for real estate transactions and more or less reckless financial ventures. Losses caused by failures in promotion of innovations were conspicuously absent.

Since 1990, foreign investors and pension funds have owned around half of the Swedish stock market. The once important anonymous small-scale investing individuals have been reduced to an unimportant group. This mirrors a decreasing Swedish ability to combine active and creative ownership with control over large companies.

Where Are the Entrepreneurs with Power Ambitions?

Sweden in the later half of the twentieth century is a society in which the established structures of business are vigorous and highly efficient in handling development problems along their established paths. Managerial hierarchies and owner groups have demonstrated an ability to discover new potential entrepreneurs in their spheres. But this structure has increasingly lost its capacity to perceive and select new business opportunities and new combinations with a potential for rapid growth. The economic elite almost exclusively consists of managers of a mature structure, and there are few signs that Swedish small-scale entrepreneurs really *wish* to engage in rapid business growth. They show little ambition to lead large firms of potential importance to the country.[7] To develop such a company, they must develop networks of contacts with banks, investors, and other companies—in short, entering a power game to join the power elite. The typical Swedish small-scale entrepreneur of today has little or no desire to do that. Had he been interested, he had ample opportunity to do so by joining an established large company and *using its established structures and networks.* You don't need to create a large family business in order to join the elite. The existing elite is open to you if you learn to play according to its rules and share its interests.

A Schumpeterian Perspective

Joseph Schumpeter left two paradigmatic pictures of capitalistic development. The first is the entrepreneur as the creative destroyer and promoter of new combinations in economic life. The other is routinization of economic change in large organizations, put forward in *Capitalism, Socialism, and Democracy* ([1942] 1976). In chapters 12 to 14 of that book, Schumpeter states that the triumph of capitalism as the dominant social system rapidly was making the entrepreneurial function obsolete. Economic progress was increasingly depersonalized. Technological progress and the core of entrepreneurship (the ability to get things done), could be achieved by professional managers within large-scale companies. Schumpeter saw this as ominous for the future of the bourgeois elite. Without a continuous supply of entrepreneurs to reinvigorate the bourgeois class it would rapidly lose its legitimacy as the leader of economic life. Some kind of "socialism" would replace it. He saw no future in ownership and control of large firms concentrated in a limited number of bourgeois families that no longer contributed active leadership to economic transformation. The future, which Schumpeter hardly longed for, was the triumph of industrial technocracy.

Swedish business life at the end of the twentieth century exhibits striking similarities to Schumpeter's predictions. The entrepreneurial function of transformation has been drastically reduced in importance, and for generations the supply of new entrepreneurs to reinvigorate the bourgeois class has been steadily reduced. Development, but not transformation, is routine work in the large companies. Ownership, but not active control, has rapidly been concentrated in financial intermediaries, which administer the savings of a large portion of the population. At least potentially, this is a form of "socialization" of ownership. Contrary to Schumpeter's predictions, a limited number of very powerful and competent owner-families remain. The old owner-families have inherited much of the prestige of the entrepreneurs. They are regarded as "industrialists" (creators of industrial jobs) who are "nationally conscious" (they are expected to keep main offices and central R&D units in Sweden), and they are believed to prefer profits in the long run rather than in the near future (they wish to leave an empire to future generations of their families).

Schumpeter's ideas about the future gave no space to the entrepreneurial function as a force *independent of established organizations.* He was optimistic about the ability of organizations to achieve future transformations through rational decision making, and he regarded the individual entrepreneur as increasingly obsolete. The Swedish experience more than half a century later casts doubts on that optimism. The industrial bureaucracies have not been able to achieve large-scale transformation of the industrial structure. Sweden is witnessing a *crisis of the entrepreneurial function* as a force behind economic and social transformation. Society itself also has a rather lukewarm attitude toward entrepreneurial behavior. The social institutions of Sweden (the tax system, labor market legislation, etc.) are not favorable to new and growing firms but are generally friendly to big business. This is in accordance with Schumpeter's theory that the long-term destruction of capitalist society is inherent in the mechanisms of that society—the stratum that supports it tends to disappear. It is difficult for a society to give a positive environment both to established groups and to potential destroyers of those groups, but if the creative destroyers of existing bourgeois interests are not allowed to do their job and join the bourgeois elite, this class will in the long run destroy itself.

NOTES

1. It summarizes the results from Glete 1987 and Glete 1994. Parts of the arguments in these books are presented in English in Glete 1989 and Glete 1993. My ideas about social elites in twentieth-century Swedish society is further developed in Glete 1991.

2. See the tables and presentation of the companies in Glete 1994, 13–19. It may be added that the 30 companies next in size would not have changed the age structure if they had been included in the analysis. See also Eliasson 1993.

3. See, for example, Carlsson et al. 1979, Sölvell et al. 1991, Ohlsson 1992, and Eliasson 1994.

4. The expression *entrepreneurial owners* is used in this essay for owners who actively use their power to exercise certain entrepreneurial functions. They are not necessarily *successful* entrepreneurs, although most entrepreneurial-owner families have their origins in an entrepreneurial success.

5. The conscious efforts of a large company to organize its branch (electrical engineering) through a "stick-and-carrot" policy toward entrepreneurs and potential entrepreneurs in this branch was a theme in my research on ASEA (Glete 1983, 1984).

6. The main work on Swedish entrepreneurs between the wars is Dahmén [1950] 1979. There is no comparable study of the post-1939 period.

7. This is emphasized in Utterback and Reitberger 1982.

REFERENCES

Carlsson, Bo, et al. eds. 1979. *Teknik och industristruktur—70-talets ekonomiska kris i historisk belysning.* Stockholm: IUI-IVA.
Dahmén, Erik. [1950] 1970. *Entrepreneurial Activity and the Development of Swedish Industry, 1919–1939.* Homewood, IL: Irwin.
Eliasson, Gunnar. 1993. "Introduction to the Conference." In *The Markets for Innovation, Ownership, and Control,* edited by Richard Day, Gunnar Eliasson, and Clas Wihlborg. Amsterdam: North-Holland.
———. 1994. "The Theory of the Firm and the Theory of Economic Growth." In *Evolutionary and Neo-Schumpeterian Approaches to Economics,* edited by Lars Magnusson. Boston: Kluwer.
Glete, Jan. 1983. *ASEA under hundra år, 1883–1983: En studie i ett storföretags organisatoriska, tekniska och ekonomiska utveckling.* Västerås: ASEA.
———. 1984. *Storföretag i starkström: Ett svenskt industriföretags omvärldsrelationer—en sammanfattning baserad på "ASEA under hundra år."* Västerås: ASEA.
———. 1987. *Ägande och industriell omvandling: Ägargrupper, skogsindustri, verkstadsindustri 1850–1950.* Stockholm: SNS.
———. 1989. "Long-Term Firm Growth and Ownership Organization: A Study of Business Histories." *Journal of Economic Behavior and Organization* 12:329–51.

————. 1991. "Ägarkoncentrationen och den politiska demokratin." In *Makten över företagen,* edited by R. Skog and R. Eidem. Stockholm: Carlsson.

————. 1993. "Swedish Managerial Capitalism: Did It Ever Become Ascendant?" *Business History* 35:99–110. Also published in *Nordic Business in the Long View: On Control and Strategy in Structural Change,* edited by K. Ullenhag. London: Frank Cass.

————. 1994. *Nätverk i näringslivet: Ägande och industriell omvandling i det mogna industrisamhället, 1920–1990.* Stockholm: SNS.

Ohlsson, Lennart. 1992. *R&D for Swedish Industrial Renewal: A Study for Policy Makers and Industrial Strategists.* Stockholm: Allmänna Förlaget.

Schumpeter, Joseph A. [1942] 1976. *Capitalism, Socialism, and Democracy.* London: Allen & Unwin.

Sölvell, Örjan, Ivo Zander and Michael E. Porter. 1991. *Advantage Sweden.* Stockholm: Norstedt.

Utterback, James M., and Göran Reitberger. 1982. *Technology and Industrial Innovation in Sweden: A Study of New Technology-Based Firms.* Cambridge, MA.

A Discourse on a Model of the Entrepreneur-Centered Economy
S. Y. Wu

1. Introduction

Despite its elegance and beauty, the neoclassical model (see Debreu 1959) has long been a subject of dissension. Critics of the model are concerned, for example, with (1) its reticence on the raison d'etre of the firm and the boundary between the firm and market, (2) whether this equilibrium model is capable of dealing with the ever changing market, and (3) its ability to discern whether economic development is driven by technological change or market extension. The standard neoclassical model's inability to deal with these issues can be seen readily by reminding the reader how the market economy is perceived by the neoclassical economist.

The economy is composed of two sets of primitive agents—the consumer and the firm. All agents are assumed to behave non-cooperatively and pursue their own self-interests in a complete and competitive market environment. Given the market prices, the consumer chooses a consumption plan to maximize his utility subject to a budget constraint, and the firm selects a production plan to maximize its profit. Demand and supply interact in the market to determine prices which clear the markets. Guided by prices within and without the firm, resources are allocated solely by the impersonal market. A state of equilibrium will emerge and this equilibrium is Pareto optimal.

This static view of the economy is also valid in a multi-period setting. In such an environment, commodities are distinguished not only by the physical characteristics but also by the time and state of nature in which the commodities are delivered. Assume all contingent markets exist and are competitive, agents will trade contingent claims (future contracts) to be carried out when a given state of nature has occurred. Under this situation, both the consumer and the firm will want to make commitments now for future delivery of commodities on the contingent basis. Futures markets which open in the current period will take the place of the spot markets which would have opened sequentially. Equilibrium of the economy occurs whenever there exists a set of futures prices under which the consumer's consumption plan maximizes his expected utility subject to his overall budget constraint, the firm's production plan maximizes its present market value, and demand is equal to supply in each and every market. Because agents, in choosing their plans, have access to the complete set of futures prices, sales are all contracted and paid for in the current period on the basis of the equilibrium contingent prices. As time elapses and events unfold, deliveries are made according to the contractual arrangements. No future use of the spot markets is necessary.

From this description of the economy, it is evident that the neoclassical model was never intended to deal with the initially posed issues. First, not only the existence of the firm is assumed but its allocative role is denied. Because all the activities in the firm and the market are guided by market prices, "the market works itself," with demand and supply interacting to determine both the employment of inputs and the distribution of products according to the universal marginal principle. The firm does not possess a separate internal decision rule and makes no independent contribution to the market outcome. The market alone allocates resources, and, as such, there exists no boundary between the firm and the market.

Second, the primary concern of neoclassical economics is not the market process per se, but the existence of an equilibrium. Because resources are owned by individuals and the individuals' endowments and preferences vary widely, the primary mission of the neoclassical economist is to show that the decentralized market is capable of reaching a mutually consistent outcome for all market participants. In other words, there indeed exists an equilibrium. Consequently, an enormous amount of energy and talent has been devoted to identifying conditions under which an equilibrium will emerge. Issues concerning the market process are pushed into the background. Once the existence of an equilibrium is assured, the only remaining important issue becomes whether the outcome of this equilibrium (or equilibria) represents an efficient and equitable allocation of society's scarce resources.

Finally, in the neoclassical framework there is no room for endogenous growth. Since the neoclassical model was developed under the premise that endowments of resources, consumer preferences, and production technologies are all given and full market information through prices is available to all participants, the market necessarily would have explored all opportunities and settled on the one that is optimal both for now and in the future. There is no possibility for improvement and change. Should the economy experience any change at all, the change must be brought about by exogenous factors such as technological improvement or population growth. Because growth takes place only through exogenous shocks, the distinction between growth induced by the technological push and by market extension (e.g., population expansion) is minimized. Inadvertently, the capitalistic market is robbed of its inherent creativity.

Recognizing the shortcomings of the standard neoclassical model, economists in recent years have endeavored to improve its realism by relaxing some of its assumptions. Frank Knight (1971) pointed out long ago that the fundamental difference between perfect and actual competition is that uncertainity is absent in the former but ubiquitous in the latter. The bulk of the contemporary literature reflects efforts to extend the neoclassical model by incorporating uncertainty. While these efforts have brought marked improvements, because the modelers insist on retaining the neoclassical perception that the market alone is capable of allocating resources the extended model remains unequipped to cope with the questions we seek to answer. An alternative model must be found.

Accordingly, we wish to call the reader's attention to a model of the entrepreneur-centered economy that overcomes these shortcomings. This model (Wu and Qin 1996) reflects the understanding that the presence of uncertainty implies that some contingent markets are absent. With the absence of these markets, resources owners no longer have access to a complete set of contingent prices and therefore lack full market information. Dissimilarity in endowments and preferences among individuals inevitably leads to disagreement on production policy. This disagreement destroys joint production and therefore causes the market to break down.

As was pointed out by Frank Knight, chaos in the marketplace also offers spirited entrepreneurial individuals opportunities to rise and restore production through their own volition. Entrepreneurs use their own subjective judgments (instead of objective knowledge) of the market to make production decisions. In this way, entrepreneurs take an active part in resource allocation. The resulting economy is thus called the entrepreneur-centered economy (Wu 1989). The perception of this economy is that:

> Consumers are the only primitive agents. They own all the resources of which land, labor and capital are tradable in the factor markets while entrepreneur services are not. Each agent holds at least a two-period decision horizon, today and tomorrow. Today is known with certainty and tomorrow is uncertain. In order to sustain consumption in the future, the agent must convert his current resources into future income. He does so by participating in production. The owner of a tradable resource obtains his income by selling his services to the firm. The entrepreneur, on the other hand, does so indirectly. He first helps to organize the firm which converts inputs into a commodity and then claims a share of the firm's profit as income after the commodity is sold in the market. The firm is organized whenever (1) a set of entrepreneurs agrees to organize themselves into a particular form and adopt a profit sharing rule, (2) the cooperative entrepreneurs settle on a specific production and financing policy, and (3) the firm acquires the necessary financing.

In the entrepreneur-centered economy, the consumer chooses his consumption, investment and production activities so as to maximize his expected utility subject to a set of appropriate constraints. The firm has no objective of its own; it merely serves as a vehicle for the entrepreneur to carry out his optimizing activities. Activities in this economy include simultaneously the consumption-investment of the consumer, the coalition formation of the entrepreneurs, the production of the firm, and the exchanges in the market. As these activities interact to bring the economy into a state of equilibrium, the prices of the commodities and the amount of financial securities are determined, the traded and non-traded resources are channeled into their employment, and the number and internal organization of firms are also determined. In this manner, the formation of the firm, the determination of resource utilization and the exchange of goods and services all become an integral part of the allocative process in this economy.

The purpose of this essay is twofold: in sections 2 and 3 I first describe the recent contributions of the relevant literature and pointed out why the proposed solutions are still unable to address adequately the issues concerning the nature of the firm, the way in which the market copes with changes, and the causes of economic development. Next, I demonstrate that the model of the entrepreneur-centered economy is naturally suited to deal with these questions. The balance of this essay is then divided into three additional sections: section 2 deals with issues concerning the firm, section 3 addresses the remaining issues, and section 4 concludes.

2.   On the Nature and Boundary of the Firm

It is commonly agreed that the presence of market uncertainty serves as the primary underlying cause for firms to exist.[1] Four immediate causes are identified in the literature: the firm is organized in order to (1) break the impasse created by a lack of consistent resource commitment among risk-averse resource owners (Knight), (2) gain the advantage of risk sharing (portfolio theorists), (3) reduce shirking by workers who engage in joint production (Alchain and Demsetz), and (4) avoid the high cost of using the market (Coase). Although all these views enjoy wide support in the literature, perhaps the Coasian theme is most popular. Ronald Coase (1937) cited transaction costs as a reason for the firm to exist. In a world of uncertainty, the resource owners must incur information costs, which the perfect market freely provides. Moreover, it is also costly to negotiate and enforce contracts. The magnitude of these uncertainty-related transaction costs will decrease if a firm is created to coordinate production. A Coasian entrepreneur is one who signs contracts with each resource owner "whereby . . . for a certain remuneration [the resource owner] agrees to obey the direction of an entrepreneur within certain limits" (391). In this way, a firm is created to coordinate production, thus enabling its activities to bypass the rule of the market.

To assert that there exists a distinct allocative role for the firm is to imply that the firm and the market become two alternative modes of resource allocation and must share this responsibility. The crucial question is how the firm and the market divide up the allocative tasks. This question is taken to be equivalent to the question of where the firm ends and the market begins. There are two approaches in the literature—the behavioral approach and the cost approach. Neither approach is wholly satisfactory.

The behaviorists (Cyert and Marsh 1963) advocate the cooperative view of the firm and claim that outside the firm, agents' relationship is short lived and they behave impersonally and noncooperatively, whereas within the firm the agents' relationship is enduring and they behave cooperatively. The behavior-based theorists insist that it is this transformation from individualistic behavior in the market to cooperative behavior in the firm that sets the firm and the market apart. Unfortunately, this approach is not satisfactory because it is not difficult to find examples of long-run-oriented contracts between independent buyers and sellers who cooperate with each other in order to exploit mutually benefical market opportunities. If so, the boundary between the firm and the market is blurred.

The cost-based theorists (Coase 1937) start with the proposition that the use of the internal decision apparatus of the firm is not without cost; otherwise, they reason that there would be no way to prevent the firm from expanding indefinitely, thus eliminating market transactions altogether. According to Ronald Coase, there exists a diminishing return to the entrepreneurial function; as the number of internal transactions increases, the probability of failure by the entrepreneur to make the best utilization of the factors of production also increases. In the words of Arrow (1974), it is the overloading of information and the decision-making capacity of the entrepreneurial authority that brings the firm to its limit.

Because there exists a cost of either using the firm or using the market, neither the firm nor the market can operate exclusively without the other. A firm will expand until the cost of organizing an extra transaction within the firm becomes equal to the cost of carrying out the same by means of the market. Thus, by substituting at the boundary, Coase and his followers solve the boundary problem between the firm and the market. Unfortunately, because of the existence of an internal inconsistency, the cost-based theory is also unsatisfactory. To see this, we need to observe that the Coasian argument involves two parts. First, the entrepreneur employs inputs authoritatively, and, second, the boundary between the firm and the market is determined by equating the marginal cost of using the firm with that of using the market. Once this boundary is identified, the marginal productivity of the entrepreneur becomes known and the market price for the entrepreneur is determined. In other words, the activities of the entrepreneur are now subject to market discipline. Because the productivity of the entrepreneur is derived from the productivities of the factors that he employs, the marginal productivity of the entrepreneur must reflect the marginal productivities of these inputs. Since the entrepreneur's own reward is subject to market discipline, it is hard to imagine that his employment of the factors of production can be immune to the same discipline. Under these circumstances, the entrepreneur's private decision rule must be superseded by the market criterion. Consequently, if one wishes to accept the second part of the Coasian argument, one must reject the first part: that the entrepreneur does allocate inputs in a purely authoritative fashion. There cannot exist a separate decision mechanism for the firm! With the entrepreneur's independent prerogative vanishing, so does the Coasian delineation of the boundary between the firm and the market.

The entrepreneur-centered theory can shed light on the nature of the two-tier (dual) allocation between firms and the market and help to settle the associated boundary issue. Based upon the brief description of this model given in the previous section, we see that, contrary to popular belief, the firm does not use nonmarket means to allocate all resources internally. Instead, it allocates only the nontradable entrepreneurial services through cooperative bargaining among entrepreneurs but allocates tradable factor services by means of the price mechanism. This fact implies that the issues of "how the firm and the market divide up the allocative role" and "where the firm ends and the market begins" are not equivalent. This is not to say that the unique way of allocating entrepreneurial services in the firm does not have any impact on the employment of other factors. On the contrary, because the allocation of the entrepreneurial services simultaneously determines the firm's production policy, it is necessarily true that this allocation determines the firm's demand for the tradable factors of production and the supply of its products. What we wish to say is that the firm's boundary had little to do with how the allocative responsibility is divided between the firm and the market. The only exception occurs whenever all factor owners have opted to act as entrepreneurs. Only in this case will the boundary of the firm serve to separate the ways that the firm and the market allocate resources (Wu 1989, chap. 6).

The preceding discussion makes it abundantly clear that the literature has erred in characterizing the precise nature of the two-tier allocative mechanism in the market economy. Because it is believed that the entrepreneur allocates all inputs of the firm by nonmarket means, the literature concludes that by simply identifying the boundary between the firm and the market one can discern the division of the allocative responsibility between the entrepreneur and the market. Since the entrepreneurs do not, in general, allocate all factors of production but their own services by nonmarket means, it is not existence of the boundary between the firm and the market that gives rise to the two-tier allocation of resources. Rather, it is through the unique way that the entrepreneurs allocate their own services that the two-tier system is manifested. Because the entrepreneurs play a central role in the firm, the allocation of their own services inevitably affects the firm's production policy and thereby indirectly affects the level of inputs employed and outputs produced. Perhaps it is this indirect effect that gives many economists the impression that all factors of production are subject to the direction of entrepreneurs.

3. On Equilibrium and Growth

Recall that the neoclassical model assumes the market is complete, all state prices are known, and the exchange rates between periods and states are well defined. Futures markets, which open in the current period, take the place of the spot markets, which would have to be opened sequentially. Exchanges are all contracted and paid for in the current period on the basis of the equilibrium futures prices. Since the futures prices in the current period provide accurate forecasts of the equilibrium spot prices for the various dates and events, equilibrium plans in today's futures markets mirror the set of equilibrium actions in the sequential spot markets. Thus, expectations are identical to realizations. This consistency between plans and actions is significant because it is only when this condition is met that today's optimal choices will remain optimal in the future and the choices made today will be truly rational. This hallmark of the Arrow-Debreu equilibrium has served as a standard for all modern neoclassical theories to emulate.

The equilibrium analyses in the post-Arrow-Debreu era incorporate uncertainty by dealing with general equilibrium in the incomplete market setting. An incomplete market, in the present context, means the absence of some futures markets. A lack of such markets requires that trading of the associated physical goods takes place sequentially in spot markets at future dates. Since equilibria among periods and states are mutually dependent, the inability of agents to accurately forecast prices that will prevail on future dates implies that the current market equilibrium is also indeterminate. Thus, due to a lack of full price information, the market is prevented from fulfilling its coordinating role. A market failure results.

Neoclassical Revisions
In recent years, mainstream economists have advocated that there indeed exist mechanisms that allow agents to forecast future prices and thereby avert this market failure. In a seminal paper, Roy Radner (1972) demon-

strates that, by using a two-step procedure, common expectations of prices among agents can indeed be assured. First, the expectations of the future environment are objectively formulated by observing the historical evolution of the market environment, which is deemed to be common knowledge, and, second, given the expected future environment and the assumed commonly known law of the market, each agent formulates expectations about future spot prices. Moreover, by virtue of these assumptions, these expectations are common to all agents. With the aid of a set of common expectations of the future spot prices and the knowledge of current prices, optimal individual plans for both the consumer and the producer will emerge. As these plans are implemented, the market would clear at each date-event pair. This result implies that plans and actions are indeed consistent.

In an attempt to soften the strong assumptions employed in this path-breaking model, a large body of literature, for example, under the rubric of rational expectations (Radner 1979) and temporary equilibrium analysis (Grandmont 1977), has emerged. Due to the lack of space, we are unable to survey this literature here. It suffices to say that these models in a variety of ways postulate that agents can start with different information about the environment and different hypotheses about the law of the market. Learning processes have to be added to allow a convergence of environmental information and the law of the market to its true self. Thus, through learning, agents adjust their behaviors and the market moves toward an equilibrium. At this equilibrium, expectations become self-fulfilling and plans and actions again become consistent.

Thus, despite the lack of some futures markets, through the agents' uncanny ability to correctly forecast future spot prices, the missing futures markets are sidestepped and an equilibrium is generated. In this regard, the Radner economy conforms closely to the Arrow-Debreu economy. The only difference is that in the Arrow-Debreu model the future is telescoped to the present, whereas in the Radner case agents, at least through learning, are all clairvoyant. In both cases, plans are made correctly with common information and unfailing expectations; all resources are efficiently allocated.

Restoration of market equilibrium notwithstanding, it is evident that the neoclassical model is devoid of endogenous growth. However, the growth phenomenon does take place under the circumstance that the economy is currently not in the steady state equilibrium (Solow 1956). Because current resources can either be used for current consumption or be invested in capital stock for the purpose of producing goods for future consumption, the issue is how consumption, and hence investment, should be determined so that the consumer's utility derived from a stream of consumption over time is maximized subject to the appropriate technological and resource constraints. Taking consumer preferences, production technology, labor endowment in each period, and initial capital endowment as given, this choice problem is well defined. Assuming that preferences and technology are convex and there are no external effects, then the consumer choice problem generates a competitive equilibrium growth path that is also efficient. On this growth path, per capital output (as well as capital stock and its price) grow at a constant rate. In the absence of any technological innovation, the per capita output converges to a steady state equilibrium value. At this point, growth of per capita output ceases to take place. Because genuine growth must be brought about by external changes in technology or the pattern of labor supply, there is no endogenous growth in this economy.

This characterization of growth in the neoclassical economy is challenged by the new growth theorists. According to these theorists, investment in knowledge (Arrow 1962; Romer 1986) or human capital (Lucas 1988) often promotes increasing returns to scale and generates external effects, thus causing sustainable endogenous growth. The basic idea is that there is a trade-off between using resources for current consumption or investing them to produce more consumption in the future. Investing resources or time for the accumulation of either knowledge or human capital not only increases their own productivities but, through spillover effects, also contributes to the productivities of other factors of production. Consequently, investing in knowledge and human capital leads to increasing returns in outputs as well as generating positive externalities. However, the presence of these external effects causes the optimal growth path to deviate from the competitive growth path. At any moment in time, investment in knowledge and human capital will lie below the optimal level. Underinvestment of these activities notwithstanding, with the presence of externality per capita output can grow monotonically over time and is sustained by the growth in knowledge and human capital.

As a consequence, the neoclassical model now depicts the economy as a perpetual growth machine capable of growing monotonically without bounds. However, this pattern of growth still lacks true endogeneity. To see this, let us use the popular metaphor that depicts the market as a preprogrammed system operating under the control of an autopilot that is designed to bring the market into equilibrium. Once this equilibrium (whether steady state or perpetual growth) is attained, no forces endogenous to the market can dislodge it. Change in this context means adjustment toward the equilibrium, not an alteration of the program. Any such program change must still be initiated from a source outside the market system. The neoclassical model's inability to deal with program changes also implies that whenever there exist multiple equilibria, the market is incapable of making a choice among them even if these equilibria are well ranked. This inability to choose is the root cause of the "coordination failure problem" referred to in the literature (Hart 1975).

Moreover, the new growth theory is found wanting for another reason. Inspection of the historical data makes it clear that no economy grows in the alleged monotonic pattern. A typical economy, instead, grows in spurts and exhibits peaks and valleys. Efforts are already under way to incorporate this phenomenon into the model (Aghion and Howitt 1992). To do so, researchers have to reach out to a much older literature for inspiration and help. It is to this literature that we now turn.

The Entrepreneur-Centered Economy Model

Long before revised neoclassical economies came into vogue, another group of economists advocated that the market failure caused by a lack of full market information could be averted with the assistance of entrepreneurs. The entrepreneur, instead of relying on the objective knowledge provided by the market, uses his subjective judgment of the market situation to make production decisions. Because of his willingness to bear the consequences associated with these decisions, according to Frank Knight ([1921] 1971), production is restored and the market revived. In addition, entrepreneurs also serve as agents of change. The presence of uncertainty places a veil over market opportunities; a state of disequilibrium prevails. The Austrian economists (Kirzner 1973) believe that in a disequilibrium situation entrepreneurs do not choose "equilibrium behaviors" but merely make plans to exploit "hitherto unnoticed" profit opportunities. As these opportunities are discovered and profits reaped, the existing plans become obsolete. Plans are modified to reflect the new market situation. In this manner, the market participants interact to generate market forces, thereby setting the market process in motion. When all profit opportunities are exhausted, the market reaches a state of equilibrium. This equilibrium is, however, not permanent. In Schumpeter's view, the capitalist economy is inherently dynamic: "It incessently revolutionizes the economics structure from within" (Schumpeter 1942, 83). The source of this revolution is economic development led by the innovator-entrepreneur (Schumpeter 1934, 74). Through innovation, imitation, and competition, the economy propels itself forward and upward.

The entrepreneur-centered economy model referred to in the introductory section represents a first attempt to formally model an economy embracing the features just mentioned. Although the two-period intertemporal equilibrium model used thus far does not explicitly include all activities that entrepreneurs perform, by extending it to a multiperiod setting the defining properities of this economy can be deduced.

Because the model is designed to explain the formation of the firm and the origin of financial securities, naturally it needs to focus on the activities in the first period. In order to meet this requirement, a temporary equilibrium methodology is adopted. Recall that temporary equilibrium is determined at any given time by the interaction of agents' current decisions and their expectations about the future. In the present case, the entrepreneur uses his judgment to formulate expectations about the future. These expectations involve not only relevant future events but also a scenario as to how his own participation in production will affect the outcome of these events. Based upon these expectations, entrepreneurs take the initiative to organize firms by playing a cooperative game with each other. At the conclusion of this game, not only firms with specific size and internal organization emerge but each firm's production policy and financial structure is also determined. As time elapses, the economy moves from one temporary equilibrium to the next.

However, temporary equilibrium in the entrepreneur-centered economy differs from that of the neoclassical economy in a fundamental way; this equilibrium does not converge to a long-run limit. When decisions are made by the entrepreneurs on the basis of judgment, the fact that the entrepreneurs' market scenarios may differ means that profits can be had not only from unexploited market opportunities but also from entrepreneurs betting against each other. The existence of betting behaviors is evidenced by the presence of bulls and bears in the same market. The optimistic bull will buy, and the pessimistic bear will sell. The result is a betting equilibrium. Because the betting equilibrium possesses properities different from the neoclassical equilibrium, the market's propensity to be in a betting equilibrium naturally implies that it will not converge to the long-run neoclassical equilibrium.

In addition, decisions based upon judgment also alter the notion of rationality. Now the discrepancy between expectations and realization may simply represent an acceptable variation of the perceived scenario or be deemed as having been caused by other agents' erroneous betting behavior; no indictment of the entrepreneur's rationality is implied, and no change in the firm's policy is warranted. However, entrepreneurs are realistic individuals; they do realize that no one is infallible and misjudgments do lead to suboptimal policy decisions. Corrections must be made when mistakes are made. Since the revision of policies is costly, rationality now requires that the choice of policy be made to minimize the long-run cost of adjustment induced by policy revisions. A change in the criterion of rationality has taken place.

The presence of entrepreneurs affects not only the nature of equilibrium but also the way in which equilibrium changes from one state to another. There are two causes of change, one passive and the other revolutionary. Passive change takes place as result of routine adjustment following a shift in the underlying market conditions. Revolutionary change, on the other hand, takes place whenever the entrepreneur through his own innovative efforts has altered the fundamental market conditions. This revolutionary change is the source of economic development.[2]

Following Schumpeter (1934, 66), economic development is defined as "carrying out new combinations"; it is a pure, endogenously generated process involving three stages: invention, innovation, and imitation. Invention is the technical discovery of new things or new ways of doing things, innovation is the successful commercialization of invention, and imitation is the market process that leads to the adoption of a new product or process. Development is initiated by the entrepreneur who commits to innovation in order to create profit opportunities for himself. "Because being an entrepreneur is not a profession" (Schumpeter 1934, 78), once an innovative act is committed, the entrepreneur loses his status as an entrepreneur. As a result, the entrepreneur does not benefit permanently from the development process; he merely serves as a catalyst for economic development. On the other hand, because this development process first destroys the existing market equilibrium and then ultimately brings the market into an equilibrium superior to its predecessor, society now attains a higher level of satisfaction as well as wealth. Since society is the ultimate beneficiary of innovation, Schumpeter characterizes economic development as a process of "creative destruction" (1942, 83).

Moreover, because economic development is initiated by the entrepreneur, the involvement of a human element in the development process makes economic development a nonroutine matter; unlike the neoclassical case, development is spontaneous and unpredictable. Schumpeter, therefore, emphasizes that economic developments occur in spurts and tend to cluster together. Because income generated from each development levels off over time, this pattern of development induces a wavelike historical income record. In this way, Schumpeter integrates the theory of economic development with the theory of the business cycle, a feat that is still emulated by present-day growth theorists (Greiner and Hanusch 1994).

Although a formal growth model under the rubric of the entrepreneur-centered economy is not yet available, the structure of the Wu-Qin model suggests that such a growth model would embrace the basic features of the Schumpeterian theory. Two aspects of the entrepreneur-centered economy model further enrich the theory of economic development.

First, in the Schumpeterian framework, innovation is always a result of an entrepreneur's conscious effort directed explicitly toward this purpose. In contrast, in the entrepreneur-centered economy, innovation may be a by-product of other entrepreneurial activities (Wu and Qin 1996). Since the firm is a coalition of entrepreneurs, each entrepreneur's share of the firm's profit depends on his relative position in the internal organization of the firm. Because an entrepreneur's relative position is determined by his contribution to the configuration of the firm's production set, each cooperative entrepreneur, in an attempt to improve his relative share of the firm's profit, will strive to bring forth an expansion of the firm's production set. Although this effort is motivated by the entrepreneur's attempt to improve his relative position within the firm, nonetheless, innovation takes place as a consequence.

Second, the entrepreneur-centered economy model sheds new light on another aspect of economic development central to classical economics but largely neglected by modern economists. Recall that the classical economist cites the extension of the market as a key source of economic development. In an entrepreneur-centered economy, this avenue of development is indeed widely employed (Wu 1989, chap. 9; 1996, chap. 1). Because entrepreneurs in this economy assume a broader role than the one envisaged by Schumpeter, besides carrying out innovations, they also bear risks and perform other creative acts. For example, in an incomplete market setting, entrepreneurs not only must convert input into outputs but also concomitantly create markets for these products. Sometimes markets can be created only by the entrepreneur's willingness to internalize some market uncertainties and by his ability to mobilize the support of complementary nonmarket institutions (e.g., legal support). Numerous new markets and institutions are still being created in this way. Markets on the Internet and financial markets for new derivatives are cases in point. Because entrepreneurs and the market complement each other in the allocation of resources, as new markets are created and the market becomes more complete the role played by the entrepreneur also adjusts to become more specialized. These adjustments, in turn, lead to the streamlining of the firm's internal organization. For example, the development of the information industry and complementary legal institutions has led to a decentralization of the firm's internal decision processes and thus greatly enhanced its efficiency. In short, because entrepreneurs contribute to technological advances as well as to the size and efficiency of the market, both technological improvements and market extensions have served to bring about economic development.

4. Concluding Remark

This essay introduces the entrepreneur-centered economy model and contrasts it with the traditional neoclassical model. The fundamental difference between the two models is the modeler's perspective of the market economy. The neoclassical economist views the economy as an automated system wherein the market works itself; in contrast, the advocator of the entrepreneur-centered model perceives the economy as an interactive system in which the market works in conjunction with the entrepreneurs. The inclusion of entrepreneurs as active players in the market place has greatly improved the generality, realism, and explanatory power of the model, at least concerning the nature of the firm, the market process, and the causes of economic development. The entrepreneur-centered economy model, therefore, merits greater attention and scrutiny. Many more implications of this model wait to be explored and much remains to be done. I hope that this brief presentation has stimulated the reader's interest in the entrepreneur-centered economy and thus has served to convert the reader into an active researcher on this topic.

NOTES

1. Another branch of the literature identifies monopoly as a reason for the firm to be an independent resource allocator. This literature has evolved to include managerial theories of the firm, agency theories, and so on. Due to lack of space, I shall not deal with these topics here.

2. We distinguish growth and development by the fact that growth can take place without the aid of any agent, while development cannot.

REFERENCES

Aghion, P., and P. Howitt 1992. A Model of Growth through Creative Destruction. *Econometrica* 60:155–73.

Alchain, A. A., and H. Demsetz. 1972. Production, Information Cost, and Economic Organization. *American Economic Review* 62:777–95.

Arrow, K. J. 1962. The Economic Implications of Learning by Doing. *Review of Economic Studies* 29:155–73.

———. 1974. *The Limits of Organization.* New York: Norton.

Coase, R. H. 1937. The Nature of the Firm. *Economica* 4:386–405.

Cyert, R. M., and J. G. March. 1963. *A Behavioral Theory of the Firm.* Englewood Cliffs, NJ: Prentice-Hall.

Debreu, G. 1959. *Theory of Value: An Axiomatic Analysis of Economic Equilibrium.* New York: Wiley.

Grandmont, J. M. 1977. Temporary General Equilibrium Theory. *Econometrica* 45:535–72.

Greiner, A., and H. Hanusch. 1994. Schumpeter's Circular Flow, Learning by Doing, and Cyclical Growth. *Journal of Evolutionary Economics* 4:261–71.

Hart, O. 1975. On the Optimality of Equilibrium When the Market Structure Is Incomplete. *Journal of Economic Theory* 11:418–43.

Kirzner, I. M. 1973. *Competition and Entrepreneurship.* Chicago: University of Chicago Press.

Knight, F. H. [1921] 1971. *Risk, Uncertainty, and Profit.* Chicago: University of Chicago Press.

Lucas, R. E., Jr. 1988. On the Mechanics of Economic Development. *Journal of Monetary Economics* 22:3–42.

Nelson, R. R., and S. Winter. 1982. *An Evolutionary Theory of Economic Change.* Cambridge: Harvard University Press.

Radner, R. 1972. Existence of Equilibrium Plans, Prices, and Price Expectations in a Sequence of Markets. *Econometrica* 40:278–91.

———. 1979. Rational Expectations Equilibrium: Generic Existence and the Information Revealed by Prices. *Econometrica* 47:655–78.

Romer, P. M. 1986. Increasing Returns and Long-Run Growth. *Journal of Political Economy* 94:1002–37.

Solow, R. 1956. A Contribution to the Theory of Economic Growth. *Quarterly Journal of Economics* 70:64–94.

Schumpeter, J. A. [1910] 1934. *The Theory of Economic Development.* Cambridge: Harvard University Press.

———. 1939. *Business Cycles.* New York: McGraw-Hill.

———. 1942. *Capitalism, Socialism, and Democracy.* New York: Harper and Row.

Williamson, O. E. 1970. The Vertical Integration of Production: Market Failure Considerations. *American Economic Review* 61:112–23.

———. 1981. The Modern Corporation: Origin, Evolution, Attributes. *Journal of Economic Literature* 19:153–68.

Wu, S. Y. 1989. *Production, Entrepreneurship, and Profits.* Cambridge: Basil Blackwell.

———. 1996. Essays on Entrepreneur-Centered Economy. Manuscript.

Wu, S. Y., and C. Z. Qin 1996. A Model of the Entrepreneur-Centered Economy. Paper presented at the sixth conference of the International Schumpeter Society, Stockholm.

Economic Efficiency with Enabling and Mandatory Law
Clas Wihlborg

The economic problems facing the economies in transition from central planning to market systems have greatly enhanced the awareness among economists of the importance of institutions governing market mechanisms. In many transition economies, the legal framework for business in a market economy must be created more or less from scratch. The design of law is an important topic for the industrialized economies as well. In the European Union (EU) much attention is paid to the development of a common legal framework that will help EU countries combating "Eurosclerosis" to remain competitive with the United States and Japan in high-tech industries.

Posner (1992) distinguishes between three types of law in a market economy. First, the "law of property" is concerned with creating and defining property rights. Second, "the law of contracts" facilitates the voluntary movement of property rights. And, third, "the law of torts" is concerned with the protection of property rights.

The focus in this essay is on the design of the law of contracts in the areas of, for example, company law, credit market law, bankruptcy law, product liability law, and labor market law. The question asked is how law most effectively contributes to the dynamic efficiency of a market economy. In particular, it is argued that dynamic markets characterized by pronounced unpredictability as to new technologies and productive organization require that laws governing explicit and implicit contractual rights and obligations be "enabling" as opposed to mandatory. Mandatory law specifies in detail contractual arrangements, and these arrangements cannot be changed unless the law is changed. Enabling law, on the other hand, leaves it to the parties of a transaction to agree on contractual terms, and these terms can be changed by mutual agreement without changes in written or case law.

Like products in the market, the contractual relations and institutions must develop over time in competition to serve market participants and social objectives. Contractual relations develop over time in business practice, explicit contracts, and legislation. Laws develop either through written law or cases. The point being made is that the dynamics of a market economy are best served by enabling law. Such enabling law does not imply the absence of law. There are informational advantages to specifying laws in some detail as "standard form contracts." Such laws are enabling if they can be changed by mutual agreement among parties to the "standard form contract." However, if law has social objectives other than economic efficiency in a dynamic sense, then enforcement of mandatory law is necessary. An egalitarian distribution of power and wealth, consumer protection, environmental protection, and enhancement of job security are examples of such social objectives of law. If noneconomic objectives of economic policy are best achieved through means other than the legal system, then it can be argued that enabling law should obtain a higher status constitutionally than mandatory law.

The concept of economic efficiency is discussed in section 1. The argument that dynamic efficiency requires enabling law is developed further in section 2. Noneconomic social objectives and the constitutional status of enabling law are discussed in section 3. Concluding comments follow in section 4.

1. Economic Efficiency

Dynamic efficiency is not a well-recognized concept in mainstream economics and is not well defined in the new schools of evolutionary economics. It is associated with innovative activity, investment incentives, and economic processes that take place out of equilibrium in the conventional static sense. Schumpeter's notion of "creative destruction" is one example.

Dosi (1993) makes a distinction between the static and the dynamic efficiency of a financial system. The static efficiency concept originates in conventional welfare analysis that abstracts from information and transaction costs. Dynamic efficiency, on the other hand, recognizes these costs and refers to "evolutionary viability." There is a trade-off between the two types of efficiency. Dosi argues that some financial systems perform better in the static dimension while other systems perform better dynamically. Eliasson (1991, 165 n) denotes as "Schumpetarian" efficiency allowing for endogenous entry and exit, taking transactions and information costs into consideration. In the following, dynamic and Schumpetarian efficiency should be seen as equivalent. Such efficiency implies that the present value of welfare is maximized, but this formal definition is not helpful from a policy perspective because of genuine uncertainty about growth processes when transactions and information costs are considerable. These costs make it essential to study how various institutional arrangements affect economic processes.

Once transaction and information costs are considered, dynamic efficiency and static efficiency (including these costs) need not be contradictory. In fact, dynamic efficiency becomes the interesting concept while static efficiency becomes nearly tautological. Deviations from static efficiency in an instant can always be explained by reference to costs associated with change. Thus, the more interesting issue is whether the economy moves over time in an efficient manner and what this means.

When discussing dynamic efficiency, it should be recognized that it is impossible for any one individual to know how the human capital of individuals is best organized to maximize a firm's intangible assets. Owners and managers of firms face genuine uncertainty about the reactions of those linked to a firm by various explicit and implicit contractual arrangements because all possible future circumstances cannot be incorporated in contracts. Possible sources of agency costs among owners, lenders, and shareholders are likely to depend on a number of technological and environmental factors that cannot easily be identified. It is never possible to say that there are no better contractual arrangements and organizational solutions available. What is thought to be best today is most likely going to change in the future. The uncertainty implies that the "best" contractual arrangements have to be determined by trial and error. Hence, contractual arrangements and organizations have to be flexible, allowing the perceived "best" contractual arrangements to change over time.[1] Just as competition among products is expected to lead to an efficient dynamic process for product development, competition among contractual and organizational arrangements is required for development of the arrangements that minimize expected future costs of agency, contracting, and enforcement at a given level of output.

This view of the dynamics of the economy implies that dynamic efficiency must be defined in terms of the system's ability to adjust to changes in preferences and productive conditions at lowest costs and, especially, to adjust to new conditions affecting the incentives of individuals to develop new explicit and implicit contractual arrangements. If, for example, such contractual arrangements do not develop in response to new informational conditions influencing potential agency costs, then the system lacks dynamic efficiency. Analogously, if new firms do not enter a market characterized by monopoly and low entry barriers, then there is dynamic inefficiency.

The difficulties of determining the degree of efficiency of a dynamic economic system has clear policy implications; competition among different organizational structures and contractual arrangements, as well as among products and services, is likely to lead to a superior organization of production from a dynamic point of view. Deviations from static efficiency in the conventional sense have little value as indicators of desirable economic policy measures. Policy measures to reduce such deviations are likely to lead to reduced incentives to find new contractual solutions to information problems and reduced incentives to acquire and use information. No planner, regulator, or legislator is able to determine the most efficient organizations, contracts, and services. Thus, the task of the regulator and the legislator should be to create the best conditions for search and competition among organizational and contractual solutions.

2. Enabling Law and Efficiency

Enabling law provides flexibility of contractual terms. These terms can be varied according to the particular needs and preferences of individuals and firms. There is no one set of rules that will meet the needs of all investors, individuals, or firms.[2]

The role of explicit law from the perspective of dynamic efficiency would be both to reduce the transaction and information costs of entering a contract that all parties would agree upon and to make changes in this contract possible when all parties so desire. In the case of, for example, enabling company law, transaction and information cost savings are achieved by company law that specifies a contract that covers most potential sources of future conflict among shareholders and between shareholders and management. The desirable specifics of contracts would vary across firms and over time, however. By making the standard form contract such as the corporate charter enabling—meaning that the charter can be changed by mutual consent—it can be adjusted depending on circumstances in different industries and in response to changing circumstances over time.

Mandatory law rules cannot represent all possible voluntarily agreed upon contracts in a wide variety of circumstances across firms, among individuals, and over time. In the case of company law, however, many scholars argue that mandatory law is necessary in order to avoid a majority of shareholders changing the terms of the contract among owners to the disadvantage of the minority that has become owners under specific contractual terms.[3] Macey (1992) counters this argument. First, a corporate charter can include provisions specifying requirements for changes in it while protecting minorities. Second, the price of ownership shares reflects the uncertainty about future contractual arrangements that could cause changes in the price of ownership shares. Thus, one aspect of enabling law is that it enables the stakeholders to seek an efficient degree of permanence of contractual terms. The standard form contract in law provides basic security for the relatively uninformed party, and it identifies potential sources of future conflict that may not be obvious without written law.

Since many investors and individuals lack experience in business deals, it is particularly important that individuals have the incentive to seek out the knowledge and information that will reduce the scope for opportunistic behavior that creates agency costs.[4] Highly detailed mandatory law specifying the terms of a contract under all or most contingencies would have the effect of reducing the incentive of contractual parties to gain an understanding of the potentially opportunistic behavior of other parties and of the contingencies that influence the success of a business venture. Mandatory law thus has an insurance dimension in the sense that it reduces the incentives for precautionary action. Hence, the incentive to seek the knowledge to develop the most efficient contractual relations is reduced. The existence of such incentives is required for dynamic efficiency, as was argued previously.

Dynamic efficiency requires enabling law for two reasons. First, the legislator cannot know the "best" mutually agreeable contract terms under a wide variety of circumstances. Second, only if law is enabling can competition among contractual arrangements exist. Thus, mandatory law is likely to be associated with efficency losses in the sense that many firms and individuals must enter into contracts that are not mutually agreeable.

Even if there are efficiency losses associated with mandatory law, could it not be argued that contract and enforcement costs would be lower with such law? These aspects of law would be of great importance in the formerly centrally planned economies, where legal expertise and enforcement capacity are scarce.

It must be recognized that all contingencies can never be specified even in the most detailed mandatory law. Questions of interpretation and applicability of contract terms will therefore arise in all cases. Absence of law of contract in combination with courts' recognition of all voluntarily agreed upon contracts is likely to be legally resource using either during the process of negotiating contract terms covering a wide range of contingencies or as a result of conflicts when contengencies are not covered. This consideration is particularly relevant for complex contractual arrangements. Standard form contracts in law would economize on these costs because the standard form contract helps parties identify potential sources of conflict. However, if the standard form is mandatory, then it is likely to be more legally resource using during enforcement because the mandatory rules would not be aligned with desirable contract terms across all firms and individuals. Fewer disputes will arise if enabling contract models are used because the contract terms will be those voluntarily agreed upon.

3. Nonefficiency Objectives of Law and the Constitutional Status of Enabling Law

If enabling law is associated with the privately most efficient contractual arrangements among users and suppliers of financial resources, then it also follows that, if company law has objectives other than such efficiency, mandatory law is necessary. In other words, mandatory law is required to achieve contractual terms that all parties would not voluntarily enter into, taking into account the price effects of various contractual terms. For example, if there is a political decision that labor unions should have a direct influence on investment decisions, then the channels of influence must be specified by mandatory law. Achieving social goals by predetermining contractual terms is often not the "first-best" method of achieving goals, however. For example, in the labor market, legal restrictions on rights to lay off persons increase the reluctance of firms to employ the particular persons protected by law. Enabling law would allow firms and labor groups to arrive at mutually agreeable conditions for layoffs while trading off these conditions against wage compensation.

An alternative to mandatory law that protects groups considered to be at an informational disadvantage is for government authorities to help the relatively uninformed to become informed, by either setting up special agencies or legislating within an enabling framework so that withholding certain kinds of information carries with it punitive damages.

If there is no conflict between designing law with the objective of achieving dynamic efficiency and achieving other noneconomic policy objectives at the lowest possible cost, then the case can be made for providing enabling law with a higher constitutional status than mandatory law. Such a constitutional rule would imply that an existing specific mandatory rule would be made invalid if legislators could agree on an enabling law that potentially conflicts with the existing mandatory rule.

A constitutional rule providing higher status for enabling than for mandatory law would be consistent with the principles of Hayek's (1979) constitutional proposals. The objective of those principles are to minimize both governments' coercion of individuals and the coercion of one individual by another. Mandatory law must imply coercion of at least one side to a contract in many cases, while enabling law definitionally implies that mutually agreed upon contracts can be sought. Thus, with enabling law government coercion would be restricted to enforcement of mutually agreed upon contracts.

4. Concluding Comments

It has been argued that a dynamically efficient system requires that law is enabling. In order to reduce transaction and information costs associated with contracting, law can specify a "standard form contract" for various contingencies, but the standard form can be changed by mutual agreement.

The most important aspect of enabling law is that it extends the principle of competition to contractual, institutional, and organizational arrangements in the economy. This competition is valuable because the knowledge required to design an efficient system does not rest with any one authority. This point gains additional weight in an economy in which efficient arrangements are likely to change over time. When law is enabling, competition among contractual arrangements would tend to favor those contracts that economize on agency costs, information costs, and transaction costs at a given level of output. In this sense, enabling law is dynamically efficient. It also economizes on enforcement costs in economies with scarce legal resources.

NOTES

I am grateful to Gunnar Eliasson for enabling comments and discussions.

1. Eliasson (1985, 1991) elaborates on the role of uncertainty and trial and error in an efficient system.

2. See Macey 1992.

3. Eisenberg 1989; McCheny 1989; Gordon 1989; Romano 1989.

4. The opposite point of view—that investors must be given substantial protection and preset rules because they lack information and experience—is often heard. This point of view is clearly static, and it ignores the fact that institutions develop and improve by learning.

REFERENCES

Day, R., G. Eliasson, and C. Wihlborg. 1993. *The Markets for Innovation, Ownership, and Control.* Stockholm and Amsterdam: IUI and North-Holland.

Dosi. G. 1988. "Institutions and Markets in a Dynamic World." *The Manchester School* 56, no. 2 (June): 119–46.

Eisenberg, M. A. 1989. "The Structure of Corporation Law." *Columbia Law Review* 89, no. 7 (Nov.): 1461–1525.

Eliasson, G. 1985. *The Firm and Financial Markets in the Swedish Micro- to Macro Model—Theory, Model, and Verification.* Stockholm: IUI.

———. 1990. "The Firm as a Competent Team." *Journal of Economic Behavior and Organization* 15 (June): 275–98.

———. 1991. "Modelling the Experimentally Organized Economy: Complex Dynamics in an Empirical Micro-Macro Model of Endogenous Economic Growth." *Journal of Economic Behavior and Organization* 16 (July): 153–82.

Eliasson, G., T. Rybczynski, and C. Wihlborg, eds. 1994. *The Necessary Institutional Framework to Transform Formerly Planned Economies.* Stockholm: IUI.

Gordon, J. N. 1989. "The Mandatory Structure of Corporate Law." *Columbia Law Review* 89, no. 7 (Nov.): 1549–98.

Hayek, F. A. 1979. *Law, Legislation, and Liberty.* Vol. B: *The Political Order of a Free People.* Chicago: University of Chicago Press.

Macey, J. 1992. *Corporate Law and Governance in Sweden: A Law and Economics Perspective.* Stockholm: SNS.

McChesney, F. S. 1989. "Economics, Law, and Science in the Corporate Field: A Critique of Eisenberg." *Columbia Law Review* 89, no. 7 (Nov.): 1530–48.

Posner, R. A. 1992. *Economic Analysis of Law.* Boston: Little, Brown and Scottsman.

Romano, R. 1989. "Answering the Wrong Question. The Tenuous Case for Mandatory Corporate Laws." *Columbia Law Review* 89, no. 7 (Nov.): 1599–1617.

PART 3

The Nature and Performance of the Firm

Bounded Rationality and Firm
Performance in the Experimental Economy
Richard H. Day

President Eliasson told us that the ambition of this conference is to clarify the microfoundations of economic growth. He asked me to talk about "the origin of firm performance: the bounded rationality hypothesis," but I have permitted myself a change in title because I want to consider not only the role of bounded rationality in firms but also the implications for understanding markets and the economic role of government.

The limitations of rationality have finally become a major topic of inquiry in economic research, but their implications for firms, markets, and government are not yet fully understood. In these remarks I want to suggest what some of these implications are. The most fundamental one is that decisions and actions within firms, households, and government agencies are essentially experimental in nature and so learning is constrained by a ubiquitous identification problem. Thus, Eliasson's phrase, "the experimentally organized economy," is an apt one.[1] The factual content of bounded rationality is hardly an issue. The issue for economists is therefore not a factual one but a methodological and theoretical one.

Our own bounded rationality as scholars leads us to look for ways of simplifying our intellectual tasks. One way to do so is to specialize; another is to assume away the complexities. The former is necessary; the latter facilitates rigorous theory; both are often misleading. Equilibrium theory, by simplifying the basic ingredients of economic decisions and exchange, makes it possible to unravel the classical conundrum of value and to explain how a decentralized system of producers and consumers who pursue their individual interests can in principle be coordinated by an appropriate price system in a manner that may have certain desirable properties. In recent years, these concepts have been used by a large number of economists as a behavioral theory by abstracting from the essentially algorithmic mechanism underlying real world institutions and by *assuming* that economies act as if they do, or actually do, satisfy equilibrium conditions at all times. In the meantime, many other economists—certainly including those in the Schumpeter Society—have continued thinking about how to model and theorize about economic behavior and exchange when they do not satisfy conditions for equilibrium. This essay summarizes my own interpretation of this algorithmic or behavioral point of view.

The next section considers the bounded rationality of people; the following one addresses the bounded rationality of firms. Then I consider the role of imagination, upon which both rationality and innovation are based. These reflections explain why individual and organizational decisions generally cannot satisfy equilibrium conditions, why markets are structured so as to make coordination possible anyway, and why the functioning of markets out of equilibrium is not in general stable. After considering the role of markets in these terms, we see why government must enter the picture and why it must play a fundamental role. The result of all this is the outlines of a general theory of the coevolution of market and state.[2] The concluding section suggests a special need for an appeal to economic history for the further development of this theory.

Boundedly Rational People

I find it useful to distinguish seven boundedly rational economizing modes: (1) explicit optimizing, (2) experimenting or trial and error searching, (3) obeying an authority (or following tradition), (4) imitating successful others, (5) acting on hunches, (6) thoughtlessly acting out of habit, and (7) acting on impulse, that is, unmotivated searching. Most of these have been recognized in the literature, and a considerable amount of experimental research has established their importance.[3] The central point is that all of them are problematic and experimental. In the case of explicit optimizing, the underlying system of understanding the "model" (or "problem") must in general be imperfect and proximate. Moreover, within the perceived problem framework the solution can in general only be approximated. Thus, an act based on explicit optimizing should be recognized as a trial, a particular way of conducting the search for efficacious behavior. It is for this reason that the other six modes provide potential alternatives for improving performance.

The existence of the alternative modes implies a higher-order selection criterion, which must determine which mode is used in any given situation. Learning—in effect—informs this selection, leading decision makers not only to modify their actions but to switch among the modes in response to experience and unfolding information. Scholars using adaptive processes, replicator dynamics, and experimental methods are finally beginning to explore the complexities of adapting behavior and evolving strategies in various types of games and economic settings.[4] It is clear from this research that (1) behavior rarely satisfies equilibrium conditions, (2) behavior does not always converge to conventional equilibria, and (3) effective or viable behavior generally leads to a mix of strategies that include unmotivated search (usually represented by intermittent random actions).

To put it even more succinctly, economic agents are in general out of economic equilibrium with respect to their external environment. Having said this, however, it is equally important to keep in mind the goal-directed nature of economizing behavior. People want to do well with respect to their needs and wants, and they try—using one of the several modes of economizing behavior—to do so. When things go badly, they may be motivated to modify their actions and possibly their mode of behavior.

Boundedly Rational Firms

What are the implications of costly, boundedly rational behavior on the nature of firms? First of all, it helps explain why firms exist. It is not only to reduce transaction costs or technical economies of scale that they exist. It is also due to the benefits of specialization. Specialization and cooperation in management should yield benefits just as they do in physical production. This is the ultimate reason for the existence of a managerial function and for the existence of firms. While some individuals in an enterprise focus on the development and application of requisite physical skills, others focus on decision making, communicating, monitoring, and coordinating. This specialization rests on cooperation. Cooperation is costly and can only be achieved through the expenditure of effort and resources.

As an enterprise grows, the managerial effort also becomes specialized and grows in complexity. The costs of learning, deciding, communicating, and coordinating grow, and all the other costs of collective action increase. According to the data assembled in Eliasson (1990) for contemporary large-scale businesses, such indirect costs exceed those of direct labor and materials. Thus, the economic allocation of resources to managerial activity emerges as a major problem for the firm. As the size of management grows, the organization and management of management becomes as challenging as managing production itself. Undertaken as it is by boundedly rational people, management must appeal to operational mechanisms that work in practice. These mechanisms, if they are to work, must allow for the frailties of human decision making, in particular, their bounded rationality.

As firms grow in complexity, it is inevitable that increasing appeal must be made to rules and standard operating procedures. These rules mediate the role of authority and provide a basis for habit, thereby economizing intelligent discretion. They liberate cognition from trivial tasks and make it available for important problem solving and creative innovation. They also reduce transaction costs by eliminating the need for bargaining, negotiating, and coordinating the various individuals in the enterprise. They form a part of the "algorithm" the firm follows in implementing its complex transactions and interactions.

Collaterally, rules and standard operating procedures introduce inertia and inflexibility, which can have a beneficial stabilizing effect by moderating the pursuit of apparently favorable opportunities that may turn out to be misguided. But, by the same token, they may prevent an efficacious response to changes that might stimulate innovation and improve efficiency. The performance of any enterprise is the result of these two polar effects. Indeed, it has been observed that the large-scale economic organizations that have emerged from the successful development of capitalism sometimes surpass the scope within which entrepreneurial management can effectively cope. Bureaucratic management, with its standard operating procedures, whose initial justification is to economize scarce creative ability and scarce decision making talent, can stifle the entrepreneurial spirit and individual initiative.

The implication, then, of bounded rationality in this context is that firms will rarely, if ever, satisfy the conditions of optimality with respect to their environments, and their human constituents will virtually never operate at a Pareto or even a Nash equilibrium. Every managerial procedure and organizational structure is a strategy on trial, and the firm as a whole adapts to its fortunes and misfortunes just as do the people who make up the firm.

Rationality, Entrepreneurship, and Imagination

Certainly, managerial systems and the administrative technologies on which they are based originated and evolved in the same way as did production technologies, through a process of invention, innovation, and diffusion. The role of these activities, which played such a key role in Schumpeter's thought, is well understood. These activities begin with the imagination: the capacity to form images of what might be and to generate actions that will lead to the embodiment of those internal images in the phenomenal external world. This ability to form and communicate images is at the foundation of human thought and language. Its creative character is a primitive quality of everyday speech.[5] Rational thought in general and economic rationality in particular rests on that same creative capacity, for most of the choice problems that occur involve a selection among imagined futures. As I put it before (paraphrasing William James), we imagine "possible scenarios of what might happen, sequences of imagined act and consequence that form conscious stories of what might be. To choose rationally is to compare imagined stories, to select one and then to design a sequence of actions that will make those stories come true."[6]

The other economizing modes also involve imagination. For example, imitation and obedience to authority require the exercise of imagination, for they require one to imagine doing oneself what another may have done or is doing or what one has been told to do.

The crucial aspect of imagination is that it involves the generation of ideas and concepts that did not exist before (at least in one's self) and contemplates the existence of things not yet present in the phenomenal world. Like all other human faculties, this creative intelligence is scattered asymmetrically throughout any population. Some are more richly endowed (and in different ways) than others. That some individuals should invent, others innovate, and still others imitate is a simple application of the economizing principle.

Inventors and entrepreneurs imagine things that do not exist and foresee practical steps that can make them happen, just as each of us does whenever we form a plan for the future and carry it out. They make possible the subsequent adoption of new techniques of production or management by "ordinary" decision makers who imitate the successful innovations by others. Instead of instantaneously jumping to a new competitive equilibrium, their adjustments follow with a lag and are distributed over time. The process then exhibits waves of adaptation and abandonment that transform societies. Bounded rationality thus explains the existence of specialized roles for work, management, invention, entrepreneurship, and imitation in *seeking* an economical allocation of resources.

The Nature of Markets

Given the bounded rationality of individuals and the imperfect coordination of participants in enterprise, given the perturbations in existing knowledge through the exercise of creative intelligence, and given the lags in adjustment that occur when knowledge depends on experience, how are we to understand the functioning of a market economy? One answer, articulated in Friedman's famous essay (1953) is that people behave *as if* they were unboundedly rational and perfectly coordinated. A second answer is Knight's extreme interpretation of Adam Smith's "invisible hand," made after Knight explicitly recognized bounded rationality. He argued that "the market" causes individual behavior to be individually rational and collectively coordinated.

Still a third answer is given in the Cassel-Muth-Lucas concept of "rational expectations," which asserts that rational agents will expect equilibrium prices (more generally, all stochastic and environmental feedback mechanisms) and will therefore carry out equilibrium actions, an argument equivalent to the assertion that people know perfectly the solution to the dual valuation problem inherent in general equilibrium and can as individuals then perfectly sole the primal resource allocation problem in a manner that is consistent among themselves and with their own expectations. More generally, the rational expectations hypothesis asserts that agents will anticipate correctly the entire working of the economy and behave optimally in a manner that accords with a Nash equilibrium throughout the entire system.[7] In that approach, markets have no real function at all. Cournot, Marshall,

Walras, Schumpeter, Keynes, Kaldor, and all the mathematical general equilibrium theorists who studied the stability of exchange economies, including Arrow, Hahn, Hurwicz, Nikaido, Uzawa, and Saari, and, indeed, any neoclassical economist worth his or her salt knows better. All of them recognized and emphasized that markets don't work in equilibrium, which is best thought of as a state that may exist in principle and has certain properties that *may* be brought about—if at all—with the passage of time. We Schumpeterians are willing to stake our careers on thinking about the contrasting adaptive, evolutionary view of markets. The fundamental theoretical question to be answered from our point of view is: "How can an economy work (or exist) when its agents are boundedly rational, when their exchanges within and among organizations are imperfectly coordinated, when their expectations are based on imperfect information, and when they are armed only with past experience, their limited understanding of it, their fallible imaginations, and hunches to aid them in anticipating the consequence of their actions?"

It makes sense to begin an inquiry into this question by observing markets in the real world. There we find that "markets" are collections of *marketing agents* such as merchants, brokers, specialists, buyers, and various managers within stores and the sales departments of individual manufacturing firms. They operate inventory, order-backlog and price-adjustment processes that buffer uncoordinated and usually inconsistent plans among consumers and producers and between buyers and sellers.[8] The inventories and order backlogs that are central to these mechanisms are in continual flux as individuals within households and firms throughout the economy adapt their behavior to unfolding events. Their adaptation includes delaying action (or queuing), planning revision, and exercising contingent tactics. These changes enable people to continue functioning when their expectations are not fulfilled and their plans are not realized.

Moreover, marketing agents set prices, "marking up" costs of production or commodity purchases so as to earn an income from their services but adjusting them when inventories or order backlogs change from their current estimated appropriate levels. Even in the absence of innovation, the system of producers, consumers, and mediators may be unstable in principle, just as they are often unstable in fact; their prices, profits, inventories, and order backlogs fluctuate persistently. The idea that markets bring about equilibria is simply wrong. They may do so, but they usually do not. Instead, they constitute more or less permanent mechanisms for mediating exchange, thereby facilating specialization and coordination out of equilibrium.

Marketing agents can be represented in a stylized fashion and studied in a formal, theoretical setting. Indeed, a start in this direction was made by Clower and Friedman (1986) and by myself (1994). The latter reference derives conditions for viable markets when they work out of equilibrium in terms of parameters of demand and supply, including the extent of the market, speeds of adjustment, initial capitalization, and initial inventory.

When innovation is present, the destabilizing forces are even more prominent. The creation of credit instruments that empower specialized enterprises to create purchasing power and allocate it to investment projects is the cornerstone of Schumpeter's theory of economic development. Financial institutions (markets) generally provide the mediating mechanisms for facilitating entrepreneurship on a wide scale. In this way, they have been essential instruments in the transformation of economy. By allocating purchasing power, they ration the application of imagination and initiative, simultaneously enabling yet regulating change. In this way, the monetary system has powerful real effects. It is far from neutral, in contrast to what is typically assumed by many macroeconomists.

Because of the imperfect coordination that is endemic both within and among economic organizations, individual and social costs are involved. Because labor is infinitely perishable, unused labor cannot be accumulated for use later: an available but unexploited hour of work is lost forever. The inventory method for buffering disequilibria on goods markets cannot be exploited on labor markets. Not only the worker must fear of his existence. The owner of property and the manager of enterprise are also exposed to market forces. In the movements of production, employment, investment, profit, and loss, no one's livelihood is guaranteed. Almost always some workers, managers, and entrepreneurs are gaining—often at the direct expense of others who are losing—as flourishing occupations take over resources from stagnant ones. Such asymmetric rewards and punishments stimulate adjustments through the reallocation of resources within the market system. These adjustments take time, however. They need not converge in theory and do not converge in fact. The new flourishing activities are accompanied by high wages and profits; the old decaying activities are accompanied by diminished relative wages and losses. It is routine in capitalist countries for entire industries to be abandoned as new ones take their place. The corollary in human terms is rapidly changing opportunities, positive or negative, and complete transformation in a way of life within a generation or even a decade.

We should not think of these costs as signs of market failure. Rather, we should think of these costs as the necessary price for coordinating a system of decentralized enterprises in workable, reasonably efficient, but imperfect fashion when all decisions and all organizations are experimental in nature. To put it succinctly, producers and consumers who act out of equilibrium can do so because market mechanisms enable them to in spite of the imbalances in their supplies and demands. Without these mechanisms, the system as a whole will not function effectively and will eventually grind down or collapse altogether. Even with them, however, and even if most individuals and firms remain viable most of the time, the continuing adaptation to experience induces unexpected changes that modify the requirements of labor and the demand for goods. When these mechanisms operate ineffectively, they cost society dearly in wasted resources.

When the discrepancies between plans and actions, between expectations and actual events caused by imbalances in demand and supply, are great enough, the compensating adjustments within the existing institutional structure for mediating exchange can take longer than is willingly endured. Moreover, the limited monopoly of economic opportunity that private property bestows upon individuals sometimes grows into highly concentrated managerial control, separated even from owners, which can involve undue coercion of those who specialize in "work" or "labor" or can lead to the plundering of the rewards of innovation and thrift by those who control, as would seem to be the case with extreme executive compensation.

Still further, as innovation occurs, new targets for imitation and new avenues for the average individual to change are generated. The long-run viability of some may be destroyed. Advantage is shifted from one pursuit to another. The fortunes of some may be expanding, while the fortunes of others are declining. These non-Pareto adjustments imply conflicts, ones that are produced by markets, not solved by them. Conflict can reach intolerable levels when the gap between those who flourish and those who stagnate widens enough.

The Role of Government

Government provides mechanisms intended to regulate imperfectly functioning institutions in the market economy by means of incentives and constraints, for redirecting the allocation of resources through taxes and subsidies, and for authorizing new insitutions of market and state to enhance economic coordination and stabilize performance. When well conceived, these mechanisms can ameliorate the individual and social costs of change by continually generating opportunity. If one set of institutions fails in this regard, another set can be invented and tried. The ultimate role of government for the market economy is to create public and/or private institutions that will eventually restore opportunity to those driven out of the market system by the market itself and to engage the voluntary participation of those unavoidably made worse off through their exposure to market forces.

Obviously, the agencies of government, like that of the market, are composed of organizations constituted with boundedly rational agents whose powers of rational thinking and amicable cooperation are severely limited. They are governed by the same modes of decision making, the same necessity for economizing on scarce cognitive and coordinating power, as are firms. They, too, *must* use rules and standard operating procedures. Government actions and organizations are, therefore, just as experimental in nature as are those of the market. In investigating and carrying out its policy experiments in response to market outcomes, the economic environment of households and firms is changed. They cannot jump immediately to a new equilibrium, however, for the same reason that they cannot do so in response to private innovations in technology and management.

"Democratic capitalism" is not a completely adequate phrase for capturing the coevolution of market and state implied by this analysis. A capitalistic enterprise need not be, and seldom is, democratic in the political sense. Indeed, excessive policization of the entrepreneurial and managerial aspects of business can impair the incentives and controls necessary for effective resource allocations. On the other hand, democracies need not—cannot and will not—rely solely on capitalistic forms of enterprise. The latter, working in disequilibrium, create too much instability, and the social cost of change is sometimes too high. For this reason, various agencies created by government inevitably emerge to augment the functioning of industry and commerce. Their fundamental functions are dual: *both to facilitate and to bound and buffer change.*

Achieving the correct blend of private and public mechanisms is a problem. It is not designed by a single act of rational thought; it cannot be brought about by either a convergent *tâtonnement* or a political revolution. It can only evolve through an experimental political-economic system that allows for the widespread application of individual discretion within various frameworks for voluntary collective action.

It is this potential for expanding the scope for individual discretion while stabilizing the inherent conflicts and social costs of rapid change that characterizes the coevolution of democratic polity and capitalistic economy. But, further, as the state offers an avenue for resource reallocation alternative to the market, it provides an additional means for the pursuit of private interest through the formation of interest groups and political coalitions. In this way, the political process itself can bring about non-Pareto adjustments in the system as a whole that reflect contending underlying values and interagent comparisons.

On Method

I believe that rigorous methods, including mathematical and econometric modeling, can be (and are being) exploited to understand this grand process. General intertemporal equilibrium theory has its place in defining the terms and conditions of optimal, perfectly coordinated behavior of agents in a decentralized system of exchange. But it should be clear that bounded rationality and imperfect coordination vitiate the use of equilibrium theory for understanding how people actually behave and how the economy works as a whole. In particular, it says nothing about how an experimental economy can find an equilibrium if one or more exist. What must be developed is an adaptive, evolutionary theory of the *dual disequilibrium dynamics of economy and state.*

But theory is not enough. The experiments produced within the private and government sectors are not controlled in the sense of laboratory experiments. So many variables interact that rigorous tools of mathematical economics and econometrics need to be augmented by broader methods of inference. It is the function of the economic historian to record and describe the trials and errors that public and private agents generate and to identify, explain, and evaluate their effects using comparative historical and comparative case study methods.[9] Economists in general and theorists in particular need to draw on this great body of work much more than we do. By carefully grounding theoretical abstractions on salient real world characteristics, our chances for understanding how economies work and for anticipating the consequences of alternative institutional innovations might be improved.

If history's lessons are as important as they are numerous, the stakes would seem to be high. The record shows that no great state or civilization has ever lasted without intervening crises and breakdowns. Those that emerge have always done so with modified structures, and those that have lasted for a significant duration have done so by means of adaptation to experience and by evolving new rules and institutions. It is not unrealistic, therefore, to hope that advances in our science might enhance the development of our own civilization and improve its chance for survival.

NOTES

1. See Eliasson (1993).

2. For an earlier version of the story, see Day (1984).

3. See Pingle and Day (1996) for recent experiments and Conlisk (1996) for a brilliant survey of findings and related issues.

4. For samples of varied approaches, see the *Journal of Economic Behavior and Organization* 22.1 (Sept. 1993); 29.1 (Jan. 1996).

5. Distinguishing the a priori capacities for and primitive characteristics of language as distinct from its creative character is a central message in the work of Noam Chomsky and his followers. See Chomsky (1966).

6. See Day (1984).

7. This is Lucas's *Models of Business Cycles* (1987).

8. I developed this view of markets in Day (1984).

9. Commons's little read piece contains the germ of this coevolutionary theory. His *Collective Action* (1950), edited by Kenneth Parsons, was an attempt to make the theory unintelligible. For an engaging survey, see Kaufman (forthcoming, 1998).

REFERENCES

Chomsky, Noam. 1966. *Cartesian Linguistics.* New York: Harper and Row.

Clower, Robert, and Dan Friedman. 1986. "Trade Specialists and Money in an Ongoing Exchange Economy." In *The Dynamics of Market Economies,* edited by R. Day and G. Eliasson. New York: Elsevier Science Publishers.

Commons, John R. 1950. *The Economics of Collective Action.* New York: Macmillan.

Conlisk, John. 1980. "Costly Optimizers versus Cheap Imitators." *Journal of Economic Behavior and Organization* 1:275–93.

———. 1988. "Optimization Costs." *Journal of Economic Behavior and Organization* 9:213–28.

———. 1996. "Why Bounded Rationality?" *Journal of Economic Literature* 34:669–700.

Cyert, Richard M., and James G. March. 1963. *A Behavioral Theory of the Firm.* Englewood Cliffs, NJ: Prentice-Hall.

Day, Richard H. 1984. "Disequilibrium Economic Dynamics: A Post Schumpeter Contribution." *Journal of Economic Behavior and Organization* 5:57–76.

———. 1994. *Complex Economic Dynamics.* Chap. 11: "Market Mediation." Cambridge: MIT Press.

Day, Richard H., and E. Herbert Tinney. 1968. "How to Cooperate in Business without Really Trying: A Learning Model of Decentralized Decision-Making." *Journal of Political Economy* 76, no. 4 (July/Aug.): 583–600.

Eliasson, Gunnar. 1990. "The Firm as a Competent Team." *Journal of Economic Behavior and Organization* 13:275–98.

———. 1993. "The Firm as a Competent Team." Chapter 8 of *The Markets for Innovation, Ownership, and Control,* edited by R. H. Day, G. Eliasson, and C. Wihlborg. Amsterdam: North-Holland.

Friedman, Milton. 1953. *Essays in Positive Economics.* Chicago: University of Chicago Press.

Kaufman, Bruce E. 1998. "Regulation of the Employment Relationship: The 'Old' Institutional Perspective." *Journal of Economic Behavior and Organization,* forthcoming.

Lucas, R. E., Jr. 1987. *Models of Business Cycles.* Oxford: Basil Blackwell.

March, James G., and Herbert Simon. 1968. *Organizations.* New York: Wiley.

Nelson, Richard, and Sidney Winter. 1982. *An Evolutionary Theory of Economic Change.* Cambridge: Harvard University Press.

Pelikan, Pavel. 1989. "Evolution, Economic Competence, and the Market for Corporate Control." *Journal of Economic Behavior and Organization* 12:279–304.

Pingle, Mark. 1995. "Submitting to Authority: An Experimental Examination of Its Effect on Decision-Making." Manuscript.

Pingle, Mark, and Richard H. Day. 1996. "Modes of Economizing Behavior: Experimental Evidence." *Journal of Economic Behavior and Organization* 29, no. 2 (Mar.): 191–209.

Schumpeter, Joseph. 1934. *The Theory of Economic Development.* Cambridge: Harvard University Press.

Simon, Herbert. 1983. *Reason in Human Affairs.* Palo Alto: Stanford University Press.

Winston, Gordon. 1989. "Imperfectly Rational Choice: Rationality as the Result of a Costly Activity." *Journal of Economic Behavior and Organization* 12:67–88.

Winter, Sydney. 1964. "Economic 'National Selection' and the Theory of the Firm." *Yale Economic Essays* 4:225–72.

———. 1975. "Optimization and Evolution in the Theory of the Firm." In *Adaptive Economic Models,* edited by R. Day and T. Groves. New York: Academic.

Routinized Innovations: Dynamic Capabilities in a Simulation Study

Uwe Cantner, Horst Hanusch, and Andreas Pyka

1. Introduction

Joseph Alois Schumpeter (1942) has been among others prominent for emphasizing that innovative activities of firms are to be considered as active and intended search processes for new technological possibilities and opportunities rather than solely accidental events. Although this statement has been a first attack on neoclassical general equilibrium theory, it is the neoclassical camp itself that has presented an approach to formalize these ideas; the *new industrial economics* (Arrow 1962, Dasgupta and Stiglitz 1980, Reinganum 1985) was born. Within a traditional cost-benefit framework, the conditions for an optimal allocation of R&D resources are derived. To do so, however, this approach has to rely on several strong assumptions, of which known technological opportunities, perfect capabilities, perfect foresight, and full information combined with weak uncertainty are the most crucial ones. Only on this basis can optimal solutions be obtained and respective firm strategies derived.

This neoclassical approach, however, has been criticized by modern innovation theory, which claims that the neoclassical assumptions about opportunities, information, and uncertainty do neglect the very nature of the innovative process: opportunities are not known ex ante, information is far from complete, uncertainty is strong, and capabilities are heterogeneous and far from perfect. On this basis, the strategic behavior of firms is not only to be seen as a response to other firms' actions — a play against competitors as in traditional industrial economics — but also as a device to play a *game against nature.*

Within this context, where strategies are not readily computable, one has to ask according to what rules do firms behave and how do they shape their strategies. The concept of *procedural rationality* (Simon 1976, Dosi and Egidi 1991) explains the behavior of actors in only very weak computable environments with a high degree of uncertainty. Accordingly, actors do not globally optimize their decisions but follow certain *routines* that provide for satisficing outcomes. In order to cope with this kind of behavior, the decision-theoretic approach of neoclassical innovation theory has to be replaced with an alternative theory, the *behavioral approach.*

On this basis, our essay investigates how different routines of innovative behavior perform. The design of those routines is derived from the techno-logical environment a firm faces—that is, opportunities, uncertainty, and appropriability conditions—from economic factors such as profits and sales, and from the individual capability and willingness to cope with (tech-nological) uncertainty. Principally, the "constructed" routines contain *fixed* and *flexible* components, the former labeled *strategies* and the latter *learn-ing rules*. Three different strategies are investigated: the *absorptive strat-egy*, in which the ability to use technological spillovers plays the central role; the *conservative strategy*, which acts rather in isolation and relies only on own research efforts; and the *imitative strategy*, which, on the contrary, relies not on own research efforts but tries to catch up by imitating best-practice technologies.

With this routine-based modeling of innovative activities, our analysis cannot look for equilibrium outcomes (with optimal R&D resource alloca-tion) but relies on simulation experiments in the tradition of Nelson and Winter (1982). Under different conditions and different flexible routines, we show that the absorptive strategy is very likely to dominate other strate-gies in the long run. Moreover, we find that learning rules focusing on technological rather than economic performance accelerate the speed of technological progress considerably.

Our analysis proceeds as follows. In section 2, we discuss the theoreti-cal foundations and explicitly introduce and explain the different strategies and the motives behind them. Section 3 describes the simulation model. Section 4 shows the most important results of different simulation runs. We close our discussion with some concluding remarks in section 5.

2.   The Design of R&D Strategies

One of the major attempts of modern innovation theory is to provide new insights into the process of technological change by dismissing the often unrealistic assumptions of traditional economic theory. There, the assump-tion of abundant technological opportunities, appropriability conditions, perfect capabilities, information, and foresight combined with an only weak uncertainty means that innovative activities are boiled down to an *optimal* R&D allocation game against competitors. Here, technological progress—banned into a "black box"—is designed so as to allow for opti-mal cost-benefit calculations. Dismissing these assumptions and taking into account that technological progress is also a *game against nature*, it is not at all clear how and along which lines firms design their R&D.

In the following, we investigate how different innovation strategies found in the literature perform in a comparative analysis. For this purpose, we first briefly discuss the technological environment that firms are facing.

Based on this, the second step provides a characterization of different R&D strategies.

Supply-Side Factors Influencing Innovation

The saying that innovative activities are (also) a *game against nature,* and thus against the unforseeable, suggests that firms invest resources mainly in order to acquire more information, which allows for better decisions and improved performance. This is done in a technological environment that is not a "black-box" but which rather has its own structural and dynamic features. Since the 1980s, innovation theory has been mainly engaged in investigating those environments that show the following main features.

Technological uncertainty.   The search for new technologies and even the improvement of existing technologies are risky and uncertain endeavors. With this uncertainty — intrinsic to the innovation process — it is impossible to predict innovative results: on the one hand, firms try to find new technological solutions for their production processes with ex ante, not anticipated, consequences; on the other hand, new unforeseen discoveries external to a firm open up totally new combinations of different and seemingly unrelated technologies.

Technological opportunities.   The developmental potential of a single technology is increasingly exhausted with progress along the respective technological trajectory. So-called intensive technological opportunities (Coombs 1988) are depleted step by step. Therefore, technological as well as scientific boundaries come into play more and more and make further improvements increasingly difficult and sometimes even impossible to achieve.

Besides intensive opportunities characterizing a specific technology, there are also "extensive technological opportunities" that arise out of *cross-fertilization* of different technologies (Mokyr 1990). New technical solutions are often created by new combinations of existing technologies. Sometimes the amalgamation of ex-ante, unrelated technologies leads to totally new technological fields — mechatronic or bionic are points in case. Therefore, "structural tensions" (Dahmén 1989) between complementary technologies may be solved in the course of time, providing for new technological opportunities.

Those mutual interdependencies have quite a number of different sources: besides new ideas and findings in academia, the manifold effects between up- and downstream productions between firms within branches, as well as between different industries, are potential sources of such *cross-fertilization.* These mutual influences come into being mainly through technological spillovers. These spillovers are possible whenever new technological know-how is not a purely private good and thus not entirely appropriable by the innovating firm.

Appropriability conditions.   Inventors should realistically anticipate receiving something less than the maximum benefits arising out of an innovation (see, e.g., Winter 1989). Imperfect appropriability conditions are responsible for this. In mainstream economics, this is a reason for a suboptimal level of innovative activity.[1] New innovation theory does not deny this but emphasizes the *idea-creating* features of knowledge spillovers.

The main argument for imperfect appropriability conditions are the "latent public good" features of newly generated technological know-how. To a large extent, this knowledge is only partly excludable and nonrival, making R&D laboratories of firms the potential source of mighty spillovers. Accordingly, this has different impacts on the incentives for R&D. On the one hand, other firms eventually can use the new knowledge, and this, of course, will reduce the respective incentives to undertake costly innovative endeavors. On the other hand, this leakage of own know-how is compensated for by the opportunity to use the know-how of other firms. The latter argument underlines the complementary character of R&D and is also based on the assumption of bounded rational behavior of agents, which leads to the perception that innovative activities do not follow a common optimizing concept but are to be taken as local search processes for which specific cumulative experiences, knowledge, and competences, as well as lock-in effects, play an important and determining role. Even within a branch, this necessarily leads to a significant heterogeneity of firms applying fuzzy sets of technologies. Because of "technological pluralism" specific R&D projects are not only substitutes but often provide for synergies and complementaries. Here, however, technological constraints, heterogeneity, and uncertainty do not allow for global optimization. Instead, in competitive environments characterized by a continuously changing technological framework firms try to struggle in other ways. By this, firms design certain strategies, which will be discusses in the following section.

Firm Strategies to Cope with Innovation

The rate of technological progress is not God-given but is determined by the uncoordinated behavior of firms that try to improve or introduce new technologies. The restrictions arising out of technological heterogeneity, uncertainty, and rationality constraints are — as just mentioned — indeed responsible for an abandonment of the global optimization principle. This, however, does not imply that there are no longer regularities in firm behavior. In their decisions, firms do not randomly allocate R&D budgets and select by chance certain research directions. Instead, they are guided in a cumulative manner by their past experiences and their built-up capabilities. Consequently, the resulting behavior is neither unique nor optimal and can be described by the concept of routines.

Routines.   Strong regular patterns in the innovative activities of firms suggest that innovative behavior is "routinized" (Nelson and Winter 1982). Firms are operating in environments characterized by a spectrum of market and technological possibilities that make it possible to overcome current constraints. Although there exists technological uncertainty with respect to the results of their actions, firms have economic expectations. Hence, within the restrictions and constraints just mentioned, firms are able to design different innovation strategies (Freeman 1982) in which they decide how to use their technical skills and resources.

These strategic decisions are guided by a "procedural rationality" (Simon 1976). Abstract questions of how to measure the marginal productivity of R&D expenditures are not on the agenda of firms, rather, questions about reasonable procedures for fixing these quantities are to be answered. Therefore, we simply regard R&D decision rules as behavioral patterns that cannot be explained by optimization, but by reference to historical circumstances, experience, and evolutionary development. Firms design and adjust their routines by the means of learning and adapting to changing environments. In this perspective, firms are learning organizations, constrained by their cognitive capabilities (Heiner 1988). They do not completely know the set of actual and future opportunities open to them and therefore cannot choose the globally best alternative; they are constrained to local opportunities.

Exploitation versus exploration. The introduction of new technologies, the improvement of existing ones, learning how to adjust behavior, and imitation of other successful actors are the most important components of improving firms' performance and strengthening their competitive advantage. Within this context, modern organizational theory points to a trade-off problem between the exploitation of existing and the exploration of new opportunities (Winter 1971, March 1991). Typically included in exploration are behaviors like search, variation, risk taking, and experimentation, whereas exploitation means refinement, production, efficiency, and execution. This is also reflected in the comparison of the returns from exploration, which are less certain and more remote in time with respect to the returns from exploitation. In the following, we introduce three general behavioral patterns and show how exploration and exploitation find a variety of expressions in different routines.

The conservative strategy. The first strategy considered is the so-called conservative strategy[2] in which all innovative efforts are concentrated exclusively on own research. This strategy neglects external technological developments insofar as it only invests in the refinement of its own specific opportunities. Thus, the technology and know-how it requires for growth and competitiveness are generated in isolation. Innovative efforts are directed into exploitation of the existing technology, that is, process improvements, and into exploration of new technologies, that is, product innovation.

The imitative strategy.   Firms applying the imitative strategy[3] do not devote resources to explorative search. Their main goal with respect to introducing new technologies is the attempt to imitate the most successful methods generated elsewhere instead of trying to innovate by themselves (Winter 1986). Thus, this strategy attempts to exploit external knowledge and opportunities. However, this does not imply that there are no R&D expenditures. Rather, imitative firms can be as research intensive as other firms are. But they are not willing to explore risky new opportunities. They want to avoid failure, and even more they want to learn from failures of competitors. Therefore, they are satisfied with not being technological leaders. According to Freeman (1982), the imitative strategy is a kind of insurance. It enables firms to react and adapt to technical change introduced by competitors.

Imitation becomes possible whenever new technological know-how is not completely appropriable by the innovating firm. In a regime of total nonappropriability of the know-how, imitative firms have the advantage of knowing and learning ex ante that the aim of their imitative efforts is a workable solution. However, technological knowledge is typically characterized by specificity, by tacitness as well as cumulativeness. "In such cases 'technology transfer' may be as expensive and time consuming as independent R&D" (Nelson 1990, 197). Therefore, it is the very nature of technological knowledge that also makes imitation a costly endeavor. Moreover, in cases of limited access to the technology to be imitated, it is very unlikely that imitation yields the same technological results as the original innovative technology (Winter 1986).

The absorptive strategy.   Firms applying the so-called absorptive strategy decide to run a mixture of explorative and exploitative search. On the one hand, they undertake research endeavors aiming at two goals that are also targeted by conservative firms: they exploitatively improve their production processes and exploratively introduce product innovations. On the other hand, they additionaly exploit external knowledge sources, not in order to imitate but to achieve cross-fertilization effects that allow them to extend the opportunity space.

It is far-fetched, however, to believe that these spillovers can be integrated into the knowledge stock of a receiving firm without costs. On the contrary, firms with an absorptive strategy have to invest a significant share of their R&D budget in scanning general (external) technological development.[4] Doing this, they expect synergistic benefits that will help them to overcome depleted technological opportunities.

In contrast to imitative firms, absorptive firms do not simply copy a successful technology but try to integrate external knowledge in order to *create* additional technological opportunities. And, contrary to conservative firms, they do not spend their total R&D budget on improving their in-house technology. Absorptive firms, rather, have to trade off short-term benefits of exploiting own specific opportunities with a mixture of long-range exploring and exploiting of external technological possibilities. In this respect, they try to avoid—at least in a dynamic perspective—situations in which the "exploitation of existing knowledge reduces the capabilities and the speed with which new alternatives can be explored" (Levinthal and March 1981).

Following this characterization of the innovative process, investing in absorptive capacity in technological, heterogeneous environments is done in order to exploit extensive technological opportunities by understanding the content of knowledge spillovers. Therefore, investing in absorptive capacity is not immediately targeted toward a specific, well-described, research purpose. In a way, it is done for precautionary reasons, allowing the firm to be prepared for unforeseen technological developments. In this context, Cohen and Levinthal (1994) refer to the words of Louis Pasteur: "Fortune favors the prepared mind."

In reality, a clear distinction between these stylized strategies is not possible. This is for several reasons: building up absorptive capabilities is often taken as a kind of by-product of "normal" R&D activities, especially with respect to technologies that are characterized by small technological distances. In these cases, conservative as well as imitative firms acquire the capability to understand and use know-how related to close neighbor technologies. But, with increasing technological distances, God-given absorptive capabilities decrease and direct efforts to acquire complementary knowledge become necessary. Unexpected, and therefore not yet realized, synergistic benefits from the combination of quite close technologies are less probable than those arising out of the combination of ex-ante different technologies. Of course, in reality firms will apply an opportunistic mixture of these strategies, some with more emphasis on conservative attitudes and others emphasizing more absorptive or imitative attitudes. For analytical purposes, we will, however, distinguish those strategies as clear-cut.

3. The Simulation Model

In this section, we present a model of a dynamic oligopoly in which firms not only compete in the market but also influence each other through their innovative activities. The firms under consideration belong to three "camps," each characterized by a fixed strategy. One group is applying the *conservative* strategy, neglecting technical development created outside its own firm boundaries. The next group behaves according to the *imitative* strategy, does not innovate itself, and instead tries to imitate the most successful technologies of its competitors. The third group contains *absorptive* firms, which attempt to integrate research results created by others to support their own R&D endeavors.

In order to represent market relationships, we choose a model of heterogeneous oligopoly as discussed in Kuenne (1992).[5] Here n firms (indexed with i, $i = \{1, \ldots, n\}$) differ in their production processes and product qualities. Firms are continuously confronted with uncertainty and try myopically to improve their technologies; they are assumed to be able to optimize their purely economic decisions statically. In this respect, knowing their demand function, they compute reaction functions, taking into account the economic decisions of their competitors. This modeling strategy allows us to focus on the technology side of behavior, whereas economic decisions are represented by a well-understood oligopolistic setting.[6] The model of heterogeneous oligopoly is standard and is described in more detail in Cantner and Pyka (1995). Regarding production techniques, we assume constant returns to scale, so consequently unit costs $c_i(t)$ are independent of output. Concerning the technology side of the model the following building blocks are relevant.

R&D investment decisions and learning rules.   Besides mere production, firm i periodically devotes investment $r_i(t)$ to research, development, and imitation. Since the development of a new technology and even the improvement of an existing one are risky and uncertain endeavors, R&D decisions are guided by "procedural rationality," allowing firms to learn and adapt their routines to changed environments. The respective routines determine a share of turnover $\gamma_i(t)$, which firms invest in R&D.

In our model, we distinguish two different methods of adjusting those routines. A first learning rule uses as a reference criterion an economic indicator, the return on turnover $\beta_i(t)$:

$$\gamma_i(t) = \gamma_0 + \omega \left(\frac{\bar{\beta}_t - \beta_i(t)}{\bar{\beta}_t} \right), \tag{1a}$$

where

γ_0 = initial value

ω = exogeneous rate of adjustment

$\beta_i(t)$ = rate of turnover

$\bar{\beta}_t$ = average rate of turnover.

Whenever firm i's own return on turnover is lower (higher) than the market average rate, the firm does rise (reduce) its share $\gamma_i(t)$. A second learning rule does not look at an economic indicator but rather uses the average relative technological positions with respect to process technology $RP_i^{PC}(t)$ and product technology $RP_i^{PD}(t)$. Both indicators are restricted to [0,1], with a value of 1 indicating the leading position:

$$\gamma_i(t) = \gamma_0 + \omega \left[1 - \frac{RP_i^{PC}(t) + RP_i^{PD}(t)}{2} \right]. \tag{1b}$$

The share $\gamma_i(t)$ determining R&D efforts is increased or decreased according to the respective technological position. In a sense, both learning rules represent a kind of satisficing behavior. If the own position — whether economical or technological — is unsatisfactory, an adjustment mechanism with respect to periodical R&D investments should ensure catching up. We compare the effects of these different learning rules in the following simulations.

Firms deciding to implement the *absorptive strategy* have additionally to decide on the respective share $\sigma_i(t)$ of the R&D budget, and invest in building up absorptive capacity $ac_i(t)$. It is plausible to assume that firms on the technological frontier cannot learn much from their competitors. Accordingly, they adjust their investment in absorptive capacity due to their relative technological position. Equation 2 formally describes this decision rule:

$$\sigma_i(t) = 1 - [RP_i^{PD}(t) \cdot RP_i^{PC}(t)]; \quad \sigma^{min} \le \sigma_i(t) \le \sigma^{max}. \tag{2}$$

There are upper and lower bounds for variable $\sigma_i(t)$: a minimum level, at which firms always invest in absorptive capacity due to exogenous spillovers from sciences and interindustrial spillovers; and a maximum level because firms do not reduce their own R&D below a certain level. Figure 1 shows this decision rule in a simplified way ($RP_i^{PC} = RP_i^{PD}$).

Process innovation.   R&D and the imitative endeavors of firms are partly directed to process innovation in order to make production techniques more efficient. The efficiency level is dependent on the know-how, and efficiency gains are represented by unit cost reductions. To reach a certain technological level, the preceding levels have to be passed through

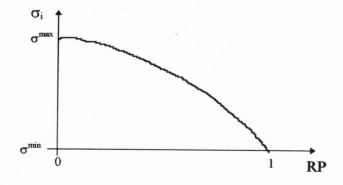

Fig. 1. Adjustment of absorptive capacity

because otherwise the relevant technological understanding cannot be achieved. Therefore, to represent the cumulative feature of technological progress the periodic R&D investments $r_i(t)$ sum up to an R&D capital stock $R_i(t)$. Besides R&D activities, the rate of technological progress depends on the degree of exhaustion of the intensive technological opportunities. To model this feature, we assume innovative success $ie_i(t)$ positive but decreasing in $R_i(t)$. To take account of technological uncertainty, the occurrence of such success is determined stochastically by an equally distributed random number ψ_t. The innovative success $ie_i(t)$ translates with a time lag of one period in unit cost reductions:

$$c_i(t) = c_0 \cdot [1 - ie_i(t - 1)], \tag{3}$$

where c_0 equals the initial value of unit costs.

For the *conservative* firms, innovative success in t is given by:

$$ie_i(t) = 1 - \text{Exp}[-\alpha \cdot R_i(t)] \qquad \text{and} \tag{4}$$

$$ie_i(t) = \begin{cases} ie_i(t) & \text{for} \quad f[R_i(t)] \geq \psi_t \\ ie_i(t - 1) & \text{for} \quad f[R_i(t)] < \psi_t, \end{cases}$$

where α equals the bending of innovation success and

$$f(R_i) = 1 - e^{-\alpha R_i}.$$

For the *absorptive* strategy, spillover effects and the ability to use them are relevant. In our model, the spillover effects are generated endogenously. For process spillovers, the variance of the unit costs $s(t)^2$ of the different firms is taken as a proxy for spillover potentials. The absorptive capacity $ac_i(t)$ necessary to integrate the knowledge content of spillovers has to be accumulated like the stock of R&D capital:

$$ac_i(t) = \sum_t \sigma_i(t) \cdot r_i(t). \tag{5}$$

Of course, the adoption of externally created technological know-how in the form of spillovers is also a cumulative process. This implies that the potential impact of spillovers is increasing with the accumulation of absorptive capacity and the increasing informational content of the spillovers already integrated.[7]

Additionally, for using spillovers the technological distance or technology gap $G_i^{PC}(t)$ in process technologies (*PC*) to the leader is relevant.[8] For

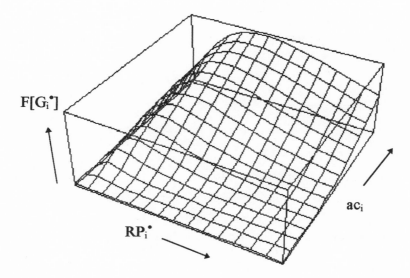

$F[G_i^*]$

ac_i

RP_i^*

Fig. 2. Spillover function

small distances, there is not much new a firm can learn; it masters the technology on its own. On the other side, firms that fall very far behind are not able to keep up with the pace of technological leaders because the respective knowledge becomes too specific. But, for in-between gaps, the spillovers have the highest impact because these firms need and could use the respective information.

The impact of technological spillovers on innovative success $F[G_i^{PC}(t)]$ is described by equation 6[9] and graphically depicted in figure 2:

$$F[G_i^{PC}(t)] = RP_i^{PC}(t) \cdot \text{Exp}\left[-\frac{RP_i^{PC}(t)}{ac_i(t)}\right], \tag{6}$$

where $F[G_i^{PC}(t)]$ equals the spillover function (process technologies).

The function of innovative success for process innovations (eq. 4) by applying the absorptive strategy is modified by a term containing the spillover pool $s(t)^2$ and the spillover function $F[G_i^{PC}]$ as a weight for the R&D capital stock. This reflects a nonlinear process, which should show the threshold effect of the impact of additional information if the necessary basis is already built up.[10]

$$ie_i(t) = 1 - \text{Exp}\left[-\alpha\left(\frac{\xi + s(t)^2}{1 + \text{Exp}\{\tau \cdot d_i(t) - F[G_i^{PC}(t)]\}}\right) \cdot R_i(t)\right] \quad \text{and} \tag{7}$$

$$ie_i(t) = \begin{cases} ie_i(t) & \text{for} & f[R_i(t)] \geq \psi_t \\ ie_i(t-1) & \text{for} & f[R_i(t)] < \psi_t \end{cases}$$

$$d_i(t) = [1 - \epsilon \cdot ac_i(t)] \cdot (1 + \theta)^t, \tag{8}$$

where

ϵ = scaling parameter

τ = difficulty in building up absorptive capacity

θ = learning parameter

$d_i(t)$ = impact of absorptive capacity

ξ = interindustry spillovers and feedbacks from the sciences.

By building up absorptive capabilities, a learning process will take place: on the one hand, there are experiences with respect to the richness of different spillover sources; and, on the other hand, an advantage in experience with the integration of external knowledge should be expected. In the model, the learning effect as well as the accumulated absorptive capacity determine the term $d_i(t)$, which is responsible for the impact of absorptive capacity.

Imitative firms try to improve their production processes by imitating the most successful technologies ie_{t-1}^{max} of their competitors. Because they are imitating already workable technologies, their endeavors are not confronted in the same way with risk and uncertainty like the innovative efforts of other firms. Nevertheless, at least some degree of appropriability suggests a stochastic determination of their imitative success. The imitative success $pcimit_i(t)$ is given by:

$$pcimit_i(t) = ieit_{t-1}^{max} \cdot \mu_t^{PC} \cdot \{1 - Exp[-\alpha \cdot R_i(t)]\}, \tag{9}$$

where

$ieit_t^{max}$ = max of innovation success of innovative firms

μ_t^{PC} = equal distributed random number

$\mu_t^{PC} \in [\mu^{min}, \mu^{max}]$.

Product innovation.   Besides improving production processes, firms engage in product innovations. These are reflected by quality improvements, which show a twofold effect. First, the mutual price dependence $h_i(t)$ of the oligopolists decreases with higher heterogeneity in quality levels. Second, successful product innovations change prohibitive prices $a_i(t)$.[11] The innovating entrepreneur i produces higher quality connected with an improvement in consumers' assessment. Other firms j experience a decrease in their individual prohibitive price because the innovation of i decreases the relative quality of their products.

The uncertainty involved in these endeavors is quite different from what we assume for process innovations. Whereas the direction and impact of process innovations along certain trajectories can be roughly expected, this does not apply to product innovations. In the literature, this context is described with the notion of "intrinsic" uncertainty: if somebody knows the results of innovative endeavors ex ante, it is no longer a product innovation. In order to model this quite different feature of product innovations, we use a *Poisson-distributed* random number.[12]

The R&D efforts devoted to product innovations are again represented by the stock of R&D capital $R_i(t)$. By this stock, firms accumulate success probability $pr_i(t)[.]$, which approximates asymptotically the mean value of the Poisson-distributed random number. The increase of success probability for *conservative* firms is characterized by positive but decreasing rates:

$$pr_i(t)[PDI = 1] = 1 - \text{Exp}[-\alpha \cdot R_i(t)]$$

$$PDI = \begin{cases} 1 \text{ for } pr_i(t) \geq \rho_t \\ 0 \text{ for } pr_i(t) < \rho_t \end{cases}$$

$$(10)$$

where

ρ_t = Poisson-distributed random number

PDI = binary variable, which takes the value 1 in the case of success.

Absorptive firms take into account the idea-creating effects of spillovers. Their probability for a product innovation is supported by learning from product spillovers. The respective spillover pool is given by the variance $s_a(t)^2$ of the prohibitive prices $a_i(t)$. The stock of R&D capital is again weighted with the spillover function $F[G_i^{PD}(t)]$ and the spillover pool. This should reflect the cross-fertilization possibility of technological spillovers in connection with product innovations:

$$pr_i(t)[PDI = 1] = 1 - \text{Exp}\left[-\alpha \left(\frac{\xi + s_a(t)^2}{1 + \text{Exp}\{\tau \cdot d_i(t) - F[G_i^{PD}(t)]\}} \right) \cdot R_i(t) \right], \quad (11)$$

where $F[G_i^{PD}(t)]$ equals the spillover function (product technology).

Imitative firms do not face the same uncertainty when they attempt to introduce a new product. They engage in imitation only if one of the competitors successfully introduced a new product. Then they accumulate a success probability in the following manner:

$$pdimit(t)[PDI = 1] = 1 - \text{Exp}[-\alpha \cdot R_i(t)] \tag{12}$$

$$PDI = \begin{cases} 1 \text{ for } pdimit_i(t) \geq \mu_t^{PD} \\ 0 \text{ for } pdimit_i(t) < \mu_t^{PD} \end{cases},$$

where μ_t^{PD} equals the equal distributed random number and $\mu_t^{PD} \in [\mu^{min}, \mu^{max}]$.

Obsolescence.   Whenever a firm succeeds in introducing a product innovation, the knowledge to master the old technology is assumed to have become irrelevant. Therefore, the old stock of R&D capital will be totally depreciated every time a product innovation occurs. The new technology shows full technological opportunities and consequently a large potential for new process innovations.

For a firm that decides to invest in absorptive capacity, a product innovation bears two additional consequences. The absorptive capacity, like the stock of R&D capital, becomes obsolete and will be depreciated. Also, the learning variable $d_i(t)$ will be set back to the initial value.

4.   Simulation Results

In our simulation experiments, we are dealing with an oligopoly containing 15 firms.[13] According to the three different strategies, these enterprises are subdivided into three "camps." For each simulation run of 200 periods, we assume that all firms start with identical unit production costs and product qualities, which are assessed equally by consumers. To avoid distortions due to the several stochastic elements, we run all simulations 30 times and calculate the respective averages. Additionally, we only present average results of the different groups. For the following discussion, we first investigate the performance of the different strategies. In a second step, we compare the impact of the two different learning rules.[14]

The strategies' performances.   Figures 3a and 3b show the development of profits for the different strategies.[15] These figures demonstrate how firms behave according to the technological learning rule (eq. 1a) and the economical learning rule (eq. 1b), respectively. In the beginning the periodic profits of the absorptive and the imitative firms are clearly below the ones of the conservative camp. Conservative firms are able to exploit the intensive technological opportunities faster. By the ongoing exhaustion of intensive opportunities, the absorptive firms are technologically catching up, which soon leads to a narrowing of profits between these two strategies. Contrary to conservative competitors struggling with nearly depleted oppor-

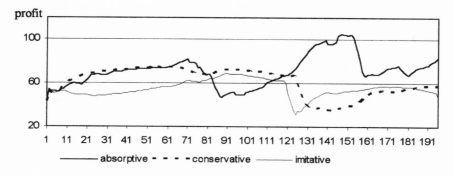

Fig. 3a. Profits in the technological scenario

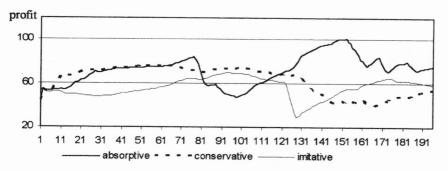

Fig. 3b. Profits in the economic scenario

tunities, absorptive firms finally are able to explore new technological potentials with the help of know-how created outside their own laboratories and transferred by technological spillovers. Technologically, this effect is depicted in the additional sharp decrease of the best-practice unit cost frontier (I) shown in figure 4 for the technological learning rule.

With respect to periodic profits, absorptive firms leapfrog their conservative competitors and are now in the leading profit position. During this period, imitative firms are in the last profit position. They are confident about imitating the technological improvements of their competitors and therefore technologically lag behind. Nevertheless, due to imitation they are able to increase their periodic profits continuously.

Obviously, the ability of absorptive firms to exploit external knowledge also supports innovative endeavors aimed at product innovation.[16] Because of their capability to integrate the know-how of technological spillovers, these firms are the first to introduce a product innovation. On the new technological trajectory, they are confronted with high unit costs depicted by the best-practice unit cost frontier (II) in figure 4. This product innovation

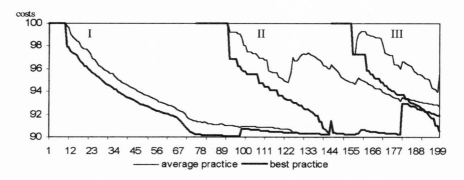

Fig. 4. Best and average practice costs

and the corresponding jump on a new trajectory leads to an initial profit erosion, which, however, does not last long. Despite the higher quality and the higher consumer assessment of product II, in the beginning of that product cycle conservative and imitative firms are able to attract some demand of the absorptive firms because of high unit costs there. But, with relatively fast cost reductions due to new technological possibilities, absorptive firms are able to gain the leading profit position again just some periods later. The technological gap between imitative and conservative firms on the second trajectory increases because they are still lagging behind in introducing product II. These increasing technological advantages finally provide for the high profit margins of the absorptive firms. Despite introducing a third technology later, they keep their leading profit position.

On the second trajectory, the self-sufficient conservative firms technologically are lagging behind even the imitative firms, which earlier introduced the new technology II. This technological advantage of the imitative strategy translates into an economic one, and even with respect to profits they leapfrog their conservative competitors. Later, however, the conservative firms are successful in catching up.

These technological and economic processes are also reflected in the concentration ratio of the heterogeneous oligopoly. Figure 5 shows the development of the CR_4 index for the two learning rules, respectively. The increase in concentration in the beginning is induced by the innovative, most successful, conservative firms and the falling behind of the imitative firms. But very soon the absorptive firms are catching up technologically, which in turn leads to a decrease in concentration. This trend changes again when absorptive firms are leapfrogging the conservative ones. In the following periods, the successful product innovation of absorptive firms is responsible for temporarily growing market shares of conservative and imitative firms. Up to this period, the four largest firms are composed of both camps, absorptive and conservative. But, with increasing success on the

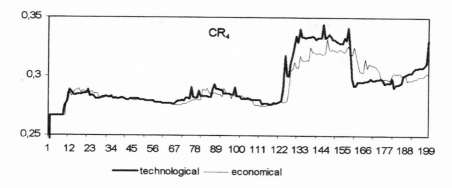

Fig. 5. Concentration ratios

second trajectory, only absorptive firms are used for CR_4. Due to their innovative success, their economic success is not only dependent on higher consumer assessment connected with higher prices but also on increasing market shares.

Another possibility for comparing the different strategies is to investigate "R&D effectiveness." Here, one has to distinguish between success in process and product innovation. Concerning the latter, firms following the absorptive strategy are always the first to introduce a new product. With respect to process innovations, figure 6 shows for the three strategies the relationship between the periodic R&D budgets and the resulting cost reductions. The learning rule applied here is the technological one, however, and the results by and large apply also to the scenario with economic learning. To interpret these figures, observations are represented by "sunflowers." The number of petals of each sunflower gives an account of the number of observations falling in a certain interval.

The following results are interesting: First, average R&D budgets are higher for the absorptive group because on the average they are more profitable and have higher market shares. Second, R&D success is higher for the other groups. This is caused mainly by three effects.

1. Higher R&D budgets allow for higher R&D stocks and consequently for a higher R&D success probability.

2. A considerable share of the R&D budgets is spent on absorptive capacity, which allows firms to exploit externally generated know-how (with equivalent effects on R&D success probability).

3. Finally, since these firms are more frequently opening up new product cycles, they exploit depleted intensive opportunities only briefly, as they can "enjoy" the refreshed opportunities offered by the new trajectory.

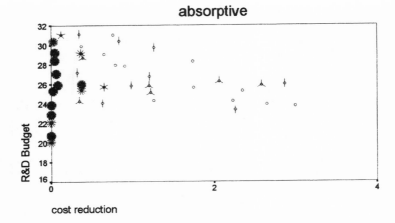

Fig. 6a. R&D effectiveness of absorptive firms

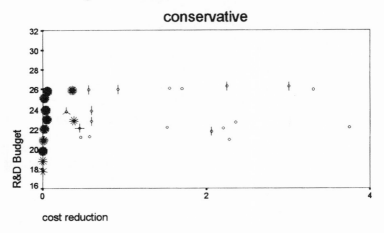

Fig. 6b. R&D effectiveness of conservative firms

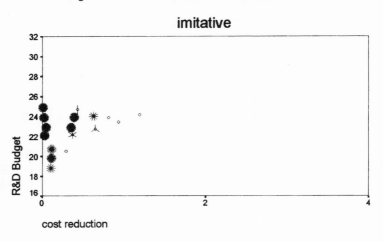

Fig. 6c. R&D effectiveness of imitative firms

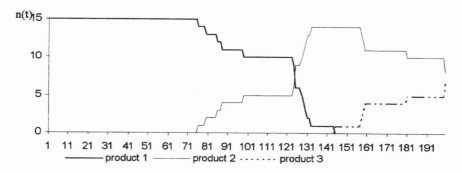

Fig. 7a. Product cycles in the technological scenario

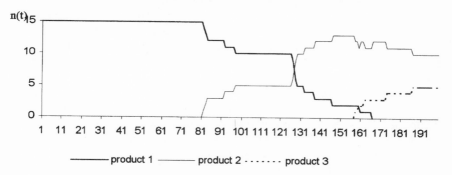

Fig. 7b. Product cycles in the economic scenario

Comparing the different learning rules.   After the introduction of the first product innovation, in the scenario of the technological-learning rule the share of the old technology is decreasing relatively fast. This is shown in figure 7a, illustrating the product cycles. Firms lagging behind the technological leaders are increasing their R&D expenditures to catch up technologically. Consequently, some periods later, one after another firm quickly introduces a new technology.

However, in the scenario of the economic-learning rule firms lagging behind in jumping on the new trajectory can temporarily increase their periodic profits due to the switching problems of the successful innovators. Doing this, they are able to increase their rate of turnover with a negative effect on their R&D endeavors. This is illustrated in figure 7b, showing the product cycles for this scenario. One can observe larger overlapping phases of the different product technologies. Some firms still stay on the first trajectory when their competitors are opening up the third product cycle.

Therefore, firms applying the economical adjustment mechanism of R&D budgets exploit their technological opportunities on a trajectory more intensely and take advantage of the short-term problems of the innovating firms. On the contrary, firms applying the technological-learning rule are accelerating the speed of innovation because they attempt to close their technological gaps with the leaders as soon as they become aware of them.

5. Conclusions

In this essay we investigate the technological and economic implications of different strategies and learning rules firms apply in pushing forward technological progress. Those strategies are not designed in an optimal—neoclassical—way but are more or less rules of thumb that have been successful in the past. The main reasons for this modeling are the inherent technological uncertainty, the technological constraints, and the bounded and procedural rationality of agents.

Within this framework three different strategies are investigated, the absorptive, the conservative, and the imitative strategies. Additionally, we distinguish between learning rules for adapting R&D budgets, which on the one hand are oriented along the economic success, and on the other hand along the technological success of the different strategies.

Comparing the different strategies, it has been a quite robust result that in the medium and long run the absorptive strategy dominates with respect to technological as well as economic performance.

With respect to the different learning rules, a clear result is that with technological learning the rate of technological progress is comparatively higher. Applying the economic-learning rule, oligopolistic competition quite often allows for sufficient economic success so that the necessity to intensify R&D activities is relatively low.

This result mirrors *in some way* the discussion between neoclassical and new innovation theory. In the former, it is the computable economic efficiency of R&D budgets, and in some sense it is static efficiency that counts. The economic-learning rule is to some degree designed in this way, although this is not to be taken literally. In the latter, however, it is the experimental character of innovative behavior and its focus on an—even only assumed—dynamic efficiency. Here, it is not present profitability but the relative technological performance that drives R&D activities, the main feature of the technological-learning rule.

APPENDIX

TABLE A1.   Parameter Values

Bending of innovation success	α	0.001
Exogeneous rate of adjustment	ω	0.01
Difficulty in building up absorptive capacity	τ	15
Interindustry spillovers	ξ	1
Scaling parameter	ϵ	0.0001
Absorptive capacity minimum	σ^{min}	0.05
Absorptive capacity maximum	σ^{max}	0.2
Upper bound of μ	μ^{max}	1
Lower bound of μ	μ^{min}	0.8
Learning parameter	θ	0.001

TABLE A2.   Initial Values

Price	$p_i(0)$	110
Share of turnover for R&D	γ_0	0.025
Costs	c_0	100
Impact of absorptive capacity	d_0	1
Prohibitive price	a_0	25
Output	$x_i(0)$	10
Number of firms	$n(0)$	15

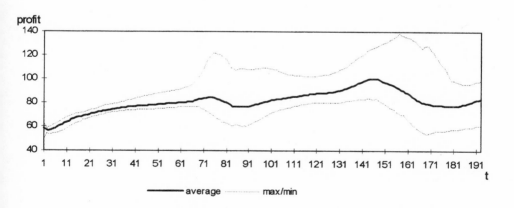

Fig. A1. Range of profit variable of the absorptive camp (economic learning rule, moving average, average standard deviation 9, 04)

In the sensitivity analysis, we test the robustness of our model (only for the case of the economic learning rule) due to several parameter variations. Thereby, always only one parameter is varied, keeping the others on their value of the reference case. The aim of this exercise is to draw attention to the ranges of parameter values for which the basic results of our investigation hold. The respective workable ranges are listed in table A3.

If the α parameter, which represents the bending of the innovation success function, takes values smaller than 0.0001, no product innovation occurs in the observed time interval. Despite staying on the first trajectory, after 35 iterations absorptive firms are head to head with the conservative firms. And after 110 iterations these absorptive firms are clearly ahead. Imitative firms are not able to hold their intermediate position. Because there is less to copy, they are in the last position during the 200 iterations. For α-values bigger than 0.01 (which means an increase by factor 10), there are no bottlenecks with respect to their own opportunities, and therefore the firms very often introduce new products. Building up of absorptive capacity leads more or less to the same success as spending all of the R&D budget in the way the conservative firms does. In this scenario, sometimes the absorptive camp and sometimes the conservative camp is in the leading profit position. Imitative firms behave quite well in this case; they do not introduce as many new products as the other camps do, and therefore they are able to exploit intensively the opportunities of a single trajectory. Under this setting, the long-term advantage of absorptive firms is not as decisive as in the reference case due to the volatility of profits.

The next parameter varied is the prohibitive price a. Values lower than 25 support the absorptive firms to some degree. Demand constraints are responsible for large gains resulting from early cost reduction. With respect to quality improvement, only these firms introduce new products. But quality improvement is connected with increasing unit costs. Under this setting, increasing costs together with demand constraints are responsible for the problems absorptive firms are confronted with after their successful product innovation. Imitative firms are able to copy improvements of their absorptive competitors, so that they even threaten the position of the conservative camp. If the prohibitive price a is higher than 25, larger profits due to increased demand make higher R&D budgets available. Therefore, both heterogeneity between agents and spillovers increase. This development clearly supports absorptive firms, which now have no severe problems in keeping their market position when introducing new products, a problem which arose due to demand constraints in our reference scenario. Conservative firms cannot exploit absorptive firms during their time in a weak position after introducing new products

TABLE A3.   Parameter Range

Parameter	Reference Value	Range
α (bending of the innovation probability)	0.001	$0.0001 \leq \alpha \leq 0.01$
a (prohibitive price)	25	$20 \leq a$
τ (slope of the R&D-weighting function)	15	$5 \leq \tau$
θ (learning parameter)	0.01	$\theta \geq 0.001$
ϵ (scaling parameter)	0.0001	$\epsilon \geq 0.00001$
ξ (interindustry and science spillovers)	1	$\xi \geq 0.1$

because of the strong competition with imitative firms. Under this setting, there is always leapfrogging between the conservative and the imitative camp.

The slope of the R&D-weighting function τ does not significantly influence the basic results. Nevertheless, one has to mention some implausible results that occur for similarly low values ($\tau \leq 5$). Here, the impact of absorptive capacity comes into action at the beginning of the learning process.

If the learning parameter θ is set at a value of 0.0001 (which means a decrease by factor 10), firms with absorptive strategies need more time to introduce their product innovation. Nevertheless, they are still the first to introduce new products. Conservative and imitative firms behave more or less in the same way. For even further decreases of θ, the conservative firms will be the first to introduce new products.

If the scaling parameter ϵ is decreased by factor 10 ($\epsilon = 0.00001$) also, the conservative firms are the first to introduce a new product. But the absorptive camp is able to catch up and even to leapfrog on the second trajectory due to the increased spillover pool.

Finally, we investigate the impact of the interindustry and science spillover parameter ξ. Our results hold for values larger than 0.1. But, even if we assume that there are no external feedbacks ($\xi = 0$), we find a long-run dominance of absorptive firms when we broaden the investigation period. In this setting, dominant absorptive firms are found in the first 200 periods if appropriability in the model is reduced and larger endogenous spillover pools are established this way.

NOTES

1. The fundamental reference is Arrow (1962).

2. In the literature, the notion of "go-it-alone" is used alternatively for this strategy. See Fusfield and Haklish (1985).

3. Freeman (1982) alternatively uses the notion of "defensive or dependent strategy."

4. Cohen and Levinthal (1989, 129) state in this respect: "When a firm wishes to acquire and use new knowledge that is unrelated to its ongoing activity, then the firm must dedicate exclusively to creating 'absorptive capacity' (i.e. 'absorptive capacity' is not a by-product)."

5. The heterogeneous oligopoly is also applied in another simulation study by Meyer, Vogt, and Vosskamp (1996).

6. Keeping in mind our investigative goal, the market framework should be not too complicated. Of course, there are more realistic, and in an evolutionary sense better-suited, market respresentations (e.g., mark-up pricing models and replicator dynamics); these, however, are not the center of interest in this essay.

7. "[L]imited competence is caused by the imperfect ability to use information, which is to be distinguished from the usually considered case of imperfect information" (Pelikan 1992, 383).

8. There is empirical evidence that the technological gap determines the capability to internalize spillover effects. Verspagen (1992) and Cantner (1995) found a bell-shaped relation between the technological gap and the ability to integrate knowledge spillovers.

9. If in the spillover function (eq. 6) the technological gap G_i^{PC} is substituted with

the gap in product technology G_i^{PD}, we get the spillover function with respect to product innovation.

10. "Learning is a process by which repetition and experimentation enable tasks to be performed better and quicker and new production opportunities to be identified" (Dosi, Teece, and Winter 1992, 191).

11. Each firm faces an individual linear demand function $p_i(t) = a_i(t) - \eta x_i(t) + [h_i(t)] n(t - 1) - 1 \Sigma_i p_i(t - 1)$ where p_i: = price of firm i; η = slope of the demand function; n = number of firms; and h_i = variable that expresses mutual price dependence.

12. This probability distribution, which in the literature is often called "the distribution of the low probability for happenings with a low probability," seems to be adequate with respect to product innovations.

13. The different parameter values are listed in the appendix.

14. The robustness of the different simulation results is tested in Cantner and Pyka (1995). There, two additional scenarios were investigated. The first scenario is a regime of high appropriability and therefore low spillover pools. In the second scenario, we lower the oligopolistic interdependence. This scenario comes close to a situation in which the firms can be considered as different industries technologically connected by interindustry spillovers. Our basic results hold under these changed settings. A detailed sensitivity analysis in the setting of this essay can be found in the appendix. Additionally, the range of the profit variable, due to numerous simulation runs, is shown there.

15. We show 5-period moving averages to make the respective curves somewhat smoother because they represent an aggregation over different firms and 30 simulation runs.

16. The effects of absorptive capacity on product innovations are described in detail in Cantner and Pyka (1995).

REFERENCES

Arrow, K. J. 1962. Economic Welfare and the Allocation of Resources for Invention. In *The Rate and Direction of Inventive Activity*, edited by R. R. Nelson. Princeton: Princeton University Press.

Cantner, U. 1995. Technological Dynamics in Asymmetric Industries: R&D, Spillovers, and Absorptive Capacity. Institut für Volkswirtschaftslehre der Universität Augsburg, Volkswirtschaftliche Diskussionsreihe, no. 143.

Cantner, U., and A. Pyka. 1995. Absorptive Capacities and Technological Spillovers II: Simulations in an Evolutionary Framework. Institut für Volkswirtschaftslehre der Universität Augsburg, Volkswirtschaftliche Diskussionsreihe, no. 141.

Cohen, W. M., and D. A. Levinthal. 1989. Innovation and Learning: The Two Faces of R&D. *Economic Journal* 99:569–96.

———. 1994. Fortune Favours the Prepared Firm. *Management Science* 40 (2): 227–51.

Coombs, R. 1988. Technological Opportunities and Industrial Organization. In Dosi et al. 1988.

Dahmén, E. 1990. Development Blocks in Industrial Development. In *Industrial Dynamics*, edited by B. Carlsson. Dordrecht: Kluwer Academic.

Dasgupta, P., and J. E. Stiglitz. 1980. Industrial Structure and the Nature of Innovative Activity. *Economic Journal* 90:266–93.

Dosi, G., et al., eds. 1988. *Technical Change and Economic Theory.* London: Pinter.

Dosi, G., and M. Egidi. 1991. Substantive and Procedural Rationality. *Journal of Evolutionary Economics* 1:145–68.

Dosi, G., D. J. Teece, and S. Winter. 1992. Towards a Theory of Corporate Competence: Preliminary Remarks. In *Technology and Enterprise in a Historical Perspective,* G. Dosi, R. Giannetti, and P. A. Toninelli. Oxford: Clarendon Press.

Freeman, C. 1982. *The Economics of Industrial Innovation.* 2d ed. London: Pinter.

Fusfield, H. I., and C. S. Haklish. 1985. Cooperative R&D for Competitors. *Harvard Business Review* 6; no. 6 (Nov./Dec.): 60–76.

Heiner, R. 1988. Imperfect Decisions and Routinzed Production: Implications for Evolutionary Modelling and Inertial Technical Change. In Dosi et al. 1988.

Kuenne, R. E. 1992. *The Economics of Oligopolistic Competition.* Cambridge, MA: Blackwell.

Levinthal, D. A., and J. G. March. 1981. A Model of Adaptive Organizational Change. *Journal of Economic Behavior and Organization* 2:307–33.

March, J. G. 1991. Exploration and Exploitation in Organizational Learning. *Organization Science.* 2 (1):71–87.

Meyer, B., C. Vogt, and R. Vosskamp. 1996. Schumpeterian Competition in Heterogeneous Oligopolies. *Journal of Evolutionary Economics* 6:411–24.

Mokyr, J. 1990. *The Lever of Riches: Technological Creativity and Economic Progress.* Oxford: Oxford University Press.

Nelson, R. R. 1990. What Is Public and What Is Private about Technology? CCC Working Papers, no. 90–9, University of California at Berkeley.

Nelson, R. R., and S. Winter. 1982. *An Evolutionary Theory of Economic Change.* Cambridge, MA: Harvard University Press.

Pelikan, P. 1992. Can the Innovation System of Capitalism Be Outperformed? In Dosi et al. 1992.

Reinganum, J. E. 1985. Innovation and Industry Evolution. *Quarterly Journal of Economics* 100:81–99.

Schumpeter, J. A. 1942. *Capitalism, Socialism, and Democracy.* 5th ed. London: Allen & Unwin.

Simon, H. A. 1976. From Substantive to Procedural Rationality. In *Method and Appraisal in Economics,* edited by S. J. Latsis. Cambridge: Cambridge University Press.

Verspagen, B. 1993. *Uneven Growth between Interdependent Economies.* Maastricht: Aldershot, U.K.: Avebury.

Winter, S. G. 1971. Satisficing, Selection, and the Innovating Remnant, *Quarterly Journal of Economics* 85 (2):237–61.

———. 1986. Schumpeterian Competition in Alternative Technological Regimes. In *The Dynamics of Market Economics,* edited by R. Day and G. Eliasson. Elsevier: North-Holland.

———. 1989. Patents in Complex Contents: Incentives and Effectiveness. In *Owning Scientific and Technical Information,* edited by V. Weil et al. New Brunswick, NJ: Rutgers University Press.

Innovation and Knowledge Spillovers:
A System cum Evolutionary Perspective
Bo Carlsson

Introduction: Why Systems?

This essay shows that a systems cum evolutionary approach to the study of the economic impact of innovation is necessary when spillovers of knowledge are important.

Economic growth is increasingly based on knowledge, and technology is the means through which it is applied to economic activity. Yet economists have been slow to integrate technology fully into their analyses. It wasn't until the 1950s when Abramovitz (1956), Solow (1956), and others discovered that increases in inputs of capital and labor alone accounted for only a fraction of macroeconomic growth that economists began to recognize the importance of technology. The unexplained residual, often referred to as the "technology factor," prompted economists to include technology as a factor in the production function. But it remained an exogenous factor. The inclusion in the late 1980s of knowledge as a factor enhancing the inputs of capital and labor (rather than as a separate factor of production) in the macroproduction function (Romer 1986, 1990; Lucas 1988) represents a small—but only a small—step forward, even though it has been widely touted as "the new growth theory." But, as Romer himself points out, the bulk of economic growth analysis has remained stuck in the world of "objects" (i.e., capital, labor, and physical material inputs) rather than "ideas" (Romer 1993).

One reason why knowledge has been neglected in economic analysis is that it is difficult to capture statistically (cf. Eliasson and Braunerhjelm in this volume). Another reason is that it is not a commodity that can be readily bought and sold in markets. Instead, exchange and transfer of knowledge take place largely outside markets. Some knowledge may be fruitfully viewed as a public good in the sense that once it is produced its use by one person or firm does not restrict its use by others. But it is not "free": the transaction costs pertaining to the transfer of knowledge are often high (especially if it is in the form of tacit knowledge), involving costly and quite specific investments (in receiver competence, transfer technology, or both) on the part of the recipient or customer. Furthermore, the transfer does not usually occur in markets but rather via nonmarket interaction. Thus, the difficulty of incorporating knowledge in the analysis of economic growth stems not only from the problem of capturing and measuring it statistically but also from the fact that it is treated as an externality.

The more knowledge intensive the activity is, the more it depends on nonmarket interaction. Therefore, clustering of activity, both geographically and in terms of interindustry linkages, while common in many industries, is particularly important in high-tech sectors such as biotechnology, electronics and computers, and software. Clustering facilitates the sharing and transfer of knowledge, competence, and skills. The recent rapid growth of literature on spillovers (see, e.g., the survey in Eliasson 1997) indicates their rising importance.

The more pervasive knowledge spillovers are, the more important it is that they be included explicitly in the analysis. The activity needs to be viewed not in isolation but in context, as part of a system. The boundaries of the system need to be drawn in such a way that "spillovers" are regarded as transactions *within* the system rather than externalities, so that the interfaces with the environment are few and the interactions across these interfaces are simple (English 1972, 2).

Systems engineers define a system as a set of interrelated components working toward a common objective. Systems are made up of components, attributes, and relationships. Components are the operating parts of a system. Attributes are the properties of the components; they characterize the system. Relationships are the links between components and attributes. The properties and behavior of each component of the set influence the properties and behavior of the set as a whole. At the same time, each component depends upon the properties and behavior of at least one other component in the set. Because of this interdependence, the components cannot be divided into independent subsets; the system is more than the sum of its parts (Blanchard and Fabrycky 1990, 2).

The systems concept is necessary in analyzing the economic impact of innovation when nonmarket synergies are important. The relative importance of market and nonmarket interaction varies from case to case and hence also the appropriate system definition. Often, a broader definition than "industry" is needed, emphasizing the fact that problem-solving activities (involving ideas and knowledge) are often much more important than the transfer of physical commodities in buyer-supplier (input-output) relationships.

With the increasing dependence of economic activity on knowledge, "markets" and "industries" capture less of the dynamics in the economy than they used to. Further, many of the most important relationships are not captured in neat statistical entities. A system consists of a core (which may or may not be an industry) and a number of actors who interact with the core but who may also be part of other systems. Thus, there may be considerable overlap among systems; each player has more than one role to play and often a different role in each system. Thus, for example, it could well be argued that the system for electronics and computers includes the entire labor force, reflecting the fact that practically every person working today is affected by electronics and computers. At the same time, of course, workers may also be part of other systems such as biotechnology or factory automation. This reflects the complexity of the economy. Each person or unit is, at least potentially, a part of several systems simultaneously and can be positively or negatively affected by developments in several different areas.

When viewing innovative economic activity in a systems framework, three things are highlighted.

1. The components (and therefore the boundaries) of the system. Whereas the units to be included are taken as self-evident in conventional economic analyses based on "industries" or "sectors," the units making up the system, as well as the system boundaries, now need to be specifically defined. Not only the various actors (individuals and firms, buyers and sellers) that normally interact in markets need to be included but also academic units, research institutes, government agencies, trade associations, and other units making up the institutional infrastructure.

2. Also, the relationships among the various components in the system need to be analyzed—specifically, the non-market-mediated interaction in the form of knowledge spillovers. In many areas of economic activity, especially the ones that are currently the most dynamic, such spillovers are pervasive; they are not rare exceptions. Therefore, they need to be included in the analysis, that is, they are part of the system.

3. The attributes or characteristics of the components need to be specified. These include the competencies and functions of the components that enhance the system's performance.

This broadens the analysis beyond the traditional primary (narrower and more static) concern of industrial organization with the competitive conditions in an industry at a given point in time. And certainly it broadens the scope for discussing economic policy.

Various Systems Approaches

Various systems approaches have been suggested in the literature. One of the first is *input-output analysis* (Leontief 1941), focusing on the flows of goods and services among sectors in the economy. Another early approach is that represented by *"development blocs"* as defined by Dahmén: "sequences of complementarities which by way of a series of structural tensions, i.e., disequilibria, may result in a balanced situation" (1989, 111). The basic idea is that, as an innovation creates new opportunities, these opportunities may not be realized (converted into economic activity) until the requisite inputs (resources and skills) and product markets are in place. Each innovation therefore gives rise to a "structural tension," which, when resolved, makes progress possible and may create new tensions, and which, if unresolved, may bring the process to a halt. Thus, while the input-output analysis is static, Dahmén's concept is dynamic, representing one of the first attempts to apply Schumpeterian analysis; it incorporates the notion of disequilibrium; and it focuses on the role of the entrepreneur. But Dahmén's approach is similar to Leontief's in that it focuses on the interwar period and is highly disaggregated, covering the structural development of 24 different industries in Sweden.

A third but much later approach is widely known as *national innovation systems* (Freeman 1988; Lundvall 1988, 1992; Nelson 1988a, 1988b, 1993; and subsequently many others). Here the framework is broadened to include not only industries and firms but also other actors and institutions, primarily in science and technology, as well as the role of technology policy. The analysis is carried out at the national level: R&D activities and the role played by universities, research institutes, government agencies, and government policies are viewed as components of a single national system.

Another approach is represented by Michael *Porter's "diamond,"* as described in his 1990 book *The Competitive Advantage of Nations*. The four sides of the diamond are made up of factor conditions (skills, technologies, capital, etc.); demand conditions (especially "competent demand" as represented by technically sophisticated customers); links to related and supporting industries; and firm strategies, structure, and rivalry. Each economic activity is viewed primarily as an industry, but it is also part of a cluster of activities and agents rather than taking place in isolation. Because of the industry focus, Porter strongly emphasizes the role of competition among actors within industries (i.e., market competition) while suppressing nonmarket interaction with entities outside the industry. In this sense, the system definition is narrower than in the national innovation system approach.

A similar approach is represented by *"sectoral innovation systems"* (Breschi and Malerba 1995; see also Malerba and Orsenigo 1990, 1993, 1995). As in Porter's analysis, the system definition here is based on "industry" or "sector." But, rather than focusing on interdependence within clusters of industries, sectoral innovation systems are based on the idea that different sectors or industries operate under different technological regimes, which are characterized by particular combinations of opportunity and appropriability conditions, degrees of cumulativeness of technological knowledge, and characteristics of the relevant knowledge base. Thus, this approach focuses on the competitive relationships among firms by explicitly considering the role of the selection environment.

Another system definition is built around the concept of *local industrial systems* as represented in AnnaLee Saxenian's study (1994) of the electronics industry in Silicon Valley in California and along Route 128 in

Massachusetts. Here the system definition is primarily geographical. The focus is on differences in culture and competition that have led to differences among the two regions in the degree of hierarchy and concentration, experimentation, collaboration, and collective learning, which, in turn, have entailed differences in the capacity to adjust to changing circumstances in technology and markets.

Finally, the approach on which I will focus in more detail here is that based on the notion of *technological systems* (Carlsson 1995, 1997). This concept is similar to Erik Dahmén's "development blocs" (1950, 1989) in that it is both disaggregated and dynamic: there are many (or at least several) technological systems in each country (thus differing from national innovation systems), and they evolve over time, that is, the number and types of actors, institutions, relationships among them, etc., vary over time (thus differing from all the other system definitions except Dahmén's). Also, national borders do not necessarily form the boundaries of the systems. In addition, the system definition focuses on *generic technologies* with general applications over many industries, thus distinguishing it from all the other approaches.

Technological systems are defined as *networks of agents interacting in a given area of technology, operating within a particular infrastructure, to generate, exploit, and diffuse technology* (Carlsson and Stankiewicz 1991). The main function of technological systems is to capture and enhance technological spillovers.

Technological systems involve market and nonmarket interaction in three types of network: buyer-supplier (input-output) relationships, problem-solving networks, and informal networks. While there may be considerable overlap between these networks, it is the problem-solving network that really defines both the nature and the boundaries of the system: where do various actors in the system turn for help in solving technical problems? Buyer-supplier linkages are important, the more so the more technical information is transmitted along with the transactions, and the less so the more commoditylike the transactions are. Sometimes the most important technical information comes from sources (e.g., universities and research institutes) separate from buyers and sellers. Sometimes the informal, mostly personal networks established through professional conferences, meetings, publications, and so on are important channels of information gathering and sharing.[1]

Technological Systems

Basic Assumptions
In recent years, a group of Swedish researchers has studied the evolution of four technological systems in Sweden: those for factory automation, elec-

tronics and computers, pharmaceuticals and biotechnology, and powder technology. To a lesser extent, the system for aircraft production has also been examined. These studies are summarized in Carlsson (1997).

Four basic assumptions underly these studies.

1. The system as a whole is the unit of analysis, not its individual components.

2. The systems are inherently dynamic and evolving but do not necessarily emerge spontaneously; their evolution can be influenced through the creation of appropriate institutions.

3. The global technological opportunities are practically unlimited; only a fraction of them can be identified in advance.

4. There is bounded rationality (limited knowledge and information-processing capability; the competence of various entities is differentiated but fairly stable and path dependent; and the search for new knowledge is local). The agents' own economic competence (the ability to identify, exploit, and expand business opportunities) is thus an important constraint and requires an experimental organization of the economy (Carlsson and Eliasson 1994, Eliasson 1991). The choice of business opportunities in the experimentally organized economy can never be "optimal"; it must always be based on limited knowledge and intuition. But it can be enhanced through the establishment of appropriate institutions. Information is more effectively gathered, processed, and interpreted and knowledge more efficiently allocated within a technological system or competence bloc than they would be if each agent acted independently.

Components and Connectivity

In each system studied, we have identified the components and boundaries and then examined their *connectivity*, that is, the networks or linkages among actors through which spillovers take place.[2] Three types of network have already been mentioned (user-supplier, problem-solving, and informal). The higher the degree of connectivity, the more effectively the competence base of each participant can be put to use. Network building can take place spontaneously, but it is often aided (and sometimes initiated) by *bridging institutions,* that is, agencies and other organizations that bring together academic institutions, research institutes, business firms, and government agencies.

Main Features

When the components and their relationships have been clarified, three characteristics of the system are explored: (1) the *nature of knowledge,* (2) the presence of sufficient *receiver competence*, and (3) the *ways in which variety is created* in the system. Together, these features determine the potential for spillovers as well as the mechanisms through which they occur.

Codified *knowledge* can be transferred more easily and over longer distances, but it is often less important than tacit knowledge, which can be transferred only through close personal interaction. Component-oriented R&D is often conducted in or in collaboration with user firms, while more architecturally oriented work is more frequently conducted by suppliers or in separate units. Some R&D processes are discovery driven (e.g., in biotechnology and pharmaceuticals), whereas others (e.g., in factory automation and industrial machinery more generally) are design driven. Thus, the nature of knowledge and the characteristics of the carriers of knowledge and of the knowledge creation process determine how knowledge is diffused, how the networks are built up, and what the institutional requirements are. The mechanisms for knowledge transfer (spillovers) include personnel moving between various entities, imitation, competent purchasing, and the establishment of new entities (Eliasson 1997).

The second feature of technological systems is *receiver competence* (Eliasson 1990), including the ability to identify and exploit ideas in the global opportunity set; this is one of the most important institutional characteristics of the systems we have studied. Investment in research and development by the big multinational firms (which are often the "prime movers") is primarily oriented toward discovering the frontier in their particular area of technology. By training their own people (functioning, as it were, as institutes of higher learning—see Eliasson 1995), by forcing their suppliers to comply with the standards required by new technology in the global market, and by sharing their knowledge in ways both planned and unplanned, these firms set in motion a series of actions that may lead to the building of new technological systems. Given the global nature of the opportunity set, it is not surprising that actors who can tap into it become technological leaders.

Third, technological systems depend for their long-term survival on *variety-creating mechanisms* (Eliasson 1984). Given the effectiveness of market selection, the perennial problem in evolutionary systems is to maintain variety in existing systems and to create new systems. "Bounded vision" (Fransman 1990) and path dependence create lock-in effects; hence, there is a need for continual new entry. This raises the critical public policy problem of how to foster a climate conducive to experimentation, tolerant of failures, and flexible enough to close down activities that do not succeed and to promote the idea that innovation has little to do with static efficiency but everything to do with effectiveness in creating new opportunities. This is an exceedingly difficult task and requires taking a long view rather than a short one.

Macroeconomic Effects of Spillovers

Micro-to-Macro Simulations

What do we lose by defining the system too narrowly and ignoring non-market interaction (i.e., spillovers)?

Evaluating system performance and systems effects is a difficult task, since it requires a complete dynamic systems model. None of the systems approaches mentioned above provides reliable answers in this respect. They are all either too narrowly defined or too loosely structured. What we have done in our study of technological systems in Sweden is to first perform case studies to determine the important system features and then analyze their macroeconomic effects through simulations on the Swedish micro-to-macro model. The results are reported in Carlsson, Eliasson, and Taymaz (1997). The micro-to-macro model is a simulation model[3] of the Swedish economy based on data for about 150 real Swedish manufacturing firms, aggregated up to the manufacturing industry totals through the use of national income account data. The primary focus of the model is on the individual firms of the manufacturing sector and how they interact and compete in markets. This sector is therefore modeled in greater detail than are other sectors: a government sector, a household sector, and a foreign trade sector. There are also sectors for agriculture/forestry/fishing, construction, oil, electricity, services, and finance, although these are not explicitly modeled at the microlevel.

We focused on the macroeconomic effects of technological spillovers and ran two sets of simulations. In one set, we explored the implications of different configurations of membership in networks through which knowledge spillovers can occur (members picked randomly or selectively within or across sectors or on the basis of specific criteria). In the other set, we reduced the intensity of receptivity and/or connectivity among network members. The results show that the simulations in which the technological spillovers are the most intensive (i.e., the first group) are the ones generally exhibiting the highest overall economic growth rates and rates of return. In the relatively short run (less than 10 years), there is little difference among the simulations at the macrolevel. But in the long run (we ran the simulations for 50-year periods) the differences are dramatic. The average GNP growth rates in the first group of simulations range from 3.3 to 3.5 percent per year. The second set of experiments shows that the performance of the economy clearly declines dramatically when both connectivity and receptivity are reduced or eliminated. The GNP growth rate declines to only 0.7 to 3.3 percent over the 50-year period in the second group.

The results of the first set of simulations suggest that it does not make much difference who the network partners are; the important thing is that networks expand the range of options available to each participant and increase the experience base upon which decisions can be made. The basic reason is the limited knowledge and experience in each firm compared with that which exists elsewhere.

The differences in results between the first and second set of simulations show that the yield on investment, whether in physical capital or knowledge, rises as a result of spillovers and that the economy grows faster. This suggests that firms learn more from each other and their environment than they do from their own in-house research and development in isolation. These results are indicative of strong systems effects due to viable combinations of innovation, learning, and spillovers.

Another feature of technological systems that has been experimentally tested is the importance of variety. In previous simulations on the Swedish micro-to-macro model, it has been demonstrated that diversity among micro-units is a prerequisite for stability at the macroeconomic level (see Eliasson 1984). If firms become too much alike, minor changes in the competitive situation can force a major portion of the firm population out of business suddenly. This is similar to Burton Klein's observation concerning the conflict between short-term static efficiency and long-term dynamic efficiency (1977). A certain amount of microinstability is required for macrostability.

These examples indicate that systems effects are important for the long-run performance of the economy. This suggests that it is necessary to understand not only the interaction among firms and other actors that takes place via markets but also that which occurs outside the market mechanisms. The latter is not only more difficult to observe; its effects are also likely to emerge only in the long run. The systems effects are particularly important in the dynamic, knowledge-based sectors of the economy. If we ignore the systems effects, we are likely to miss (or misunderstand) the true dynamics in the economy.

Deindustrialization: Too Narrow a View of the Industrial System

Another example that illustrates the same point but from the opposite direction is the following: if the industrial system is too narrowly defined, the causes and effects of structural changes may be completely misunderstood.

The fact that the share of total employment and/or output represented by manufacturing industries has shrunk over the last several decades has sparked a debate in several countries concerning "deindustrialization." But in a broader industrial systems perspective the "deindustrialization" phenomenon largely disappears. In fact, some of the most interesting and dynamic new developments in the economy are occurring in the intersection between manufacturing and private services (Eliasson et al. 1990).

In a recent study, Karaomerlioglu and Carlsson (1997) analyze the development of manufacturing and producer service industries in the United States over the period 1975–95. Producer services represent some of the most knowledge-intensive activities that are a part of or closely related to manufacturing industry: for example, legal, accounting, engineering, and data processing services. Karaomerlioglu and Carlsson examine the factors that have contributed to the growth of producer services and find that unbundling, that is, the shift of some activities from manufacturing to producer services, is an important explanation for the observed pattern. They also show that the producer service industries are the most important suppliers to manufacturing and vice versa. In 1994, purchases of producer services represented 72 percent of nonmanufactured inputs to manufacturing industries, while manufactured goods represented 54 percent of nonproducer service inputs to producer service industries. At the same time, manufacturing industries purchased 67 percent of producer services sold outside the producer service industries, and these industries, in turn, purchased 28 percent of the manufactured goods sold to industries other than manufacturing itself.

Thus, the two industries should be examined jointly to understand the structural changes in the economy. The study shows that if this is done the joint employment share of manufacturing and producer services has been reduced only slightly in the United States, from 45 to 41 percent, over the period 1975–95—hardly a precipitous decline. A similar finding was reported in a recent Swedish study: the combined share of manufacturing and producer services in Sweden's GNP stayed virtually constant (varying between 44.0 and 51.0 percent, with no observable time trend), over the period 1950–91 (Sjöholm 1993).

This suggests that the widely observed "decline of manufacturing" is largely a matter of statistical definition. By using too narrow a definition of manufacturing, one is likely to miss the systems effects.

Conclusion

This essay has attempted to demonstrate that in the presence of significant knowledge spillovers among industries, firms, and other actors in the economy it is important to define the economic activities in such a way that spillovers cannot only be included in the analysis but also taken fully into account rather than being treated as externalities. Various systems approaches that have been suggested in the literature were compared briefly. The technological systems approach, representing both a dynamic and a disaggregated perspective and being technology- rather than industry- or nationally based, was discussed in more detail. The results of some simulations on a micro-to-macro model were presented, indicating that the macroeconomic effects of technological spillovers are substantial. It was also shown that the commonly observed decline of manufacturing output and employment as a share of the total economy largely disappears when the manufacturing and producer service industries are considered together as a system.

NOTES

This essay was written within the framework of the research project Sweden's Technological Systems and Future Development Potential. Financial support from the Swedish National Board for Industrial and Technical Development (Nutek) is gratefully acknowledged.

1. A closely related concept is that of competence blocs. Whereas technological systems focus on the supply side, competence blocs are defined from the demand (product or market) side as the total infrastructure needed to create, select, recognize, diffuse, and exploit new ideas in clusters of firms (Eliasson and Eliasson 1996, 14).

2. The main players in the commercial arena are usually easy to identify, and the main suppliers of material inputs are as well. The sources of immaterial (knowledge) inputs are more difficult to identify. A full mapping of all the system components may require extensive gathering of both primary data (through interviews) and secondary data concerning the educational system and other aspects of the institutional infrastructure (including public policy agencies) in each field.

3. The model was built originally by Gunnar Eliasson and colleagues at the Industrial Institute for Economic and Social Research (IUI) with important contributions in recent years by Erol Taymaz and Gérard Ballot. For an overview of the model, see Carlsson and Taymaz (1995); for a more complete description, see Eliasson (1978, 1985, 1991), Albrecht et al. (1989), Bergholm (1989), and Taymaz (1991).

REFERENCES

Abramovitz, Moses. 1956. "Resources and Output Trends in the United States since 1870." *American Economic Review* 46 (1): 5–23.
Albrecht, James, F. Bergholm, G. Eliasson, K. A. Hanson, C. Hartler, M. Heiman, T. Lindberg, and G. Olavi. 1989. *MOSES Code.* Research Report, no. 36. Stockholm: Industriens Utredningsinstitut (IUI).
Andersson, Thomas, P. Braunerhjelm, B. Carlsson, G. Eliasson, S. Fölster, L. Jagrén, E. Kazamaki Ottersten, and K. R. Sjöholm. 1993. *Den långa vägen — den ekonomiska politikens begränsningar och möjligheter att föra Sverige ur 1990-talets kris* [The long road: the limitations and possibilities for economic policy to bring Sweden out of the 1990s crisis]. Stockholm: IUI.
Bergholm, Fredrik. 1989. *MOSES Handbook.* Research Report, no. 35. Stockholm: IUI.
Blanchard, Benjamin S., and Wolter J. Fabrycky. 1990. *Systems Engineering and Analysis.* Englewood Cliffs, NJ: Prentice-Hall.
Breschi, Stefano, and Franco Malerba. 1995. "Sectoral Innovation Systems: Technological Regimes, Schumpeterian Dynamics, and Spatial Boundaries." Paper prepared for the conference Systems of Innovation Research Network, Söderköping, Sweden, 7–10 September.

Carlsson, Bo, ed. 1989. *Industrial Dynamics: Technological, Organizational, and Structural Changes in Industries and Firms.* Boston and Dordrecht: Kluwer Academic.

———, ed. 1995. *Technological Systems and Economic Performance: The Case of Factory Automation.* Boston and Dordrecht: Kluwer Academic.

———, ed. 1997. *Technological Systems and Industrial Dynamics.* Boston and Dordrecht: Kluwer Academic.

Carlsson, Bo, and Gunnar Eliasson. 1994. "The Nature and Importance of Economic Competence." *Industrial and Corporate Change* 3 (1): 687–711.

Carlsson, Bo, Gunnar Eliasson, and Erol Taymaz, 1997. "Micro-Macro Simulation of Technological Systems: Economic Effects of Spillovers." In Carlsson 1997.

Carlsson, Bo, and Rikard Stankiewicz. 1991. "On the Nature, Function, and Composition of Technological Systems." *Journal of Evolutionary Economics* 1 (2): 93–118.

Carlsson, Bo, and Erol Taymaz. 1995. "The Importance of Economic Competence in Economic Growth: A Micro-to-Macro Analysis." In Carlsson 1995.

Dahmén, Erik. 1950. *Svensk industriell företagarverksamhet* [Swedish industrial entrepreneurial activity]. Stockholm: IUI.

———. 1970. *Entrepreneurial Activity and the Development of Swedish Industry, 1919–1939.* American Economic Association Translation Series. Homewood, IL: Richard D. Irwin. Translation of Dahmén 1950.

———. 1989. " 'Development Blocks' in Industrial Economics." In Carlsson 1989.

Dosi, Giovanni, C. Freeman, R. R. Nelson, G. Silverberg and L. Soete, eds. 1988. *Technical Change and Economic Theory.* London: Pinter.

Eliasson, Gunnar, ed. 1978. *A Micro-to-Macro Model of the Swedish Economy.* IUI Conference Reports, no. 1978:1. Stockholm: IUI.

———. 1984. "Micro Heterogeneity of Firms and Stability of Growth." *Journal of Economic Behavior and Organization* 5:249–74.

———. 1985. *The Firm and Financial Markets in the Swedish Micro-to-Macro Model: Theory, Model, and Verification.* Stockholm: IUI.

———. 1990. "The Firm as a Competent Team." *Journal of Economic Behavior and Organization* 13 (3): 273–98.

———. 1991. "Modeling the Experimentally Organized Economy: Complex Dynamics in an Empirical Micro-Macro Model of Endogenous Economic Growth." *Journal of Economic Behavior and Organization* 16 (1–2): 153–82.

———. 1995. *Teknologigenerator eller nationellt prestigeprojekt? Exemplet svensk flygindustri* [Technology generator or a national prestige project? The example of the Swedish aircraft industry]. Stockholm: City University Press.

———. 1997. "General Purpose Technologies, Industrial Competence, and Economic Growth—with Special Emphasis on the Diffusion of Advanced Methods of Integrated Production." In Carlsson 1997.

Eliasson, Gunnar, and Åsa Eliasson. 1996. "The Biotechnological Competence Bloc." *Revue d'Économie Industrielle* 78 (4): 7–20.

Eliasson, Gunnar, S. Fölster, T. Lindberg. T. Pousette, and E. Taymaz. 1990. *The Knowledge Based Information Economy.* Stockholm: IUI.

English, J. Morley. 1972. *Economics of Engineering Social Systems.* New York: Wiley.

Fransman, Martin. 1990. *The Market and Beyond: Cooperation and Competition in*

Information Technology in the Japanese System. Cambridge: Cambridge University Press.

Freeman, Christopher. 1988. "Japan: A New National System of Innovation?" In Dosi et al. 1988.

Karaomerlioglu, Dilek C., and Bo Carlsson. 1997. "Manufacturing in Decline? A Matter of Definition." Working paper, Department of Economics, Case Western Reserve University, February. Mimeo.

Klein, Burton H. 1977. *Dynamic Economics.* Cambridge: Harvard University Press.

Leontief, Wassily W. 1941. *The Structure of the American Economy, 1919–1929: An Empirical Application of Equilibrium Analysis.* Cambridge: Harvard University Press.

Lucas, Robert. 1988. "On the Mechanics of Economic Development." *Journal of Monetary Economics* 22 (1): 3–42.

Lundvall, Bengt-Åke. 1988. "Innovation as an Interactive Process: From User-Supplier Interaction to the National System of Innovation." In Dosi et al. 1988.

———, ed. 1992. *National Systems of Innovation: Towards a Theory of Innovation and Interactive Learning.* London: Pinter.

Malerba, Franco, and Luigi Orsenigo. 1990. "Technological Regimes and Patterns of Innovation: A Theoretical and Empirical Investigation of the Italian Case." In *Evolving Technology and Market Structure,* edited by A. Heertje and M. Perlman. Ann Arbor: University of Michigan Press.

———. 1993. "Technological Regimes and Firm Behavior." *Industrial and Corporate Change* 2 (1): 45–71.

———. 1995. "Schumpeterian Patterns of Innovation." *Cambridge Journal of Economics.* 19 (1) (February): 47–65.

Nelson, Richard R. 1988a. "National Systems of Innovation: Preface." In Dosi et al. 1988.

———. 1988b. "Institutions Supporting Technical Change in the United States." In Dosi et al. 1988.

———. ed. 1993. *National Systems of Innovation: A Comparative Analysis.* Oxford: Oxford University Press.

Porter, Michael E. 1990. *The Competitive Advantage of Nations.* New York: Free Press.

Romer, Paul. 1986. "Increasing Returns and Long-Run Growth." *Journal of Political Economy* 94:1002–37.

———. 1990. "Endogenous Technological Change." *Journal of Political Economy* 98 (1): 71–102.

———. 1993. "Idea Gaps and Object Gaps in Economic Development." *Journal of Monetary Economics* 32:543–73.

Saxenian, AnnaLee. 1994. *Regional Advantage: Culture and Competition in Silicon Valley and Route 128.* Cambridge: Harvard University Press.

Sjöholm, Kent Rune. 1993. "Den reviderade industrisektorn" [The manufacturing sector revised]. Appendix 1 in Andersson et al. 1993.

Solow, Robert M. 1956. "A Contribution to the Theory of Economic Growth." *Quarterly Journal of Economics* 70 (1): 65–94.

Taymaz, Erol. 1991. *MOSES on PC: Manual, Initialization, Calibration.* Stockholm: IUI.

Knowledge Sources in Biotechnology through the Schumpeterian Lens

David B. Audretsch and Paula E. Stephan

Joseph Schumpeter emphasized throughout his works that the links between sources of knowledge, how that knowledge is appropriated, and who appropriates it are anything but trivial. In his 1911 treatise, Schumpeter argued that the gap between those firms creating knowledge and those appropriating it triggered a process of creative destruction. But by 1942 Schumpeter had modified his theory, arguing instead that: "innovation itself is being reduced to routine. Technological progress is increasingly becoming the business of teams of trained specialists who turn out what is required to make it work in predictable ways" (132). According to this later Schumpeter (1942), the integration of knowledge creation and appropriation bestowed an inherent innovative advantage upon giant corporations: "Since capitalist enterprise, by its very achievements, tends to automize progress, we conclude that it tends to make itself superfluous— to break to pieces under the pressure of its own success. The perfectly bureaucratic giant industrial unit not only ousts the small- or medium-sized firm and 'expropriates' its owners, but in the end it also ousts the entrepreneur and expropriates the bourgeoisie as a class which in the process stands to lose not only its income but also, what is infinitely more important, its function" (134). In linking knowledge inputs, incentives for appropriation, and innovative output together within the boundaries of the large corporation, Schumpeter anticipated what more recently has been termed by Zvi Griliches (1979) the *model of the knowledge production function.*

As we showed in our 1996 paper, upon which this essay is based, in recent years a large number of start-up companies have developed in biotechnology. These new biotech start-ups are examples of a broader class of firms, which depend for birth and growth on knowledge inputs (Audretsch 1995). The existence and continued growth of such biotechnology firms seemingly challenges the model of the knowledge production function, which was expressed by Schumpeter some 50 years ago. Where do such new and small firms obtain the requisite knowledge inputs?

The purpose of this essay is to determine whether the earlier or later Schumpeter was correct. We do this by examining sources of new knowledge and the incentives confronting economic agents in biotechnology. In particular, we use a new data base, drawn from the prospectuses of initial public offerings, to examine the founders of biotechnology firms and compare them with other university scientists linked to biotechnology firms.

The results suggest that the earlier Schumpeter may have been more prescient than the later Schumpeter. While the knowledge production function may still hold, it apparently does not hold in the manner implied by Schumpeter's writings in 1942. Instead of becoming routinized, innovative activity, at least in biotechnology, has led to a considerable chasm between those entities creating new economic knowledge and those appropriating it. Thus, new economic knowledge can be observed to *spill over* from the source and be applied by third-party agents and firms.

New Economic Knowledge

Production

The starting point for most theories of innovation is the firm.[1] In such theories, the firms are exogenous and their performance in generating technological change is endogenous.[2] For example, in the most prevalent model found in the literature of technological change, the model of the *knowledge production function,* formalized by Zvi Griliches (1979), firms exist exogenously and then engage in the pursuit of new economic knowledge as an input into the process of generating innovative activity.

The most decisive input in the knowledge production function is new economic knowledge. And, as Cohen and Klepper conclude, the greatest source generating new economic knowledge is generally considered to be R&D.[3] Certainly a large body of empirical work has found a strong and positive relationship between knowledge inputs such as R&D, on the one hand, and innovative outputs on the other.

The knowledge production function has been found to hold most strongly at broader levels of aggregation. The most innovative countries are those with the greatest investments to R&D. Little innovative output is associated with less-developed countries, which are characterized by a paucity of production of new economic knowledge. Similarly, the most innovative industries also tend to be characterized by considerable investments in R&D and new economic knowledge. Not only are industries such as computers, pharmaceuticals, and instruments high in R&D inputs that generate new economic knowledge, but they also are high in terms of innovative outputs (Audretsch 1995). By contrast, industries with little R&D, such as wood products, textiles, and paper, tend to produce only a negligible amount of innovative output. Thus, the knowledge production model linking knowledge-generating inputs to outputs certainly holds at the more aggregated levels of economic activity.

Where the relationship becomes less compelling is at the disaggregated microeconomic level of the enterprise, establishment, or even line of business. For example, While Audretsch (1995) found that the simple correlation between R&D inputs and innovative output was 0.84 for four-digit standard industrial classification (SIC) manufacturing industries in the United States, it was only about half, 0.40 among the largest U.S. corporations.

The model of the knowledge production function becomes even less compelling in view of the recent wave of studies revealing that small enterprises serve as the engine of innovative activity in certain industries. These results are startling, because, as Scherer (1991) observes, the bulk of industrial R&D is undertaken in the largest corporations; small enterprises account for only a minor share of R&D inputs. Thus, the knowledge production function seemingly implies that, as the *Schumpeterian hypothesis* predicts, innovative activity favors those organizations with access to knowledge-producing inputs—the large incumbent organization. The more recent evidence identifying strong innovative activity raises the question of where new and small firms get their innovation-producing inputs, that is, their knowledge.

One answer, proposed by Audretsch (1995), is that, although the model of the knowledge production function may still be valid, the implicitly assumed unit of observation—at the level of the firm—may be less valid. The reason why the knowledge production function holds more closely for more aggregated degrees of observation may be that investment in R&D and other sources of new knowledge spills over for economic exploitation by third-party firms.

The Appropriability Problem Revisited

A large literature has emerged focusing on what has become known as the *appropriability problem*.[4] The underlying issue revolves around how firms that invest in the creation of new economic knowledge can best appropriate the economic returns from that knowledge (Arrow 1962). Audretsch (1995) proposes shifting the unit of observation away from exogenously assumed firms to individuals—agents with endowments of new economic knowledge. As J. de V. Graaf (1957) observed nearly four decades ago:

> When we try to construct a transformation function for society as a whole from those facing the individual firms comprising it, a fundamental difficulty confronts us. There is, from a welfare point of view, nothing special about the firms actually existing in an economy at a given moment of time. The firm is in no sense a 'natural unit'. Only the individual members of the economy can lay claim to that distinction. All are potential entrepreneurs. It seems, therefore, that the natural thing to do is to build up from the transformation function of men, rather than the firms, constituting an economy. If we are interested in eventual empirical determination, this is extremely inconvenient. But it has conceptual advantages. The ultimate repositories of

technological knowledge in any society are the men comprising it, and it is just this knowledge which is effectively summarized in the form of a transformation function. In itself a firm possesses no knowledge. That which is available to it belongs to the men associated with it. Its production function is really built up in exactly the same way, and from the same basic ingredients, as society's.

But when the lens is shifted away from focusing upon the firm as the relevant unit of observation to individuals, the relevant question becomes: *how can economic agents with a given endowment of new knowledge best appropriate the returns from that knowledge?*

The appropriability problem confronting the individual may converge with that confronting the firm. Economic agents can and do work for firms, and, even if they do not, they can potentially be employed by an incumbent firm. In fact, in a model of perfect information with no agency costs, any positive economies of scale or scope will ensure that the appropriability problems of the firm and individual converge. If an agent has an idea for doing something different than is currently being practiced by the incumbent enterprises—both in terms of a new product or process and in terms of organization—the idea, which can be termed an innovation, will be presented to the incumbent enterprise. Because of the assumption of perfect knowledge, both the firm and the agent would agree upon the expected value of the innovation. But, to the degree that any economies of scale or scope exist, the expected value of implementing the innovation within the incumbent enterprise will exceed that of taking the innovation outside of the incumbent firm to start a new enterprise. Thus, the incumbent firm and the inventor of the idea would be expected to reach a bargain splitting the value added to the firm contributed by the innovation. The payment to the inventor—either in terms of a higher wage or some other means of remuneration—would be bounded between the expected value of the innovation, if it is implemented by the incumbent enterprise on the upper end, and by the return that the agent could expect to earn if he used it to launch a new enterprise on the lower end. Or, as Frank Knight (1921, 273) observed more than 70 years ago: "The laborer asks what he thinks the entrepreneur will be able to pay, and in any case will not accept less than he can get from some other entrepreneur, or by turning entrepreneur himself. In the same way the entrepreneur offers to any laborer what he thinks he must in order to secure his services, and in any case not more than he thinks the laborer will actually be worth to him, keeping in mind what he can get by turning laborer himself."

Thus, each economic agent would choose how to best appropriate the value of his endowment of economic knowledge by comparing the wage he would earn if he remains employed by an incumbent enterprise, w, to the expected net present discounted value of the profits accruing from starting a new firm, π. If these two values are relatively close, the probability that he would choose to appropriate the value of his knowledge through an external mechanism such as starting a new firm, *Pr(e),* would be relatively low. On the other hand, as the gap between w and π becomes larger, the likelihood of an agent choosing to appropriate the value of his knowledge externally by starting a new enterprise becomes greater, or

$$Pr(e) = f(\pi - w) \tag{1}$$

Asymmetric Knowledge, Transaction Costs,
and the Principal-Agent Relationship

As Knight (1921), and later Arrow (1962) emphasized, new economic knowledge is anything but certain. Not only is new economic knowledge inherently risky, but substantial asymmetries exist across agents both between and within firms (Milgrom and Roberts 1987). This is to say that the expected value of a new idea, or what has been termed here a potential innovation, is likely to be anything but unanimous between the inventor of that idea and the decision maker, or group of decision makers,[5] of the firm confronted with evaluating proposed changes or innovations. In fact, it is because information is not only imperfect but also asymmetric that Knight (1921, 268) argued that the primary task of the firm is to process information in order to reach a decision: "With the introduction of uncertainty—the fact of ignorance and the necessity of acting upon opinion rather than knowledge—into this Eden-like situation (that is a world of perfect information), its character is entirely changed. . . . With uncertainty present doing things, the actual execution of activity, becomes in a real sense a secondary part of life; the primary problem or function is deciding what to do and how to do it."

Alchian (1950) pointed out that the existence of knowledge asymmetries would result in the inevitability of mistaken decisions in an uncertain world. Later, Alchian and Demsetz (1972) attributed the existence of asymmetric information across the employees in a firm as resulting in a problem of monitoring the contribution accruing from each employee and setting the rewards correspondingly. This led them to conclude that: "The problem of economic organization is the economical means of metering productivity and rewards" (783).

Combined with the bureaucratic organization of incumbent firms to make a decision, the asymmetry of knowledge leads to a host of agency problems spanning incentive structures, monitoring, and transaction costs. It is the existence of such agency costs, combined with asymmetric information, that not only provides an incentive for agents with new ideas to appropriate the expected value of their knowledge externally by starting new firms but also offers a propensity that varies systematically from industry to industry.

Coase (1937), and later Williamson (1975), argued that the size of an (incumbent) enterprise will be determined by answering the question Coase (1937, 30) articulated: "The question always is, will it pay to bring an extra exchange transaction under the organizing authority?" In fact, Coase (24) pointed out that: "Other things being equal, a firm will tend to be larger the less likely the (firm) is to make mistakes and the smaller the increase in mistakes with an increase in the transactions organized."

Holmstrom (1989) and Milgrom (1988) have pointed out the existence of what they term a *bureaucratization dilemma,* where: "To say that increased size brings increased bureaucracy is a safe generalization. To note that bureaucracy is viewed as an organizational disease is equally accurate" (Holmstrom 1989, 320).

To minimize agency problems and the cost of monitoring, bureaucratic hierarchies develop objective rules. In addition, Kreps (1991) has argued that such bureaucratic rules promote internal uniformity and that a uniform corporate culture, in turn, promotes the reputation of the firm. These bureaucratic rules, however, make it more difficult to evaluate the efforts and activities of agents involved in activities that do not conform to such bureaucratic rules. As Holmstrom (1989, 323) points out: "Monitoring limitations suggest that the firm seeks out activities which are more easily and objectively evaluated. Assignments will be chosen in a fashion that are conducive to more effective control. Authority and command systems work better in environments which are more predictable and can be directed with less investment information. Routine tasks are the comparative advantage of a bureaucracy and its activities can be expected to reflect that."

Williamson (1975, 201) has also emphasized the inherent tension between hierarchical bureaucratic organizations and the ability of incumbent organizations to appropriate the value of new knowledge for innovative activity outside of the technological trajectories associated with the core competence of that organization: "Were it that large firms could compensate internal entrepreneurial activity in ways approximating that of the market, the large firm need experience no disadvantage in entrepreneurial respects. Violating the congruency between hierarchical position and compensation appears to generate bureaucratic strains, however, and is greatly complicated by the problem of accurately imputing causality." This leads Williamson (205–6) to conclude: "I am inclined to regard the early stage innovative disabilities of large size as serious and propose the following hypothesis: An efficient procedure by which to introduce new products is for the initial development and market testing to be performed by independent investors and small firms (perhaps new entrants) in an industry, the successful developments then to be acquired, possibly through licensing or merger, for subsequent marketing by a large multidivision enterprise. . . . Put differently, a division of effort between the new product innovation process on the one hand, and the management of proven resources on the other may well be efficient."

This model analyzing the decision of how best to appropriate the value of new economic knowledge confronting an individual economic agent seems useful when considering the actual decision to a new firm taken by entrepreneurs. For example, Chester Carlsson started Xerox after his proposal to produce a (new) copy machine was rejected by Kodak. Kodak based its decision on the premise that the new copy machine would not earn very much money, and in any case Kodak was in a different line of business—photography. It is perhaps no small irony that this same entrepreneurial start-up, Xerox, decades later turned down a proposal from Steven Jobs to produce and market a personal computer because it did not think that a personal computer would sell and, in any case, it was in a different line of business—copy machines (Carrol 1993). After 17 other companies turned down Jobs for virtually identical reasons, including IBM and Hewlett Packard, he resorted to starting his own company, Apple.

Similarly, IBM turned down an offer from Bill Gates, "the chance to buy ten percent of Microsoft for a song in 1986, a missed opportunity that would cost $3 billion today."[6] IBM reached its decision on the grounds that "neither Gates nor any of his band of thirty some employees had anything approaching the credentials or personal characteristics required to work at IBM."[7]

Divergences in beliefs with respect to the value of a new idea need not be restricted to what is formally known as a product or even a process innovation. Rather, the fact that economic agents choose to start a new firm due to divergences in the expected value of an idea applies to the sphere of managerial style and organization as well. One of the most vivid examples involves Bob Noyce, who founded Intel. Noyce had been employed by Fairchild Semiconductor, which is credited with being the pioneering semiconductor firm. In 1957, Noyce and seven other engineers quit en masse from Schockley Semiconductor to form Fairchild Semiconductor, an enterprise that in turn is considered the start of what is today known as Silicon Valley. Although Fairchild Semiconductor had "possibly the most potent management and technical team ever assembled" (Gilder 1989, 89), "Noyce couldn't get Fairchild's eastern owners to accept the idea that stock options should be part of compensation for all employees, not just for management. He wanted to tie everyone, from janitors to bosses, into the overall success of the company. . . . This management style still sets the standard for every computer, software, and semiconductor company in the Valley today. . . . Every CEO still wants to think that the place is run the way Bob Noyce would have run it" (Cringley 1993, 39). That is, Noyce's vision of the firm excluded the dress codes, reserved parking places, closed offices, and executive dining rooms, along with the other trappings of status that were standard in virtually every hierarchical and bureaucratic

U.S. corporation. But when he tried to impress this vision upon the owners of Fairchild Semiconductor he was flatly rejected. The formation of Intel in 1968 was the ultimate result of the divergence in beliefs about how to organize and manage a firm.

The key development at Intel was the microprocessor. When longtime IBM employee Ted Hoff approached IBM and later DEC with his new microprocessor in the late 1960s, "IBM and DEC decided there was no market. They could not imagine why anyone would need or want a small computer; if people wanted to use a computer, they could hook into time-sharing systems" (Palfreman and Swade 1991, 108).

The Geography of Sources and Incentives

Sources

The emergence of a recent literature (re)discovering the importance of economic geography[8] might seem paradoxical in a world increasingly dominated by e-mail, faxes, and electronic communications superhighways. Why should geographic proximity matter when technology has advanced in a manner that has drastically reduced the cost of transmitting information across geographic space? The answer posited by Audretsch and Feldman (1996), Audretsch and Stephan (1996), and Feldman (1994a, 1994b) is based on a key distinction between *information,* on the one hand, and *tacit knowledge* on the other. While the cost of transmitting information may be invariant to distant, the cost of transmitting knowledge, especially tacit knowledge, rises along with distance.[9] Geographic location and proximity to the source matter in the transmission of tacit knowledge because face-to-face contact is the most effective and economical mode of transfer. Thus, Glaeser, Kallal, Scheinkman, and Schleifer (1991, 1127) characterize the Marshall-Arrow-Romer model as suggesting that "intellectual breakthroughs must cross hallways more easily than oceans and continents."

This model is consistent with anecdotal evidence. For example, a survey of nearly 1,000 executives located in America's 60 largest metropolitan areas ranked Raleigh/Durham as the best city for knowledge workers and innovative activity.[10] *Fortune* reports: "A lot of brainy types who made their way to Raleigh/Durham were drawn by three top research universities. . . . U.S. businesses, especially those whose success depends on staying atop new technologies and processes, increasingly want to be where hot new ideas are percolating. A presence in brain-power centers like Raleigh/Durham pays off in new products and new ways of doing business. . . . Dozens of small biotechnology and software operations are starting up each year and growing like *kudzu* in the fertile business climate."[11]

Considerable evidence has been found suggesting that location and proximity clearly matter in exploiting knowledge spillovers. Not only have Jaffe, Trajtenberg, and Henderson (1993) found that patent citations tend to occur more frequently within the state in which they were patented than outside of that state, but Audretsch and Feldman (1996) found that the propensity of innovative activity to cluster geographically tends to be greater in industries in which new economic knowledge plays a more important role.

In studying the networks in California's Silicon Valley, Saxenian (1990, 96–97) emphasizes that it is communication between individuals that facilitates the transmission of knowledge across agents, firms, and even industries, and not just the high endowment of workers' knowledge that is conducive to innovative activity.

> It is not simply the concentration of skilled labor, suppliers and information that distinguish the region. A variety of regional institutions— including Stanford University, several trade associations and local business organizations, and a myriad of specialized consulting, market research, public relations and venture capital firms—provide technical, financial, and networking services which the region's enterprises often cannot afford individually. These networks defy sectoral barriers: individuals move easily from semiconductor to disk drive firms or from computer to network makers. They move from established firms to startups (or visa versa) and even to market research or consulting firms, and from consulting firms back into startups. And they continue to meet at trade shows, industry conferences, and the scores of seminars, talks, and social activities organized by local business organizations and trade associations. In these forums, relationships are easily formed and maintained, technical and market information is exchanged, business contacts are established, and new enterprises are conceived. . . . This decentralized and fluid environment also promotes the diffusion of intangible technological capabilities and understandings.[12]

Of particular importance in providing a source of innovation-generating knowledge are research scientists at universities. Jaffe (1989) and Audretsch and Feldman (1996) find that knowledge created in university laboratories spills over to the generation of commercial innovations in the private sector. This evidence suggests that spillovers from university research contribute substantially to the innovative activity of private corporations. Similarly, Link and Rees (1990) find that private corporations are able to exploit their university-based associations to generate innovations.

Biotechnology companies are overwhelmingly defined by their scientists. Many of these scientists, particularly senior scientists with strong reputations, do not work for the company full time but instead are members of university faculties. These university-based scientists fulfill a variety of roles within biotechnology companies. Some are founders, others serve as members of scientific advisory boards (SABs), while still others serve as directors of an SAB.

The degree of knowledge and the nature of that knowledge, in terms of whether it is comprised of a relatively high degree of tacit knowledge or information, varies according to the role played by the scientist. Founders of new biotechnology firms presumably seek out venture capitalists in order to appropriate the expected economic value of their tacit knowledge. By contrast, scientific advisers provide links between scientific founders and other researchers doing work in the area. In particular, they provide a signal of firm quality to the scientific and financial communities. An effective way to recruit young scientists is to have an SAB composed of the leaders in the field. George B. Rathman, president and CEO of Amgen, attributes much of the company's success to an SAB of "great credibility" whose "members were willing to share the task of interviewing the candidates for scientific positions." Rathman goes on to point out that the young scientists that Amgen recruited would not have come "without the knowledge that an outstanding scientific advisory board took Amgen seriously" (quoted in Burrill 1987, 77).

Thus, the geographic dimension of the link between a scientist and a biotechnology firm should be shaped by the nature and quality of the knowledge inherent in the role played by the scientist. If the scientist is involved in the transfer of scientific knowledge with a relatively high component of tacit knowledge—as will be the case when the scientist is a founder of the firm—he should tend to be located in the same geographic region as the firm. By contrast, when the scientist is involved in the transfer of information for signaling purposes—as will be the case when he is a member of a SAB—he does not have to be located in the same region as the firm. Thus, the exact geography of the linkages between scientists and biotechnology firms should reflect the underlying role played by the scientist and the type of information or knowledge that is being transferred.

Incentives

A necessary condition for a scientist to work with a biotechnology firm is that the firm be aware of the capabilities of the scientist. The dispersion of such information is clearly shaped by the geographic breadth of the scientist's network (contacts). Scientists with limited networks are more likely to be constrained to participate within a local rather than a nonlocal sphere. This suggests that, other things being equal, a younger person is more likely to be involved with a local than with a nonlocal firm.

The career life-cycle theory of scientists developed by Levin and Stephan (1991), Stephan and Levin (1992), and Stephan (1996) suggests that the incentives confronting scientists to appropriate the value of their human knowledge shapes the decision to invest in basic research versus commercialization. According to these theories, in the early stages of their lives scientists invest in human capital in order to build a reputation, while in the later stages of their careers scientists trade or *cash in* their reputation for economic return. That is, early in their careers, scientists invest in the creation of knowledge in order to establish a reputation reflecting the scientific value of that new knowledge; with maturity, scientists cash in by seeking ways to appropriate the economic value of that new knowledge.

The life-cycle theory of scientific careers implies that the younger scientists who have a higher opportunity cost of being absent from their laboratories will tend to focus on contacts with private companies within their own geographic regions. By contrast, older scientists should tend to have a greater propensity to travel outside their regions.

Evidence

Measurement

To identify the links between knowledge sources, the incentives confronting individual scientists, and where the knowledge is commercialized, we rely upon a data base developed by Paula Stephan and documented in Audretsch and Stephan (1996). The data base consists of data collected from the prospectuses of biotechnology companies that prepared an initial public offering (IPO) in the United States between March 1990 and November 1992. The firms and their locations are listed in table 1. A total of 54 firms affiliated with 445 university-based scientists were identified during this time period. By carefully reading the prospectuses, it was possible to identify the names of university-based scientists affiliated with each firm, the role that each scientist plays in the firm, and the name and location of their home institutions. Universities and firms were then grouped into regions, which are generally larger than a single city but considerably smaller than a state. Certain areas, for example, metropolitan New York, cross several state lines.

Role of Scientists

Only 138 of the 445 links observed between scientists and biotechnology companies are local in that the scientist and firm are located in the same region. This suggests that geographic proximity does not play an important role for links between biotechnology companies and scientists in general. However, as table 2 shows, the geographic link between the scientist and the founder is influenced by the particular role played by the scientist in working with the firm. Most strikingly, 57.9 percent of the scientist-firm links were local when the scientist was a founder of the firm, while 42.1 percent were nonlocal. By contrast, when the scientist served as a member

TABLE 1. Location of Biotech Firms by Region

Firm	Number of University-Based Scientists	Scientists from within Region Number	%
San Francisco Bay Area, CA			
Anergen	5	4	80.0
Applied Immune Sciences	8	1	12.5
Biocircutis	4	2	50.0
Biotime	6	2	33.3
Cell Genesis	16	2	12.5
COR Therapeutics	15	5	33.3
Cygnus	5	1	20.0
Genelabs Technologies	13	6	46.2
Genpharm	15	0	0.0
Gilead Sciences	7	1	14.3
Neurex	22	6	27.3
Oclassen Pharmaceuticals	7	1	14.3
Protein Design Labs	7	4	57.1
Sciclone	8	7	87.5
Systemix	7	2	28.9
Total	145	44	30.3
San Diego, CA			
Amylin	10	3	30.0
Corvas	9	3	33.3
Cytel	9	1	33.3
Genta	19	1	5.2
Idec Pharmaceuticals	2	1	50.0
Immune Response	7	2	28.6
Ligand Pharmaceuticals	7	4	57.1
Protein Polymer Technologie	7	1	14.3
Vical	7	3	42.3
Total	77	21	27.2
Boston, MA			
Alpha-Beta Technology	7	7	100.0
Cambridge Neuroscience	10	4	40.0
Creative Biomolecules	11	4	36.4
Cytotherapeutics	14	4	28.6
Epigen	8	2	25.0
Immulogie	11	5	45.5
Matritech	8	3	37.5
Sepracor	7	3	42.8
Seragen	3	3	100.0
Vertex Pharmaceuticals	6	6	100.0
Total	85	41	48.2

TABLE 1—*Continued*

Firm	Number of University-Based Scientists	Scientists from within Region	
		Number	%
Philadelphia, PA			
Affinity Biotech	5	1	20.0
Cephalon	5	1	20.0
DNX	5	2	40.0
Magainin Pharmaceuticals	6	2	33.3
Medarex	6	0	0.0
Zynaxis	4	2	50.0
Total	31	8	25.8
Metropolitan New York			
Alteon	6	4	66.6
Biomatrix	6	1	16.7
Biospecifics Technologies	5	2	40.0
Medicis	9	0	0.0
Regeneron Pharmaceuticals	13	2	15.4
Total	39	9	23.0
State of Maryland			
Genetic Therapy	7	0	—
Univax Biologics	6	1	16.7
Total	13	1	7.7
Seattle, WA			
Cell Pro	7	2	28.6
Boulder, CO			
Somatogen	4	1	25.0
State of Kansas			
Deprenyl	6	0	0.0
Research Triangle, NC			
Sphinx Pharmaceuticals	6	2	33.3
Los Angeles, CA			
Watson Pharmaceuticals	9	0	0.0
Dallas, TX			
Corntech	10	1	10.0
Houston, TX			
Argus Pharmaceuticals	13	8	61.5
TOTAL	445	138	31.0

TABLE 2.   Role of Scientist

	Founder	SAB	Major Stock
Nonlocal	16	249	20
($n = 307$)	(42.1)	(68.2)	(51.3)
Local	22	116	19
($n = 138$)	(57.9)	(31.8)	(48.7)
Total	38	365	39
χ^2	14.04**	.562	5.25*

* Significant at the .02 level or better.
** Significant at the .01 level or better.

on the SAB, only 31.8 percent of the links were local, while 68.2 percent were nonlocal. This disparity suggests that the nature of the knowledge transmitted between the university and the biotechnology firm may be different between scientists serving as founders and those serving on a SAB. Presumably it is the difference in the nature and quality of the knowledge being transferred from the university to the company that dictates a higher propensity for local proximity in the case of the founders, but not for SAB members.

Scientist Incentives

In addition to the role played by the scientist in working with a biotechnology company, the incentives confronting the scientist may also shape whether the firm-scientist link is local or not. The results in Audretsch and Stephan (1996) suggest that, as the theory predicts, the specific role played by the scientist in the biotechnology firm clearly shapes the geographic dimension of the contact. In particular, those scientists serving as founders of biotechnology firms have a significantly higher propensity to be located in the same region as the firm than do those who are not founders. According to the marginal effect, a shift in status from nonfounder to founder increases the likelihood of a contact being local by more than 20 percent. The combined impact of serving as a founder or chair of a SAB is slightly larger.

In addition, several variables reflecting the impact of the life cycle on incentives to engage in a local versus long-distance link are included. The negative and statistical coefficient of the age variable suggests that older scientists have a greater incentive than do their younger counterparts to engage in contacts with biotechnology firms located outside of the regions of their universities. The marginal effect of an additional year is to increase the probability of a scientist commuting by 0.6 percent. This means that the impact of an additional decade is to increase the probability of a scientist commuting by 6.0 percent.

In addition, having been awarded a Nobel Prize significantly increases the propensity for the scientist to engage in local contacts with biotechnology firms. This may reflect the willingness of venture capitalists and other key members of new biotechnology start-ups to locate close to a Nobel Prize recipient, thereby suggesting that, for scientific start-ups, drawing power overwhelms general reputational effects. On the other hand, there is no evidence that the citation history of a scientist influences the propensity of a scientist to engage in local versus nonlocal contacts. This presumably reflects the offsetting effects of reputation and drawing power.

To control for any specific regional effects, two dummy variables, the first taking on a value of one for scientists located in California and the other taking on a value of one for scientists located in the Northeast, are included. Inclusion of these regional-specific dummies suggests that scientists located in the Northeast tend to be insular in their propensity to engage in contacts with firms located in their specific area. This does not appear to be the case for scientists located in California.

Conclusions

One of the puzzles in the literature on innovation and technological change is that small and new firms are able to innovate even in the absence of substantial investments in R&D. The presence of innovative output without knowledge-generating inputs seemingly contradicts the main assumption underlying the knowledge production function. One resolution of this paradox is that new economic knowledge spills over from the source creating that knowledge to independent agents or firms.

But how exactly do such knowledge spillovers take place, and what are the mechanisms by which knowledge created by one economic entity is transmitted to a different entity? While the previous literature has had little to say about the actual mechanisms facilitating knowledge externalities, this essay suggests at least one mechanism—through the networks created by scientists in linking firms with knowledge creating at universities. Because a fair number of these scientists not only work with biotechnology firms but actually found the firms, this also suggests that the assumption underlying the model of the knowledge production function may not always be valid. The findings in this essay challenge the assumption implicit in the knowledge production function—that firms exist exogenously and then endogenously seek out and apply (knowledge) inputs to generate innovative output. Although this may be valid some, if not most, of the time, our results suggest that, at least in some cases, it is the knowledge embodied in individual economic agents and groups of economic agents that is *exogenous,* and in an effort to appropriate the returns from that knowledge the spillover of knowledge from its source involves *endogenously* creating a new firm.

But if new economic knowledge does in fact spill over beyond the boundaries of the source, what keeps it from continuing to spill over across geographic space? After all, there is surely no physical equivalent of the Berlin Wall impeding the flow of knowledge beyond city, county, state, and even country borders. That is, why should new economic knowledge stop spilling over once the process has started? As the *Economist* points out: "The death of distance as a determinant of the cost of communications will probably be the single most important economic force shaping society in the first half of the next century . . . [since] any activity that relies on a screen or a telephone can be carried out anywhere in the world."[13]

But to conclude that the telecommunications revolution has trivialized the economic cost of transmitting information across geographic space is to confuse the crucial distinction between information and tacit knowledge. Perhaps an unanticipated impact of the telecommunications revolution has been to shift the comparative advantage of high-cost, knowledge-rich countries away from information-intensive economic activities and toward knowledge-intensive activities.

Such a view is consistent with the findings that the importance of geographic proximity is clearly shaped by the role played by the scientist. This presumably reflects qualitative differences in the types of information and knowledge transferred from the universities to biotechnology firms by scientists. Geographic proximity to the source matters when knowledge spillovers are informal and tacit in nature. But, when information is transmitted through formal ties between scientists and firms, geographic proximity is not necessary, since face-to-face contact does not occur by chance but instead is carefully planned.

NOTES

An earlier version of this essay was presented at the 1996 International Schumpeter Society meetings, June 3–5, 1996, Stockholm, Sweden. We are grateful to the participants for helpful suggestions and comments. All errors and omissions remain our responsibility.

1. For reviews of this literature, see Baldwin and Scott (1987), Cohen and Levin (1989), Scherer (1984, 1992), and Dosi (1988).

2. See, for example, Scherer (1984, 1991), Cohen and Klepper (1991, 1992a, 1992b), and Arrow (1962, 1983).

3. Cohen and Klepper (1991, 1992a, 1992b).

4. See Cohen and Levin (1989) and Baldwin and Scott (1987).

5. For example, as of 1993 a proposal for simply modifying an existing product at IBM had to pass through 250 layers of decision making to gain approval ("Überfördert und Unregierbar," *Der Spiegel,* no. 14, 1993, 127).

6. "System Error," *The Economist,* September 18, 1993, 99.

7. Paul Carrol (1993), "Die Offene Schlacht," *Die Zeit,* no. 39, September 24, 18.

8. See for examples Krugman (1991a, 1991b), Lucas (1993), Romer (1990), Audretsch and Feldman (1996), Feldman (1994a, 1994b), and Audretsch and Stephan (1996).

9. *Fortune* ("The Best Cities for Knowledge Workers," November 15, 1993, 44–57) notes that "business is a social activity, and you have to be where important work is taking place" (46).

10. The survey was carried out in 1993 by the management consulting firm of Moran, Stahl, & Boyer of New York City.

11. *Fortune* (see n. 9) also reports: "What makes the (triangle) park work so well is a unique nexus of the business community, area universities, and state and local governments. . . . It is home to more than 34,000 scientists and researchers and over 50 corporate academic and government tenants specializing in microelectronics, telecommunications, chemicals, biotechnology, pharmaceuticals, and environmental helath sciences" (46).

12. Saxenian (1990, 97–98) claims that even the language and vocabulary used by technical specialists is specific to a region: "[A] distinct language has evolved in the region and certain technical terms used by semiconductor production engineers in Silicon Valley would not even be understood by their counterparts in Boston's Route 128."

13. "The Death of Distance," *Economist,* September 30, 1995, 39.

REFERENCES

Alchian, Almerin. 1950. "Uncertainty, Evolution, and Economic Theory." *Journal of Political Economy* 58:211–21.

Alchian, Almerin, and H. Demsetz. 1972. "Production, Information Costs, and Economic Organization." *American Economic Review* 62:777–95.

Arrow, Kenneth J. 1962. "Economic Welfare and the Allocation of Resources for Invention." In *The Rate and Direction of Inventive Activity,* edited by R. R. Nelson. Princeton: Princeton University Press.

———. 1983. "Innovation in Large and Small Firms." In *Entrepreneurship,* edited by J. Ronen. Lexington, MA: Lexington Books.

Audretsch, David B. 1995. *Innovation and Industry Evolution.* Cambridge: MIT Press.

Audretsch, David B., and Maryann P. Feldman. 1996. "R&D Spillovers and the Geography of Innovation and Production." *American Economic Review* 86, no. 3: 630–40.

Audretsch, David B., and Paula E. Stephan. 1996. "Company-Scientist Locational Links: The Case of Biotechnology." *American Economic Review* 86, no. 3: 641–52.

Baldwin, William L., and John T. Scott. 1987. *Market Structure and Technological Change.* New York: Harwood Academic.

Burrill, G. Steven. 1987. *Biotech 88: Into the Marketplace.* San Francisco: Arthur Young High Technology Group.

Carrol, Paul. 1993. "Die Offene Schlacht." *Die Zeit,* no. 39 (24 September), 18.

Coase, R. H. 1937. "The Nature of the Firm." *Economica* 4, no. 4: 386–405.

Cohen, Wesley M., and Steven Klepper. 1991. "Firm Size versus Diversity in the Achievement of Technological Advance." In *Innovation and Technological Change: An International Comparison,* edited by Z. Acs and David B. Audretsch. Ann Arbor: University of Michigan Press.

———. 1992a. "The Tradeoff between Firm Size and Diversity in the Pursuit of Technological Progress." *Small Business Economics* 4, no. 1: 1–14.

———. 1992b. "The Anatomy of Industry R&D Intensity Distributions." *American Economic Review* 82, no. 4: 773–99.

Cohen, Wesley M., and Richard C. Levin. 1989. "Empirical Studies of Innovation and Market Structure." In *Handbook of Industrial Organization,* vol. 2, edited by R. Schmalensee and R. Willig. Amsterdam: North-Holland.

Cringley, Robert X. 1993. *Accidental Empires: How the Boys of Silicon Valley Make Their Millions, Battle Foreign Competition, and Still Can't Get a Date.* New York: Harper Business.

Dosi, Giovanni. 1988. "Sources, Procedures, and Microeconomic Effects of Innovation." *Journal of Economic Literature* 26, no. 3: 1120–71.

Feldman, Maryann P. 1994a. *The Geography of Innovation.* Boston: Kluwer Academic.

———. 1994b. "Knowledge Complementarity and Innovation." *Small Business Economics* 6, no. 5: 363–80.

Gilder, George. 1989. *Microcosm.* New York: Touchstone.

Glaeser, Edward L., Hedi D. Kallal, Jose A. Scheinkman, and Andrei Shleifer. 1992. "Growth of Cities," *Journal of Political Economy* 100, no. 4: 1126–52.

Graaf, J. de V. 1957. *Theoretical Welfare Economics.* Cambridge: Cambridge University Press.

Griliches, Zvi. 1979. "Issues in Assessing the Contribution of R&D to Productivity Growth," *Bell Journal of Economics* 10, no. 1: 92–116.

Holmstrom, Bengt. 1989. "Agency Costs and Innovation." *Journal of Economic Behavior and Organization* 12:305–27.

Jaffe, Adam B. 1989. "Real Effects of Academic Research." *American Economic Review* 79, no. 5: 957–70.

Jaffe, Adam B., Manuel Trajtenberg, and Rebecca Henderson. 1993. "Geographic Localization of Knowledge Spillovers as Evidenced by Patent Citations." *Quarterly Journal of Economics* 63, no. 3: 577–98.

Knight, Frank H. 1921. *Risk, Uncertainty, and Profit.* New York: Houghton Mifflin.

Kreps, David. 1991. "Corporate Culture and Economic Theory." In *Positive Perspectives on Political Economy,* edited by J. Alt and K. Shepsle. Cambridge: Cambridge University Press.

Krugman, Paul. 1991a. "Increasing Returns and Economic Geography." *Journal of Political Economy* 99, no. 3: 483–99.

———. 1991b. *Geography and Trade.* Cambridge: MIT Press.

Levin, Sharon G., and Paula E. Stephan. 1991. "Research Productivity over the Life Cycle: Evidence for Academic Scientists." *American Economic Review* 81, no. 4: 114–32.

Link, Albert N., and John Rees. 1990. "Firm Size, University Based Research, and the Returns to R&D." *Small Business Economics* 2, no. 1: 25–32.

Lucas, Robert E., Jr. 1993. "Making a Miracle." *Econometrica* 61, no. 2: 251–72.

Merton, Robert. 1957. "Priorities in Scientific Discovery: A Chapter in the Sociology of Science." *American Sociological Review* 22, no. 6: 635–59.

Milgrom, Paul. 1988. "Employment Contracts, Influence Activities and Organization Design." *Journal of Political Economy* 96, no. 1: 42–60.

Milgrom, Paul, and John Roberts. 1987. "Information Asymmetries, Strategic Behavior, and Industrial Organization." *American Economic Review* 77, no. 2: 184–93.

Nelson, Richard R., and Sidney G. Winter. 1982. *An Evolutionary Theory of Economic Change.* Cambridge: Harvard University Press.

Orsenigo, Luigi. 1989. *The Emergence of Biotechnology: Institutions and Markets in Industrial Innovation.* New York: St. Martins.

Palfreman, Jon, and Doron Swade. 1991. *The Dream Machine: Exploring the Computer Age.* London: BBC Books.

Romer, Paul. 1990. "Endogenous Technological Change." *Journal of Political Economy* 68: 71–102.

Rose, Frank. 1989. *West of Eden: The End of Innocence at Apple Computer.* New York: Viking.

Saxenian, AnnaLee. 1990. "Regional Networks and the Resurgence of Silicon Valley." *California Management Review* 33, no. 1: 89–112.

Scherer, F. M. 1984. *Innovation and Growth: Schumpeterian Perspectives.* Cambridge: MIT Press.

———. 1991. "Changing Perspectives on the Firm Size Problem." In *Innovation and Technological Change: An International Comparison,* edited by Z. J. Acs and D. B. Audretsch. Ann Arbor: University of Michigan Press.

———. 1992. "Schumpeter and Plausible Capitalism." *Journal of Economic Literature* 30, no. 3: 1416–33.

Schumpeter, Joseph A. 1911. *Theorie der wirtschaftlichen Entwicklung. Eine Untersuchung über Unternehmergewinn, Kapital, Kredit, Zins und den Konjunkturzyklus.* Berlin: Duncker and Humblot.

———. 1942. *Capitalism, Socialism, and Democracy.* New York: Harper and Row.

Stephan, Paula E. 1996. "The Economics of Science." *Journal of Economic Literature* 34, no. 3: 1199–1235.

Stephan, Paula E., and Stephen Everhart. 1997. "The Changing Rewards to Science: The Case of Biotechnology." *Small Business Economics* 9.

Stephan, Paula E., and Sharon G. Levin. 1992. *Striking the Mother Lode in Science.* New York: Oxford University Press.

Tirole, Jean. 1986. "Hierarchies and Bureaucracies." *Journal of Law, Economics, and Organization* 2, no. 3: 181–214.

Williamson, Oliver E. 1975. *Markets and Hierarchies: Antitrust Analysis and Implications.* New York: Free Press.

Zucker, Lynne G., Michael R. Darby, and Jeff Armstrong. 1995. "Intellectual Capital and the Firm: The Technology of Geographically Localized Knowledge Spillovers." National Bureau of Economic Research (NBER) Working Papers, no. 4,946. Mimeo.

Zucker, Lynne G., Michael R. Darby, and Marilynn Brewer. 1994. "Intellectual Capital and the Birth of U.S. Biotechnology Enterprises." National Bureau of Economic Research (NBER) Working Papers, no. 4,653. (February) Mimeo.

R&D as Premarket Selection: Managing Uncertainty in Genetic Engineering and Broadband

Maureen McKelvey

Formalized research and development (R&D) in firms is argued to play important strategic roles in (1) identifying opportunities to innovate and (2) interpreting environmental conditions.[1] If firms act upon opportunities to innovate, the resulting innovations, defined as novelties of economic value, allow the firm to gain advantage and survive. Based on an explicitly evolutionary approach, R&D is thus seen as a special category of firm activity, which integrates internal decision making about technology with an interpretation of external conditions. This essay argues that R&D can be premarket selection, and it specifies selection criteria and selection mechanisms involved in R&D processes.[2]

Using R&D activities to link successfully strategic decisions about the firm's current and future capabilities with an interpretation of environmental conditions is not so easy, and R&D management therefore faces a number of challenges. These challenges arise particularly because managers and researchers want to influence the rate and direction of technical change under conditions of uncertainty. For example, they have to make decisions about whether to engage in R&D and which R&D projects to initiate, continue, and discontinue, that is, how to allocate resources among different formal searching and learning activities. It is not clear which project will lead to functioning technical alternatives or to "winning," respective "losing," innovations in future market selection.

This essay explores the role of R&D as premarket selection by developing an evolutionary conceptual framework for technology management. The questions address whether, and in what ways, R&D is premarket selection as well as the relative success of internal (to the firm) selection mechanisms in R&D projects. The concepts and analytical tools developed are used to analyze two illustrative R&D projects. As R&D management faces great challenges in high-tech projects, two such projects are explored here. They are the American biotechnology firm Genentech's use of genetic engineering to make a human growth hormone (hGH) and the Swedish telecommunication firm Ericsson's use of the asynchronous transfer mode (ATM) technique to develop large, broadband exchanges (switches) for data transmission. Genetech developed genetic engineering as the basis of production for what was an existing pharmaceutical, that is, a new source of supply. Ericsson attempted to further develop their large fixed telephone exchanges by using the ATM technique.[3] ATM is a novel way to compact and transfer data, and the basic idea is that it can handle all types of data communication (telephone, computer, TV, etc.) on the same lines (*Tele Special Issue* 1990a). The two R&D projects thus involve different industries, under somewhat different competitive conditions.

These R&D projects were chosen because they both involve expensive search activities in highly uncertain and rapidly changing technologies. Moreover, there are similarities in how the two technologies create economic value, such that the technologies have use, or value, in relation to a combination of other technologies. In these two specific projects, genetic engineering creates economic value in relation to biological production methods for pharmaceuticals whereas the ATM technique creates value in relation to telephone exchange hardware, cables, computer programs, services, and so on. We can thus make a distinction between the core technology (genetic engineering and the ATM technique) and all the necessary complementary technologies. These together are seen to constitute a systemic technology in the sense that a number of different "technologies" are linked together (Hughes 1983, Rosenberg 1982).

Another reason why these two R&D projects were chosen was a conscious desire to examine not only a success but also a failure in terms of the resulting innovation. The Genentech R&D project was successful, leading to a pharmaceutical product (Genentech sold $216 million of Protropin/Nutropin in 1995), whereas the Ericsson R&D project was mostly abandoned in December 1995 after 6 billion SEK (approximately $895 million) had been invested in R&D and when there were more than 1,000 engineers working on the project.[4] The illustrative cases were thus consciously chosen to examine what both successes and failures may say about R&D as premarket selection.

Conceptual Framework

A reflected, evolutionary approach based on the peculiarities of socioeconomic evolution—such as human intentionality—is the starting point here.[5] An evolutionary perspective is used because it allows us to analyze the interactions between factors internal to the firm and those factors external to it; these together determine the competitive success of the firm. In relation to knowledge production, evolution can be summarized as three principles and one assumption (McKelvey 1996, chap. 3).

1. There are multiple attempts to generate novelty, leading to a diversity of alternatives.
2. The transmission and retention of knowledge, techniques, and

behavior among agents (individuals or organizations) are useful to generate and select among technical alternatives.

3. Selection among alternatives is a social process.

4. There is an assumption of nonoptimization, wherein selection occurs in relation to local environments.

The three principles are used here to analyze and interpret the various functions that R&D can fulfill in the firm as well as to indicate why the "fit" between internal R&D decision making and external selection criteria can be closer or further apart. It is proposed here that R&D in firms can fulfill three functions. The first two functions of R&D are well known in the literature, whereas this chapter contributes by proposing and discussing the third function, namely, premarket selection. R&D can play a role in the following.

1. *Generating novelty.* R&D is a collective effort directed toward the generation of novelty relevant to the firm (Coombs et al. 1987). That novelty may be new to the world, new to the firm, and/or a modification of existing knowledge and techniques.

2. *Inheritance of knowledge.* R&D activities allow the firm to develop and maintain competences (knowledge) and to monitor knowledge developed elsewhere. Cohen and Levinthal (1990) analyze this as "absorptive capacity." The argument is that firms must perform some search and learning activities in-house, thereby developing their technical competences, in order to interpret and be able to act upon technical developments occurring external to the firm. Rosenberg (1990) and Pavitt (1991) develop similar arguments in order to analyze why some firms devote a proportion of R&D to basic research.

3. *Selecting among alternatives.* This essay explores the role that R&D can play in premarket selection. R&D may do so by developing and implementing internal (to the firm) selection criteria, which, in turn, influence technical change. In that firms are interpreting and "betting" on various combinations of economic and technical characteristics of innovation during R&D, they are selecting among alternatives before any sort of market selection occurs. These internal firm selection criteria are then implemented through selection mechanisms such as technical testing routines, choices made by management, and interpretation of future markets. The firm starts using these internal selection criteria before market selection, but external selection feeds back and indicates which strategies and choices are (were) viable. The cases will illustrate how premarket selection occurs.

Selection criteria for innovations include market and technical characteristics (Kline and Rosenberg 1986) and are here further divided into two categories, external and internal to the firm. For the current analysis, external selection criteria are assumed to operate through some form of market competition, so that, if an innovation fulfills the required conditions, the firm can sell it and in the long term survive. Less well adapted innovations usually disappear from the market. Internal selection criteria are defined as characteristics that the firm uses to direct its in-house search and learning activities, thereby influencing the rate and direction of technical change. The firm uses its interpretation of external selection criteria (environmental conditions) in order to a priori influence the generation of novelty.[6] The firm, however, can be more or less successful in its attempts to influence technology.

This concept of internal to the firm, premarket selection processes is important theoretically for at least two reasons. First, it underscores the diversity of firms necessary in evolutionary economics (Nelson 1990). Second, instead of relying on the concept of random mutations for introducing novelty, it also relies on concepts like consciousness and bounded rationality.

Uncertainty, R&D, and Selection

Innovation processes involve uncertainty due to the nature of technical change and market selection (Dosi 1984). In economics, uncertainty is often seen as synonymous with risk. Eliasson (1990) interprets Knight's (1921) distinction between risk as insurable (and hence calculable), versus uncertainty as a genuine lack of knowledge, in order to argue that when the firm makes subjective judgments it turns uncertainty into subjectively defined risk. Although this transformation of uncertainty into subjective risk can be important for understanding firms, evolutionary economics also clearly differentiates between risk in this sense of calculable and uncertainty in the sense of not being able to know what the future might bring (Dosi et al. 1988). In innovation processes, what is particularly interesting is that market and technical uncertainty mutually influence each other. Four types of uncertainty relevant for R&D are visible from an evolutionary perspective.

1. Due to the ex-post nature of selection, uncertainty remains about which environmental conditions (or selection criteria) will be most important in the future.

2. In contrast to biological evolution, humans try to interpret selection criteria a priori. This implies that the firm's perceptions are important. Uncertainty therefore exists about how well firms' perceptions will actually represent existing and future conditions.[7] In this case, firm learning implies both gathering information and evaluating it.

3. There is also uncertainty related to technical change, such that

it may not be clear that a desired function can be developed at all nor which design will turn out to be suited to demand. Managers and researchers do make a priori calculations and judgments about the size and type of R&D investments, but they cannot be certain of the outcome of that investment. Even R&D with a definite purpose and goal may thus lead to unexpected results.[8]

4. Similarly, there is true uncertainty about the economic importance of an innovation. Although the firm has some information about the current, external, market selection criteria, the firm has no—and logically cannot have—reliable information about the economic impact of its innovation. In other words, the innovation opportunity cannot be (completely) specified in advance.

What is particularly challenging about innovations are the mutual influences between technical and market uncertainty. Managers must often make trade-offs in R&D between them. For example, a higher level of technical sophistication in a product (whether a good or a service) often commands a higher price but may thereby reduce sales and profits.[9] On the other hand, buyers may prefer high technical sophistication, so that, if the firm has developed a less technically sophisticated but lower-cost alternative, it may find few buyers.

Seeing R&D management as an attempt to reduce uncertainty implies that firm learning is a crucial factor in this selection process. Learning may occur explicitly in R&D or less formally in other parts of the firm. Basically, as time passes, the firm should learn more about external selection criteria in order to focus its innovation process (R&D, knowledge collection, etc.) on alternatives likely to be well adapted. This is why learning about which strategies did—or did not—work under various conditions can be crucial to future success in an environment (Langlois and Everett 1994, 11).

However, instead of assuming that learning will decrease uncertainty, it is proposed here that learning can increase, decrease, or leave uncertainty unchanged. When market conditions or technology are stable, learning leads to the reduction of uncertainty. The firm develops a better understanding of what types of innovations are likely to succeed in that environment. However, when environmental conditions or technology are changing relatively rapidly, then it is not clear what effect learning will have on the level of uncertainty. Learning during R&D can involve generation of novelty, and therefore it can increase uncertainty if new alternatives are developed. Greater diversity can lead to greater uncertainty about which will be selected. The level of uncertainty can be evaluated before, during, and after R&D projects.

Seven sets of concepts are discussed and used in the next two sections in relation to the two illustrative R&D cases. The concepts are: (1) market uncertainty; (2) technical uncertainty in core technology, complementary technologies, and external technical developments; (3) trade-offs between technical and market considerations; (4) relative distance to firm competences; (5) degree to which a systemic technology should be developed in-house; (6) internal (to the firm) selection criteria; and (7) internal (to the firm) selection mechanisms.

The two cases are of Genentech and Ericsson. Genentech is an American biotech firm, now owned by the Swiss pharmaceutical firm Hoffman-LaRoche. It was founded in 1976 by the venture capitalist Swanson and the basic scientist Boyer in order to exploit the commercial potential of genetic engineering. Their initial ambition was to sell R&D contracts to established companies and thereafter move into the production of pharmaceuticals (Swanson 1986). Two of their first R&D contracts, done for pharmaceutical firms, were to use genetic engineering to produce insulin and human growth hormones in bacteria. In 1978–79, Genentech managed to express a small amount of each protein on a lab scale, but the first sales of this type of insulin were in 1982 and of hGH in 1985 (McKelvey 1996). Genentech sells hGH on the American market, due to arrangements with Kabi (now Pharmacia Upjohn), which commissioned the original R&D contract for hGH. Being a biotechnology firm, they have had a tradition of being R&D intensive and even of doing basic research.

Ericsson is a large, Swedish telecommunications equipment firm, successful internationally. Their major product markets are in "advanced systems and products for wired and mobile communications in public and private networks." (Ericsson Annual Report 1989, 1994) and were previously also in electronic defense systems. Of Swedish business groups in 1995, Ericsson spent the highest percentage of sales revenue on R&D, namely 16.2 percent, which was also highest total amount at 13 million SEK, or $1.9 billion (*Ny Teknik* 1995b, 18).[10] Ericsson has traditionally been an early mover into new technologies relevant to their products; for example, they developed an AXE system, a new generation of telephone exchanges based on digital technology and computer programming, in collaboration with other Swedish actors (Vedin 1994). Ericsson subsequently decided in 1989 to develop the next generation of telephone exchanges based on the ATM technique in a broadband frequency (*Ny Teknik* 1995b). They were to do so with the firm Ellemtel, then jointly owned with Televerket (now Telia), the government-owned, fixed telephone operator. This is the R&D project that was abandoned in December 1995, although Ericsson is continuing to develop and market some smaller products relevant to broadband transmission.

A vital question here is whether, and which, premarket selection processes in firms lead to innovations better or less well adapted to environmental conditions. To what extent do managers and researchers in R&D projects interpret external selection criteria (existing, changing, new) when developing innovations? How and to what degree can they use their interpretations to influence the rate and direction of technical choices used or developed in-house? Such an approach should help us understand what it is that explains why some firms are more successful than others.

Uncertainty in the Genentech and Ericsson R&D Projects

Three types of uncertainty are introduced in this section and used to analyze the Genentech and Ericsson R&D projects.

1. Market Uncertainty

The first type of uncertainty involves the firm's ability to interpret market conditions. The level and type of market uncertainty should be considered in relation to R&D investment decisions and relative success. In particular, market uncertainty can be formulated as comparisons of the envisioned innovation relative to other products. Is a new product likely to substitute for an existing one? Will (do) buyers demand technical characteristics similar to those existing or are new ones emerging? Are the buyers used to similar products or does the innovation open the possibility of reaching new categories of buyers? The level of substitution for existing products versus true novelty obviously influences market uncertainty.

Even though sales and marketing personnel can play a more direct role, R&D does give information about technical characteristics relevant to innovation opportunities. It does so by monitoring, identifying, and developing technical possibilities, which can then be used to analyze the likely price elasticity of products relative to the level of technical sophistication.

Genentech identified both an existing market for hGH and a potentially larger market (McKelvey 1996, chap. 8). Genetic engineering would be a substitute source of supply for an existing pharmaceutical, that is, existing hGH extracted from pituitary glands and given to children suffering from dwarfism. When Genentech made a decision to sell it in 1980, the American market was estimated to be about $10 million, and the world market about $100 million. The potential market was expected to be much larger, however, because pituitary hGH was always in short supply for children suffering from dwarfism at the same time that medical studies had indicated other uses as well.[11] Thus, Genentech management could discern that rDNA hGH could substitute for an existing product, could expand the size of that market due to previous supply constraints, and could be used for new treatments and hence open new markets. Afterward, it turned out that these alternative uses of hGH—particularly for children who have "normal" amounts of hGH but are short—skyrocketed. In 1995, the world market was approximately $1 billion and the U.S. market $300 million (*Financial Times* 1995, 17). Genentech has about 75 percent of the U.S. market.

There remained, however, some market uncertainty due to users' perceptions of genetic engineering per se, even though genetically engineered hGH is identical to that produced in the body.[12] Would they believe that the "natural," that is pituitary, product was superior to the genetically engineered (e.g., rDNA) version? However, even if users' perceptions were negative, it was known that demand would far exceed supply of the pituitary version. Moreover, the perceived relative superiority of pituitary and rDNA hGH did an abrupt switch in 1985 when a rare and deadly viral infection was found in some former pituitary hGH patients, leading to a ban in many countries. The whole market was then wide open for the rDNA hGH.

Ericsson's new, large, ATM-based telephone exchange would also be a replacement for an existing product with a larger (expected) future market. Here, in contrast to Genentech, Ericsson was already in the market with competing products, although buyers and users would require new and different characteristics of the ATM innovation. At the same time, telecommunications operators (the traditional buyers of Ericsson's equipment) were being deregulated and consequently changing their demands on technology, and the new broadband exchanges would also have to satisfy new categories of buyers and operators as well as those using the hardware to provide (other) services. Each group could have different technical specifications, for example, in the rate of data transmission. Thus, over time, the changing composition of buyers and users and the subsequent changing technical characteristics demanded have increased uncertainty about how to define the appropriate balance of technical characteristics and price.

Moreover, Ericsson faced competition not only with other ATM-based exchanges but with the alternative of upgrading already installed data transmission networks such as telephone lines, TV cable, and computer networks.[13] The firm could also decide to make only some components rather than the whole exchange system. In 1995, Ericsson management decided to cancel this project partly because this market had not grown as fast as expected. Growth has instead been in smaller ATM exchanges, particularly those used in local-area nets. The 1995 management decisions thus focused on reducing market uncertainty by concentrating on current market demands rather than future ones.

2. Technical Uncertainty—Core, Complementary, and External

The second group of questions involves technical uncertainty, here divided into three categories: core technology, complementary technologies, and direction and rate of external technical developments. The distinctions are important because the level and the location of uncertainty influence how difficult it is for the firm to make the "right" bet. For example, instead of trying to choose one winning combination of all technologies from the beginning of the project, the firm may find it more important to increase flexibility by increasing the number of alternatives.

The level of uncertainty in the core technology.   Is there one collectively agreed upon technical function and solution or are there many? In addition, we want to know if diversity is increasing or decreasing. Utterback and Abernathy (1975) argue in their product life-cycle model that uncertainty is greatest intitially. Various actors are proposing a number of technical alternatives, but later one dominant design emerges and competition is then over cost reductions rather than alternative designs. However, R&D activities can also involve searching and learning about new technical possibilities and dead ends, thereby increasing diversity. If the firm chooses a core technology that afterward turns out to be inadequate, then we can expect the whole R&D project to fail.

The level and type of uncertainty in complementary technologies.   In addition to a core technology, many complementary technologies are needed. Rosenberg (1982) and Hughes (1983) have each argued that technology is systematic in the sense that many technologies must work together in order for, say, a car to function. In systemic technologies, problems in "bottlenecks," respectively "reverse salients," block further development of the system and thereby focus attention on solving the problems and thereby advancing the system as a whole.

Relevant questions are: what level and types of uncertainty exist in the complementary technologies? Is the firm innovating within one uncertain core technology, which is then integrated into existing and well-understood complementary technologies? Does the firm have to develop many complementary technologies? Does integration of the core and complementary technologies lead to new, unexpected problems?

If the complementary technologies are known and not changing much, we expect innovation to be relatively easier than if they must also be developed or are very complex and changing rapidly. In the former case, the firm can concentrate its energy on the core technology and integration. In the latter case, management may need to concentrate on flexibility of alternatives in the system rather than locking into one bet.

The rate and direction of relevant, external, technical change.   This question addresses whether, and to what extent, the firm has to monitor and learn from external knowledge producers while being stimulated by the external environment to develop new competences. How rapidly and what types of competing technical alternatives are being developed? Does diversity of external developments increase or decrease during the duration of the R&D project? Do competitors have very different paradigms?

The greatest technical uncertainty in Genentech's R&D project initially involved the core technology genetic engineering. Before Genentech's more basic scientific experiments in 1979, it was not even clear that such bacteria could make human proteins. Having shown it was possible, there were still questions—up through the early 1980s—about whether the process would be commercially viable. More specific questions involved whether these bacteria would produce a high enough percentage of the desired protein, with the correct physical characteristics, and whether the protein could be adequately purified from contaminants and variations. However, over the period of the R&D project, genetic engineering became generally accepted as a viable technical method of production, but only for specialized, high-price (or high-value-added) products.[14]

In contrast, Genentech scientists doing R&D to integrate the genetically engineered bacteria into existing biological production systems thought that the complementary technologies would involve little uncertainty. "At first we thought it [fermentation] would be the same. What you're going to do is insert a gene in *E. coli* [bacteria] and tell the *E. coli* to express it so it'll be the same" (Lin 1993; see also McKelvey 1996, chap. 7). They soon discovered, however, that integrating genetic engineering with complementary technologies like fermentation and protein purification led to many new challenges requiring additional R&D investment.

Meeting these challenges often involved changes in the complementary technologies and/or the core technology. For example, Genentech researchers tried to modify genetic engineering aspects like the promoter (that is, the start signal) in order to improve the bacteria and thereby increase yield. Thus, although Genentech researchers initially thought standard complementary techniques and technologies could be used, they soon found that each new project required modifications and improvements specific for that use.

Moreover, identification of problems in turn drove forward improvements in analytical methods. These are interesting in relation to internal selection criteria because changing them redefined what technical modifications would be considered acceptable in the next round. The analytical methods became more and more sensitive to impurities and variations, thereby raising the standards. Those engaged in this R&D never knew if what today was considered "good enough" would tomorrow be considered inadequate (Fryklund 1992). Improvements in the complementary technologies turned out to be necessary, even though many of these were relatively small modifications. Integration of genetic engineering and complementary technologies enabled the identification of bottlenecks, later solved, and hence directed the path of in-house technical change.

As to external technical change, Genentech was one of the absolute leaders in the commercialization of genetic engineering. Other firms had joined them by the early to mid-1980s and shared quite similar paradigms about the general technological solutions needed to produce such pharmaceuticals. Nonetheless, alternative compositions of genetic engineering techniques have to some extent been firm specific, and these differences have become greater over the years (McKelvey 1996, chap. 9). Moreover, external developments have continued to lead to improvements in alternative methods of pharmaceutical production such as tissue extraction and chemical synthesis, which are alternative technological trajectories. In short, genetic engineering has become an accepted production method for some pharmaceuticals, but alternative core technologies, particularly chemical synthesis, are still very viable for other pharmaceuticals.

The Ericsson project probably experienced as much technical uncertainty about whether the core ATM technique would function in practice in 1989 as Genentech did over genetic engineering in 1979. The difference, however, was that by 1989 major actors, including international standardization organizations, had agreed that ATM was "the 'target solution' for future broadband networks" (*Tele Special Issue* 1990b, 12; *Tele Special Issue* 1990a; *Tele* 1989).[15] This general, collective agreement about the core technology still holds. Nevertheless, ATM has neither been developed nor introduced as fast and widely as expected, and other technological alternatives are still being developed.

Despite agreement over the approach, it was also clear that using the ATM technique in broadband telephone exchanges would be complex and would require development of many complementary technologies. In particular, more efficient ways of managing the routing of information and deconstruction and reconstruction of data from cells were needed.[16] As a result, the ATM technique for broadband communication placed much higher technical requirements on complementary technologies—such as computer programming and processors—than were available in 1989.

Moreover, Ericsson felt it should develop the majority of complementary technologies in-house, although naturally based on monitoring of external developments. For example, to be able to handle the complexities of information management for flexible data transmission, Ericsson (Ellemtel) decided from the beginning to use the then new, object-oriented programming approach and the computer language C++. It also decided to build its own Unix-based computer, as those available in 1989 did not have the necessary capacity. Thus, Ericsson's initial strategy was to build a whole new systemic technology, based on uncertain core and complementary technologies.

Finally, Ericsson was also a fairly early mover into the core technology. During the duration of the R&D project, however, external developments by universities, competitors, firms in related sectors, and so on, as well as new demands of potential buyers and users, led to rapid technical change. This means that it has been difficult for the firm to monitor all external developments and keep up with them in-house. Moreover, some choices that Ericsson initially perceived as the obvious way to proceed have proved less well suited for its purposes than alternatives generated later. External developments have thus meant challenges to the core technology. These rapid developments in alternative systemic technologies have been partly due to competition over whether telephone systems (i.e., Ericsson's traditional competence), TV systems, and/or computer networks (local, firm-level, or national) will carry the data of the future (*IEEE Spectrum* 1996, *Ericsson Review* 1993). Nonetheless, major firms still invest massively in ATM for telephone exchanges and believe it will dominate future broadband environments, even though basic-research-oriented groups are already working on faster alternatives (*Tele* 1995, 17; *Ny Teknik* 1994).

What is more striking is that some of Ericsson's (Ellemtel's) choices of complementary technologies to be developed in-house have been bypassed by later, external technical developments (*Ny Teknik* 1995a; *Computer Sweden* 1996, 2; *Tele* 1994). For example, Ellemtel's development of its own computers and processors seems expensive (in terms of R&D investment and production) and inadequate today compared with commercially available computers, which easily handle the information requirements of ATM. This was an apparent mistake in judging the rate of technical change in the computer industry. However, it may have been necessary initially to get the ATM technique to work at all.

Moreover, by 1995, the experiences of various industrial actors—including Ericsson but also many others—have indicated that object-oriented programming involves significant difficulties and complexities, especially when programming large, complex bodies of code such as those necessary for telephone exchanges.[17] Problems often center around the difficulty of programming in several layers; for example, there are difficulties in designing reusable code as well as follow-on errors resulting from the inheritance of code for a later (similar) function. Similarly, the decision to use the computer language C++ might have seemed "obvious" in 1989, but it has presented some significant problems in identifying and fixing programming errors in the huge, very complex programs necessary for the ATM technique (*Computer Sweden* 1996, 2).[18] Thus, Ericsson's initial choices about the specifics of the complementary technologies have been challenged by later external changes in knowledge and technologies.

3. Trade-offs between Technical and Market Considerations

Finally, we want to know about trade-offs made between market and technical considerations. These trade-offs should be visible when the firm chooses the level of R&D investment because the firm may choose to follow one technical trajectory, which emphasizes one set of trade-offs over another, or to develop a set of alternatives.

Management in the Genentech R&D project apparently emphasized technical improvements (McKelvey 1996, chap. 8). This is indicated by comparisons with the pharmaceutical firm Kabi, which simultaneously (and partly in cooperation with Genentech) developed rDNA hGH for the international market. For example, Kabi was very cautious, and continued with clinical testing until it felt certain that purity was high enough, due to the crucial importance of perceptions of safety in pharmaceuticals. Genentech went ahead and did a phase 1 clinical test in 1981 because existing analytical methods showed purity. Individuals receiving their rDNA hGH had some mild reactions, which led some critics to question the validity of the genetic engineering approach in general. However, these problems also spurred creative development of analytical methods necessary to identify these unexpected problems, which were soon solved.

Moreover, in a later stage of R&D, Genentech continued to integrate new technical improvements in order to improve yield. In contrast, Kabi decided at one point that the current production system was adequate and not to incorporate subsequent technical changes; it instead concentrated on getting government approval for the pharmaceutical in order to get a jump on the market. Despite Genentech's emphasis on technical considerations, whenever technical improvements were introduced in R&D, there was a clear awareness of the costs of implementing the improvement relative to expected benefits either as improved characteristics of the product or for the reduction of production costs.

How Ericsson made technical versus market trade-offs during the R&D project is somewhat less clear, although there seems to have been a clear shift from an emphasis on technical superiority to market considerations. Criticism has been voiced that technical considerations had too much influence over the goals of the R&D project; in other words, new technical possibilities were allowed to continually redefine the goals and specifications of the innovation rather than setting technical goals in advance and then finding solutions (*Ny Teknik* 1995a, *Elektroniktidningen* 1995). This can be interpreted as too much technical flexibility and too little understanding of market considerations.

When, however, the Ericsson management decided to discontinue the large-scale ATM exchange project, the trade-off was the opposite. The decision was based on a more short run approximation of the costs of doing further R&D when market growth was slower than anticipated. The growing market has been mostly within local-area nets, which are important for corporate users and comprised a market initially targeted by American firms. In contrast, Ericsson and European firms have concentrated more on developing large exchanges, ones relevant for both corporate users and public telecommunications—that is, households (*Tele Special Issue* 1990a, *IEEE Spectrum* 1996). Ericsson decided to concentrate on smaller products within the broadband technology, which can be sold in the near-term future (*Elektroniktidningen* 1995, *Nätvärlden* 1996, *Ny Teknik* 1995a). The current Ericsson strategy is thus to concentrate on products close to the market, including components of an ATM exchange, and on improving its existing AXE exchange. This trade-off emphasizes today's market considerations rather than technical developments for future markets.

Internal Firm Criteria in Genentech and Ericsson R&D

Four groups of questions about internal firm selection criteria are proposed in order to analyze how, and how well, R&D management in firms uses internal selection criteria to direct internal technical change and to choose among externally developed alternatives.

4. Distance to Firm Competences

The distance—in terms of the firm's competences and experiences—is defined in terms of the firm's competences and experiences, and hence is the relationship between the new R&D project/innovation and previous R&D projects/products. Relative distance to previous firm competences and products is important because it helps identify the extent to which previous firm choices influence current technical change in a R&D project. We expect this influence to be of value to the firm when knowledge and technological developments are cumulative and follow a similar trajectory but to be problematic when there is a discontinuity. In the latter case, the firm can lose flexibility and becomes locked into a technological trajectory inappropriate for the new project and its (projected) environment. Does the firm have a general paradigm about how to design a similar systemic technology? How close is the previous internal selection criteria and solutions to those found necessary in the new R&D process? To what extent does the R&D follow existing routines rather than develop flexibility? These help us analyze how close or far away the new knowledge base(s) are from existing firm competences.

As Genentech was a start-up biotech firm, it had no previous products and few comparable R&D projects, and so the concept of distance between this project and previous firm competences has little meaning. However, parallel with the rDNA hGH project, Genentech was engaged in the initial R&D for production of rDNA insulin for the firm Eli Lilly as well as having R&D contracts with other firms (McKelvey 1996, chap. 8). Both the insulin and hGH projects focused on improving yield and purity. Moreover, the technical approaches to problem solving were quite similar in, for example, specific genetic-engineering aspects like promotors, and Genentech tried to develop standardized complementary technologies relevant for more than one project. It strove for standardization but had to modify core and complementary technologies for each R&D project. The distance between contemporary R&D projects was thus quite close, meaning that similar competences were being developed and could be shared.

In contrast, the established firm Ericsson had previously developed a similar systemic technology. Its closest major product was the AXE telephone exchange for fixed telecommunications (Vedin 1994, Tele 1993), which the ATM broadband exchange would eventually replace for some users while attracting new users as well (*Ny Teknik* 1995a, *Tele Special Issue* 1990a, *Tele* 1993). Although based on different core techniques, the two products have a similar general paradigm of system design, which may be specific to the firm. Both systems were intended to emphasize flexibility, leave open the possibility of adding later technical improvements and meet new demands, make components into interchangeable modules, and so on. Moreover, in both systems Ericsson strove to be a technical pioneer, as indicated by examples in the types of signals used (for AXE, completely digital instead of analogue; for broadband, ATM), computer programming (for AXE, high level language instead of machine code as well as modular program code with defined interfaces; for broadband, object-oriented instead of normal programming architecture), special processors for both AXE and ATM, and so on. Two other important similarities were that a majority of R&D investment went into computer programming and both R&D projects were initially carried out in collaboration with the jointly owned R&D firm Ellemtel.

5. Degree to Which a Systemic Technology Should Be Developed In-House

A systemic technology (core and complementary technologies) can all be developed inside the firm or else some parts can be developed internally and some parts externally. This group of questions analyzes the extent to which the firm developed knowledge and technical change in-house versus its reliance on external technical changes. We expect that firms should have different strategies about whether or not to develop the system in-house, depending on levels of uncertainty about core and complementary technologies, on rates and the complexity of external technical change, and on costs of in-house R&D. To what degree does the innovation involve a systemic technology? Does the firm wish to develop a whole new system or only some components? What is the rationale for its choice?

The Genentech R&D project directly involved a production process, and so the firm wanted control over the whole system, not least to comply with government safety regulations for pharmaceuticals (although it would have been possible to license production to others). Control over the production system does not mean, however, that everything should be, or was, developed in-house. Quite the contrary, for Genentech R&D used existing knowledge, techniques, and machines as much as possible for complementary technologies like purification and analytical methods. However, as noted, integrating genetic-engineering and biological production methods led to a number of new challenges requiring additional R&D activities and leading to new techniques. In this process, different alternatives of genetic engineering and complementary technologies were tested in-house, based on internal developments or the in-house modification of knowledge and techniques developed externally—usually in universities.

Similarly, Ericsson wanted to develop a complete systemic technology, but its system would be a new product. It wanted a whole new broadband communications system based on ATM, at least that was the plan up until December 1995. It had choices about whether it wanted to develop the whole system or just some components. However, at the same time that Ericsson (Ellemtel) was focused on developing a complete system in-house it closely monitored external developments and was, for example, involved in a number of European-level, collaborative R&D projects (*Tele Special Issue* 1990b, 1990c, 1990d). Its systemic technology required the further development and/or modification of a large number of uncertain complementary technologies as well as the design of complex interactions among them.

6. Internal Selection Criteria

Internal (to the firm) selection criteria are defined as those the firm uses to choose among technical alternatives. The firm can use these criteria either to integrate an improvement into a functioning system or to steer technical change in a particular direction. Which criteria are used by R&D managers and researchers in order to choose among technical alternatives? In what ways does that knowledge have to be modified to fit the needs of the firm? When generated in-house, what types of demands are placed on the direction of technical change? These questions specifically address the direction, rate, and type of knowledge and technical change identified as desirable in the R&D project.

When deciding to introduce an improvement or a new alternative, Genentech researchers have stressed the importance of the size of the change in terms of its impact on cost and/or characteristics of the product (McKelvey 1996, chaps. 7, 8). For example, when a genetic-engineering technique (new to the firm) was found to increase protein yield, the improvement was integrated if it more than covered the costs of the change and/or introduced a new, desirable, product characteristic. An example of the latter is an improvement that made rDNA hGH identical to pituitary hGH.

The Genentech case also indicates internal selection criteria that were designed to influence the direction of technical change in-house. Certain criteria appear as general for Genentech's R&D work within different areas like genetic engineering, protein purification, analytical methods, and so on (McKelvey 1996, chap. 7). These criteria include the characteristics: reliable, can be replicated, easy to use, less expensive, and standardized (e.g., possible to use for a number of similar projects). Just as the industrialization trend in factory production was toward interchangeable and mass-produced mechanical parts, so, too, the techniques and methods used in Genentech should be replicable and standardized.

In making choices about the direction of technical change, the Ericsson R&D project involved a similar rationale, striving for reliability, ease of use, standardization, and decreased costs. For example, Ellemtel further developed a method to use object-oriented programming for the whole programming cycle, including specification of the project in advance, construction, testing, and maintenance of code (*Tele* 1993).[19] The reason for doing so was that this method should increase the reusability of code, standardize tasks, increase reliability, and thereby lower costs. By using higher-level languages and formal methods during programming, Ericsson wanted to be able to reuse the code even under a new system. For example, if a new computer language and/or process were later introduced, reuse would increase flexibility and the range of possible choices. In comparison, programming code to perform tasks possible in the existing AXE system cannot be moved to the new telephone exchanges and must instead be developed anew (*Tele* 1993, 21).

Although the rationale was the same as Genentech's, Ericsson seems to have had more difficulty in developing technology that fits its criteria. This difference may be related to the increasing rate of technical change in core and complementary technologies. Technologies are malleable to different degrees.

7. Internal Selection Mechanisms

Finally, there are internal selection mechanisms, which implement internal selection criteria. What internal firm selection mechanisms can be identified? Which have more influence than others on the rate and direction of technical change? Why? To what extent can management decisions influence technical change? These address the extent to which management can or cannot implement its goals with R&D.

Genentech management was committed to this R&D project, indicating strong mechanisms to continue technical change. For example, resources were found to continue R&D (and clinical testing), even when unexpected challenges arose involving increased costs. Moreover, many decisions about which paths of technical development to emphasize in in-house R&D were based on judgment about the relative market and technical benefits. For example, Genentech researchers improved the university-developed analytical method of silver staining according to the firm's internal selection criteria. It would have been technically possible to do so earlier, but the cost of the technique and modifying it was judged as too high relative to expected returns. However, when existing analytical methods were incapable of identifying contaminants and variations causing clinical reactions, then resources were found to invest in R&D to make this university-based technique relevant to the needs of the firm.

Similarly, in Ericsson, the management decision to scrap the large broadband exchange project was a strong internal selection mechanism. During the R&D project, however, some have argued that the problem was not too much management influence but too little, for new technical possibilities continually redefined the goals of the project rather than leading to the analysis of technical possibilities relative to future market demands (*Ny Teknik* 1995a).

Another selection mechanism common to both R&D projects is the vital role played by testing methods and routines. In the case of Genentech's rDNA hGH, testing routines compared the output of the production process with an ideal hGH molecule, with what was known about pituitary hGH, and with patients' reactions to rDNA hGH. Testing routines such as analytical methods enabled the firm to see problems with complementary or core technologies and then gave it some idea of how to modify them. Much of Genentech's R&D effort went into improving, and to some extent developing new, testing routines. Its testing methods were in turn tools used to influence the direction of other in-house technical changes.

In the case of Ericsson as well, testing routines have been a crucial means of deciding which would work in the system and of selecting between existing alternatives. Ericsson's testing routines have in particular involved verifying, testing, and debugging code because computer programming is the major cost of developing telephone exchanges. The testing is intended to verify what does and does not work in the computer program, and it mostly influences further programming (rather than other types of technology).

Conclusions

The preceding comparison of the Genentech and Ericsson R&D projects as premarket selection are summarized in table 1. The Genentech project led to a successful innovation, whereas the Ericsson project was canceled before reaching its goals. For each of the seven points, table 1 indicates the similarities and differences between the two R&D projects. What can we learn from this specific comparison?

For the first, the less successful R&D project involved more uncertainty than the successful one did. There has been more market uncertainty

TABLE 1. Comparison of Two R&D Projects as Premarket Selection

Criteria \ Firm	Genentech	Ericsson
1. Market uncertainty	Low —substitute for existing —expand existing —new markets Decrease over time	Medium —new uses —new characteristics —competition with existing Remain medium over time —new time horizon?
2. Technical uncertainty Core technology	High —work at all? —commercially viable? Decrease over time	High (but apparent collective agreement) Remain high
Complementary technology	Low —use existing Increase over time —modify for each new use	High general uncertainty —new demands on tech. Remain high over time —rapid external technical development
External technological developments	Firm as leader Decrease over time —similar paradigm —new uses of the tech. —other core tech.	Firm as leader Increase over time —rapid tech. change in core and complementary tech.

3. Trade-offs between market and technical considerations	Placed technical before market in R&D
	Even so, only implement tech.
	  change if reduces cost and/or
	  improves product
		Placed technical before market in R&D
		Criticisms:
		—too flexible?
		—too tech. oriented?
		Reason to stop R&D: market before
		  technical

4. Relative distance to firm competences	None (new firm) Similar contemporary R&D projects —objectives and approach —firm sees itself as leader	Close to existing —new tech. and competences —similar design and tech. characteristics —firm sees itself as leader

5. Develop systemic technology in-house?	Yes
	—control over production
	—use and modify existing tech.
	—participate in and monitor
	  external developments
		Yes
		—product
		—control of development, design
		  in-house
		—participate in and monitor external
		  developments

6. Internal selection criteria For existing alternatives To influence direction of technical change	Decrease cost Increase performance Replicable Reliable Standardized Ease of use Decreased cost	Decrease cost Increase performance Replicable Reliable Standardized Ease of use Decreased cost Flexible Modular
7. Internal selection mechanisms	Management commitment to project Testing (analytical method)	Management —too weak during R&D? —strongest when canceled Testing of computer programs

in relation to which technical characteristics will be demanded by new and/ or future users—and more technical uncertainty about complementary technologies. Moreover, the pace of external technical and knowledge development has been very rapid. New R&D investment in the firm and in other organizations has led to more technical alternatives being generated, hence greater diversity and more uncertainty. R&D management in the successful project led to a reduction of uncertainty, whereas the less successful involved more experimenting and monitoring of external trends.

Second, the less successful project involved a wider span of new core and complementary technologies. Nonetheless, this firm had had experience with similar products and technologies, and it mostly used an existing paradigm for the innovation. In this case, the principles for how the systemic technology should function were approximately the same, but new areas of technical competence were necessary. The successful innovation also required a range of complementary technologies, but these were not changing as rapidly, and the start-up firm hired persons with competences or cooperated with other firms.

For the third, the internal selection criteria to steer in-house technical change were approximately the same in the two R&D projects. The less successful project did have two additional ones (e.g., flexibility and modular), but these are probably related to the type of technologies involved. However, a more clear difference is that the less successful firm had more difficulty in stimulating technical change that followed its criteria. This implies that there are different levels of difficulty in actually modifying technical change to meet internal selection criteria.

Finally, in both R&D projects, management decisions were, as expected, a strong selection mechanism, but testing was also very important for choosing among alternatives. The less successful project involved a rather dramatic switch from emphasizing technical considerations (potentially under conditions of too little management control) to emphasizing market considerations, especially current rather than future markets. This switch in evaluation criteria rapidly depreciated the value of search for future (or potential) innovations relative to products that could be developed quickly. The time horizon for returns shifted.

A vital remaining question is whether these differences between success and failure arose from too little—or too much—commitment and investment in in-house R&D or whether the explanation lies with the type of technology involved and the rate of external technical change.

In that only two R&D projects have been compared here, no general conclusions can be drawn about the circumstances underlying why one R&D project will successfully link strategic management decisions with external selection criteria in an innovation while another will fail. We can make a few hypotheses worth testing in a larger number of cases. They include:

1. If the firm bets on the "wrong" core technology, the whole R&D project will be a failure.

2. If the firm bets on the "wrong" complementary technologies, it may be possible to change trajectories.

3. If technical uncertainty is high in all dimensions, management should emphasize flexibility, and keeping options open, rather than locking into one alternative.

4. Moreover, in this situation the firm should develop more incentives to monitor external developments and should let that influence the direction of in-house technical change.

5. Finally, the trade-off between market and technical considerations is often related to the question of time, or when the R&D project is expected to show a return. Radical projects may incur losses over a longer period, so if they are failures they cost much money, but if they are successful they have the potential to lead to large gains.

The final concluding remarks address how this essay could be used to influence our, or firms', thinking. For the first, an evolutionary approach has been used here to identify a third function of R&D, namely, developing internal firm selection criteria and mechanisms, which influence technical change. This function has not previously been explicitly discussed in the literature about R&D.

Second, this essay has developed concepts and questions about the links between market and technical uncertainty and about premarket selection. With a larger number of cases, the categories could be used to examine hypotheses about why some R&D projects are more likely to generate successful innovations than others. This analysis would include factors internal as well as external to the firm. It is also proposed that firms should explicitly use the concepts and questions developed here in order to better evaluate and manage R&D projects.

Finally, this approach has theoretical implications for evolutionary economics because it is a step away from assuming the overwhelming importance of random mutations and instead illuminates premarket selection processes in firms.

NOTES

This research was financed by the Swedish Council for Planning and Coordination of Research (FRN, Forskningsrådsnämnden), "Swedish Innovative Activities in High Technology," Project 9–15–5, Dnr. 950692.

1. However, it is not assumed that all R&D projects actually do so. Whether and how well specific R&D projects fulfill these functions is instead an empirical question.

2. Nelson (1987) argues that understanding selection mechanisms is crucial and

one of the major challenges of a socioeconomic evolutionary approach. Specifying them avoids tautologies such as "those which survive are best because the best survive." Instead, we must be able to specify conditions of selection as well as how fast and efficiently the process winnows among diversity.

3. Within Ericsson, this project had the temporary name of "AXE-N," but to avoid confusion with the existing AXE telephone exchange system, the terms "ATM" and "broadband exchange" are used here.

4. Genentech information is from the *Financial Times* (1995, 17), and Ericsson information is from *Ny Teknik* (1995a).

5. Readers interested in the similarities and differences between biological and socioeconomic evolution are referred to McKelvey (1996), which also refers to the relevant evolutionary literature.

6. See McKelvey (1997a), which makes the argument that in general human beings interpret environmental conditions, and therefore their intentionality, a priori influences the novelty generated.

7. This is why learning about current conditions and technical conditions that were/were not selected is also important.

8. There are, however, different levels of uncertainty; more uncertainty is involved the further away the novelty is from current routines and knowledge.

9. The higher price commanded may be possible in a longer or shorter run due to factors such as monopoly conditions, patents, and/or early-mover advantages.

10. Ericsson spends the highest total amount if the Swiss-Swedish multinational ABB is excluded.

11. These include treating children in the normal height range but short as well as other conditions such as burns, wounds, retention of muscle mass, and so on.

12. The initial rDNA versions differed slightly (by one amino acid).

13. Moreover, the level of technical sophistication demanded was expected to be high, although there would be competition over price, including costs of installation, maintenance, and upgrading. Technical sophistication had to be high if the broadband system was to compete as a future-oriented system, which, once installed, could function for many years and satisfy new, as yet unformulated demands.

14. The main use of genetic engineering in pharmaceuticals seems to be as a research tool rather than the basis of production (McKelvey, 1997b).

15. Agreement was over the general ATM approach and how to divide data into standard-sized cells. Each cell consists of a header field with addressing (routing) information and an information field with data.

16. The basic problem, already identified in 1989, was that if one ATM cell would arrive out of order or get lost (sent to the wrong place) then the whole message might be disturbed; the severity of the problem would depend on the type of data being sent. For example, direct contact between human beings such as telephone conversations are much more sensitive to such disruptions and lags than is transmission of text between computers.

17. The problems of programmer freedom and follow-on errors are compounded in an object-oriented approach because each module of computer programs is supposed to be used for multiple (similar) tasks and hence is inherited.

18. Problems arose not least because C++ gives the programmer much freedom, meaning that their own bits of code can influence processes well beyond the task at hand. Such problems can be compared with characteristics of much more

recent computer languages used in the object-oriented approach, such as Hot Java. These restrict each individual programmer's degree of freedom and thereby make it easier for a group of programmers to develop and debug a large, complex body of code.

19. Eriksson further developed the Swedish method ObjectOry into a specific method for telephone systems, called Software Design Process (SDP).

REFERENCES

Cohen, W., and D. Levinthal. 1990. "Absorptive Capacity: A New Perspective on Learning and Innovation." *Administrative Science Quarterly* 35:128–52.
Computer Sweden. 1996. "C++ sänkte Ericsson" [C++ sunk Ericsson]. 2.
Coombs, R., P. Saviotti, and V. Walsh. 1987. *Economics and Technological Change.* London: MacMillan.
Dosi, Giovanni. 1984. *Technical Change and Industrial Transformation.* New York: Macmillian.
Dosi, Giovanni, Christopher Freeman, Richard Nelson, Gerald Silverberg, and Luc Soete, eds. 1988. *Technical Change and Economic Theory.* London: Pinter.
Elektroniktidningen. 1995. "Gunnar Eriksson ska sätta fart på Ellemtel" [Gunnar Eriksson will get Ellemtel moving]. No. 10: 17–18.
Eliasson, Gunnar. 1990. "The Firm as a Competent Team." *Journal of Economic Behavior and Organization* 13:275–98.
Ericsson Annual Report. 1989.
———. 1994.
Ericsson Review. 1993. "The Telecom Evolution in the Broadband Era." No. 1.
Financial Times. 1995. "Eli Lilly and Genentech Settle Dispute: Settles 8-Yr Dispute with Genentech over the Rights to a Growth Hormone." 6 January.
Fryklund, Linda. 1992. Interview with the author, November 25, Stockholm. Director of R&D Peptide Hormones, Kabi, Stockholm, Previously department head of the Recip Hormone Laboratory and head of Growth Factors Research at KabiVitrum.
Hughes, Thomas. 1983. *Networks of Power: Electrification of Western Society, 1880–1930.* Baltimore: Johns Hopkins University Press.
IEEE Spectrum. 1996. "Technology Highlights, 1996: Communications." Institute of Electrical and Electronics Engineers, Inc., January 1996. Vol. 33.
Kline, S., and N. Rosenberg. 1986. "An Overview of Innovation." In *The Positive Sum Strategy,* edited by R. Landau and R. Rosenberg. Washington, DC: National Academy Press.
Knight, Frank. 1921. *Risk, Uncertainty, and Profit.* Boston: Houghton-Mifflin.
Langlois, Richard, and Michael Everett. 1994. "What is Evolutionary Economics?" In *Evolutionary and Neo-Schumpeterian Approaches to Economics,* edited by Lars Magnusson. Boston: Kluwer Academic.
Lin, Norm. 1993. Senior Scientist, Cell Culture, and Fermentation R&D, Genentech. Interview with the author, January 11, South San Francisco.
McKelvey, Maureen. 1996. *Evolutionary Innovations: The Business of Biotechnology.* Oxford: Oxford University Press.
———. 1997a. "Using Evolutionary Theory to Define Systems of Innovation." In

Systems of Innovation: Technologies, Institutions, and Organizations, edited by Charles Edquist. London: Pinter.

———. 1997b. "Coevolution in Commercial Genetic Engineering." *Industrial and Corporate Change.* 6, no. 3 (forthcoming).

Nätvärlden. 1996. "Ericsson växlar ner efter misslyckade ATM-satsning." No. 1: 45–47.

Nelson, Richard. 1987. *Understanding Technical Change as an Evolutionary Process.* Amsterdam: North-Holland.

Nelson, Richard, and Sidney Winter, 1982. *An Evolutionary Theory of Economic Change.* Cambridge: Belknap Press of Harvard University Press.

Ny Teknik. 1994. "Efterföljaren till ATM finns redan hos svenska forskare" [Successor to ATM already under development by Swedish researchers]. 24:14–15.

———. 1995a. "Ericsson ger upp framtidens telenät" [Ericsson gives up the telephone net of the future]. 50–52:4–5.

———. 1995b. "Ericsson fortforande bäst på FoU" [Ericsson still best at R&D]. 19:18–20.

Pavitt, Keith. 1991. "What Makes Basic Research Economically Useful?" *Research Policy* 20, no. 2:109–19.

Rosenberg, Nathan. 1982. *Inside the Black Box: Technology and Economics.* Cambridge: Cambridge University Press.

———. 1990. "Why Do Firms Do Basic Research (with Their Own Money)?" *Research Policy* 19, no. 2: 165–74.

Schumpeter, Joseph. 1968. *The Theory of Economic Development.* Cambridge: Harvard University Press.

Swanson, Robert. 1986. "People Make Decisions as Owners." In *Biotech 86, at the Crossroad: A Survey of an Industry in Evolution, Including Interviews with Industry Pioneers and the New Generation of Managers.* Arthur Young High Technology Group.

Tele. 1989. "Ellemtel's aktiviteter inom bredband" [Ellemtel's activities in broadband], no. 4: 37–41.

———. 1993. "Utveckling av programvara: Mijlardbelopp på spel i nya programvarupottan" [Development of computer programs: billions at stake], no. 4: 17–22.

———. 1994. "Objektorientering—rapport från verkstadsgolvet" [Object-oriented programming—report from the floor], no. 4: 46–47.

———. 1995. "PARC-Bredband. Sex grundläggande problem att lösa" [PARC-broadband: six fundamental problems to solve], no. 2: 14–17.

Tele Special Issue. 1990a. "ATM—When, Where, How—and Why?" Tele Network Department Special Issue, 49–53.

———. 1990b. "RACE: Atmospheric." Tele Network Department Special Issue, 12–19.

———. 1990c. "RACE: Software Technologies, Best." Tele Network Department Special Issue, 42–44.

———. 1990d. "RACE: Software Technologies, Arise." Tele Network Department Special Issue, 45–48.

Utterback, James M., and William J. Abernathy. 1975. "A Dynamic Model of Product and Process Innovation." *Omega* 3, no. 6: 639–56.

Vedin, Bengt-Arne. 1994. "Så blev AXE ett sjumilakliv" [How the AXE exchange took a large step forward]. *Daedalus* (Stockholm) 42–79.

Technology Level, Knowledge Formation, and Industrial Competence in Paper Manufacturing

Staffan Laestadius

1. Introduction

The academic analysis of industrial innovations, competitiveness, and technology policy has been heavily focused on a "science and technology perspective" (S&TP) based on highly aggregated data on R&D spending and patent statistics. The many publications from the Organization for Economic Cooperation and Development (OECD) and Department of Science, Technology, and Industry (DSTI; within the OECD) illustrate that phenomenon (see OECD 1994). A recent EU document, the *Green Paper on Innovation,* adopts a similar S&TP (EU 1995). And Swedish government reports in this field are worried that Sweden, compared with its trading partners, is too specialized on "simple commodities from basic industries" (LU 1994).

The empirical foundation for many of these intellectual exercises is the very detailed R&D statistics that are produced for the OECD area and are based on a data collection procedure standardized through the well-known *Frascati Manual* (OECD 1993). These R&D data, available on country and industry levels, are attractive not only because they make quantitative analyses possible but also because they can be related to production, trade, and patent statistics. The excessive use of these data illustrates the common political and academic tendency to overemphasize what you can see and neglect what is not statistically visible. These data should of course be used; the role of academics, however, should be to place them in a proper perspective.

The use of R&D statistics may illustrate this. Although somewhat modified over the years, the OECD classification of industries with respect to their technology level identifies 22 industries in the OECD, which are ranked according to their average R&D intensity and classified into four categories: high tech, medium high, medium low, and low tech (OECD 1994, 231).

At the top end of this scheme you can find industries like aerospace, computers, electronics, and pharmaceuticals, which all have R&D intensities exceeding 10 percent (R&D expenditure/production). In the very low-tech bottom, on rank 20 of 22, you can find the pulp, paper, and printing industry. The average R&D intensity of this industry is 0.3 percent of production in that sector.

From this S&TP, Sweden is a medium or low-tech producer and exporter compared with many other OECD countries (Edquist 1993, 42; Ohlsson 1992, 27ff.). This is partly due to the heavy Swedish specialization in the pulp and paper (p&p) industry. The situation is similar for Finland. The Balassa indices for pulp and paper are 3.8 and 8.1 for Sweden and Finland, respectively. Not only are these figures extreme for the p&p industry within the OECD; advanced industrialized countries usually are not that highly specialized in single industries on that level of aggregation (OECD 1995, 172).

Other indices, however, point in different directions. In general, Swedish R&D intensity (more than 3 percent of GDP) is among the highest within the OECD area (OECD 1995, 146). Sweden is also one of the countries spending most (relative to its population, GDP, etc.) on information and communication technology (OECD 1992, 12; EITO 1995, 406), indicating an ability to take advantage of these technologies, if not to export them.

Added to that, it can be argued that differences in R&D intensities between p&p and printing, differences in the mix between them in various countries, and, finally, real differences in the industry's R&D intensities between countries for a long time have been neglected in aggregate analyses.[1]

These phenomena constitute the context for a research project in progress: "Is Sweden a high-tech or low-tech industrial country?" *The first part* of that project deals with the overall methodological problems of the standard science and technology perspective. Is the low score in R&D intensity in production and exports the result of different classifications of R&D between industries? More fundamentally, does measured R&D intensity reflect innovative activity (Laestadius 1996b)?

In *the second part* of the research project, we study the fundamentals of industrial knowledge formation, technology, and industrial competence in a broader perspective than measured as R&D spending. In this part of the project, the processes of knowledge formation, paths followed by technological development, and the complexity of technical systems are studied on a detailed level by looking "inside the black box" of technology (cf. Rosenberg 1982, 1995). This "bottom-up approach" is necessary for the academic understanding of industrial and technical development.

Initially, a pilot study of the industrial competence of a small welding company was carried out (Laestadius 1994). The study on paper technology presented here also belongs to this second ambition of the research project.

Eight paper mills and seven plants for paper machinery and equipment have been visited. I have studied the production systems and interviewed about 90 engineers, process operators, and other staff responsible for research and technological developments.[2] The results provide a new picture of knowledge formation in paper technology, of learning, and of innovation.

2. Industrial Competence as Systems Competence

Engineers, technicians, and operators interviewed in this project and engaged in paper technology identify their competence as a *systems competence,* that is, a competence to run and develop complete, complex, technical systems. Many of the respondents with experience in other industries (automotive, steel, and nuclear power) are of the opinion that the complexity is higher in paper technology than in many other engineering and process industries.

For the purpose of this study, we can identify two different systems. The first is the technological system at large, that is, the *wide* cluster related to the production chain of paper and including parts of the forest industry, manufacturers of paper machinery, consultants, manufacturers of process- and control equipment and so on (cf. Carlsson 1995, chap. 2). Second, I identify the *narrow* system related to the paper machine and the plant where it is situated. Both these systems may be called sociotechnical systems, rather than technical in a narrow sense, although the enormous artifact, the paper machine, is more in focus in an analysis made narrow than in one made wide.

The sections that follow focus on the plant. In section 3, I describe the narrowly defined system, and in section 4 I concentrate on knowledge formation and competence in that system. Section 5 analyzes the different technological strategies chosen by four paper mills. In section 6, however, I include some extensions to the wider context of knowledge formation within paper technology—a questions that is analyzed in more depth in the larger study of which this is a part (Laestadius 1996a). Section 7 contains the conclusions.

3. The Paper-Making System, Narrowly Defined

Paper making starts with collecting fibers—natural or recycled. Through mechanical procedures and/or heat and chemical processes, they are dissolved into a suspension of <1 percent fiber content. The rest is mainly water.

After various screening and washing processes, this suspension is ejected from a headbox between two lips onto an endless moving wire web (or between two) through which the water can be drained. After the initial drainage on the web, the paper "in spe" is forwarded to a press section where the dry content is increased to about 50 percent before it moves to a long drying section consisting of maybe 50 drying cylinders heated with steam. After that follows sections for calandering, coating, and winding.

For newsprint, which is by far the most important single quality, this process is carried out at a speed of 1,300 to 1,700 meters per minute (m/min) in modern paper machines, which have wire widths of about nine to 10 meters. The paper, produced at about 14,000 m^2/min, typically has a density of 45 g/m^2 and a thickness of 70 μm. In board manufacturing, the speed is lower and the formation more complicated, as these qualities often are made up of many different layers.

The characteristics of the system may be summarized by four technological circumstances:

The dimension paradox
The circulation system
The control system (a result of the first two)
The digital character of the continuous process

The *dimension paradox* consists of the fact that a paper machine, on one hand, is an enormous artifact, usually more than 200 meters long and costing 200 to 500 million U.S. dollars to install, depending on the need for supply systems. On the other hand, this enormous artifact with its heavy components is supposed to work with extremely high precision. This can be illustrated by the fact that the expected normal deflection of a 10 meter roll in the press section is about 3 millimeters. That is about the same as 40 to 50 layers of newsprint paper, of which the tolerance in the final thickness is about +/− 0.5 μm. Roughly that also gives the tolerances for the deflection control of the press section and calandering rolls. If the paper, due to insufficient deflection control or other reasons (e.g., too little water somewhere along the 10 meter wide pulpjet ejected onto to the wire web), is allowed to deviate, say, +3 μm, it will accumulate at the winder in the end of the paper machine and may cause an intolerable 60 millimeter local increase in the radius.

The *circulation system* in paper making is part of the core technology. Between 90 and 99.5 percent of all material handled in a paper plant is water, which has to be taken care of, cleaned, and recirculated. A lot of energy is demanded in the pumping, filtering, and separation processes, and the control problem is very exacting. Because of the large water content in the suspension, even small relative contents of fines or chemicals in the drained and recirculated water will have an enormous potential impact on the paper. Such pollution also tends to accumulate over time, causing instability and potential quality problems, which can take hours to stabilize as the water is recirculated.

The *control system* is vital to handle the instability of the process. One way to illustrate the complexity of the system is to describe it from the hardware side: at SCA Ortviken in northern Sweden, the whole system consists of 135 integrated central processing units (CPUs) coordinating 2,000 motor control systems, 1,700 instrument control systems, 1,400 valves, and another 3,600 indicators. This is done with help of 21,500 digital imports, and 7,700 digital outports, and another 10,000 analog in- and outports.

Another way to illustrate the complexity is through an analysis of the control problem related to the dimension paradox just mentioned. To keep the paper, which is manufactured at a speed of about 100 km/h within allowed specifications, the system has to continuously change and balance a vector of parameters. Among the core parameters is the dilution profile at the maybe 130 nozzles at the headbox, the pressure profile at the set of hydraulic pressing elements in the press section, the transverse profile of wetting and steam blowing over the paper roll, and the profile of the pressure of the maybe 60 hydraulic elements expanding the diameters of the calander rolls from inside the end of the process.

Within certain limits, there is a large set of possible vectors of parameter settings that result in an acceptable paper but with different characteristics according to quality, manufacturability, and runnability at the customers' process equipment.

This process industry, in which a tube-based process via the headbox is transformed into a continuous mechanical one, also has a *digital character* in the sense that the whole system must be working at exactly the same time and continuously running at (more or less) full speed in order to avoid problems. As there are no possibilities to exchange or repair parts of the system while running, and there are virtually no possibilities to balance production with intermediate stocks; the whole system is either running at full speed or not in use.[3]

4.   The Knowledge Formation and Competence of a Paper-Making Plant

The competence of a paper-making plant has two dominant systemic elements. There is a short-term *running competence* and a long-term *developmental competence*. Both are connected through *learning*. The plant must develop the ability to learn from experiences and transform these not only into excellent performance in the short run but also into knowledge of importance for long-term technical development of the entire system. Such learning corresponds to the *learning-by-using* concept developed by Rosenberg (1982, chap. 6). Following Rosenberg, we can identify two main categories of knowledge.

Disembodied knowledge seems to be of great importance in the daily running of paper mills. This knowledge develops within individuals as it grows in the organization as a whole, that is, becomes a part of the plant culture into which newly recruited employees are initiated. Through daily practice, disembodied knowledge is transferred between the employees. Part of this knowledge is also tacit.

The knowledge necessary to run a paper machine, although based on well-known and internationally available technology, is unique at the paper machine level. Every paper machine is a complex compromise between old and new subsystems connected according to locally developed traditions and modified over the years. It is also a synthesis between the experiences of the user plant and the equipment producer. The combination of the uniqueness of the paper machines and differences in company/plant cultures means very different performance (with high impact on profits) even for similar machines located in different plants.

With *embodied knowledge,* we, like Rosenberg, identify the transformation of experiences out of daily running into new or modified artifacts. This embodiment is a central part of traditional engineering science and typically takes the form of incremental modification of existing systems. This process is also heavily dependent on the technological characteristics of the production process (the capital structure). High fixed costs direct inventive activities toward disembodied and incremental embodied innovations, while capital-demanding changes in technology are accumulated as invisible (tacit) knowledge in the organization until it — if ever — is mobilized in the design of new processes.

Although most of the heavy mechanical parts of a paper machine are used for decades, continuous innovative creativity and successful incremental fine tuning of hundreds of subsystems determines whether the plant will be profitable or not.

Long-term developmental competence makes the paper mill a strong user or a *competent purchaser,* which puts high pressure on the equipment manufacturers to improve equipment and provide new technical solutions, thus moving the technology frontier forward. This role is based on a capacity to absorb and fit new technology into the existing system. But it is also achieved through an ability to identify, articulate, and communicate experiences and formulate more or less precise demands on the equipment companies. Usually this *demand-forming* process is concentrated through the project team, which is organized to be the user partner in the design and construction of a new paper machine.[4]

The results of these learning processes can, with regard to short-term running competence, be illustrated by the performance of the Braviken Paper Mill in Sweden. Figure 1 shows the normalized average daily production figures for the two paper machines (PM 51 and PM 52) in Braviken. As can be seen, both machines have increased their production by about 50 percent since their installation. The rate of increase is also obviously decreasing.

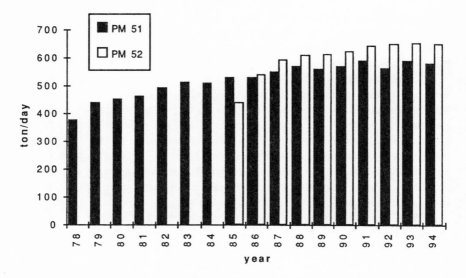

Fig. 1. The running performance of PM 51 and 52 at Braviken

The main explanation behind this production increase is disembodied knowledge. Braviken is a good example of Salter-type (1960, 1966) investments. Almost all capital costs are related to the first installment phase, thus creating a well-defined vintage capital. PM 52 is more or less a slightly upgraded version, including the embodied experiences from PM 51. The succeeding minor investments are of replacement character; they may be related to incremental (embodied) innovations, but interviews with the staff do not indicate that these are of crucial importance for productivity. Because of the high and fixed capital costs involved, the shapes of the learning curves, the daily production, and the running hours per year are extremely important for the profitability of the plant.

5. Four Strategies Based on Different Learning Experiences

Although Braviken was the world's leading newsprint manufacturer some years ago, its learning by using through disembodied knowledge is not enough to compensate for the low productivity of the old vintages of its PMs. The productivity potential of the existing platforms has been almost exhausted, although (not shown here) they are still competitive on the international newsprint market.

The strategy chosen by Braviken was to add another newsprint machine to the existing two. The new PM was installed in June 1996, following an eighteen-month purchasing and specification period of intensive user-producer relations between the Braviken staff and Voith-Sulzer, the main equipment supplier. This installment embodies the experiences of the staff at Braviken in combination with the experiences of other actors in the paper technology system widely defined.

The older paper machines will continue to produce newsprint, but they will concentrate on the thinner directory qualities for which extremely high speed is less important. The strategy is to consolidate the extremely production-oriented plant culture and the advanced experience of news-print manufacturing. From a *technological point of view,* this strategy can be interpreted as a "moderate early adopter strategy," moderate because the installation includes no revolutionary innovations regarding raw materials, product, or process technology. Nor will Braviken become a pilot plant for any radically new technology. The strategy is early because Braviken has included in its new paper machine four advanced subsystems already exist-ing on the market, although not in combination or used for newsprint. From a *strategical point of view,* the continued concentration on relatively low-priced newsprint, based on a high proportion of energy-consuming thermo-mechanical pulp made of virgin wood fibers, can be viewed as risky. A further analysis of this, however, falls outside the scope of this essay.

Parallel to this, the competitor Ortviken (SCA) has chosen another strategy. This plant invested in a paper machine that can produce light-weight-coated (LWC) quality (i.e., by coating the paper with a thin layer of clay before it is calandered). At least four reasons can be identified behind this strategy: first, Ortviken never managed to run its earlier paper ma-chines with the high productivity and running time necessary for newsprint (as Braviken could); second, the good local availability of chemical and mechanical pulp based on natural fiber compared with recycled fiber; third, the size of the plant site not allowing the wire width necessary to compete in the newsprint market; and, fourth, the overall corporate (SCA) strategy of transferring newsprint production to Aylesford, closer to the sources of recycled fiber in the London area.

And this competitor, Aylesford Newsprint, works under totally dif-ferent conditions. Instead of—like Braviken—using a 40/60 relation of recycled and natural fibers, this Kent-based plant has developed an energy-saving process for the treatment of ordinary household paper waste, converting it to pulp and further to a totally recycled fiber-based (RCF) newsprint quality with an electricity demand of about one-sixth of the demand in virgin fiber-based thermo-mechanical pulp preparation. The process has been designed and developed at Aylesford in cooperation with consultants and built up with equipment from more than a dozen major machine builders. At the end of the process, this SCA-controlled plant has, however, installed a paper machine composed of well-tested "old" technology. The competence of this plant lies in the treatment of recycled fibers and the high quality of the newsprint produced from that.

Another plant to compare is Haindl Papier in Schongau, which combines the qualities of Braviken and Aylesford. Like the former, it has a tradition of high speed and high productivity, giving it a top position in the informal global ranking list. In this extremely clean production site, any pulp, paper, or water found outside the tubes or the paper machines signals that something is wrong and has to be corrected.

Like Aylesford, the Schongau plant has designed and developed an extremely energy-saving recycling process, the pulp of which makes up about 85 percent of the material content of its newsprint. Unlike the other plants, Schongau, however, has adopted a pilot plant strategy. Several times it has been the test plant for new equipment (mainly from Voith) and thus has accepted the start-up problems connected with the pilot versions of new machinery. This has been remunerated with reductions in installment costs, but it has also created a high development competence and a capacity to absorb and utilize new technology among the employees at Schongau, which has allowed the plant to reduce drastically the otherwise frequent use of consultants for process design and redesign in connection with new installments.

These plants, which all exhibit low R&D expenditures, have chosen four different strategies in technological development and maintaining and advancing their industrial competence. None of this information surfaces through a superficial analysis of their R&D intensities.

6. The Context of Learning and Knowledge Formation: Changing Relations

New technologies and industrial competence do not grow out of plant cultures in isolation. Although this essay focuses on plants, the context for their development processes should at least be touched upon.

First, for *technical reasons* the development of paper is largely carried out in the form of *user-producer collaboration*. The monitoring of the process in its entirety is traditionally allocated to the paper mill — the experiences of which have to be communicated to the equipment producers. Also, the fact that laboratory results cannot, without much further work, be transformed into down-scaled pilot plants or full-scale production units usually necessitates cooperation. The enormous costs of full-scale development work — often connected with production losses at the test plant — also add to the arguments for cooperation. My field studies clearly indicate that these development projects — usually the most expensive parts of the whole process — are seldomly counted as R&D. In fact, only about 20 percent of the costs in the development projects studied were registered as R&D in the accountancies of either the producer or the user of the equipment.

Second, the paths followed in the development of paper technology exhibit strong inner dynamics reinforced by the *thought styles* (Laestadius 1992, Douglas 1986) dominating within the profession and the industry, although there are differences between countries, regions, plants, and corporations. These cultures have their roots in the local resource endowments, which have always provided the opportunities to grasp and set the problems to be overcome by paper makers. Two hundred years ago, the shortage of recycled fibers (rag) was a serious bottleneck for the expansion of the industry. This shortage also directed inventive activity for many decades (Hills 1988, chaps. 9–10). Today the problems are different.

The Scandinavian countries (and Canada) are relatively abundant in natural fibers. As mentioned, these countries are also highly specialized in production and export of pulp and paper products. This, of course, fits well in standard foreign trade theory. The availability of virgin wood fiber, water, and cheap energy has influenced the industrial strategies developed and technological paths followed.

In the rest of Europe, the situation is — and has for a long time been — different and more related to facing selective disadvantages (cf. Porter 1990).

The competence in paper making in Aylesford illustrates this phenomenon. With its origins in paper production out of fibers from rag in the seventeenth century, the Maidstone area in Kent managed to keep its competitiveness in paper making well into the 1960s. Maidstone was in fact until then the single largest paper-producing district in Europe — although the industry gradually shifted to wood fiber during the second half of the nineteenth century (Lewis 1967).

With no advantages in virgin wood fibers and facing high energy prices, Aylesford (and the rest of Kent) gradually lost its competitiveness to Scandinavian producers. The paper makers in Kent were thus forced to use and de-ink recycled fibers that they had tested during World War I, and again, with improved methods, during World War II. In 1982, they pioneered the converting of a newsprint machine to 100 percent recycled fibers. The company was in decline, however, and was sold to SCA, which has contributed with capital and management.

Third, there is also a user-producer relation between paper plants and their customers. The buyers may, for example, demand higher runnability, lower weight, higher opacity, or totally new qualities. Although these user-producer relations are concerned with the *product* for both parties involved, they have significant implications for their *processes.* For printing papers and newsprint alike, the design of the product and the production process is highly integrated. This integration of product and process development tells a lot about the character of technical development, especially in mature industries/technologies. The fact that a sheet of paper (or a pill?) has a simpler appearance than a mobile telephone does become irrelevant. The important thing to consider is the complexity of the competences involved at the different stages in the production chain as a whole (Laestadius 1996b, chap. 46ff.).

7. Conclusions

The weak links between R&D and technological development in paper technology. The technology level and knowledge formation in the paper industry can only marginally be measured in the form of R&D investments (cf. Laestadius 1996, chap. 3).

The use of R&D indicators for comparative analyses of technology levels, competitiveness, and knowledge formation will therefore be misleading in this case and probably in many other cases as well. This problem can to some extent be removed with new and better routines of bookkeeping, new definitions in the *Frascati Manual,* and so on. Fundamentally, however, such modifications of statistics will not solve the problem. The important differences in the character of knowledge formation between industries probably cannot be captured within the R&D framework.

These differences are partly related to *the origin* of knowledge formation in various industries. Unlike some "high-tech" industries like pharmaceuticals (Eliasson and Eliasson 1996), paper technology does not originate in academia but in improved craft and traditional engineering skills on the shop floor. A typical paper machine installment demands (on the purchaser's side) the equivalent of about 100 qualified engineers working for about a year on designing, constructing, specifying, programming, controlling, and integrating the system. Through advanced user-producer relations, they interact with the equipment producers, the details of which I do not analyze in this essay. This kind of intellectual activity is usually not included in R&D spending. Virtually nothing of the 10 to 15 million U.S. dollars spent by Braviken on process development and user-producer interaction during its recent installation project (5 percent of total project costs) was registered as R&D.

Within a pharmaceutical company, on the other hand, such a concentration of qualified people (with backgrounds in engineering and the natural sciences) in a development project will surely be identified as R&D.[5]

Partly, this also originates in the *organization* of new installations and development activities. The fact that many of these activities take place in direct relation to new installments seems to mean that the costs get lumped together with the usually huge investment costs.

This difference, finally, relates to *the character* of the knowledge-formation process itself. Analytical development activities count as R&D, but synthetical ones do not. The concept of *analytical activities* corresponds to normal practice in the natural sciences. To a large extent, this consists of a narrowing of the focus to isolated phenomena and concentrating efforts on understanding and explaining the inner details of the system. This is very close to the understanding of the creation of new knowledge, that is, "real" R&D from a S&TP.

Synthetical activities, on the other hand, are directed toward building and designing systems through integrating components into complex wholes. This usually necessitates the understanding of the subsystems, although the intellectual efforts are directed toward the system and its interfaces rather than its components. The traditional Schumpeterian understanding of innovations as new combinations in fact is very close to our concept of synthetical activities.

Paper technology — like other mature technologies — is highly synthetical, that is, basically directed toward integrating different subsystems to make them work together. Consider the design of a paper production unit like the new Braviken PM 53: virtually nothing is new in this gigantic paper machine installation. All the different subsystems have been individually described in the literature. In various combinations and shapes, most of them are already installed somewhere in the world. The thermo-mechanical-chemical processes are all known in principle and practice, although there are varieties in, for example, pressure, temperature, and the shapes of the grinding bars.

But the process as a whole system is new; there exists no identical process or system elsewhere, although there are similar ones. A lot of incremental innovations, like the geometry of the nips in the press section, make the process unique, although not radically new. The particular design of the whole, and the competence to master it, are what matters for performance.

R&D activities, paths of technological development, and industrial strategies — some final reflections. The increasing concerns for environmental and energy conservation problems make it natural to conclude that current global tendencies toward increased use of recycled fibers will continue. Increasing energy costs will push this development to include new technologies of screening, for example, third-round fibers from fifth round and using them in various products or different layers (Culichi and Rossi 1995). Over time, this will also challenge processes and products that are still based on virgin wood fibers.

Plants specializing in virgin fibers will thus face the need to transfer their technical development of processes and products to market segments that are easier to defend against attacks from recycled fiber products. The obvious fact that new fibers, at least to some extent, must be fed into the system will not necessarily allow the energy-demanding natural fibers to compete all over the present product range.

Although future development can follow many paths, one possible scenario may be very Schumpeterian, indeed. Stagecoach owners did not develop the railroads. Consequently, we should not expect those dominating the state of paper technology today to lead in the future: actors not building their competence on the abundance of natural fibers and energy but on the shortage of these inputs and a closeness to recycled fibers and expensive energy may be the true innovators of future paper technology. Recent development (e.g., in biotechnology) challenges established processes, industries, and countries.

This scenario may or may not be true. However, the possible structural change discussed previously will probably not be visible through shifts over time or in differences between countries in R&D intensities. As shown in the case of paper, the low R&D intensities in some mature industries, at least, are not comparable with the figures from academically based high-tech undertakings. And the interesting differences in industrial strategies (not analyzed in this essay) between Finnish and Swedish forest-based industries — both with much higher R&D figures within the forest industry than in other countries — are also hidden behind these popular science and technology indicators (cf. Ojainmaa 1994, Peterson 1996).

Understanding the development and the international competitiveness of the paper industry in Sweden (or Finland or Canada) thus necessitates a more disaggregated level of analysis and a more ambitious look into the black box of technology than we economists usually are willing to admit.

NOTES

This essay has improved thanks to the comments of the discussant, Prof. Peter Swann (Manchester), and of my colleague, Prof. Gunnar Eliasson at Kungl Tekniska Högskolan.

1. Data on this are, however, available (cf. OECD 1995, 162). See also Laestadius (1996a, chap. 7.1).

2. The paper plants studied hitherto (although with different intensities) are Aylesford Newsprint (United Kingdom), Braviken Paper Mill (Sweden), Haindl Papier Schongau Werk (Germany), Hylte (Sweden), Italcarta (Italy), Jämsenkoski (Finland), Ortviken (Sweden), and Skoghall (Sweden). In this paper I do not give detailed references to the interviews made.

3. Even extremely well managed paper machines need at least 400 hours per year to exchange outworn parts. Thus, in reality, paper machines are not available more than 95 percent of the hours in a year.

4. The analysis of the complexity of demand forming processes has benefited from Hollander (1995).

5. In 1992, the Swedish pharmaceutical industry reported a R&D intensity of 30.4 percent, which is by far the highest R&D intensity for any industry in any country in the world (OECD 1995, 163).

REFERENCES

This paper is also based on interviews with about 90 persons responsible for R&D, technological development, process control, and the running of paper machines at eight paper mills and several R&D units and equipment producers.

Carlsson, Bo, ed. 1995. *Technological Systems and Economic Performance: The Case of Factory Automation.* Dordrecht: Kluwer Academic.

Culichi, P., and S. Rossi. 1995. "New Screening Concepts for Recycled Fibres: Experiences at SCA Italcarta Mill." Conference paper, 48th AITP Congress, November.

Douglas, Mary. 1986. *How Institutions Think.* Syracuse, NY:

Edquist, Charles. 1993. *Innovationspolitik för förnyelse av svensk industri* [Innovation policy for the renewal of Swedish industry]. Tema T Reports, no. 33. Linköping: Linköping University.

Eliasson, Gunnar, and Åsa Eliasson. 1996. *The Pharmaceutical and Biotechnological Competence Bloc.* Research Report (TRITA-IEO R 1996:3), Dept. of Industrial Economics and Management. Stockholm: Kungl Tekniska Högskolan.

EITO. 1995. *European Information Technology Observatory 95.* Frankfurt am Main: EITO Group.

EU. 1995. "Green Paper on Innovation." *Bulletin of European Union* 5:S

Hills, Richard L. 1988. *Papermaking in Britain, 1488–1988.* London: Athlone.

Hollander, Ernst. 1995. *Varför var det så segt? Om lågriskkemi, miljödriven innovation och kravformning* [The enigmatic time pattern of environmental innovation]. Diss. (TRITA-IEO R 1995:7) Stockholm; Kungl Tekniska Högskolan.

Laestadius, Staffan. 1992. *Arbetsdelningens dynamik* [The dynamics of the division of labor]. Lund: Arkiv Förlag.

———. 1994. *Ramnäs Ankarkätting AB—världsledande tillverkare av avancerad lågteknologi* [Ramnäs Anchor Chains, Inc.—world's leading manufacturer of advanced low-tech products]. (TRITA-IEO R 1994:2). IEO Research Report. Stockholm: Kungl Tekniska Högskolan.

———. 1996a. *Vid "lågteknologins" frontlinjer* [At the front lines of "low technology"]. Research Report. (TRITA-IEO R 1996:8) Stockholm: Kungl Tekniska Högskolan.

———. 1996b. *Är Sverige lågteknologiskt?* [Is Sweden low tech?]. IEO Research Report. (TRITA-IEO R 1996:2). Stockholm: Kungl. Tekniska, Högskolan.

Lewis, P. W. 1967. "Changing Factors of Location in the Papermaking Industry as Illustrated by the Maidstone Area." *Geography* 52, no. 3: 280–93.

LU. 1994. *Näringslivets tillväxtförutsättningar till 2010* [Conditions for industrial growth until 2010]. Långtidsutredningen 1994, suppl. 6. Stockholm: Ministry of Finance.

OECD. 1992. *Information Technology Outlook, 1992.* Paris: OECD.

OECD. 1993. *Frascati Manual, 1993: Proposed Standard Practice for Surveys of Research and Experimental Development.* Paris: OECD.

OECD. 1994. *Science and Technology Policy: Review and Outlook, 1994.* Paris: OECD.

OECD. 1995. *Industry and Technology: Scoreboard of Indicators, 1995.* Paris: OECD.

Ohlsson, Lennart. 1992. *R&D for Swedish Industrial Revival.* Stockholm: Ministry of Education and Research.

Ojainmaa, Kaisa. 1994. *International Competitive Advantage of the Finnish Chemical Forest Industry.* Research Report (C 66). Helsinki: ETLA.

Peterson, Christer. 1996. *Finsk ingenjörskonst och svenskt imperiebyggande* [Finnish engineering competence and Swedish industrial empire building]. Stockholm: SNS Förlag.

Porter, Michael. 1990. *The Competitive Advantage of Naitons.* London: Macmillan.
Rosenberg, Nathan. 1982. *Inside the Black Box.* Cambridge: Cambridge University Press.
———. 1994. *Exploring the Black Box.* Cambridge: Cambridge University Press.
Salter, W. E. G. [1960] 1966. *Productivity and Technical Change.* Cambridge: Cambridge University Press.

Innovator Typologies, Related Competencies, and Performance

John R. Baldwin and Joanne Johnson

This essay classifies small and medium-sized firms by innovator type and explores the complementary strategies in management, marketing, human resources, and financing that are adopted by each innovator type. It also investigates differences in the performance of each group of firms.

Innovation types are chosen as the broad theme around which the essay is based for several reasons. First, studies of innovation regimes (Lundvall 1992, Nelson 1993) have emphasized the differences across nations, industries, and firms. Firms can focus on their existing customers or on new markets. They can concentrate on introducing new or improved products; they can devote their efforts to improving the efficiency of the production of their existing products; or they can introduce radically new processes. Some will focus just on product innovations, others just on process innovations, and still others will combine both product and process innovations. Thus, firms differ substantially in their innovation stances.

The second reason that an innovation taxonomy is used here is because others who have studied the relationship between the strategy that a firm adopts and its success have found it to be a useful way to classify information on firm activity. Because firms are complex entities pursuing heterogeneous policies, a classification methodology is required to reduce the complexity of the analysis of the factors associated with success. Miller (1988) builds on the classification systems of Ansoff and Stewart (1967), Freeman (1974), and Miles and Snow (1978), which focused primarily on the production system of the firm—batch, assembly, continual process—and argues that it is the innovativeness of each that adds the necessary additional dimension for understanding differences among firms.

Others have chosen to reduce the dimensionality of the classification task by examining the determinants of success within a particular industry, size class, or technological emphasis. Chaganti (1987) finds that attention to production costs is associated with success in small firms in the industry growth stage, competitive pricing is associated with small-firm success in the mature industry stage, and aggressive marketing strategies are associated with success in small firms in the declining industry stage.

This focus on the life-cycle model of product-process innovations has also been used by Hayes and Pisano (1994) and the Ministère de l'Industrie (1995) to suggest that manufacturing and innovation strategies will differ across the life cycle of a product or industry, with the early stages of the life cycle being driven primarily by product innovation while process innovation becomes relatively more important in the later stages of the product life cycle. The importance of the life cycle of a product market that was emphasized by Kuznets (1953) is also stressed by Gort and Klepper (1982), who argue that the stage of the life cycle affects the type of strategies that will be found in an industry.

While innovation *in general* is related to success (Baldwin et al. 1994, Nelson 1993, Mowery and Rosenberg 1989, Utterback et al. 1988), the type of innovation *in particular* may affect a firm's probability of success. It may also be the case that certain conditions—firm characteristics or strategic orientations—are necessary for success and that these vary across innovator types. For example, firm size is emphasized in the Schumpeterian literature as being a key to success. In previous studies, success has also been related to export activity (Edmonds and Khoury 1986), merger activity (Reid 1969), and human resource strategies (Rosenbloom and Abernathy 1982). The type of competencies in the area of financing, human resources, and management that are necessary complements to an innovation strategy may be constant irrespective of the market within which a firm is operating, or they may vary across innovator types.

This essay builds on the life-cycle literature and uses an innovation taxonomy to study the strategy profiles of firms. Firms are classified into four basic types based on their innovation strategies. These different innovation types conform to the product life-cycle model that others have described. Differences across innovation types both in terms of success and complementary strategies in marketing, finance, and human resources are then explored.

In the following sections, the existence of distinct innovation types is first established. Subsequently, differences in the complementary strategies and the performance of firms in each of the innovation groups are explored. A brief description of the data, which are taken from the Survey of Growing Small- and Medium-Sized Enterprises (GSME), is presented in the next section.

The Data

Two types of data are used in this essay. Survey data are used to evaluate the emphasis that firms place on different strategies and activities. Administrative data on these firms are used to provide objective information on the size of firms, their rates of growth, and their profitability, so as to evaluate how strategies differ by a firm's performance.

Administrative Data Measuring Success

Administrative firm-level data on sales, assets, employment, profits, and equity for both 1984 and 1988 were used to calculate objective measures of success for firms in the survey. These provide measures of profitability, growth, or market-share change. In order to take into account the multidimensionality of success and to recognize that many of these dimensions are not independent of one another, a large number of measures were combined via principal component analysis into a general success index.[1] The variables included in the analysis are presented in table 1. Measures of market-share change, labor productivity, and profit/sales margins are weighted most heavily in the principal component used here to capture success.

Survey Data

The second source of data that was utilized to perform this analysis comes from the Survey of Growing Small- and Medium-Sized Enterprises. The survey was conducted in 1992, using firms that grew in sales, assets, and employment over the last half of the 1980s. Small and medium-sized firms were defined as having less than 500 employees and less than 100 million dollars in assets in 1984. The sample was drawn from all major industrial sectors, with the exception of public administration. The survey of 2,157 firms was conducted by mail with telephone follow-up. The response rate was 69 percent. Only those firms that answered each question, and for

TABLE 1. Weighting Factors in the General Success Index

Factors	Weight
Output-share change	0.48
Asset-share change	0.49
Equity-share change	0.42
Profit-share change	0.31
Labor-share change	0.21
Change in profits/assets relative to industry	−0.02
Change in profits/equity relative to industry	−0.01
Change in profits/sales relative to industry	0.30
Change in sales/assets relative to industry	−0.03
Change in sales/labor relative to industry	0.16
Equity/assets in 1984	−0.05
Profits/assets in 1984	0.02
Profits/equity in 1984	0.02
Profits/sales in 1984	−0.26
Sales/assets in 1984	0.03
Sales/labor in 1984	−0.14

Source: Baldwin et al. 1994, 59.

which there are corresponding administrative data, amounting to some 661 firms, are used in this study.

The survey investigates the competencies of firms in a variety of areas—their characteristics, activities, and strategic emphases—across a range of industries. Answers to two types of strategy questions allow us to gauge the types of competencies that firms develop.[2] First, respondents indicated the importance they attributed to a variety of factors that contributed to their success, including marketing, technology policy, human resources, and management practices. Respondents scored these factors on a scale of 0 to 5, with 0 corresponding to *not applicable,* 1 to *unimportant,* 2 to *slightly important,* 3 to *important,* 4 to *very important,* and 5 to *crucial.* Second, firms rated their performance relative to their competitors with regard to prices, quality of products, customer services, costs of production, R&D spending, labor climate, and employee skill levels, using a scale of 0 to 5, with 0 corresponding to *not applicable,* 1 to *much worse,* 2 to *somewhat behind,* 3 to *about the same,* 4 to *somewhat better,* and 5 to *much better.* Additionally, questions pertaining to the exporting, investment, training, and innovating activity of firms were also posed. Finally, the importance of various sources of innovation were investigated.

Strategy Types

Data on a number of competencies are developed here. These include such areas as innovation, marketing, human resources, financing, and management. In addition, the firm's innovative stance is carefully investigated. Since the survey contains a number of questions that probe each area, principal component analysis was used to summarize the wealth of data available.[3] The following sections describe the variables that were used in this procedure and the resulting constructs that are employed to investigate the relationship between a firm's innovation strategy and the other competencies and activities that it pursues. The first examines the taxonomy of innovation types that is used in the remainder of the essay. Then summary measures of investment, marketing, human resource policy, financing, and management strategies are developed in turn.

Innovation

The first strategic variable to be analyzed is the innovativeness of the firm. Previous research (Baldwin et al. 1994) found that innovation is strongly related to success, though it did not attempt to provide a comprehensive classification of the different innovation strategies that firms pursue, as is done in this analysis. Technological improvements in communication and transportation, coupled with globalization of markets, have exposed Canadian firms to intense competition. The most successful firms are those that outperform their competitors by continually introducing new products and processes.

A large number of both subjective and objective measures of innovative activity are available from the GSME survey. In addition to traditional questions, such as the number of employees in an R&D unit and expenditures on R&D, subjective questions relating to the innovative stance of the firm and the importance of innovation-related strategies are also employed. Firms rated their R&D spending relative to their competitors on a scale of 0 to 5 (0 corresponding to *not applicable,* 1 to *much worse,* and 5 to *much better*). They also scored the importance of R&D innovation capability or the ability to adopt technology, on a scale of 0 to 5, as a factor in past growth. Questions on general development strategies queried firms on the importance they attribute to strategies related to developing new technology, using others' technology, using new materials, using existing materials more efficiently, reducing labor or energy costs, just-in-time inventory control, and process control. Finally, the stimulus for innovative activity was sought by asking firms to rate a variety of factors—both internal and external—on a scale of 0 to 5, in terms of the importance of that factor as a source of innovation.

Principal component analysis was used to summarize the dimensionality in the set of variables capturing innovative activity. As will be demonstrated, the first three principal components correspond to three different innovation types. The mean scores of each of the variables that were used to define the components are reported in table 2 (the standard errors are reported in the appendix, table A1).

The first prototype, the *product innovator,* represents firms that emphasize product innovation as opposed to process innovation. These firms devote a significant proportion of their investment spending to product innovation. They place a high value on strategies related to continually developing and offering new products. They pay little attention to enhancing their technological capabilities or improving their production efficiency.

The second prototype is the *comprehensive innovator.* This component weights all of the innovation variables positively. Firms that score high on this component are those that are innovative in a broad sense—firms that are seeking to innovate both their products and processes and draw on a variety of sources for innovative ideas. They perceive that their capabilities with regard to technology (both developing new technologies and using others' technology), R&D innovation, reducing energy costs, using new materials, just-in-time inventory control, and process control are critical factors contributing to their success, and they obtain innovative ideas from a number of sources (marketing, management, the R&D unit, and patents).

The third component is the *process innovator.* Firms that rank high on this principal component are those that are primarily devoted to process innovation. These are firms that perceive their success to be dependent on

TABLE 2. Average Scores on Innovation-Related Variables for Firms in Each of the Groups

Variables	Product innovator	Comprehensive innovator	Process innovator	Non-innovator
Percentage of investment devoted to product innovation	12.9%	7.7%	5.2%	1.2%
Percentage of investment devoted to process innovation	2.4%	1.5%	2.8%	1.0%
Importance of R&D innovation capabilities as a factor in success	1.9	2.7	1.7	0.6
Importance of ability to adopt technology as a factor in success	2.4	3.5	3.0	2.4
R&D spending relative to competitors	1.8	2.4	1.6	0.8
Importance of strategies related to:				
Developing new technology	1.7	3.3	2.0	1.0
Refining others' technology	1.5	2.9	1.8	1.1
Using others' technology	1.8	3.1	2.4	1.9
Improving own technology	1.9	3.6	2.6	1.8
Using new materials	0.8	3.4	2.3	1.4
Using existing materials more efficiently	0.9	3.9	3.0	2.1
Cutting labor costs	1.4	4.1	3.8	3.0
Reducing energy costs	0.5	3.6	3.3	2.2
Introducing new products in existing markets	3.2	4.0	2.8	2.2
Introducing new products in new markets	2.9	3.8	2.2	1.8
Range of products relative to competitors	3.5	3.9	3.2	3.0
Frequency of introduction of new products relative to competitors	3.2	3.6	2.6	2.1
Importance of factors as a source of innovation				
R&D unit	1.3	2.2	0.4	0.3
Production unit	1.2	3.2	0.6	1.3
Marketing unit	1.9	3.7	0.6	1.8
Management	2.2	3.9	1.0	2.7
Related firms	0.8	1.3	0.1	0.4
Canadian patents	1.0	1.4	0.0	0.2
Foreign patents	1.0	1.2	0.0	0.1
Government contracts	0.8	2.1	0.1	1.3
Competitors	1.5	3.3	0.3	2.4
Customers	2.4	4.4	0.7	3.4
Suppliers	1.7	3.9	0.5	2.8

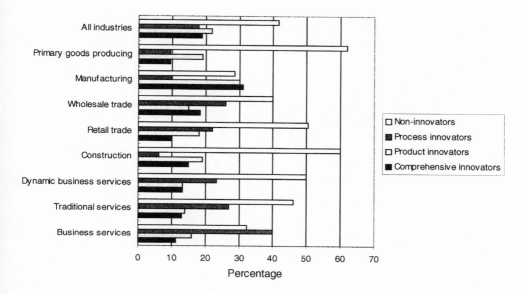

Fig. 1. Industry breakdown by firm type

continually enhancing their technological capabilities and improving their production efficiency by using new materials, using existing materials more efficiently, and reducing their labor and energy costs. These firms place little value on developing new products.

Some 19 percent of the sample consisted of product innovators, 19 percent were comprehensive innovators, and 20 percent were process innovators. Membership in a particular innovative group is not solely determined by broad industry groups. While manufacturing industries are slightly more likely to be found in the innovative groups relative to services industries, firms in each of the industries are distributed across each of the innovative groups (fig. 1).

In order to interpret the differences in the policies that occur across the innovative types and within each type, it is useful to think of the three innovation components as corresponding to different stages in the product life cycle. The product innovators are those who focus purely on product development. At this stage in the product life cycle, product specifications are changing so quickly that firms have not yet had time to focus on process technology. Comprehensive innovators are those firms that have begun to combine rapid product evolution with improvements in process technology. The process innovators operate in the third stage of the product life cycle, when product specifications have more or less stabilized and a firm's attention is concentrated on moving down the cost curve via process innovations. Firms that do not score highly on any of these innovation principal components operate in the fourth and final stage of the product life cycle—the mature stage in which product and process innovation occurs less frequently.

Investment and Production Costs

In order to both adopt new technologies and maintain properly functioning equipment, firms must invest in new machinery, equipment, and production facilities. The extent to which firms maintain and enhance their production capabilities is measured by whether the firm incurred any investment expenditures in the 1991 reference year and the percentage of sales that were devoted to investment expenditures.

Marketing

Several indicators of the marketing strategy of the firm are available from the survey. Firms rated (on a scale of 0 to 5) the importance of strategies related to maintaining current products in current markets and introducing current products in new markets. They also rated themselves in comparison to their competitors in terms of price, quality, customer service, and flexibility in responding to customer needs. The first principal component index constructed from these six variables, referred to here as the *comprehensive traditional marketer,* is used to summarize the importance that the firm attributes to marketing in general. The weights assigned to each variable were relatively similar, thereby indicating that they have about the same importance.

This measure captures the broad marketing stance of the firm. In addition, exporting behavior is used here to represent a separate and specific market orientation of the firm. Developing a significant export market allows firms to reduce risks by diversifying across dissimilar markets and to prolong the marketability of their products. Therefore, in addition to measuring the broad marketing efforts of firms, the export activity of the firm is used here as a separate variable to represent this specific aspect of its sales orientation.

Human Resources

As increased skill levels become an increasingly important element in many economic activities, the importance that a firm gives to enhancing its human resources becomes more critical to success. The survey provides evidence about several different facets of firms' competencies in this area. Firms rated (on a scale of 0 to 5) both their labor climate and their labor skills relative to those of their competitors. They also rated the importance of labor skills as a factor contributing to their past growth. Additional questions elicited the value that firms attribute to various human resources strategies: continuous staff training, innovative compensation packages, and other means of staff motivation. As was the case with marketing, the first principal component was used to generate a *comprehensive labor* index that captures the emphasis a firm gives to human resources. Once again, a relatively similar weighting is assigned to each of the six underlying variables.

In addition to examining the emphasis on human resources in a broad sense, the activities that the firm undertakes to improve its human resources are of particular interest. Actions taken to either improve existing skills or teach new skills should result in workers either being able to perform their existing tasks better or being able to perform new tasks. Both contribute to superior performance. To capture this, a binary variable indicating whether or not the firm engaged in training, as well as the expenditures on training per employee in the firm, are also included in the analysis.

Financing

The structure of, and attention to, financing are also likely to be factors that affect the success of the firm. The structure of financing is represented here by the types of financing instruments used and the sources of that financing.

There are two types of financing instruments measured by the survey: debt and equity. Debt is divided into short and long term. Two types of equity are captured by the survey: share capital and retained earnings. Three summary statistics are used to represent the capital structure of the firm—the percentage of net assets (assets minus accounts payable) attributable to debt, share capital, and retained earnings. The omitted variables for the types of financing are deferred taxes and other types of financing (i.e., contributed surplus and shareholder advances).

Firms are also distinguished by the sources of their financing—whether from retained earnings, accounts payable, financial institutions, venture capital firms, public equity markets, governments, affiliates, deferred taxes, or other individuals. Some of these are more traditional sources of financing, while others are more innovative sources of financing. Innovative firms are typically perceived to have greater problems in raising capital because of the difficulty in evaluating the prospects of the company and the lack of hard collateral to back knowledge-based assets. It is, therefore, hypothesized that sources that specialize in evaluating the special risks involved (venture capitalists, equity markets) are more likely to provide capital to innovators when the problems of evaluation require specialized intermediaries.

Financing sources are summarized here with two variables—the percentage of financing from financial institutions and from innovative sources (venture capital, public equity, and affiliates). The omitted variables for the sources of financing are accounts payable, government, individuals, (not elsewhere specified), and other miscellaneous sources. Principal component analysis is used to generate the financing types. Three typologies of financing structures are evident (table 3).

The first financial structure typology is *high-debt diversified financing.* Firms that score high on this principal component typically have a high percentage of assets that is attributable to debt, little in the way of retained earnings, and a focus on both innovative and more traditional bank sources of financing.

The second principal component is *low-debt, high-share capital, innovative financing.* Firms here have relatively little debt, rely on share capital, and derive a large portion of their financing from innovative sources such as public equity, venture capital, and related firms. They draw little of their financing from traditional sources such as banks.

The third principal component is *low-debt, high-share capital, bank financing.* Firms that score high on this component have low debt-asset levels and hold large amounts of share capital. While this group has relatively less debt, most of it is derived from banks.

In addition to the structure of financing, the strategic emphasis given to financing is also included in the analysis. Firms rated (on a scale of 0 to 5) the importance of access to capital and the cost of capital as a contributor to their growth. These two additional variables on the strategic orientation of the firm with respect to financing are used to complement the summary measures on financial structure that are derived from the principal component analysis.

Management

Finally, the management strategy of the firm is likely to be associated with success. Four questions from the survey were used to gauge the importance of management. As the broadest indicator of the importance of manage-

TABLE 3. Weights for Financing Principle Components

Financing	High-Debt Diversified Financing	Low-Debt Innovative Financing	Low-Debt Bank Financing
Type of financing			
Debt as a percentage of net assets	0.66	−0.19	−0.24
Share capital as a percentage of net assets	0.22	0.54	0.58
Retained earnings as a percentage of net assets	−0.69	0.04	0.11
Source of financing			
Percentage of financing from venture capital, public equity, and affiliates	0.16	0.64	0.04
Percentage of financing from financial institutions	0.13	−0.50	0.77

ment, firms rated the importance of management skills to the growth of the firm. They also rated the importance of several specific management strategies, including improving management incentives through compensation schemes, innovative organizational structure, and total quality management (TQM). The first three responses were closely related and thus were combined to form a *comprehensive management* variable using the first principal component of these variables. The last, the importance of TQM, is a very specific management strategy with a different dimension than the others, and it is included as a separate variable.

Analyzing the Factors Related to Success

Regression Analysis

This section establishes the importance of innovation to success. Accordingly, the general success index was regressed on the variables that summarize the firms' posture in the areas of innovation, human resources, management, marketing, and financing previously described (all values of the components are standardized). The results of an OLS regression, presented in table 4, corroborate the previous findings of Baldwin et al. (1994). It is clear that innovation is strongly related to success. Firms that adopt a comprehensive innovation strategy—that is, firms that strive to develop both new products and processes—are more likely to be successful. Firms that focus on process innovation by introducing new technologies, adding new inputs, and improving the efficiency of use of their existing inputs are also more likely to be successful. Conversely, firms that concentrate just on product innovation, without giving sufficient attention to improving their production processes, are less likely to be successful, although this result is statistically insignificant.

None of the measures relating to marketing, investment, production, human resources, and management are significantly related to success. This does not imply that capabilities in these areas are unimportant. Rather, it indicates that once the effects of innovation and other significant factors on success are taken into account additional emphasis in these areas is unrelated to success.

All three of the financing principal components are positively associated with success. The two low-debt components are most strongly associated with success. Each of these components weight share capital heavily. Successful firms are those that derive a significant amount of their net assets from share capital. These firms do not have to rely on retained earnings to finance their activities. The relationship between the measure of success and the value of the third principal component—high debt-long-term debt-bank financed—is positive though weaker and less significant than the other finance principal components. This component negatively

TABLE 4.   A Simple Analysis of the Factors Relating to Success

Variable	Parameter Estimate	Standard Error	Probability Value
Intercept	−0.4443	0.2329	0.0569**
Innovation			
Comprehensive innovator PC	0.2026	0.0899	0.0247*
Process innovator PC	0.1441	0.0637	0.0241*
Product innovator PC	−0.0962	0.0653	0.1414
Investment and production			
Percentage of firms incurring investment expenditures	−0.0580	0.1423	0.6835
Percentage of sales invested	−0.0007	0.0034	0.8453
Human resources			
Comprehensive labor PC	−0.1182	0.0586	0.0439
Percentage of firms offering formal training	0.0836	0.1381	0.5454
Training expenditures per employee in the firm	−0.0001	0.0001	0.1464
Management			
Comprehensive management PC	−0.0692	0.0661	0.2957
Total quality management	0.0811	0.0499	0.1042
Marketing			
Comprehensive traditional marketing PC	−0.0687	0.0475	0.1487
Percentage of sales exported	0.0096	0.0035	0.0057***
Financing			
High-debt diversified financing	0.1007	0.0437	0.0215*
Low-debt innovative financing	0.3002	0.0558	0.0001***
Low-debt bank financing	0.2145	0.0668	0.0014***
Importance of access to capital	0.1435	0.0653	0.0285*
Importance of cost of capital	−0.1032	0.0627	0.1004
Size at start of period			
Assets ($000), 1984[a]	0.0595	0.0214	0.0056***
Sales ($000), 1984[a]	−0.0353	0.0151	0.0197*
F-statistic	5.723	—	0.0001
Adjusted R^2	0.1636	—	—

[a]Canadian dollars
* Significant at the 5 percent level.
** Significant at the 10 percent level.
*** Significant at the 1 percent level.

weights retained earnings. Once again, firms that rely heavily on retained earnings do less well.

The importance that the firm attaches to financing also contributes to the success of the firm. Firms that value access to capital more highly are typically more successful than other firms. On the other hand, firms that are more concerned about the cost of capital (after having corrected for differences in the perceived importance of access to capital) are less successful—though the coefficient is much less significant. One explanation for this is that growth generally requires greater share capital, which is a more expensive form of capital, and firms that are overly concerned about the cost of capital are imposing restrictions on their abilities to obtain financing. Finally, firm size is related to success. Firms that have a strong asset base in the earlier part of the period used to derive performance data were significantly more successful than those with a weaker asset base. The relationship between sales and success in the multivariate model is the reverse (and statistically significant). If the model is recalculated omitting either sales or assets, the remaining variable is found to be insignificant, that is, if the model is run without the asset variable, the sales variable is no longer significant. The positive and significant sign on assets, in combination with the negative and significant sign on sales, indicates that, while size contributes to success, firms that expand their sales base without a concurrent increase in their asset base are less likely to be successful.

Strategies by Innovation Type

Previous work with the GSME survey (Baldwin et al. 1994) has found that the success of firms in the sample was strongly related to the innovative stance that they adopted, but it did not distinguish the type of environment that firms faced. Some authors (e.g., Miller 1988) have argued that the route to success is dependent on the environment in which the firm operates, the characteristics of the firm, and the particular strategic thrust of the firm. One of the major differences that firms face is the innovative environment (Gort and Klepper 1982). Therefore, the next section groups firms by innovation type. To do this, firms were ranked according to their scores on each of the three innovation principal components. Firms that scored in the top quartile—the top 25 percent—in any of the three principal components were deemed to be innovative. Firms that scored in the top quartile of one component only were assigned to that component. A small number of firms that scored high on more than more component were assigned to the component in which their scores most resembled the average score of the uniquely assigned innovators. All other firms were classified as noninnovative.

The average measures of performance by innovator type are presented in table 5 (the appendix, table A2, contains standard errors). The emphasis given to different strategies pursued by firms in each innovation group are presented in table 6 (the appendix, table A3, contains the standard errors).

Product Innovators

Product innovators represent firms operating in the first stage of the product life cycle. These firms focus on continually introducing new products (table 2). They do not pursue an aggressive technology or cost-reduction strategy. The product innovators are less successful, across a broad range of performance measures, than are the other two groups of innovators (table

TABLE 5.   Performance Measures of Firms

Performance Measure	Product Innovator	Comprehensive Innovator	Process Innovator	Non-innovator
Score on success index	−0.054	0.266	0.050	−0.183
Number of employees, 1984	23	21	18	23
Number of employees, 1988	47	49	39	45
Share of change in employ-ment, 1984 to 1988[a]	0.34	0.61	0.35	0.25
Sales, 1984	$ 2,231	$ 2,656	$ 1,817	$ 2,434
Sales, 1988	$ 5,581	$ 6,322	$ 4,405	$ 5,590
Share of change in sales, 1984 and 1988[a]	0.06	0.11	0.06	0.05
Assets, 1984	$ 1,086	$ 1,311	$ 858	$ 1,327
Assets, 1988	$ 3,185	$ 3,348	$ 2,500	$ 3,856
Share of change in assets, 1984 to 1988[a]	0.05	0.09	0.05	0.04
Profits, 1984	$ 107	$ 106	$ 65	$ 86
Profits, 1988	$ 147	$ 304	$ 213	$ 180
Share of change in profits, 1984 to 1988[a]	0.22	0.07	0.02	0.19
Labor productivity, 1984	$ 116	$ 123	$ 116	$ 127
Labor productivity, 1988	$ 126	$ 118	$ 123	$ 133
Change in profits/sales rela-tive to industry, 1984 to 1988	185%	96%	370%	89%

[a]Measured in percentage points

5). Their product differentiation has paid off in terms of increases in their share of industry profits. However, their lack of emphasis on improving production efficiency has prevented them from realizing market-share gains comparable to those of comprehensive innovators or the efficiency gains that have rewarded process innovators with strong growth in profit/sales margins relative to the industry average.

The commitment of product innovators to introducing new products is associated with intense investment activity. Almost half of product innovators incurred investment expenditures in 1991 (table 6). These firms were more likely to invest than were process innovators and noninnovators, and a larger portion of investment expenditures went into investments in R&D product innovation.

Product innovators stress product innovation but place little value on strategies related to maintaining existing products in current markets. This is in marked contrast to the comprehensive innovators, who place higher scores both on traditional strategies with respect to existing products and on aggressive strategies with respect to new products, and the process innovators, who score higher in the traditional marketing areas. This difference in emphasis substantiates the view that product innovators are at the head of the product life cycle, where firms tend to possess new products.

TABLE 6.   Strategies across Types of Firms

Strategy	Product Innovator	Comprehensive Innovator	Process Innovator	Non-innovators
Investment and production				
Percentage of firms incurring investment expenditures	47.0%	52.0%	35.0%	32.0%
Percentage of sales invested	5.0%	3.0%	7.0%	3.0%
Marketing				
Comprehensive traditional marketing PC	−0.05	0.73	−0.09	−0.26
Maintaining current products in current markets	2.8	4.0	3.6	3.2
Introducing current products in new markets	3.0	3.8	2.9	2.5
Price relative to competitors	3.2	3.3	3.0	3.1
Quality relative to competitors	4.0	4.3	3.9	3.8
Customer service relative to competitors	4.1	4.3	4.0	4.0
Flexibility in responding to customer needs	4.0	4.3	4.0	3.9
Percentage of sales exported	13.0%	11.0%	7.0%	4.0%
Human resources				
Comprehensive labor PC	−0.26	0.98	−0.01	−0.32
Labor climate relative to competitors	2.4	3.2	2.9	2.7
Labor skills relative to competitors	3.5	3.7	3.5	3.5
Importance of labor skills to past growth	3.0	3.8	3.7	3.2
Importance of continuous training	2.8	3.6	2.9	2.7
Importance of innovative compensation packages	2.4	3.2	2.2	2.1
Importance of other staff motivation strategies	3.0	3.9	3.1	2.9
Percentage of firms offering formal training	51.0%	60.0%	42.0%	45.0%
Training expenditures per employee in the firm	$ 683	$ 482	$ 248	$ 324
Financing				
High-debt diversified financing	0.20	0.26	−0.03	−0.19
Low-debt innovative financing	0.33	0.11	−0.18	−0.12
Low-debt bank financing	0.11	−0.04	0.03	−0.05
Financing instrument—as a percentage of net assets				
Total debt	47%	59%	44%	34%
Short-term debt	23%	28%	20%	16%
Long-term debt	24%	31%	22%	19%
Share capital	14%	9%	5%	5%
Retained earnings	31%	22%	42%	53%
Other types of financing instruments	8%	10%	7%	7%
Sources of financing—as a percentage of total financing				
From financial institutions	23%	25%	28%	26%
From venture capital, public equity, affiliates	10%	10%	5%	5%
From other sources	67%	65%	67%	69%
From foreign sources	5%	2%	0	1

(continued)

TABLE 6—*Continued*

Strategy	Product Innovator	Comprehensive Innovator	Process Innovator	Non-innovators
Importance of accessing financing	2.6	3.4	3.0	2.7
Importance of cost of financing	2.6	3.4	3.0	2.7
Management				
Comprehensive management PC	−0.13	0.92	−0.03	−0.34
Importance of management skills to growth	3.5	3.9	3.5	3.3
Improving management incentives via				
compensation schemes	2.2	3.1	2.1	2.0
Innovative organizational structure	2.2	3.5	2.5	2.1
Total quality management	2.63	4.25	3.33	2.84
Size at start of period				
Assets, 1984	$ 1,086	$ 1,311	$ 858	$ 1,327
Sales, 1984	$ 2,231	$ 2,656	$ 1,817	$ 2,434

Their strategic emphases is reflected in their competitive stance. These firms score about the same as process innovators or noninnovators in traditional areas of price, quality, customer service, and flexibility in responding to customer needs. However, they significantly outperform the process innovator and noninnovator groups in terms of the range of products offered and the frequency with which they introduce new products.

As is the case for both comprehensive and process innovators, firms that are product innovators require employees who are both adaptable and highly skilled. Their investment activity and the originality of their products suggest that they will also make ongoing investments in training. This is the case. The incidence of training in this group is second only to that of comprehensive innovators. Furthermore, these firms expend the highest amount on training per worker. While these firms are clearly committed to upgrading the skills of their employees, perhaps surprisingly, they lag behind the other firms in terms of their commitment generally to human resource strategies. The average score among firms in this group on the comprehensive labor PC is lowest among the three innovative groups and only slightly higher than that of the noninnovators.

Product innovators give a higher score to the low-debt, high-share capital, innovative financing prototype than they do to the other financing components. Examination of their financial structure reveals that they depend more heavily on share capital, innovative financing, and financing from foreign sources than do firms in other groups. Product innovations require investments in marketing, research, and machinery and equipment, often for completely untried products that may be market failures. Product innovators exist at the first and perhaps riskiest stage in the product life cycle. Product innovators, due to their greater riskiness, require more share capital and tend to utilize innovative, less-traditional sources of financing such as venture capitalists, public equity, and related firms.

Comprehensive Innovators

The second group of firms, the comprehensive innovators, adopt a broad approach to innovation (table 2). They score higher in each of the areas that measure the innovation stance of a firm (with the exception of the percentage of investment devoted to R&D) than firms in each of the other groups.

Comprehensive innovators score highest on the general index that weights several different measures of performance (table 5). Comprehensive innovators enjoyed stronger growth in their share of industry sales and assets over the 1984 to 1988 period than all other firms. This growth enabled these firms to expand their share of the industry's employment faster than firms in the other groups.

The ongoing change in these firms necessitates continual investments, and consequently they are more likely to invest than are other firms. However, these changes appear to be incremental in nature, since these firms devote a smaller share of their sales to investment than other firms do.

Comprehensive innovators place more emphasis on the innovative, more aggressive measures of market development than do firms in other groups, as indicated by their score on the product development measures included in the innovation index (table 2). They also score higher than other firms on the traditional marketing strategies. Their score on the measure that captures their emphasis on traditional marketing capabilities—the comprehensive traditional marketing PC—is significantly greater than that of any of the other three groups. They also score higher on each of the factors included in the broad marketing measure. They place more emphasis on both maintaining current products in current markets and introducing current products in new markets. As a result, they are more competitive with respect to price, quality, customer service, and flexibility in responding to customer needs, all traditional means of competing. Similarly, they are outmatched, in terms of percentage of sales exported, only by the product innovators.

The ability to innovate continually—to implement new processes and produce new products—depends critically on a highly adaptable, skilled, and committed work force. This is evidenced by the emphasis this group places on enhancing their human resources, both in terms of their general emphasis on human resources (as indicated by the value of the comprehensive labor PC) and their scores in each of the subcategories that are unmatched by any of the other innovative groups. Comprehensive innovators give more credit to their labor skills for their success than do other firms. They give more emphasis than other innovator types to strategies related to enhancing their human resources—either through training, innovative compensation packages, or other means of motivating their staff. Firms in this group exhibit the highest incidence of formal training. While they spend less on training per employee than product innovators do, they spend more than process innovators and noninnovators. Their training efforts are well rewarded—they boast both a superior labor climate and better labor skills than do their competitors.

Financing is also critical for these firms. The inherent riskiness of continually implementing new processes and offering new products demands extra attention to financing. They place a greater emphasis on both access to capital and the cost of capital than do firms in other groups.

Comprehensive innovators as a group score highest on the high-debt diversified financing prototype. In keeping with this, they have the highest debt/asset ratio and the lowest percentage of share capital and retained earnings.

The low debt/asset strategy that was weighted first by their predecessor in the product life cycle—the product innovators—comes second for the comprehensive innovators. Like their predecessors, they also make use of innovative sources of financing. Nevertheless, there is evidence of a transition, since they have increased their reliance on debt and they have begun to increase the percentage of financing that comes from financial institutions. It may be argued that the second stage in the product life cycle that is represented by comprehensive innovators is less risky than the previous product innovation stage. The fact that there is some process innovation undertaken suggests that there has been some maturation beyond simple, rapid, product development. Hence, these firms are able to turn more to debt, a less expensive form of financing. Firms at this stage are also probably better able to signal their potential to financiers because they are more successful across a wide range of indicators.

In keeping with the balanced approach taken elsewhere, comprehensive innovators also pay more attention to management than do other firms. They seek to improve their performance in every area. These firms place a higher value on innovative organizational structures, management incentive compensation packages, and adherence to total quality management. The relationship between attention to management strategies and innovation involves a complex feedback loop—firms with good management choose to adopt successful strategies, like introducing new products and processes, while introducing new products and processes requires good management to overcome organizational problems that invariably arise due to change.

In summary, comprehensive innovators also adopt a strategy that places greater stress on all of the other functional areas. To succeed, these firms need to do everything well.

Process Innovators

The third group of firms consists of process innovators. These are firms that focus on developing new technologies and improving their input use (table 2). These firms place less value on developing new products than either product or comprehensive innovators do.

The emphasis on continually refining processes is well rewarded: this group of firms is the second most successful using the broad measure of success (table 5). They not only gain market share, but their focus on improving production efficiencies enables them to realize the highest gains in profit/sales ratios relative to others in their industry.[4]

Continual improvements in processes require investments on the part of the firm. Process innovators engage in investment less frequently than do comprehensive or product innovators but more frequently than non-innovators (table 6). However, the investments that they do make are typically larger, and on average they expend a greater proportion of their sales on investment. This accords with the view that process innovators invest discontinuously in large, lumpy increments.

Given that these firms focus on improving their production processes and introduce fewer new or improved products, it is not surprising to find that they lag behind both the comprehensive and product innovators in terms of the emphasis they place on aggressive, innovative, market development strategies. In contrast, they place relatively more emphasis on the traditional marketing strategy of maintaining current products in current markets than do product innovators and score approximately the same as the product innovators and the noninnovative firms in the traditional areas of price, quality, customer service, and flexibility in responding to customer needs.

Process innovators attribute part of their success to the skill level of their workers. They score second only to comprehensive innovators on the comprehensive labor PC and on most of the human resource subcategories. However, their training efforts, as measured by expenditure per employee, fall short of those in other firms. These are firms that are able to acquire skilled labor without having to exert greater than normal efforts to train—probably because process innovation is more routinized. The technology skills required come from organized labor markets and universities.

Process innovators do not have high scores on any of the three financing principal components. Indeed, they receive a large negative weight on the low-debt, high-share capital, innovative financing component, primarily because they possess the smallest amount of share capital and the least amount of innovative financing of any group except noninnovators. They rely more heavily on retained earnings than does either of the two innovative groups and turn more to banks for the remaining financing that they require. The established nature of their products is probably in part responsible for their greater reliance on traditional means of financing.

The process innovators come second only to the comprehensive innovators in terms of the importance that they attribute both to the cost of capital and access to financing as factors that contributed to their growth.

The TQM philosophy is built on the belief that the route to success involves continually improving quality and efficiency. This means searching out new inputs or better ways of using existing inputs, enhancing human resources, and utilizing information technologies to improve quality. The scores of process innovators in each of these areas is consistent with their purported emphasis on the TQM philosophy. These firms typically attribute more importance to the other management strategies than do product innovators and noninnovators—as is evidenced by their score on the comprehensive management PC.

Noninnovators

The fourth group consists of traditional (noninnovator) firms (table 2). These firms tend to devote little attention to either product or process innovation. These firms score the lowest on the general success index (table 5). They also lag the innovators in each of the individual categories that went into the overall index. These firms are still successful. They are included in the survey sample, which means that they grew over the 1984 to 1988 period. However, their success is inferior to that of firms that are introducing new products or processes. As previously noted, these differences are not closely related to the industry in which these firms are located.

Given their lack of emphasis on developing new or improved products or processes, noninnovators are the least likely to incur investment expenditures, and they spend little when they do invest (table 6). They are the group that relies most on retained earnings as a source of funds and as a result score negatively on the three financing principal components. Their marketing strategy is a traditional one—their marketing efforts are concentrated relatively more heavily on maintaining their existing products in their existing markets than is the case for all but process innovators. However, their overall emphasis on marketing is the weakest among the four groups of firms. Not surprisingly, they are generally the least competitive in the traditional areas of competition such as price, quality, customer service, and flexibility in responding to customer needs. As these firms essentially concentrate on performing traditional activities in an unchanged manner, they have less of a need for training than other firms do, and they are generally the least concerned about human resource strategies. Given the absence of change and their lack of emphasis on strategies in most areas, it is not surprising to find that noninnovators also place the least emphasis on management and are the least successful.

Conclusion

Utilizing a taxonomic approach that classifies firms by innovation type improves our understanding of the nature of innovation and its relationship to such measures of success as profitability, market-share growth, and productivity gain.

While there are some similarities in that all innovation groups are successful, there are many differences in terms of strategic emphases. Product innovators represent firms operating in the first stage of the product life cycle. In this stage, the product is still new, and its characteristics and production techniques are unlikely to be settled. This is an inherently risky stage of the life cycle, and probably accounts for the fact that these firms are, on average, the least successful of all the innovators. These firms focus on continually developing new or improved products. They concentrate less on process innovation than either of the other two innovative groups. Training is undertaken to impart the skills required to develop new or improved products. The inherent risk of product innovation requires attention to financing. These firms rely significantly more on equity and foreign financing. Finally, as is the case with other innovators, attention to management strategies is greater than is the case in noninnovating firms. Their emphasis on product differentiation generates superior profit gains for them. However, the lack of attention to production efficiencies is accompanied by lagging profit/sales performance relative to process innovators and weaker market-share gains than comprehensive innovators.

The second stage in the product life cycle may be characterized as one in which there is both product and process innovation. This stage is represented by comprehensive innovators. Continuous change in this group requires ongoing investment spending and training to upgrade both equipment and worker skills. The frequent introduction of new products requires emphasis on marketing strategies. The inherent riskiness of innovative activity demands attention to financing, in particular, long-term financing that allows firms to compensate for their relatively small size, while surviving a volatile environment. However, these firms, unlike product innovators, typically rely more on debt financing. One can argue that this is because firms operating in the first stage are typically more risky, or because comprehensive innovators are typically more successful. However, the argument over the causality is an esoteric one, as risk and success are closely related. Finally, the inherent instability caused by these ongoing changes requires superior management capabilities. Comprehensive innovators tend to outperform other firms in each of these areas and are rewarded with stronger growth in sales, market share, and employment size.

Process innovators focus on developing new technologies and improving their input use while placing little value on developing new products or seeking out new markets. As such, they tend to invest more heavily in new equipment, value their human resources more than noninnovators do, and concentrate their marketing strategies solely on maintaining their current products in current markets. While their activities are subject to changes associated with process innovation, the degree of change is less than that for comprehensive innovators. Consequently, they place more emphasis on management strategies than noninnovative firms but less than comprehensive innovators do. These firms are typically rewarded with stronger growth in sales, assets, and profit/sales ratios than those in all but the comprehensive innovator group.

The last group of firms, the noninnovators, place little value on strategies related to either product or process innovation. As they are undergoing the least amount of change, they are less likely to incur investment expenditures and they are less likely to devote resources to upgrading either their equipment or human resources. Similarly, the lack of change in this group requires less attention to marketing and management strategies. This group of firms lags the others in virtually all performance areas.

The innovator typologies tell two stories—that innovation is more successful than lack of innovation and that comprehensive (product/process) innovation is more successful than either product or process innovation alone. The latter may simply occur because firms engaging in comprehensive innovation are always more successful than firms that master only half the innovation process—either just product or just process innovation. However, this interpretation of the survey's findings ignores the substantial literature that suggests that the appropriate innovation strategy varies across the product life cycle and the empirical evidence that each of these innovation types is appropriate to a particular phase in the life cycle. If the product, product/process, and process innovative groups are taken to represent the successive stages in the product life cycle, differences in strategies simply reflect differences in the required strategies at different points in the life cycle.

Perhaps the most interesting evidence on differences across the life cycle occurs in the financial strategies that are pursued. The three innovative stages demonstrate an evolution of the financial structure of the firm. In the first stage, which is quite risky, product innovators emphasize two strategies, which have in common an emphasis on share capital. Both also rely heavily on innovative sources of financing.

In the next phase of the product life cycle, comprehensive innovators continue to stress the low-debt strategy using innovative financing that was pursued in the previous, product-innovator stage. However, the strategy that reflects higher debt/asset ratios becomes more important as the nature of firms' activities in this stage becomes less risky and firms become more successful.

In the third stage of the product life cycle, process innovators no longer pursue innovative sources of financing. Their stage in the life cycle has enabled them to build retained earnings, and this now becomes the most important financing instrument. They also move back to lower debt/asset ratios and increase their use of bank financing.

The final implication of the analysis pertains to the patterns of success that have been observed across firms by innovation type. While one index of success is used throughout, firms in the three innovative stages are each characterized by different aspects of success. Profit growth is highest for product innovators, but these firms gain market share relatively slowly. Firms in the second stage—comprehensive innovators—show both profit growth and market-share growth, but they do not exhibit the highest increases in productivity. Firms in the third stage show market-share growth and growth in profit/sales margins. Firms are, therefore, not only heterogeneous in terms of strategy but also in terms of outcomes. They provide different bundles of characteristics to investors who have different preferences for growth as opposed to profitability.

APPENDIX

TABLE A1.   Standard Errors of Estimates of Mean Scores on the Innovation-Related Variables

	Product innovator	Comprehensive innovator	Process innovator	Non-innovator
Percentage of investment devoted to product innovation	2.71%	1.91%	1.64%	0.09%
Percentage of investment devoted to process innovation	1.12%	0.42%	1.15%	0.05%
Importance of R&D innovation capabilities as a factor in success	0.16	0.13	0.15	0.07
Importance of ability to adopt technology as a factor in success	0.16	0.09	0.12	0.09
R&D spending relative to competitors	0.16	0.15	0.15	0.08
Importance of strategies related to:				
Developing new technology	0.17	0.11	0.15	0.09
Refining others' technology	0.15	0.14	0.14	0.09
Using others' technology	0.16	0.12	0.13	0.10
Improving own technology	0.17	0.12	0.14	0.10
Using new materials	0.12	0.10	0.14	0.09
Using existing materials more efficiently	0.13	0.08	0.13	0.11
Cutting labor costs	0.15	0.08	0.08	0.09
Reducing energy costs	0.09	0.11	0.12	0.10

(continued)

	Product innovator	Comprehensive innovator	Process innovator	Non-innovator
Introducing new products in existing markets	0.13	0.07	0.14	0.10
Introducing new products in new markets	0.15	0.10	0.15	0.10
Range of products relative to competitors	0.14	0.11	0.12	0.09
Frequency of introduction of new products relative to competitors	0.15	0.11	0.14	0.10
Importance of following factors as a source of innovation				
R&D unit	0.17	0.16	0.10	0.05
Production unit	0.14	0.14	0.11	0.10
Marketing unit	0.16	0.11	0.11	0.10
Management	0.16	0.09	0.14	0.10
Related firms	0.14	0.16	0.04	0.07
Canadian patents	0.14	0.15	0.01	0.04
Foreign patents	0.14	0.14	0.01	0.03
Government contracts	0.12	0.15	0.06	0.10
Competitors	0.14	0.10	0.07	0.09
Customers	0.17	0.06	0.12	0.09
Suppliers	0.15	0.10	0.09	0.09

TABLE A2. Standard Errors of Estimates of Mean Scores on the Success Variables

Success Variable	Product Innovator	Comprehensive Innovator	Process Innovator	Non-innovator
Score on success index	0.149	0.171	0.149	0.080
Number of employees, 1984	2.6	2.5	2.7	2.1
Number of employees, 1988	4.7	4.3	4.4	3.3
Share change in employment, 1984 to 1988[a]	0.09	0.12	0.07	0.03
Sales, 1984	$ 325	$ 713	$ 362	$ 291
Sales, 1988	$ 705	$ 1,356	$ 581	$ 615
Share change in sales, 1984 and 1988[a]	0.01	0.02	0.01	0.01
Assets, 1984	$ 281	$ 421	$ 194	$ 237
Assets, 1988	$ 645	$ 747	$ 571	$ 1,026
Share change in assets, 1984 to 1988[a]	0.02	0.02	0.01	0.01
Profits, 1984	$ 26	$ 17	$ 10	$ 18
Profits, 1988	$ 54	$ 53	$ 25	$ 42
Share change in profits, 1984 to 1988[a]	0.22	0.10	0.05	0.15
Labor productivity, 1984	$ 11	$ 15	$ 13	$ 12
Labor productivity, 1988	$ 11	$ 9	$ 9	$ 12
Change in profits/sales relative to industry, 1984 to 1988	144%	81%	350%	89%

[a]Measured in percentage points

TABLE A3. Standard Errors of Estimates of Mean Scores on the Strategy Variables

Strategy Variable	Product Innovator	Comprehensive Innovator	Process Innovator	Non-innovator
Investment and Production				
Percentage of firms incurring investment expenditures	4.5%	4.5%	4.1%	2.8%
Percentage of sales invested	1.2%	0.7%	2.6%	1.0%
Marketing				
Comprehensive traditional marketing PC	0.12	0.09	0.14	0.09
Maintaining current products in current markets	0.17	0.09	0.11	0.11
Introducing current products in new markets	0.14	0.09	0.13	0.10
Price relative to competitors	0.09	0.10	0.08	0.06
Quality relative to competitors	0.08	0.07	0.10	0.06
Customer service relative to competitors	0.10	0.07	0.10	0.06
Flexibility in responding to customer needs	0.09	0.06	0.10	0.07
Percentage of sales exported	2.4%	2.1%	1.7%	0.8%
Human resources				
Comprehensive labor PC	0.17	0.10	0.13	0.09
Labor climate relative to competitors	0.16	0.14	0.13	0.09
Labor skills relative to competitors	0.12	0.09	0.08	0.06
Importance of labor skills to past growth	0.14	0.09	0.11	0.08
Importance of continuous training	0.13	0.08	0.12	0.08
Importance of innovative compensation packages	0.14	0.10	0.14	0.08
Importance of other staff motivation strategies	0.13	0.08	0.12	0.08
Percentage of firms offering formal training	4.5%	4.4%	4.3%	3.0%
Training expenditures per employee in the firm	$ 258	$ 91	$ 50	$ 71
Financing				
High-debt diversified financing	0.09	0.21	0.05	0.09
Low-debt innovative financing	0.14	0.12	0.10	0.06
Low-debt bank financing	0.11	0.10	0.08	0.05
Financing instrument—as a percentage of net assets				
Total debt	4.3%	14.0%	3.0%	5.7%
Short-term debt	2.7%	7.9%	2.0%	2.6%
Long-term debt	3.2%	6.6%	2.6%	3.9%
Share capital	3.1%	2.4%	1.4%	1.0%
Retained earnings	5.9%	14.2%	3.2%	5.9%
Other types of financing instruments	1.8%	1.7%	1.4%	1.0%
Sources of financing—as a percentage of total financing				
From financial institutions	2.8%	2.3%	2.6%	1.8%
From venture capital, public equity, affiliates	2.0%	2.0%	1.4%	0.9%
From other sources	3.1%	2.6%	2.7%	1.9%
Financing from foreign sources	1.6%	1.1%	0.1%	0.3%
Importance of accessing financing	0.14	0.11	0.13	0.09
Importance of cost of financing	0.14	0.11	0.14	0.09
Management				
Comprehensive management PC	0.12	0.09	0.12	0.08
Importance of management skills to growth	0.12	0.08	0.10	0.08
Improving management incentives via compensation schemes	0.13	0.11	0.14	0.09
Innovative organizational structure	0.14	0.10	0.14	0.09
Total quality management	0.17	0.08	0.14	0.10
Size at start of period				
Assets, 1984	$ 281	$ 421	$ 194	$ 237
Sales, 1984	$ 325	$ 713	$ 362	$ 291

NOTES

This essay represents the views of the authors and does not necessarily reflect the opinions of Statistics Canada.

1. For futher discussion of the success index, see Baldwin et al. (1994).

2. For a discussion of the merits of the approach that was used, see Baldwin and Johnson (1996).

3. Limited space has meant that only a subset of the detailed tables listing the component weights are included here. See Baldwin and Johnson (1997) for more detailed results.

4. Caution should be exercised in interpreting differences in the profit/sales variable since the standard error of the estimate is large—see table A2. However, when combined with the other variables, the higher values on this measure of success make process innovators the second most successful group using the overall index.

REFERENCES

Ansoff, Igor H., and John M. Stewart. 1967. "Strategies for a Technology Based Business." *Harvard Business Review* 45, no. 6 (Nov.-Dec.): 71–83.

Baldwin, J. R., W. Chandler, C. Le, and T. Papailiadis. 1994. *Strategies for Success: A Profile of Growing Small and Medium-Sized Enterprises (GSMEs) in Canada.* Catalogue 61–523ER. Ottawa: Statistics Canada.

Baldwin, J. R., and J. Johnson. 1996. "Business Strategies in Innovative and Non-Innovative Firms in Canada." *Research Policy* 25:785–804.

———. 1997. "Differences in Strategies and Performance of Different Types of Innovators." Analytical Studies Research Papers, no. 102. Ottawa: Statistics Canada.

Chaganti, Radha. 1987. "Small Business Strategies in Different Industry Growth Environments." *Journal of Small Business Management* 25, no. 2: 61–68.

Edmonds, S. E., and S. L. Khoury. 1986. "Exports: A Necessary Ingredient in the Growth of Small Business Firms." *Journal of Small Business Management* (Apr.): 54–65.

Freeman, C. 1974. *The Economics of Industrial Innovation.* Harmondsworth: Penguin.

Gort, M., and S. Klepper. 1982. "Time Paths in the Diffusion of Product Innovations." *Economic Journal* 92:630–53.

Hayes, R. H., and G. P. Pisano. 1994. "Beyond World-Class: The New Manufacturing Strategy." *Harvard Business Review* 72, no. 1 (Jan.-Feb.): 77–86.

Kuznets, S. 1953. *Economic Change.* New York: Norton.

Lundvall, B. 1992. *National Systems of Innovation: Towards a Theory of Innovation and Interactive Learning.* London: Pinter.

Miles, Raymond E., and Charles C. Snow. 1978. *Organizational Strategy, Structure, and Process.* New York: McGraw-Hill.

Miller, Alex. 1988. "A Taxonomy of Technological Settings with Related Strategies and Performance Levels." *Strategic Management Journal* 9, no. 3: 239–54.

Ministère de l'Industrie. 1995. *Les Technologies Clés pour L'industrie Française.* Paris: Ministère de l'Industrie.

Mowery, D. C., and N. Rosenberg. 1989. *Technology and the Pursuit of Economic Growth.* Cambridge: Cambridge University Press.

Nelson, R., ed. 1993. *National Innovation Systems: A Comparative Analysis.* New York: Oxford University Press.

Reid, Samuel R. 1969. "Is the Merger the Best Way to Grow?" *Business Horizons* 12, no. 1 (Feb.): 41–50.

Rosenbloom, R. S., and W. J. Abernathy. 1982. "The Climate for Innovation in Industry." *Research Policy* 11, no. 4: 209–25.

Utterback, J. M., M. Meyer, E. Roberts, and G. Reitberger. 1988. "Technology and Industrial Innovation in Sweden: A Study of Technology-Based Firms Formed between 1965 and 1980." *Research Policy* 17, no. 1: 15–26.

Competencies, Innovation, and Profitability of Firms

Aija Leiponen

1. Introduction

It is a well-known, stylized fact that there are persistent differences in performance among firms in an industry (see Mueller 1986 and Geroski and Jacquemin 1988, among others). Equilibrating market forces work ineffectively enough to allow some firms to outperform others consistently. Hence, in order to understand industrial dynamics, economists need to come to grips with firm dynamics and behavior. It is maintained here that firm dynamics in the long run is driven to a large extent by innovation and learning, which are thus the fundamental dynamic processes about which we should be concerned.

In recent years, the students of technological change have increasingly started to focus on internal workings of firms (see Cohen 1995). This research draws both from resource-based (e.g., Penrose 1959, Wernerfelt 1984) and evolutionary (Nelson and Winter 1982) views of the firm, which suggest that there are some organization-specific assets, like knowledge, accumulated over long periods of time, which give rise to differences between firms. Despite these efforts, the roles of knowledge and capabilities in industrial economics remain underdeveloped. It has proven difficult to generalize across firms and industries. Mainly, the analyses consist of often insightful but industry-specific case studies (see, e.g., ICC 1994). This study attempts to go further in assessing more general economic implications of competencies.

The profitability implications of competencies acquired through education and innovation are assessed in this essay. In addition, some light is shed on the differences in the determinants of profitability between innovating and noninnovating firms and also between product- and process-innovating firms. In the next section, I discuss the conceptual framework underlying the analysis. Section 3 presents the empirical model and the method of estimation. The data set is described in section 4. Section 5 discusses the estimation results, and section 6 concludes.

2. Dynamic Competencies and Firm Performance

Geroski and Machin (1993) and Geroski et al. (1993) have argued that innovating and noninnovating firms are generically different because innovation is a process that transforms the capabilities of firms in a fundamental way. Hence, innovation should be understood as a process, not only a product of R&D investment. Knowledge accumulated in the innovation process gives rise to a firm-specific effect, which makes the evolution of innovating firms very different from that of the noninnovators. However, this view does not really explain how innovation comes about in the first place, nor does it specify the interaction of capabilities and innovation.

To understand the origins of innovation, I maintain that firm evolution should be viewed as a process of accumulating useful organizational knowledge with the help of dynamic competencies. Dynamic competencies mean the capabilities to learn, solve problems, and, in particular, find new problems to solve (Dosi and Marengo 1994). Dynamic competencies are based on simpler (static) skills related to techniques, communication abilities, and so forth, which are used in the organizational context to acquire relevant new information, understand it, and apply it in interaction with other members of the organization.

Due to technological progress and changes in competitive conditions, abilities to learn, adapt, and innovate are seminal. Technological and market evolution sets about a process of creative destruction of knowledge, so the firm cannot rely on knowledge created in the past. Instead, the competence base needs to be continuously upgraded through investment in skills, capabilities, and learning. Learning abilities, in particular, enhance the efficiency of adaptation ("dynamic efficiency"; cf. North 1990), which enables the firm to react and adjust swiftly to changes in the environment.

The dynamic capabilities framework (Teece, Pisano, and Shuen 1997) holds that a firm's profitability and market share are determined by its relative position, compared to competitors, with respect to strategic assets. Strategic assets include technological assets, complementary assets like distribution channels and manufacturing capabilities, and financial and institutional assets. Because strategic assets are largely firm specific, there are usually no markets for them. Therefore, they need to be developed internally. The development of strategic assets involves internal dynamic processes like integration of knowledge sources, learning, and reconfiguration of the organization.

The dynamic capabilities approach is closely related to the resource-based view of the firm, but it emphasizes the *dynamics* of knowledge accumulation as the key process underlying performance. The approach also maintains that the firm has some degree of deliberation in determining its knowledge strategy. Furthermore, the firm has to keep investing in competencies, in order to renew the knowledge base, if it desires to continue on an innovative path. In short, there is some room for strategic choice. Nonetheless, a successful strategy has to take into account the path dependencies that constrain and define the set of profitable opportunities available.

The problem with incorporating dynamic capabilities into more general empirical analysis is that they are based on firm-specific definitions. To overcome this, even if running the risk of being too general, the focus here is on learning abilities and innovation, which underlie the creation of strategic assets. Learning follows from the operation, interaction, and cooperation of the organization. Learning can be facilitated, for instance, by investing in education, training, and organizational design. Innovation, on the other hand, is also an interactive process, which integrates skills, learning abilities, R&D, and external knowledge sources.

I argue, along the lines of Cohen and Levinthal (1989), that relevant prior knowledge is useful for assimilating new knowledge. Similarly, prior experience in learning and solving problems during schooling facilitates learning on the job. Education provides employees with basic technical, communication, and social skills, and, most importantly, it enhances their learning abilities. Thus, the role of education in building dynamic competencies is to provide a set of tools and a solid base for further learning. Education should not be viewed as a "factor of production" but rather as a "factor of learning." In addition, dynamic competencies acquired through education imply more efficient learning in a multitude of directions. A wide basis of general knowledge makes it easier to adopt a new direction of learning.

Accumulation of knowledge is by no means automatic. Initially, the firm's management has to be "visionary" enough to perceive opportunities, which necessitates investment in knowledge. Then the firm takes on an innovative, or knowledge-intensive, strategy. It invests in R&D, which enables it to develop knowledge internally and absorb it from the outside. Simultaneously, it has to make sure that the employees are capable of using, applying, producing, and marketing the firm's products and technologies. Technology and competencies complement each other in different stages of the production process as well in product development, manufacturing, and marketing. This is related to Teece's (1986) idea that profiting from innovation necessitates that the firm has complementary assets in place. In a dynamic perspective, products, technology, and competencies coevolve because their coherence has to be maintained. Moreover, there is important feedback from competencies to technological change via the innovation process. To sum up, competencies affect profitability directly through enhanced learning and adaptation and indirectly through the process of innovation.

The preceding discussion can be translated into the following hypotheses.

1. Innovation improves economic performance, provided that complementary competencies are available.

2. Competencies increase the dynamic efficiency of the firm, which is reflected in consistently better profitability.

3. Different types of skills and competencies complement one another, thus conditioning the positive effects on profitability of each.

4. Competencies are essential for the innovation process, that is, competencies and innovation are complementary.

5. Innovative firms are more dependent on accumulating competencies due to their knowledge-intensive strategy.

3.   The Empirical Model and the Method of Estimation

Next the model is formulated for the empirical analysis. It augments the market structure–firm performance approach with indicators of innovation and competencies. The model asserts that a firm's profitability is a function of its knowledge assets, lagged profitability, and a few firm- and industry-specific characteristics.

The basic model reads

$$\pi_{i,t} = \alpha \pi_{i,t-1} + \beta' X_{i,t} + \eta_i + \delta_t D_t + \varepsilon_{it}, \tag{1}$$

where $\pi_{i,t}$ denotes the profitability of firm i in period t and $X_{i,t}$ are the explanatory variables. α, β, and δ are parameter vectors to be estimated, η_i is a firm-specific fixed effect, D_t are time dummies to capture macroeconomic shocks, and ε is a serially uncorrelated,[1] white noise error term. More specifically,

$$\pi_{i,t} = \alpha \pi_{i,t-1} + \beta_1 \mathbf{COMP}_{i,t} + \beta_2 \mathbf{INN}_{i,t} + \beta_3 \mathbf{FIRM}_{i,t}$$
$$+ \beta_4 \mathbf{INDUSTRY}_{i,t} + \eta_i + \delta_t D_t + \varepsilon_{it}, \tag{2}$$

where notation is as presented previously. Vectors **COMP** and **INN** consist of measures for competencies and innovations (dynamic technological capabilities), respectively. **FIRM** and **INDUSTRY** vectors include a set of available proxies to control for firm and industry-specific differences in performance.

The analysis is carried out with the generalized method of moments (GMM), a two-stage weighted least squares estimator for panel data utilizing instrumental variables, as it was presented by Arellano and Bond (1991). The fact that the model includes a lagged dependent variable, fixed effects, and predetermined explanatory variables implies endogeneity and autocorrelation. Moreover, using this type of firm data may give rise to heteroskedasticity. GMM, however, enables consistent estimation of dynamic models in spite of heteroskedasticity and autocorrelation, which would blur the results if a method such as least squares fixed effects were used. Furthermore, GMM is particularly suitable for short panels.

The model is estimated in differences to cancel out firm-specific, time-invariant, fixed effects:

$$\Delta \pi_{i,t} = \alpha' \, \Delta \pi_{i,t-1} + \beta' \, \Delta X_{i,t} + \delta' \, \Delta D_t + \Delta \varepsilon_{it}. \tag{3}$$

Among the firm characteristics, there are some predetermined explanatory variables, which have to be instrumented. The Arellano-Bond method constructs the instrumental variable matrix utilizing all the linear moment restrictions. The lagged values of the dependent variable become valid instruments thanks to the second-order serial uncorrelation of error terms. π_i dating from $t - 2$ and before are valid instruments for $\pi_{i,t}$. For the predetermined explanatory variables, the values lagged one period are used as instruments. For the strictly exogenous variables, lagged differences are valid instruments.

The crucial assumption regarding the consistency of estimates is exactly the second-order serial uncorrelation of error terms. This will be tested and reported in the estimation results. Also, the validity of instruments is checked with the Sargan test for overidentifying restrictions (see Arellano and Bond 1991 for more about these).

4. The Data

The data set is compiled by Statistics Finland and consists of firm-level data on the levels of education and financial state of a sample of Finnish manufacturing firms (two-digit SIC level). These data are combined with domestic patent applications and an innovation survey. The survey was carried out in 1991. It contains 489 manufacturing firms, including the 100 largest firms and a random sample of the rest of the population. In this study, I had to content myself with a time series of 209 firms for the period 1985–93 (every other year) for financial information and patent applications and 1987–93 for educational data (see table 1).[2]

The dependent variable *profitability* is measured with net profit margins (NET). The competence indicators include the levels and fields of education. Their interactions are considered to assess the presence of complementarities. Interactions are expected both between different levels and fields of skills and innovation and skills. Innovation, an indirect measure of dynamic technological capabilities, is described by three dummy variables for firms undertaking either product innovation, process innovation or both, and by domestic patent applications.

TABLE 1.   Variables

Vector	Variable	Definition
COMP	HIGH	Share of employees with higher education degree, % (1987–93)
	POST	Number of employees with postgraduate degree (1987–93)
	TECH	Share of employees with technical or natural scientific degree, % (1987–93)
	HITECH	Share of employees with higher technical or natural scientific degree, % (1987–93)
	POST*HIGH	Interaction terms
	PAT*POST	
	POST*TECH	
	PAT*HITECH	
INN	PROD	Dummy variable for new products launched successfully in markets between 1989 and 1991 (1991)
	PROC	Dummy for significant process innovations realized between 1989 and 1991 (1991)
	COMPR	Dummy variable for firms realizing both product and process innovation ("comprehensive innovation")
	PAT	Number of domestic patent applications (1985–93)
FIRM	SALES	Sales turnover, million Finnmarks (1985–93)
	MS	Market share, % (1987–93)
	KINT	Capital intensity: machinery, equipment, etc., on the balance sheet in proportion to sales, % (1985–93)
INDUSTRY	CON3	Three-firm concentration ratio in the industry, % (1987–93)
	$KINT_I$	Capital intensity in the industry, % (1987–93)
PROFITABILITY	NET	Net profit margin (net profit in proportion to sales), % (1985–93)

Firm-specific differences in size and growth patterns are taken into account with three indicators: sales, market share, and capital intensity. Market share is measured as the proportion of the firm's sales to the total sales in the domestic two-digit industry. Hence, it is not an exact proxy for firms that operate in several industries, have a significant share of their sales abroad, or for which a more narrow industry classification is more relevant. However, for the time being I have no access to more accurate data.

Sales and capital intensity are instrumented because they are assumed to be predetermined, that is, influenced by past profitability. Market share is not available for the year 1985 (due to a change in classification practices); otherwise, it would have been instrumented as well. Industry specificities are controlled for with concentration ratio and capital intensity in addition to industry dummy instruments. Time dummies are used as well, but they are not reported.

5. Estimation Results

All Firms

By and large, competence and innovation variables are positively associated with profitability (table 2), supporting hypotheses 1 and 2, albeit with some interesting exceptions. Higher education (HIGH), general technical skills (TECH), and higher technical skills (HITECH) correlate consistently positively with profitability, although only HITECH is statistically significant.

Research skills measured by the POST variable affect profits through the interaction effects with other competence variables. One of the most robust outcomes is that higher educated employees complement doctoral-level researchers, in line with hypothesis 3. The interaction term is positive and very significant. A sufficient amount of people with general competencies are necessary to make R&D activities, in which the POST employees tend to work, economically useful. Employees in other activities have to be capable of utilizing the results of R&D. A similar kind of interaction can be found with the technical skills and doctoral employees (POST*TECH). Moreover, higher technical and research skills interact with innovation activities. This is suggested by the strongly negative coefficients on PAT*POST and PAT*HITECH. However, the nature of the interaction cannot be properly determined with the data at hand.

The innovation dummies show some intriguing behavior. The comprehensive innovation dummy (COMPR) is consistently a positive and significant determinant of profitability. However, separating the effects of product and process innovation reveals that product innovation tends to have adverse effects on profit margins, whereas process innovation is equally positively related to them. This result may arise from life-cycle effects (Cohen and Klepper 1996). Product innovators are on average significantly smaller than process innovators in the sample. At an early stage in the cycle, firms may be more concerned with creating new products and expanding, even to the detriment of profits, than fine tuning their processes and hence improving efficiency and profitability. However, firm size (sales) and market share are accounted for, and size is also instrumented, which should control to some extent for the life-cycle differences between small and large firms.

The results with respect to process innovation are quite different. It has a rather stable and strongly positive effect on profitability throughout the specifications. This could reflect the fact that process innovations are more likely to be accumulated as firm-specific organizational knowledge than product innovations, and hence the return might be more easily appro-

TABLE 2. Estimation Results for Net Profit Margins ($N = 209$)

Vector	Variable	(1) Coeff. (t-stat)	(2) Coeff. (t-stat)	(3) Coeff. (t-stat)	(4) Coeff. (t-stat)	(5) Coeff. (t-stat)	(6) Coeff. (t-stat)	(7) Coeff. (t-stat)
	CONST	−1.159* (−2.326)	−2.438* (−3.309)	−2.013* (−2.290)	−1.439 (−1.475)	−2.078* (−2.297)	−1.816* (−2.084)	−2.268* (−3.316)
	NET_{t-1}	0.081 (1.372)	0.112 (1.829)	0.056 (0.874)	0.048 (0.740)	0.058 (0.874)	0.056 (0.895)	0.122* (2.065)
INN	COMPR		2.194* (2.265)					2.087* (2.186)
	PROD			−5.512* (−3.698)	−6.181* (−4.510)	−4.297* (−4.022)	−4.925* (−3.586)	
	PROC			5.895* (4.454)	5.976* (5.040)	5.196* (4.763)	4.957* (4.073)	
	PAT_{t-1}	0.054* (2.734)	0.029 (1.236)	0.078* (3.882)	0.178* (4.391)	0.189* (3.598)	0.228* (3.425)	0.172* (2.772)
COMP	HIGH	0.305 (1.078)	0.407 (1.421)	0.208 (0.733)	0.179 (0.660)			
	POST	−0.453* (−2.241)	−0.707* (−2.391)	−0.093 (−0.217)	−1.377* (−2.103)	−1.023 (−1.362)	−0.842 (−1.810)	−1.294* (−4.545)
	TECH	0.040 (0.489)	0.056 (0.675)			0.037 (0.440)		
	HITECH						0.769* (2.639)	0.891* (3.080)
	POST*HIGH	0.037* (4.530)	0.043* (3.822)	0.023* (2.058)	0.096* (3.438)		0.061* (3.533)	0.069* (5.477)
	PAT*POST				−0.006 (−4.098)	−0.004 (−3.287)		
	POST*TECH					0.043 (2.085)		
	PAT*HITECH						−0.007* (−5.093)	−0.006* (−5.286)

(continued)

TABLE 2—Continued

Vector	Variable	(1) Coeff. (t-stat)	(2) Coeff. (t-stat)	(3) Coeff. (t-stat)	(4) Coeff. (t-stat)	(5) Coeff. (t-stat)	(6) Coeff. (t-stat)	(7) Coeff. (t-stat)
FIRM	MS	1.128*	1.149*	1.875*	1.659*	1.361*	1.823*	1.318*
		(3.608)	(4.041)	(4.715)	(3.996)	(3.335)	(4.742)	(3.561)
	SALES	0.001	0.001	0.001	−0.001	−0.0003	−0.0001	0.0002
		(1.013)	(1.456)	(1.579)	(−1.003)	(−0.435)	(−0.256)	(0.460)
	KINT	−0.222*	−0.237*	−0.189*	−0.218*	−0.195*	−0.185*	−0.237*
		(−5.807)	(−5.475)	(−4.702)	(−5.013)	(−4.736)	(−4.231)	(−5.418)
INDUSTRY	CON3	0.081	0.087	0.053	0.055	0.082	0.079	0.101*
		(1.771)	(1.908)	(1.147)	(1.209)	(1.731)	(1.722)	(2.176)
	$KINT_I$	−0.046	−0.092*	−0.073	−0.066	−0.077*	−0.097*	−0.106*
		(−1.437)	(−2.567)	(−1.877)	(−1.701)	(−2.024)	(−2.572)	(−2.947)
Test statistics (d.f.)	Second-order serial correlation	−0.547	−0.49	−0.137	−0.198	−0.500	−0.118	−0.361
		(153)	(153)	(153)	(153)	(153)	(153)	(153)
	Wald test for joint significance	254.93	228.88	237.40	188.79	258.27	160.63	178.62
		(11)	(12)	(12)	(13)	(13)	(13)	(12)
	Sargan test	33.39	29.01	27.65	28.97	30.68	28.11	29.10
		(35)	(34)	(33)	(33)	(33)	(33)	(34)

*Significant at the 95% level, two-tailed test.

priated. In any case, the hypothesis by Geroski and Machin (1993) and Geroski et al. (1993) that innovation is always associated with better profitability is not immediately confirmed. Moreover, educational competence variables seem to be as relevant proxies for capability accumulation as are the innovation variables. More detailed research on different innovation processes is needed to understand their interactions with capabilities.

The coefficient of the lagged dependent variable, NET_{-1}, is positive (although not significant). This suggests that firms that have been performing well continue to do so. There does not seem to exist any strong mechanism balancing the profits, at least not in the short run. Among the economic control variables, firm capital intensity (KINT) and capital intensity in the industry ($KINT_I$) are significantly negatively associated with profits, which may capture the poor productivity of the heavy investment carried out in many Finnish industrial firms during the boom of the late 1980s. As expected, profits increase with market share and the concentration of the industry.

The overall validity of the model is good, according to the Wald test of joint significance. In all the cases reported in table 2, NET_{-1}, SALES, and KINT are assumed to be predetermined, and they have been instrumented in the optimal way. Additional instruments are used for the industry dummies. The validity of the instruments is tested with the Sargan test. Under the null hypothesis of valid instruments, the Sargan test statistic is asymptotically distributed as chi-square. In all specifications, the null can be accepted within a 95 percent confidence interval. The null hypothesis of the second-order autocorrelation test is no autocorrelation, and the statistic is asymptotically distributed as $N(0,1)$. The critical value for 95 percent confidence in having no serial correlation is $+/-1.96$, and estimations here do not come close to these limits. The estimates should thus be consistent.

Innovators versus Noninnovators

In this subsection, the nature of innovation is further examined. It was hypothesized that profiting from innovation requires complementary capabilities. Hence, the skills and competencies needed for profitable business may be different for innovators and noninnovators. To assess this hypothesis, I study the determinants of profitability separately for innovating and noninnovating firms. Innovators include the comprehensive innovators (both product and process innovation); noninnovators carried out neither type.

According to the results in table 3, the determinants of profitability are indeed different for innovating and noninnovating firms. Overall, patenting and educational competencies are more important for the profitability of innovators.[3] Patenting is negatively related to noninnovators' profit rates. Only higher technical skills (HITECH) are robustly significant for

TABLE 3. Profitability of Innovators versus Noninnovators

Variable	(1)	(2)	(3)	(4)	(5)	(6)
	Innovators (N = 278)			Noninnovators (N = 176)		
	Coeff. (t-stat)	Coeff. (t-stat)	Coeff. (t-stat)	Coeff. (t-stat)	Coeff. (t-stat)	Coeff. (t-stat)
CONST	−0.991* (−2.234)	−1.001* (−2.190)	−1.219* (−2.798)	0.279 (0.349)	0.840 (1.108)	0.566 (0.731)
NET_{t-1}	−0.040 (−0.903)	−0.042 (−1.022)	−0.016 (−0.412)	0.442* (3.466)	0.400* (3.587)	0.312* (3.043)
PAT_{t-1}	0.133* (6.876)	0.136* (7.177)	0.030* (2.040)	−3.143* (−3.996)	−2.628* (−3.281)	−1.014* (−2.027)
HIGH	0.516* (2.432)			−0.038 (−0.183)		
POST	−1.780* (−3.436)	−1.824* (−3.699)	−1.323 (−1.934)	−3.335 (−1.372)	−4.124 (−1.617)	−5.808* (−2.217)
HITECH		0.685* (2.836)	0.650* (2.667)		1.970* (2.797)	1.542* (2.552)
POST*HIGH	0.080* (4.663)	0.076* (4.882)	0.037* (2.032)	0.373* (2.020)	0.332 (1.466)	0.262 (1.059)
PAT*POST	−0.006* (−10.132)			−6.107* (−4.732)		
PAT*HITECH		−0.006* (−10.541)			−0.433* (−3.565)	
MS	0.382 (0.368)	0.990 (1.092)	0.749 (1.112)	−3.072 (−1.196)	−4.734* (−2.337)	−7.359* (−3.706)
SALES	0.006* (1.966)	0.004 (1.487)	0.005* (2.129)	−0.010 (−0.997)	−0.006 (−0.811)	−0.030* (4.135)
KINT	−0.125 (−1.860)	−0.143* (−2.355)	−0.091 (−1.443)	−0.417* (−14.210)	−0.441* (−12.276)	−0.382* (−14.039)
CON3	−0.010 (−0.237)	−0.013 (−0.357)	−0.031 (−0.770)	0.382* (4.567)	0.383* (4.822)	0.358* (4.867)
$KINT_I$	−0.082* (−2.204)	−0.090* (−2.623)	−0.097* (−2.628)	−0.105* (−2.361)	−0.096* (−2.334)	−0.079 (−1.902)
Second-order serial correlation	−0.781 (80)	−0.692 (80)	−0.961 (80)	−0.741 (44)	−1.149 (44)	−0.895 (44)
Wald test for joint significance	281.18 (11)	292.50 (11)	171.20 (10)	1,845.95 (11)	10,633.25 (11)	10,520.24 (10)
Sargan test	36.053 (35)	36.66 (35)	34.48 (36)	24.15 (21)	23.71 (21)	25.92 (22)

*Significant at the 95% level, two-tailed test.

noninnovators' profits. The coefficient is also larger for noninnovators. Instead, the interaction term POST*HIGH is in most cases not significant for noninnovating firms, while for the innovators, higher education (HIGH), higher technical skills (HITECH), and research skills (POST) are all very significant. Again, the positive effect of research skills is conditioned by general skills in the form of higher education. For both groups, the interaction between skills and current patenting are strong and significant, suggesting that technological competencies do not necessarily translate into better profitability if coherent accumulation of other competencies does not take place.

Profitability of noninnovating firms seems to be determined mainly by factors other than competencies. The autoregression term (NET_{t-1}) is significant, suggesting that successful noninnovators tend to remain successful due to factors outside the model. Interestingly, market share correlates negatively with their profit rates. Furthermore, the negative impact of firm capital intensity is strong compared to that of innovating firms. On the other hand, positive effects of industry concentration are more important, too.

NET_{t-1} is insignificant for the group of innovators. The size of the firm is an important determinant of profitability for innovators, again pointing to the life-cycle differences among firms. Market share and concentration do not come into play with respect to innovating firms' profitability.

To sum up, profitability of innovating firms is influenced differently by the factors considered than that of noninnovating firms, which lends support for hypotheses 4 and 5. In particular, the role of education in the accumulation of competencies is more important for innovators. Economic performance of innovating firms relies to a significant extent on the employees' competencies.

Product Innovators versus Process Innovators

This subsection briefly investigates, whether there are also differences between different kinds of innovators. The profitability model is estimated separately for product-innovating and process-innovating firms. A companion essay (Leiponen 1996b) found that product and process innovation are associated with different competencies. The analysis was based on a taxonomy of different types of innovation and requisite competencies by Malerba and Orsenigo (1993). Now I examine whether the observed differences in competencies required carry over to profiting from product and process innovation.

In spite of some overlap in the two groups, the results indeed reveal differences in the determinants of profitability between product and process innovators. The coefficients indicate that patenting is more important for product innovators, although the coefficient is positive and significant for both groups. This is in accordance with Levin et al. (1987); protection of intellectual property via patenting is more useful for product innovation. Higher education is more relevant for process innovators, whereas the magnitude of the coefficients on research skills (POST) and the POST*HIGH interaction term are larger and more significant for product innovators.

Among the control variables, main differences include the fact that the profitability of process innovators is more affected by market share, and firm capital intensity decreases the profit margins of product innovators more seriously (see table 4).

In conclusion, even with this limited and overlapping sample of firms, the result emerges that the accumulation of capabilities in product-innovating firms is different from that in process-innovating firms. However, a more thorough inspection of the innovation processes, and how

TABLE 4.   Determinants of Profitability for Product and Process Innovators

Variable	(1) Product Innovators ($N = 315$) Coeff. (t-stat)	(2) Process Innovators ($N = 355$) Coeff. (t-stat)
CONST	−1.062*	−1.004*
	(−2.240)	(−2.462)
NET_{t-1}	0.034	−0.067
	(0.646)	(−1.072)
PAT_{t-1}	0.188*	0.095*
	(4.381)	(4.003)
HIGH	0.366	0.747*
	(1.640)	(3.648)
POST	−1.355*	−0.407
	(−2.075)	(−1.584)
POST*HIGH	0.074*	0.035*
	(3.309)	(2.265)
PAT*POST	−0.006*	−0.003*
	(−6.638)	(−3.248)
MS	0.738	0.912*
	(0.736)	(4.214)
SALES	0.004	0.0002
	(1.808)	(0.457)
KINT	−0.121*	−0.004
	(−7.078)	(−0.078)
CON3	−0.021	0.006
	(−0.485)	(0.155)
$KINT_I$	−0.065*	−0.114*
	(−2.014)	(−2.385)
Second-order serial correlation	−0.979	−0.689
	(89)	(99)
Wald test for joint significance	483.48	187.23
	(11)	(11)
Sargan test	35.09	42.87
	(35)	(35)

*Significant at the 95% level, two-tailed test.

their results are incorporated in the organization, would be needed to understand the kinds of competencies needed and accumulated in each.

6. Conclusions

Overall, educational competencies and technological capabilities have a considerable role as determinants of the profitability of manufacturing firms. Evidence was found of the positive but in some cases conditional effect of competencies on profitability. In addition, there are interesting interactions between competencies and innovation. Education measures seem to capture some aspects of internal knowledge accumulation in firms. The interpretation advanced here is that skills acquired in education are useful because they facilitate building organizational knowledge via learning and interacting on the job.

The interaction between the employees with a postgraduate degree, which reflects the research orientation of the firm, and other types of competencies is significant. In order for postgraduate employees to improve profitability, there need to be sufficiently general competencies in the firm. This is intuitive; even very ambitious and productive research and development may not be useful unless there are enough competencies in other parts of the organization to make use of the knowledge produced and to enable communication and interaction between R&D and marketing, production, and administration. This suggests that there exist substantial complementarities between different types of competencies. To confirm these preliminary results, complementarities would need to be modeled and estimated more explicitly.

Factors influencing the profitability of innovating firms differ from those influencing noninnovators. Both educational competencies and patenting were more important for innovators, whereas the profitability of noninnovators correlated more robustly with previous performance and firm- and industry-specific economic variables. This supports the idea that complementary capabilities are necessary in order to successfully profit from innovation.

Some differences in the determinants of profitability of product versus process innovators were detected as well. The coefficients of research competencies and their interaction with general higher education are larger and more significant for product innovators. Instead, higher education contributes more significantly to the profitability of process innovators. These results are tentative but could be interpreted in the following way: complementarities between research competencies and general capabilities are more important in profiting from product innovation, whereas process innovation tends to rely on learning on the job, which is enhanced by general skill level.

The empirical analysis has shortcomings, particularly arising from the availability of data. A reasonably detailed analysis would require more accurate firm-level data on innovation processes and better measures for competencies. Industry specificities should also be considered more carefully. Furthermore, in order to fully grasp the dynamics of knowledge accumulation and lags involved, longer time series are needed.

Interesting issues to consider in future work would be the complementarities between organizational design, technological change, and competencies. Innovation studies have emphasized the importance of integrating crucial knowledge sources inside and outside the firm (see, e.g., Iansiti and Clark 1994). Knowledge integration necessitates establishing communications channels and integrative routines. What kind of organizational choices are associated with different types of innovation, and which type of competencies are needed therein? Finally, the organizational aspects of complementary capabilities needed in successfully profiting from innovation would be an important theme to explore.

NOTES

1. Because the model is an AR(1) process, only second-order serial uncorrelation is required.

2. There is thus one more observation of the dependent variable and predetermined control variables than exogenous competence variables. These are "used" for the lagged dependent variable and instrumentation. The number of firms in the data set was reduced from 489 to 209 for the lack of time series; for the panel data at least four of the five observations for each firm were required. For more about the data and a descriptive analysis, see Leiponen 1996a.

3. The firm may have applied for patents during 1985–93 even if it did not innovate between 1989 and 1991.

REFERENCES

Arellano, Manuel, and Stephen Bond. 1991. Some Tests of Specification for Panel Data: Monte Carlo Evidence and an Application to Employment Equations. *Review of Economic Studies* 58:277–97.

Arrow, Kenneth. 1994. The Production and Distribution of Knowledge. In *The Economics of Growth and Technical Change,* edited by G. Silverberg and L. Soete. Aldershot: Edward Elgar.

Asplund, Rita, and Synnöve Vuori. 1996. *Labour Force Response to Technological Change: An Analysis of Finnish Manufacturing in 1980–1994.* Helsinki: Research Institute of the Finnish Economy.

Baldwin, John R., and Joanne Johnson. 1996. Business Strategies in More- and Less-Innovative Firms in Canada. *Research Policy* 25, no. 5: 785–804.

Bartel, Ann P., and Frank R. Lichtenberg. 1987. The Comparative Advantage of Educated Workers in Implementing New Technology. *Review of Economics and Statistics* 69, no. 1: 1–11.

——. 1991. The Age of Technology and Its Impact on Employee Wages. *Economics of Innovation and New Technology* 1, no. 3: 215–31.

Cohen, Wesley. 1995. Empirical Studies of Innovative Activity. In *Handbook of the Economics of Innovation and Technological Change,* edited by P. Stoneman. Oxford: Blackwell.

Cohen, Wesley, and Steven Klepper. 1996. A Reprise of Size and R&D. *Economic Journal* 106 (July): 925–51.

Cohen, Wesley, and Daniel A. Levinthal. 1989. Innovation and Learning: The Two Faces of R&D. *Economic Journal* 99 (Sept.): 569–96.

Dosi, Giovanni, and Luigi Marengo. 1994. Some Elements of an Evolutionary Theory of Organizational Competencies. In *Evolutionary Concepts in Contemporary Economics,* edited by R. W. England. Ann Arbor: University of Michigan Press.

Geroski, Paul A., and Alexis Jacquemin. 1988. The Persistence of Profits: A European Comparison. *Economic Journal* 98 (June): 375–89.

Geroski, Paul A., and Steve Machin. 1993. Innovation, Profitability, and Growth over the Business Cycle. *Empirica* 20:35–50.

Geroski, Paul A., Steve Machin, and John Van Reenen. 1993. The Profitability of Innovating Firms. *RAND Journal of Economics* 24, no. 2: 198–211.

Henderson, Rebecca M. 1994. The Evolution of Integrative Capability: Innovation in Cardiovascular Drug Discovery. *Industrial and Corporate Change* 3, no. 3: 607–30.

Iansiti, Marco, and Kim B. Clark. 1994. Integration and Dynamic Capability: Evidence from Product Development in Automobiles and Mainframe Computers. *Industrial and Corporate Change* 3, no. 3: 557–605.

ICC. 1994. *Industrial and Corporate Change* 3, no. 3. Special issue on capabilities.

Klepper, Steven. 1996. Entry, Exit, Growth, and Innovation over the Product Life Cycle. *American Economic Review* 86, no. 3: 562–83.

Kline, S. J., and Nathan Rosenberg. 1986. An Overview of Innovation. In *The Positive Sum Strategy,* edited by R. Landau and N. Rosenberg. Washington, DC: National Academy Press.

Leiponen, Aija. 1996a. *Education, Tenure, and Innovation in Finnish Manufacturing Firms.* Discussion Papers, no. 561. Helsinki: Research Institute of the Finnish Economy.

——. 1996b. *Education and Innovative Capabilities.* Discussion Papers, no. 562. Helsinki: Research Institute of the Finnish Economy.

Levin, Richard C., Alvin K. Klevorick, Richard R. Nelson, and Sidney G. Winter. 1987. Appropriating the Returns from Industrial R&D. *Brookings Papers on Economic Activity* 3:783–820.

Lundvall, Bengt-Åke, ed. 1992. *National Innovation Systems: Towards a Theory of Innovation and Interactive Learning.* London: Pinter.

Malerba, Franco, and Luigi Orsenigo. 1993. Technological Regimes and Firm Behaviour. *Industrial and Corporate Change* 2, no. 1: 45–71.

Montgomery, Cynthia A. 1995. *Resource-Based and Evolutionary Theories of the Firm: Towards a Synthesis.* Boston: Kluwer Academic.

Mueller, Dennis. 1986. *Profits in the Long Run.* Cambridge: Cambridge University Press.

Nelson, Richard R., and Sidney G. Winter. 1982. *An Evolutionary Theory of Economic Change.* Cambridge and London: Harvard University Press.

North, Douglass C. 1990. *Institutions, Institutional Change, and Economic Performance.* Cambridge: Cambridge University Press.

Penrose, Edith. 1959. *The Theory of the Growth of the Firm.* Oxford: Blackwell.

Schmalensee, Richard. 1989. Inter-Industry Studies of Structure and Performance. In *Handbook of Industrial Organization,* edited by R. Schmalensee et al. Vol. 2. Amsterdam: Elsevier.

Stoneman, Paul, ed. 1995. *Handbook of the Economics of Innovation and Technological Change.* Oxford: Blackwell.

Teece, David J. 1986. Profiting from Technological Innovation: Implications for Integration, Collaboration, Licensing, and Public Policy. *Research Policy* 15:285–305.

Teece, David J., and Gary Pisano. 1994. Dynamic Capabilities: An Introduction. *Industrial and Corporate Change* 3, no. 3: 537–56.

Teece, David J., Gary Pisano, and Amy Shuen. 1997. Dynamic Capabilities and Strategic Management. *Strategic Management Journal* 18, no. 7: 509–33.

Wernerfelt, Birger. 1984. A Resource-Based View of the Firm. *Strategic Management Journal* 5:171–80.

Firm Performance, Innovation, and Technological Spillovers: A Cross-Section Analysis With Swiss Firm Data

Spyros Arvanitis and Heinz Hollenstein

1. Introduction

This essay explores the impact of knowledge capital (computed on the basis of firm patent counts and R&D expenditure) and patent as well as R&D spillovers on output and productivity at the firm level in the usual setting of a Cobb-Douglas production function for Swiss manufacturing. We introduce spillovers from R&D or patents on the basis of material flows between sectors. In a further version, international R&D as well as patent spillovers from eight technologically highly developed countries are taken into consideration.

Moreover, we exploit systematically qualitative firm data on the innovation process in order to investigate some additional aspects of the knowledge-performance relationship. To this end, first, we try to get a more differentiated picture of the spillover mechanism by taking account of appropriability, technological potential, and the effects of various external knowledge sources (users, suppliers, universities, etc.) on the basis of firm-specific data. Second, we use specific inputs of innovative activity at the firm level to qualify knowledge capital by taking account of its heterogeneity. The firm data used in the study (except patent data) come from the 1990 Swiss Innovation Survey conducted in the manufacturing sector.

The results point to the existence of substantial spillovers from other domestic industries as well from those of foreign trade partners. In addition, we find that the extent of protection from imitation as well as the specific use of various external knowledge sources exert a significant influence on the magnitude of the impact of knowledge capital on firm performance. Lastly, it is shown that the heterogeneity of knowledge capital, in this case represented by innovation inputs, matters for firm performance.

2. Theoretical Background and the Empirical Model

Basic Model

The usual approach to studying the impact of technological knowledge on economic performance at the firm level is the production function framework (see, e.g., Griliches 1979 and Hall and Mairesse 1995). It is assumed that the production function for manufacturing firms can be approximated by a Cobb-Douglas function with the three inputs, labor L, physical capital C, and knowledge capital K:

$$Q_i = A \, L_i^\alpha \, C_i^\beta \, K_i^\gamma, \tag{1}$$

where Q_i denotes value added of firm i. The parameter of particular interest is γ, the elasticity of value added with respect to knowledge capital.

Introduction of Knowledge Spillovers (Extended Model)

A crucial aspect of innovative activity is the generation of new knowledge, which to some extent has the character of a public good. This gives rise to externalities ("spillovers"), which are a central theme in the literature on innovation in industrial economics (see, e.g., Spence 1984, Cohen and Levinthal 1989, and Geroski 1995).

A general though rather simplistic way to address this externality problem is to assume the diffusion of new private knowledge as leading to a "spillover pool of knowledge" from which other economic actors can draw information useful for their own innovative activities. To this purpose, the production function framework is extended to include an additional input for knowledge capital that the firm does not generate itself but collects from different sources (see Griliches 1979, 1992):

$$Q_i = A \, L_i^\alpha \, C_i^\beta \, K_i^\gamma \, KE_i^\delta, \tag{2}$$

where KE equals knowledge spillover. Thus, the total impact of knowledge on firm output is measured by $\gamma + \delta$, the sum of the effects of a firm's own knowledge capital and the knowledge obtained by spillovers from enterprises and institutions of the firm's economic environment.

A general formulation for the spillover capital as a (weighted) sum of the knowledge capital of a firm's relevant economic environment (knowledge pool) is given by following expression (see Griliches 1979, 1992):

$$KE_i = \Sigma_j \, w_{ij} \, K_j; \quad i \neq j, \tag{3}$$

where w is a weighting variable to be further specified.

What should such a weighting variable be based on? Broadly speaking, two distinct concepts of knowledge spillovers have been applied in recent literature. According to the first one, spillover knowledge is related to flows of intermediate and/or capital goods and is assumed to be proportional to the value of the stream of goods between firms/industries (see, e.g., Terlekyj 1980 and Wolff and Nadiri 1993). In the second concept, the weights in equation 3 are some measure of scientific and technological "distance" among firms and industries (see, e.g., Jaffe 1986, Englander et al. 1988, and Harhoff 1994b).

Sources of Heterogeneity: Appropriability, Technological Opportunities, and Innovation Inputs in the Extended Model

Of course, the concept of a knowledge spillover capital as a free good, equally accessible to all firms, has several weaknesses and needs further refinement. We want to focus here on three particular aspects that have received special attention in the recent literature on innovation (see, e.g., Cohen 1995). First, strategies of appropriation and their effectiveness are not equal across firms and industries. This means that the extent to which a firm's private knowledge "spills" into the pool depends decisively on the firm's own actions. The effectiveness of patent protection, secrecy, time leads, complexity of design, and so on may render more difficult the diffusion of information and contribute to a better appropriation of the returns of a firm's innovative efforts. Second, the magnitude of spillovers may be related to the amount of external knowledge available or anticipated to be available to a firm, thus the number of existing or anticipated technological opportunities (e.g., the potential of a certain technology or technological field). Third, the extent to which external knowledge can be utilized from a firm for its own innovative activity depends crucially on its "absorptive capacity" (Cohen and Levinthal 1989), which is a function of the "productivity" of external knowledge with respect to the firm's own innovative activity (Levin and Reiss 1988) and/or the amount of available knowledge capital in the firm (Cohen and Levinthal 1989). Further, we may hypothesize that the channels by which new knowledge can reach a firm (e.g., customers, suppliers, competitors, and universities) may also be important for its absorptive capacity (Cohen and Levinthal 1989; see also Mansfield 1985).

In order to test empirically some of these effects, which are measured by qualitative variables (ordinal scale), we include "switch" variables (a functional equivalent for interaction terms in case of qualitative variables) for the knowledge stock with respect to measures for appropriability, technological opportunities, and so on in the basic model (indirect impact on firm output):

$$q_i = a + \alpha l_i + \beta c_i + \gamma_I \left(k_i / X_{ij} > d \right) + \gamma_{II} \left(k_i / X_{ij} \le d \right), \tag{4}$$

where, in logarithmic form, X_{ij} is a qualitative measure, for example, for appropriability; d indicates a threshold for the qualitative variable X_{ij}; and the index j refers to the various qualitative measures used in the empirical analysis. As a consequence, we get separate coefficients of the knowledge stock variable for the two categories ($X_{ij} \leq d$; $X_{ij} > d$) we take into consideration for each ordinal variable (γ_{I} and γ_{II}, respectively).

For the conceptualization of these qualitative measures we draw heavily on our earlier work on the determinants of innovation activity (see, e.g., Arvanitis and Hollenstein 1996). We generally expect that these factors will increase the impact of knowledge capital on firm performance.

In order to relax the hypothesis of homogeneous knowledge capital, we use a group of characteristics of innovative activity that may affect the type of knowledge capital used in a firm.[1] The structure of inputs required for the generation of new products and processes (e.g., research, development, engineering/design, follow-up investment in physical capital, and organizational adjustment) may reflect particular features of a firm's knowledge capital. To test these effects, we use again the approach of equation 4.

3.   Data and Variable Specification

Data Set

The firm data set used in this study was constructed by matching the information from three distinct sources, that is, data on innovative activity and R&D expenditure (1988–90) from a survey of Swiss manufacturing firms conducted by the Center for Research of Economic Activity of the Swiss Federal Institute of Technology in November 1990 (see Arvanitis et al. 1992); patent data (1982–90) from the patent data bank of the Ifo-Institute for Economic Research, Munich; and data on sales as well as labor, material, and wage costs (1988–92) from a complementary survey conducted by our institute.

Corrections for the Labor and Capital Variables

Labor and physical capital measures have been corrected for double counting of personnel and equipment used in R&D activities (Schankerman 1981). Specifically, we computed labor input as the total number of full-time employees minus the number of employees working in research and development. The correction for R&D employees proved to be important; it caused approximately a doubling of the value of the coefficient of the patent capital variable (see Hall and Mairesse 1995 for similar findings). We also corrected for R&D equipment by assuming that the share of the capital expenses for R&D equipment equals the value-added share of total R&D expenditure. This correction increased the patent capital coefficient only by about 3 percent.

Construction of Patent and R&D Capital Variables

The knowledge capital variables were computed according to the "perpetual inventory method." We used a depreciation rate of 0.25 for the construction of patent capital variables.[2] No time series for R&D expenditures were available. In order to be able to compare our results with the bulk of existing studies considering only R&D variables, we constructed a crude approximation for the R&D capital on the basis of the cumulated R&D expenses for the period of 1988–90, which were distributed linearly over this period and depreciated with a (rather high) rate of 0.33. The effect of the initial stock of knowledge capital is not important for our estimations because of the use of a relatively large depreciation rate. We also experimented with several time lags between the dependent variable and the patent stock variable. Within a range of four years (1987 to 1990) the coefficients of the patent variables are almost constant; hence, the mean lag seems to be about 3.5 years, in accordance with the findings of other studies (see, e.g., Pakes and Schankerman 1984 and Hall et al. 1986).

Construction of Spillover Measures

We computed variables for *domestic* R&D and patent spillover variables (IORDSO, IOPATSO) on the basis of material flows between two-digit industries in manufacturing. Our formulation of these spillovers (see table 1) assumes that the amount of information gained from supplier k's R&D or patents is proportional to its importance in industry j's (to which the focusing firm i belongs) input structure and its R&D or patent capital (see Terlekyj 1980 and Wolff and Nadiri 1993).

The *foreign* R&D spillover variable (FRDSO) was constructed by the procedure described in Coe and Helpman (1995) on the basis of intraindustry trade flows between countries with high R&D intensity (see table 1). It is assumed that the knowledge gain from supplier country k's R&D depends on the country-related import structure of the domestic two-digit industry j (to which the focusing firm i belongs) weighted with the import share of this industry.

A somewhat modified procedure was used to construct the *foreign patent* spillover variable (FPATSO). Patent stocks at the industry level were not available; thus, we computed patent capital measures at the country level by the "perpetual inventory method" with a depreciation rate of 0.25 on the basis of the sum of yearly "external" and "resident" patent applications for the eight countries to be taken into consideration (see OECD 1993). The reason for considering the sum of these two flow variables is that the ratios of external and internal patent applications vary strongly among countries.[3]

TABLE 1.   Construction of Spillover Variables

Spillover Variable	Comment
Domestic spillovers	
$\text{IORDSO}_i = \Sigma_k v_{jk} \text{KRD}_k - \text{KRD}_i$	v_{jk}: share of material input of industry j delivered by industry k
	KRD_k: R&D capital of industry k
	KRD_i: R&D capital of firm i
	k: $1, \ldots, 15$ (two-digit industries); firm i belongs to industry j
$\text{IOPATSO}_i = \Sigma_k v_{jk} \text{KPAT}_k - \text{KPAT}_i$	KPAT_k: patent capital of industry k
	KPAT_i: patent capital of firm i
Foreign spillovers	
$\text{FRDSO}_i = \text{imp}_j \Sigma_m \text{imp}_{jm} (\text{RDE}_{jk}/0.15)$	imp_j: share of imports of industry j
	imp_{jm}: share of imports of industry j coming from country m
	RDE_{jk}: R&D expenditure of industry j in country m
	m: $1, \ldots, 8$ (United States, Japan, Germany, France, Italy, Britain, Holland, Sweden)
	j: $1, \ldots, 11$ (two-digit industries); firm i belongs to industry j
$\text{FPATSO}_i = \text{imp}_j \Sigma_k \text{imp}_k \text{KPAT}_k$	imp_k: share of imports from country k
	KPAT_k: patent capital of country k

Sources: Imports at the industry and country level: *Swiss Foreign Trade Statistics;* input-output linkages (two-digit industries): input-output table of the Swiss economy for 1990 (KOF/ETH; unpublished); patent data (Swiss two-digit industries): sample of 707 manufacturing firms (see sec. 3); R&D expenditures (Swiss two-digit industries): *Swiss R&D Statistics;* R&D expenditures (two-digit industries; several countries): *Research and Development Expenditure in Industry, 1973–92* (OECD, 1995); patent data (several years and countries): *Basic Science and Technology Statistics* (OECD, 1993). For data at the firm level, see section 3.

4.   Empirical Results

Basic Model and Technological Spillovers

Basic Model. Estimations of equation 1 in logarithmic form yielded coefficients for the labor variable that amount to about 0.55 (cols. 1 and 2 in table 2). The corresponding coefficient for physical capital is considerably smaller (0.38 to 0.45; cols. 1 and 2) than the labor coefficient, though larger than in most similar studies using book values as the capital measure.

We estimated equation 1 with both types of knowledge capital (patent and R&D capital). We obtain an elasticity of knowledge capital with respect to value added of 0.053 in case of patent capital and 0.067 in case of R&D capital (cols. 1 and 2 in table 2). The coefficients of both knowledge variables (patent and R&D capital) are positive and statistically significant (5 percent level) for all estimations reported in table 2.[4] Thus, there is a

TABLE 2.   Impact of Knowledge Capital and Technological Spillovers on Firm Value-Added (OLS estimates)

Explanatory Variable	Basic Model		Domestic Spillovers		Foreign Spillovers	
	1	2	3	4	5	6
Constant	3.232*	3.564*		2.726*	2.927*	1.929*
	(0.169)	(0.226)		(0.515)	(0.745)	(0.584)
l	0.558*	0.552*	0.558*	0.559*	0.558*	0.558*
	(0.050)	(0.076)	(0.077)	(0.050)	(0.050)	(0.050)
c	0.445*	0.380*	0.408*	0.443*	0.445*	0.446*
	(0.040)	(0.047)	(0.054)	(0.040)	(0.040)	(0.040)
kpat	0.053*		0.073*	0.058*	0.053*	0.053*
	(0.020)		(0.027)	(0.021)	(0.020)	(0.020)
krd		0.067*				
		(0.026)				
iordso			0.288*			
			(0.020)			
iopatso				0.136		
				(0.142)		
frdso					0.062*	
					(0.031)	
fpatso						0.133*
						(0.066)
N	309	309	170	309	309	309
Adjusted R^2	0.971	0.963	(0.999)	0.971	0.971	0.971
SER	0.287	0.291	0.294	0.286	0.287	0.286

Note: The lower-case letters denote the logarithms of the variables. l: number of full-time employees at the beginning of 1992 (less R&D employees); c: capital income, 1992 (less c multiplied by the R&D intensity [value added]); krd: R&D capital, 1990 (depreciation rate of 33 percent); kpat: patent capital, 1990 (depreciation rate of 25 percent). Heteroscedasticity-robust coefficients: (White procedure, standard errors in parentheses). Thirteen industry dummies (two-digit).
*Significant at the .05 level.

discernible contribution of knowledge capital to firm performance measured by value added.[5] Nevertheless, compared to elasticity estimates for other countries at the firm level our figures are rather low (for recent similar studies, see Harhoff 1994a as well as Hall and Mairesse 1995).

Domestic Spillovers. We estimated several versions of equation 2 with both knowledge capital variables and two different measures of domestic spillovers, one for patent and one for R&D externalities. The coefficient of labor input remains almost unchanged, that for physical capital drops somewhat, and the impact of the knowledge variables increases to some extent; on the whole, the parameters of the basic model are not much affected when spillovers are taken into account.

We obtain statistically significant positive coefficients for R&D spillovers with both knowledge capital variables. We report here only the result with patent capital (0.288; col. 3 in table 2). The elasticity of the patent spillover variable is also positive but not statistically significant (0.136; col. 4). The effect of the R&D spillover variable is considerably larger than the effect of a firm's own R&D or patent capital. It is difficult to assess the plausibility of this result because there are few other studies with which we can directly compare it. On the whole, there is a general tendency in most studies for the spillover effect to be larger than that of a firm's own knowledge capital, but it is not clear by what magnitude (see, e.g., Goto and Suzuki 1989, Jaffe 1986 and Harhoff 1994b).

   Foreign Spillovers. Patent and R&D spillovers of foreign knowledge exert a positive, statistically significant effect on firm output. The coefficient of the spillover variables takes the value of 0.062 and 0.133 for R&D and patent spillovers, respectively, when patent stock is used as the knowledge variable (cols. 5 and 6 in table 2). Foreign patent spillovers are stronger than foreign R&D spillovers. For both kinds of spillovers, we find elasticities that are larger than those of the firm's own knowledge capital. A comparison of the results shows that the effects of domestic spillovers are larger than those of foreign spillovers. Most existing studies on foreign technological spillovers are at the country level; thus, a comparison with our results is difficult. At any rate, foreign spillovers appear to have in most studies a stronger impact on firm output than the firm's own knowledge capital (see, e.g., Mohnen 1992 and Rogers 1995).

Impact of Appropriability, Technological Opportunities, and Specific Innovation Inputs

Table 3 contains the results with respect to pairs of "switch" variables of knowledge capital constructed in order to capture the effects of the following determinants of innovative activity (and as a consequence of firm-specific knowledge capital) on firm performance: the overall appropriability measure (APPR); a proxy for the general technological potential relevant to the firm's innovative activity (TPOT); a variable for the specific contribution of external knowledge to firm's own generation of innovative knowledge (EXTINT); a measure of the extent of acquisition of external knowledge from foreign sources (EXTF) (as a special feature of EXTINT); and, alternatively to EXTINT, qualitative measure for the importance of a number of external sources of knowledge for the firm's innovative activity.[6]

   We expected a positive impact of APPR, EXTINT, and EXTF on the output for product as well as process innovations. The empirical results confirmed these expectations only partly. For product innovations, the coefficient of the patent stock variable for firms with high appropriability (APPR) is considerably larger than that for firms with low appropriability and also larger than the coefficient for all firms when we do not distinguish between high and low imitation protection. Thus, a high effectiveness of appropriability strategies with respect to products leads to a larger contribu-

TABLE 3. Indirect Impact of Appropriability and Technological Opportunities on Firm Value Added

X	Product		Process	
	$\gamma_I \ (k_i/X_{ij} > 3)$	$\gamma_{II} \ (k_i/X_{ij} \leq 3)$	$\gamma_I \ (k_i/X_{ij} > 3)$	$\gamma_{II}(k_i/X_{ij} \leq 3)$
APPR[a]	0.087*	0.029	0.040	0.059*
	(0.032)	(0.016)	(0.025)	(0.023)
TPOT[b]	0.067*	0.041		
	(0.025)	(0.025)		
EXTINT[c]	0.033	0.060*	0.081*	0.043
	(0.021)	(0.023)	(0.028)	(0.022)
EXTF[d]	0.070*	0.048*	0.095*	0.046*
	(0.033)	(0.021)	(0.033)	(0.020)
Knowledge sources				
USER (customers/users of products)	0.055*	0.049	0.019	0.056*
	(0.021)	(0.037)	(0.034)	(0.021)
SUPP (suppliers of materials/equipment)	0.027	0.057*	0.059*	0.051*
	(0.021)	(0.022)	(0.028)	(0.023)
COMP (competitors)	0.052*	0.054*	0.021	0.054*
	(0.025)	(0.025)	(0.052)	(0.021)
UNIV (universities/ scientific laboratories)	0.089*	0.035*	0.030	0.057*
	(0.019)	(0.016)	(0.017)	(0.022)
ASSOC (professional associations/ conferences)	−0.026	0.056*	−0.052	0.055*
	(0.029)	(0.021)	(0.067)	(0.020)
EXPERT (recruitment of experts)	0.058*	0.045	0.045	0.058*
	(0.024)	(0.025)	(0.027)	(0.024)
PAT (patent disclosures/ licenses)	0.057	0.052*	0.015	0.059*
	(0.034)	(0.022)	(0.020)	(0.022)
ACQUIS (acquisition of other firms)	0.069	0.048	0.033*	0.059*
	(0.041)	(0.021)	(0.015)	(0.023)
COOP (subsidiaries/ joint ventures, etc.)	0.053*	0.012	0.075*	0.020
	(0.020)	(0.014)	(0.028)	(0.018)

Note: All variables (except COOP, which is a dummy variable) reflect assessments of the surveyed firms measured on a five-point Likert scale and have been measured separately for product and process innovations (except TPOT). The threshold d in equation 4 was set to the value 3. Separate model estimations were conducted for each pair of "switch" variables (e.g., kpat/APPR > 3 and kpat/APPR ≤ 3). We report only the coefficients of the pairs of "switch" variables. Heteroscedasticity-robust standard errors are printed in brackets under the estimated coefficients. Thirteen industry dummies (two-digit) are included in the regression equations. A two-tailed t-test (five percent threshold) was performed for the difference of the parameters of every pair of switch variables used in the estimations. There is a statistically discernible difference in the coefficients of all variables included in this table except COMP (product).

[a]APPR: overall measure of the extent to which innovations can be protected from competition by means of patents, secrecy, lead time, and so on.

[b]TPOT: general technological potential, that is, scientific and technological knowledge relevant to the firm's innovative activity.

[c]EXTINT: specific contribution of external knowledge to the firm's own innovative activity.

[d]EXTF: extent of acquisition of external knowledge from other countries.

*Significant at the .05 level.

tion of knowledge input to a firm's output. This is not necessarily the case for new processes; the coefficient for firms with low appropriability is even larger than that for firms with high appropriability and of about the same magnitude as for all firms. This means that firms do not need imitation protection for new production techniques to be economically successful in applying them, a result that seems to be plausible.

The results for technological potential (TPOT) and foreign external knowledge (EXTF) are highly plausible as well. The positive impact of TPOT is considerable, and knowledge capital is more productive in firms that use much foreign knowledge; in the latter case, this effect is stronger for processes than for products. A high contribution of external knowledge to a firm's own innovative activity leads only in case of new production techniques to a larger than "average" impact on performance (EXTINT for process innovation). We have difficulty explaining the results with EXTINT for product innovations because we cannot find any plausible argument for this finding, which also contradicts the general pattern of the results we obtained for the single knowledge sources (see next paragraph).

For new products, the intensive use of six out of a total of nine external knowledge sources is associated with a higher contribution of patent stock to output; the largest elasticities of patent stock are found for knowledge from universities, research institutions, and scientific literature (0.089; UNIV) as well as from acquisitions (0.069; ACQUIS). For two of the knowledge sources (suppliers and professional associations), the coefficient of the highly intensive users is lower than that for firms that do not use much information from these two sources. This is not surprising because suppliers' knowledge is of minor importance for the generation of new products and information from professional associations refers to technical standards and general knowledge available to every firm. We could not find any specific influence of COMP (knowledge from firms in the same industry) on the coefficient of the patent capital variable. For the generation of process innovations, we get a different pattern with respect to external knowledge used compared with that in the case of new products. For seven out of a total of nine external knowledge sources, high intensity of use does not lead to a more productive patent stock. This is particularly plausible in the case of knowledge from users of firms' products, which has only a distant and indirect relationship to know-how concerning production techniques. Information from suppliers of materials and equipment (SUPP) and cooperating firms (COOP) yield a considerable (indirect) contribution to firm output by raising the elasticity of the patent capital variable to 0.059 resp. 0.075. An explanation for the estimates for the other sources can possibly be found in the nature of the type of knowledge capital we have mainly used in this study; patent stock captures primarily the innovative activity directed to the generation of new products because most patents refer to products and not to processes. Estimations not presented here on the basis of the R&D capital variable (which reflects product innovation to a much lesser degree) show a different picture: the coefficients of "switch" variables for EXTINT are of similar magnitude for both product and process innovations. On the whole, it seems that the use of external knowledge does not contribute much to a higher productivity of knowledge capital in the case of process innovations.

In order to qualify knowledge capital and take account of its heterogeneity, we distinguish five types of inputs that may be used to generate new products and processes: research, development, engineering/design, follow-up investment, and organizational inputs. For product innovations, firms with high development inputs show also a high elasticity of patent stock (see table 4), whereas high research inputs do not yield larger coefficients of the patent capital variable. About the same pattern as in research can be observed for the other three innovation inputs. Thus, development is a dominant (and highly productive) feature of innovative activity of Swiss manufacturing. On the other hand, the productivity of process-oriented innovative activity depends not only on high development inputs but also on inputs in engineering, additional investment linked to innovation, and organizational adjustment, which seems to be quite compatible with changes of work organization implied by major changes of production technology. Research, again, is not as productive for process innovation as for other inputs, which is more plausible than in case of new products.[7]

TABLE 4.   Indirect Impact of Several Inputs of Innovation on Firm Value-Added

	Product		Process	
X	$\gamma_I\ (k_i/X_{ij} > 3)$	$\gamma_{II}\ (k_i/X_{ij} \leq 3)$	$\gamma_I\ (k_i/X_{ij} > 3)$	$\gamma_{II}\ (k_i/X_{ij} \leq 3)$
R (research)	0.031	0.057*	0.041*	0.055*
	(0.019)	(0.022)	(0.017)	(0.022)
D (development)	0.087*	0.015	0.062*	0.051*
	(0.029)	(0.017)	(0.028)	(0.022)
ED (engineering/design)	0.042	0.066*	0.077*	0.047*
	(0.024)	(0.025)	(0.034)	(0.021)
FI (follow-up investment)[a]	0.031	0.058*	0.053*	0.053*
	(0.017)	(0.023)	(0.018)	(0.026)
OA (organizational adjustment)[b]	0.045	0.055*	90.071*	0.041
	(0.023)	(0.022)	(0.028)	(0.024)

Note: See note to table 3. There is a statistically discernible difference in the coefficients of all variables included in this table except "investment linked to innovation" (process).

[a]Additional investment linked to innovation (trial production, training, market analysis, investment in plant, machinery and equipment linked to new products and processes).

[b]Organizational adjustment due to the introduction of new products and processes.

*Significant at the .05 level.

5. Summary and Conclusions

We obtain positive estimates of knowledge capital on the basis of either R&D or patent data and positive coefficients of the domestic R&D spillover variables (also positive but statistically not significant coefficients for the corresponding patent spillovers); in both cases the coefficients are larger than that of knowledge capital stock. Foreign patent and R&D spillovers exert a positive effect on firm output, a finding similar to those reported in most studies dealing with international spillovers at the country level.

Our results based on qualitative data on innovation activity show that the degree of appropriability, the amount of external knowledge available to the firm, and the specific use of certain knowledge sources (universities, firm acquisitions, experts, patent disclosures, and users for products; co-operating firms and suppliers for processes) exert a significant positive influence on knowledge capital's impact on firm performance. Development inputs dominate the innovative activity of Swiss manufacturing firms; for process innovations, engineering-oriented and organizational inputs are also important. On the whole, the use of the qualitative measures of several characteristics of innovative activity proved to be informative with respect to knowledge capital heterogeneity, thus adding to our knowledge regarding the channels through which technical progress enhances performance.

NOTES

The research reported in this essay was supported by the Swiss National Science Foundation and the Swiss Federal Ministry of Economic Affairs.

1. We present here only a part of our analysis, referring to several characteristics of innovative activity such as objectives and technical orientation of innovations and extent of "innovativeness" of new products and processes (see Arvanitis and Hollenstein 1997 for more detailed results).

2. In accordance with the findings of most other empirical studies (see, e.g., Hall and Mairesse 1995), the particular choice of depreciation rate does not effect the estimation results considerably.

3. On the other hand, we commit a measurement error by double counting the patents applied for both at home and abroad. We assume that the first type of error (different ratios of external and internal patents) is much more important.

4. Alternative estimations with a cross-section for 1988 yielded a labor coefficient of 0.54, a capital coefficient of 0.46, and a knowledge coefficient (patent) of 0.06.

5. We obtain similar results using sales, labor productivity, or total factor productivity as a performance variable.

6. The tightness of the relation between EXTINT and the set of external knowledge sources was investigated by estimating an ordered probit model with EXTINT

as dependent variable and USER, . . . , COOP as right-hand variables; all coefficients of the knowledge sources variables were found to be positive and statistically significant at the 5 percent level (see Arvanitis and Hollenstein 1992).

7. It seems that the argument that patent capital variables do not reflect adequately the process-oriented innovative activity must be somewhat relaxed with respect to this type of variable.

REFERENCES

Arvanitis, S., A. Frick, R. Etter, and H. Hollenstein. 1992. *Innovationsfähigkeit und Innovationsverhalten der Schweizer Industrie.* Bern: Bundesamt für Konjunkturfragen.

Arvanitis, S., and H. Hollenstein. 1992. "Das Innovationsverhalten schweizerischer Industrieunternehmen. Eine ökonometrische Untersuchung anhand von Firmendaten für input-, output- und marktergebnis-orientierte Indikatoren unter besonderer Berücksichtigung der Firmengrösse," *KOF/ETH-Arbeitspapier* (Zurich) 41: (unpublished working paper).

———. 1996. "Industrial Innovation in Switzerland: A Model-Based Analysis with Survey Data." In *Determinants of Innovation and Diffusion: The Message from New Indicators,* edited by A. Kleinknecht. London: Macmillan.

———. 1997. "The Impact of Innovation and Technological Spillovers on Firm Performance: Evidence from Swiss Manufacturing." Mimeo.

Coe, D. T., and E. Helpman. 1995. "International R&D Spillovers." *European Economic Review* 39:859–87.

Cohen, W. M. 1995. "Empirical Studies of Innovative Activity." In *Handbook of Innovation and Technological Change,* edited by P. Stoneman. Oxford: Blackwell.

Cohen, W. M., and D. A. Levinthal. 1989. "Innovation and Learning: The Two Faces of R&D." *Economic Journal* 99:569–96.

Englander, A. S., R. Evenson, and M. Hanazaki. 1988. "R&D, Innovation, and the Total Factor Productivity." *OECD Economic Studies* no. 11: 156–91.

Geroski, P. A. 1995. "Do Spillovers Undermine the Incentive to Innovate?" In *Economic Approaches to Innovation,* edited by S. Dowrick. Aldershot: Edward Elgar.

Goto, A., and K. Suzuki. 1989. "R&D Capital, Rate of Return on R&D Investment, and Spillover of R&D in Japanese Manufacturing Industries." *Review of Economics and Statistics* 71:555–64.

Griliches, Z. 1979. "Issues in Assessing the Contribution of Research and Development to Productivity Growth." *Bell Journal of Economics* 10:92–116.

———. 1992. "The Search for R&D Spillovers." *Scandinavian Journal of Economics* 94S:29–47.

Hall, B. H., Z. Griliches, and J. A. Hausman. 1986. "Patents and R and D: Is There a Lag?" *International Economic Review* 27:265–83.

Hall, B. H., and J. Mairesse. 1995. "Exploring the Relationship between R&D and Productivity in French Manufacturing Firms." *Journal of Econometrics* 65: 263–93.

Harhoff, D. 1994a. "R&D and Productivity in German Manufacturing Firms." ZEW Discussion Papers, no. 94–01, Mannheim. Mimeo.

———. 1994b. "Searching for R&D Spillovers among German Manufacturing Firms." Paper prepared for the ZEW workshop Productivity, R&D, and Innovation at the Firm Level, June 24–25, Mannheim.

Jaffe, A. B. 1986. "Technological Opportunity and Spillovers of R&D: Evidence from Firms' Patents, Profits, and Market Value." *American Economic Review* 76:984–1001.

KOF/ETH. 1996. *Input Output Table of the Swiss Economy for 1990.* Zurich: KOF/ETH.

Levin, R. C., and P. C. Reiss. 1988. "Cost-Reducing and Demand-Creating R&D with Spillovers." *Rand Journal of Economics* 19:538–56.

Mansfield, E. 1985. "How Rapidly Does New Industrial Technology Leak Out?" *Journal of Industrial Economics* 34:217–23.

Mohnen, P. 1992. *The Relationship between R&D and Productivity Growth in Canada and Other Major Industrialized Countries.* Ottawa: Canada Communications Group.

OECD. 1993. *Basic Science and Technology Statistics.* Paris: OECD.

———. 1995. *Research and Development Expenditure in Industry, 1973–92.* Paris: OECD.

Pakes, A., and M. Schankerman. 1984. "The Rate of Obsolescence of Patents, Research Gestation Lags, and the Private Rate of Return to Research Resources." In *R&D, Patents, and Productivity,* edited by Z. Griliches. Chicago: University of Chicago Press.

Rogers, M. 1995. "International Knowledge Spillovers: A Cross-Country Study." In *Economic Approaches to Innovation,* edited by S. Dowrick. Aldershot: Edward Elgar.

Schankerman, M. 1981. "The Effects of Double-Counting and Expensing on the Measured Returns to R&D." *Review of Economics and Statistics* 63:454–58.

Spence, M. 1984. "Cost Reduction, Competition, and Industry Performance." *Econometrica* 25:101–21.

Swiss Federal Statistics Office. 1993. *Swiss R&D Statistics, 1992.* Berne: Federal Statistics Office.

———. 1994. *Swiss Foreign Trade Statistics, 1994.* Berne: Federal Statistics Office.

Terlekyj, N. 1980. "Direct and Indirect Effects of Industrial Research and Development on the Productivity Growth on Industries." In *New Developments in Productivity Measurement and Analysis,* edited by J. N. Kendrick and B. N. Vaccaras. Chicago: University of Chicago Press.

Wolff, E. N., and M. I. Nadiri. 1993. "Spillover Effects, Linkage Structure, and Research and Development." *Structural Change and Economic Dynamics* 4:315–31.

Relevance, Nature, and the Outcome of Innovation Activities: Evidence from the Italian Innovation Survey

Rinaldo Evangelista, Giulio Perani, Fabio Rapiti, and Daniele Archibugi

1. Introduction

Although technological change is one of the main determinants of long-term economic development, our knowledge of some of its most crucial aspects is still incomplete. The following are some issues that have not yet been fully explored.

1. How many firms do innovate and what factors determine the probability that a firm will introduce innovations?
2. What is the nature of innovative activities performed and the amount of financial resources devoted to innovation?
3. What amount of firms' output is affected by innovation?

In this essay, we provide fresh empirical evidence on these three issues using data on more than 22,000 firms provided by the Italian Innovation Survey.[1] Although the results presented in this work are likely to reflect the peculiarities of the Italian productive and technological structure, we also believe they highlight some more general features of innovation activities in manufacturing.

The essay is organized as follows: section 2 analyzes the spread of innovation phenomenon in the manufacturing sector, looking at percentages of innovating firms across main industries and firm size classes. Section 3 quantifies the importance of the different sources of innovation. The innovative contribution of small and large firms is analyzed in section 4, while section 5 analyzes the output of innovation by looking at the quantity and quality of new and improved products. The main findings of this work and some policy implications are drawn in the final section.

2. The Spread of Innovation in the Manufacturing Industry

One of the first aims of innovation surveys is to establish how widespread the innovative phenomenon is within the industrial structure.

Table 1 shows for the manufacturing sector as a whole and for the main industrial sectors and firm size classes the number of firms participating in the survey, the percentages of those firms that have introduced innovation in the period 1990–92, and the percentage of sales and employees ac-

TABLE 1.   Innovating and Noninnovating Firms by Firm Size and Industry

	Total Firms	Innovating Firms on Total Firms (%)		Employees of Innovating Firms on Total Firms (%)		Sales of Innovating Firms on Total Firms (%)	
Classes of employees							
20–49	15,109	25.9		27.5		29.1	
50–99	4,142	40.8		41.6		43.0	
100–199	2,012	48.0		48.7		47.8	
200–499	1,041	58.5		59.8		67.3	
500–999	292	74.0		74.5		79.1	
1,000 and over	191	84.3	.	91.5		95.9	
Total	22,787	33.3		61.5		70.7	
Industrial sectors							
Aerospace	31	67.7	(1)	99.0	(1)	99.5	(1)
Office machinery	48	64.6	(2)	94.4	(2)	97.6	(2)
Radio, TV, tele-communications	249	59.8	(3)	91.9	(3)	93.4	(4)
Pharmaceuticals	198	56.1	(4)	78.6	(8)	80.6	(8)
Precision instruments	435	50.3	(5)	65.8	(12)	67.7	(12)
Mechanical machinery	2,713	48.9	(6)	70.5	(10)	75.4	(10)
Chemicals (excluding pharmaceuticals)	561	45.6	(7)	78.8	(7)	80.9	(6)
Motor vehicles	445	44.7	(8)	91.5	(4)	92.0	(5)
Synthetic fibers	31	41.9	(9)	82.9	(5)	80.7	(7)
Rubber and plastic	866	41.8	(10)	63.6	(13)	65.1	(14)
Oil	89	39.3	(11)	81.2	(6)	97.5	(3)
Electrical machinery	989	38.7	(12)	67.7	(11)	72.5	(11)
Printing and publishing	732	38.3	(13)	54.7	(16)	53.7	(16)
Paper	496	38.3	(14)	58.5	(15)	63.5	(15)
Metals	643	37.9	(15)	60.8	(14)	65.2	(13)
Metal products	2,874	33.4	(16)	42.4	(19)	45.6	(19)
Other transport	272	32.7	(17)	75.1	(9)	75.5	(9)
Food, drink, tobacco	1,501	31.2	(18)	53.0	(17)	51.5	(17)
Mineral and nonmineral processing	1,486	29.7	(19)	47.1	(18)	49.1	(18)
Wood	622	28.8	(20)	36.6	(22)	26.1	(23)
Textiles	2,008	28.1	(21)	38.0	(20)	41.9	(20)
Other manufacturing	1,679	26.0	(22)	36.7	(21)	40.2	(21)
Leather and footwear	1,486	18.8	(23)	24.6	(23)	27.9	(22)
Clothing	1,991	11.3	(24)	17.8	(24)	18.0	(24)

Source: Istat 1995.
Note: Ranking is in parentheses.

counted for by innovating firms in 1992. The table shows that only one-third of the firms involved in the survey have introduced innovation during the three-year period considered.[2] The innovative phenomenon has involved, however, a much larger portion of the Italian industrial structure, 61.5 percent of employees and 70.7 percent of turnover of the manufacturing industry covered by the survey being concentrated in innovating firms. The table shows that there are significant differences in the percentage of innovating firms across different size classes and industrial sectors. Only one-fourth of the firms with less than 50 employees have innovated during the period 1990–92, while 84.3 percent of firms with over 1,000 employees have introduced innovations. Industries that show the highest percentages of innovating firms are aerospace (67.7 percent); office machinery (64.6 percent); and radio, TV, and telecommunications (59.8 percent). Also at the industry level a more effective indicator of the actual economic relevance of the innovation phenomenon is given by the percentage of sales and employees of innovating firms. In sectors such as aerospace, office machinery, and radio, TV, and telecommunications, innovating firms concentrate more than 90 percent of the employees and sales of these industries, while in most of the industries producing traditional consumer goods the percentages of employees and sales accounted for by innovating firms remain quite low.

On the whole, table 1 confirms that industrial sectors and firm size prove to be important factors for determining the presence of innovation activities within firms. This kind of evidence however, does not allow us to test whether large firms are more likely to be innovative independently of the industry in which they operate.

To check whether any sectoral and size "composition effects" exist, we have estimated two logit equations in which the mere presence-absence of the innovative phenomenon (eq. 1) and R&D activities (eq. 2) are considered as the independent variables (see table 2). In both equations, as regressors we used firm size (measured by the logarithm of the number of employees) and the industrial sector to which the firms belonged (expressed by 24 sectoral dummy variables). Another two variables were included as controlling factors, namely, the geographical location of the firm (identified by five regional dummies) and the fact that the firm belongs to an industrial group.[3]

The coefficients of the different independent variables allow us to estimate (through a logistic transformation) the probability that a firm with given characteristics (size, sector, geographical area, membership of a group) will be innovative or perform R&D. In the case of the dummy variables, the coefficient can be interpreted as a gross index of the relative importance of the characteristic of the firm taken into account by the dummies.[4]

The regressions have an acceptable capacity to interpret the phenomenon. Firm behavior is predicted by the model in 70 percent of the cases in

TABLE 2. Probability of Carrying Out Innovative Activities and R&D (logit estimates)

Dependent Variables	Equation 1: Presence of Innovative Activities		Equation 2: Presence of R&D Activities	
Number of observations	22,787		22,787	
Concordant	70.0%		77.5%	
Discordant	29.7%		22.1%	
−2 Log L	2774		3725	
Score	2641		3837	
Intercept	−3.972		−6.114	
Belonging to an industrial group	0.166		0.327	
Not belonging to an industrial group	reference		reference	
Log of employees	0.578		0.742	
Northwest	0.771		1.361	
Northeast	0.454		1.496	
Center	0.208		1.127	
South	0.067*		0.612	
Islands	reference		reference	
Office machinery	1.486	(1)	1.927	(1)
Aerospace	1.276	(2)	1.544	(3)
Radio, TV, telecommunications	1.212	(3)	1.578	(2)
Precision instruments	0.962	(4)	1.415	(4)
Mechanical machinery	0.875	(5)	1.219	(5)
Pharmaceuticals	0.71	(6)	1.097	(6)
Rubber and plastic	0.648	(7)	0.637	(10)
Chemicals (excluding pharmaceuticals)	0.584	(8)	0.894	(7)
Motor vehicles	0.579	(9)	0.800	(8)
Printing	0.558	(10)	−0.700	(18)
Paper	0.467	(11)	−0.221*	(21)
Electrical machinery	0.435	(12)	0.776	(9)
Metal products	0.411	(13)	0.262	(13)
Oil	0.324**	(14)	0.572	(12)
Metals	0.296	(15)	0.021**	(16)
Wood	0.203*	(16)	−0.130**	(22)
Other transport	0.17**	(17)	0.254	(14)
Food, drink, tobacco	0.16*	(18)	−0.129**	(23)
Mineral and nonmineral products	0.116**	(19)	0.086**	(15)
Clothing	−0.913	(20)	−1.287	(19)
Leather and footwear	−0.319	(21)	−0.225	(11)
Synthetic fibers	−0.06**	(22)	0.599*	(20)
Textiles	−0.015**	(23)	−0.279	(17)
Other manufacturing	reference		reference	

Source: Elaboration on the Istat data base.

Note: Ranking is in parentheses. Significant at least at 95% level unless indicated by asterisks.

*Significant only at 90 to 95% level.

**Not significant at 90% level.

equation 1 and 77.5 percent of the cases in equation 2.[5] The probability of a firm's being both innovative and performing R&D increases monotonically with firm size and increases considerably for industrial sectors that are usually labeled as those characterized by high technological opportunities, namely, aerospace; radio, TV, and telecommunications; precision instruments; mechanical machinery; and pharmaceuticals. These results confirm, therefore, that the industry in which firms are located and firm size are important factors for explaining the presence of innovating activities, irrespective of one another.

3. The Different Sources of Innovation in the Manufacturing Industry

The multiform nature of innovative activities and their sectoral specificity have been underlined in a vast amount of literature (e.g., Pavitt 1984, Kline and Rosenberg 1986, von Hippel 1988, Archibugi et al. 1991). Besides activities generating new technological knowledge, special attention has also been devoted to processes of technology adoption and diffusion (e.g., OECD 1992, Evangelista 1996).

The Italian Innovation Survey (and CIS), providing data on firms' innovation expenditures sustained for carrying out a wide range of activities, allows us to measure the relative importance of the various innovation sources. Table 3 shows the breakdown of firms' total innovation expenditure for the manufacturing sector as a whole and across main firm-size classes. The picture that emerges from the table is very clear-cut. Industrial innovative activities consist, first and foremost, of the purchase and use of "embodied" technologies, which accounts, for the manufacturing sector as a whole, for 47 percent of total expenditure on innovation, and, second, of efforts to generate and develop new knowledge inside firms, as measured

TABLE 3.   Innovation Expenditure by Firm Size (% values)

Classes of Employees	R&D	Patents and Licenses	Design	Tooling Up and Trial Production	Marketing	Innovative Investment
20–49	14.9	1.5	9.4	7.7	1.9	64.6
50–99	16.3	1.3	8.4	8.5	1.7	63.8
100–199	19.8	1.7	12.8	9.0	2.2	54.5
200–499	27.6	2.2	9.1	9.6	2.2	49.3
500–999	26.0	1.6	13.4	8.1	1.3	49.6
1,000 and over	46.7	0.8	4.8	5.7	1.2	40.8
Total	35.8	1.2	7.4	6.9	1.5	47.2

Source: See table 1.
Note: Rows add up to 100 percent.

by the percentage of innovative spending for R&D activities (35.8 percent). The other innovation components (design and trial production, the purchase of patents and licenses, and marketing) play a relatively minor role.[6]

The importance of the different sources of innovation in business strategies is, however, strongly influenced by the size of the firms and the industry in which firms operate. Table 3 shows that small firms have a high propensity to innovate by acquiring machinery and plants against the greater propensity of large firms to internally generate new technologies. For firms with fewer than 50 employees, R&D activities account for as little as 15 percent of total innovation expenditure against a percentage close to 47 percent in the case of firms with more than 1,000 employees. Data on investment show an opposite pattern. Innovative investments of firms with less than 200 employees account for more than 50 percent or more of total innovation expenditures.

Table 4 allows us to look in detail at the importance of the different sources of innovation across industries. The table allows us to identify industries traditionally defined as science based in which activities aimed at generating new technological knowledge play a fundamental role. Office machinery and computers; radio, TV, and telecommunications; pharmaceuticals; and precision instruments allocate over 50 percent of their innovation expenditure to R&D. The importance of design is much higher than the manufacturing average in aerospace, in the sectors that produce specialized machinery and instruments, and in traditional sectors such as clothing. The acquisition of new machinery and plants is by far the prevalent source of technology for most traditional consumer goods sectors, such as wood, textiles, leather and footwear, food, metal products, and capital-intensive sectors such as printing and publishing, paper, metals, rubber and plastic, and motor vehicles.

The last two columns of table 4 show two indicators of innovation intensity, namely, total innovation costs and the R&D expenditures sustained by innovating firms in each industry divided by the total number of employees in each sector. It is interesting to note that, with the exception of few capital-intensive sectors that invest heavily in the acquisition of new machinery and equipment, the ranking of industries does not change if it is measured through a traditional indicator based on R&D expenditure or using a more comprehensive innovation indicator such as total innovation expenditure per employee. In particular, all science-based industries remain the leading actors in technological change, irrespective of the indicator used.

4.   The Role of Small and Large Firms in Innovation

The relationship between innovation and firm size has been dealt with over the last two decades by a vast amount of empirical literature (for an over-

TABLE 4. Innovation Expenditure and Innovative Intensity by Industry

Industrial Sectors	Breakdown of Innovation Expenditure (% values)[a]						Innovation Intensity			
	R&D	Patents and Licenses	Design	Tooling Up and Trial Production	Marketing	Investment	Innovation Expenditure per Employee[b]		R&D Expenditure per Employee[b]	
Office machinery	64.8	0.1	4.5	17.2	1.0	12.4	34.7	(1)	22.5	(1)
Motor vehicles	36.7	0.2	1.9	3.2	0.2	57.8	27.6	(2)	10.1	(4)
Radio, TV, telecommunications	66.1	0.8	12.9	5.3	1.2	13.7	25.7	(3)	17.0	(2)
Oil	6.8	1.0	8.5	4.3	0.2	79.2	24.7	(4)	1.7	(12)
Aerospace	39.3	5.0	12.1	22.7	0.7	20.2	23.7	(5)	9.3	(5)
Pharmaceuticals	66.7	4.5	4.3	4.4	2.1	18.0	22.7	(6)	15.1	(3)
Metals	8.1	0.4	6.7	4.6	0.3	79.9	16.7	(7)	1.4	(13)
Chemicals (excluding pharmaceuticals)	42.9	1.1	3.6	3.9	4.5	43.9	11.3	(8)	4.9	(7)
Precision instruments	54.0	1.4	12.4	8.9	2.0	21.3	9.5	(9)	5.1	(6)
Other transport	21.8	0.4	20.7	7.3	5.7	44.2	7.7	(10)	1.7	(11)
Synthetic fibers	30.6	2.4	2.0	7.1	2.3	55.6	7.7	(11)	2.4	(9)
Electrical machinery	30.4	1.1	14.6	8.8	2.1	43.0	7.2	(12)	2.2	(10)
Paper	7.2	0.4	4.7	4.6	1.4	81.7	7.2	(13)	0.5	(18)
Mechanical machinery	36.0	1.9	15.0	11.8	2.2	33.1	7.0	(14)	2.5	(8)
Printing and publishing	7.9	3.7	6.2	4.0	1.0	77.2	6.3	(15)	0.5	(20)
Rubber and plastic	19.8	1.4	9.4	10.1	2.0	57.3	5.6	(16)	1.1	(14)
Nonmineral products	12.8	1.4	8.0	8.6	1.9	67.3	5.4	(17)	0.7	(17)
Food, drink, tobacco	17.5	0.8	6.4	5.8	2.8	66.7	4.6	(18)	0.8	(15)
Metal products	12.3	1.4	8.8	8.1	1.9	67.5	4.2	(19)	0.5	(19)
Wood	9.7	0.7	3.7	6.5	1.3	78.1	3.7	(20)	0.4	(23)
Other manufacturing	20.8	0.9	6.5	7.9	2.8	61.1	3.6	(21)	0.8	(16)
Textiles	12.2	0.5	8.9	8.8	1.9	67.7	3.5	(22)	0.4	(21)
Leather and footwear	15.5	1.3	8.4	8.6	2.8	63.4	2.5	(23)	0.4	(22)
Clothing	16.5	1.3	25.1	11.1	18.9	27.1	1.4	(24)	0.2	(24)
Total	35.8	1.2	7.4	6.9	1.5	47.2	9.9		3.5	

Source: See table 1

Note: Ranking is in parentheses.

[a] Rows add up to 100 percent.

[b] 1992 millions of Italian lire (see appendix). Total innovation costs have been divided by the total number of employees in each sector, including both innovating and noninnovating firms.

view, see Cohen 1995). On empirical grounds, the analysis of the role small and medium-sized firms play in technological change may be approached in three different ways.

   1. By comparing the innovation intensity of large and small firms, considering innovating firms only
   2. By considering the relative contribution of large and small firms to the overall innovation performances of a given economic system
   3. By considering the innovation intensity of large and small firms, including both innovating and noninnovating firms

The data provided by the Italian survey allow us to analyze the relationship between innovation and firm size on the basis of all three methodologies described previously. The results are shown in table 5. The first two columns show data on firms' expenditure per employee, taking into account total innovation and R&D expenditure, respectively, for the sample of innovating firms only. Column 2 confirms that large firms are much more R&D intensive than small ones (see, e.g., Soete 1979); this is hardly surprising since R&D is an innovative source that requires a minimum threshold and it does not "capture" the innovative effort typical of small firms. But, when a much more comprehensive indicator such as total innovation expenditure is considered (col. 1 of table 5), it emerges that innovative small firms are not substantially disadvantaged compared with their larger competitors. In fact, the data show a U-shaped curve: firms with fewer than 100 employees are more innovative than firms in the intermediate size groups, despite the fact that their innovative intensity is still lower than that

TABLE 5.   Intensity and Concentration of Innovative Activities by Firm Size

Classes of Employees	Innovating Firms		Total Firms		Concentration of Technological Activities and Sales (innovating firms, % values)		
	Innovation Expenditure per Employee	R&D Expenditure per Employee	Innovation Expenditure per Employee[a]	R&D Expenditure per Employee[a]	Innovation Expenditure	R&D Expenditure	Sales
20–49	14.7	2.2	4.0	0.6	8.1	3.4	15.0
50–99	12.3	2.0	5.1	0.8	6.8	3.1	9.6
100–199	11.7	2.3	5.7	1.1	7.3	4.0	10.3
200–499	11.8	3.3	7.1	1.9	10.2	7.9	12.9
500–999	16.4	4.3	12.2	3.2	11.2	8.1	8.2
1,000 and over	18.3	8.5	16.7	7.8	56.4	73.6	43.9
Total	15.7	5.6	9.7	3.5	100.0	100.0	100.0

Source: See table 1.

Note: Data are expressed in 1992 millions of Italian lire (see appendix).

[a]The index considers the employees of both innovating and noninnovating firms to the denominator, whereas the nnovation expenditure of innovating firms alone is obviously shown to the numerator.

of firms with more than 1,000 employees.[7] This result is totally consistent with the analyses of Pavitt, Robson, and Townsend (1987) and Acs and Audretsch (1990), which have taken into account the universe of innovating firms without considering firms that do not introduce innovations.

However, the indicators shown in the first two columns of table 5 fail to take into account that the number of innovating firms considerably differs between small and large firms. This aspect is crucial when the role in innovation of large and small firms needs to be assessed.

Columns 3 and 4 of table 5 report, respectively, the average values per employee of innovation expenditure and R&D expenditure for all firms participating in the survey. The positive relationship between innovation intensity (in a broad sense) and firm size strongly reemerges. The average innovation expenditure per employee for firms with over 1,000 employees is 16.7 million lire, while for firms with 20 to 50 employees it is only 4 million lire. This difference has to do with the fact that, although small innovating firms are not less innovative than large firms, they are not representative of the overall productive universe of small firms. This is confirmed by looking at the last three columns of table 5, which allow us to assess the effective economic and technological weight of small enterprises in the Italian manufacturing industry. The role of the 5,602 innovating firms with fewer than 100 employees appears rather limited. These firms account for only 15 percent of total innovation expenditure and just 6.5 percent of R&D expenditure. The technological weight of small firms is thus much lower than their economic weight in terms of turnover (25 percent).

5. The Output Generated by Innovation

In the previous two sections, we have focused on the inputs devoted by firms to innovation. The innovation intensity of firms and industries can also be measured according to output indicators. The Community Innovation Survey offers a significant indicator of innovation output, namely, the part of a firm's total sales due to innovation, which provides direct information on how a firm, an industry, or even an economic system as a whole has changed its production output in relation to innovation.

Table 6 shows the distribution of sales according to the nature of the innovations introduced, broken down by industries. Looking at the manufacturing sector as a whole, as much as 62.5 percent of sales have not been affected at all by innovation. If we exclude the office machinery sector, even in high-tech industries there is a remarkable share of noninnovating sales. The most remarkable result is represented by chemicals and pharmaceuticals, with a share of noninnovating sales that reaches 70 percent. The data also allow us to break down innovative sales between process innovations,

TABLE 6.   Distribution of Total Sales According to the Type of Innovation Introduced (% values)

Industrial Sectors	Percentage of Sales				
	Not Innovated	Innovated by Process Innovations	Innovated by Incremental Product Innovations	Innovated by Significantly New Products	Total Sales
Office machinery	19.1	7.9	16.4	56.6	100
Electrical machinery	50.9	13.6	20.3	15.2	100
Radio, TV, tele- communications	43.2	20.4	23.0	13.4	100
Aerospace	37.7	24.7	12.6	25.0	100
Chemicals (excluding pharmaceuticals)	69.2	12.9	11.4	6.5	100
Pharmaceuticals	70.1	8.5	8.7	12.7	100
Synthetic fibers	58.3	13.5	19.4	8.9	100
Mechanical machinery	56.7	11.9	19.0	12.4	100
Precision instruments	57.9	9.4	18.6	14.1	100
Motor vehicles	53.4	7.4	24.6	14.6	100
Other transport	41.3	19.5	23.2	16.1	100
Rubber and plastic	64.1	15.0	13.2	7.7	100
Metals	53.3	37.9	6.0	2.8	100
Printing and publishing	63.1	28.2	3.6	5.1	100
Paper	69.7	15.2	9.7	5.4	100
Food, drink, tobacco	78.3	13.0	5.8	2.9	100
Textiles	74.9	13.2	6.7	5.3	100
Clothing	86.5	8.7	2.6	2.3	100
Leather and footwear	82.1	7.1	4.8	6.0	100
Wood	84.4	9.2	3.0	3.4	100
Metal products	73.0	14.6	6.9	5.5	100
Mineral and nonmineral products	77.2	11.5	7.0	4.3	100
Other manufacturing	73.9	11.7	8.0	6.4	100
Oil	63.4	18.3	10.2	8.0	100
Total	62.5	18.2	10.7	8.6	100

Source: See table 1.

Note: Distribution includes the sales of noninnovating as well as innovating firms.

incremental product innovations, and significantly new products. Also, these data (shown in table 6) highlight, first and foremost, the gradual and incremental nature of firms' innovative activities: 18.2 percent of turnover was innovated by introducing process innovations and 10.7 percent through the introduction of incremental improvements of preexisting products. Only the remaining 8.6 percent of turnover of the Italian manufacturing sector referred to totally new products.

A further qualification of the quality of innovations can be assessed by taking into account the degree of novelty of the products introduced. Table 7 shows that only a very small fraction of economic output is affected by

TABLE 7. Sales According to the Degree of Novelty of the Product Innovations Introduced (% values)

Industrial Sectors	New for the Firm	New for the Italian Market	New in Absolute Terms
Office machinery	17.2	24.0	15.5
Electrical machinery	5.5	8.5	1.2
Radio, TV, telecommunications	8.7	2.8	1.9
Aerospace	2.3	15.7	7.0
Chemicals (excluding pharmaceuticals)	4.1	2.3	0.2
Pharmaceuticals	4.9	5.1	2.7
Synthetic fibers	5.0	3.6	0.2
Mechanical machinery	6.2	2.9	3.3
Precision instruments	8.6	3.0	2.5
Motor vehicles	1.5	9.3	3.8
Other transport	6.1	7.6	2.4
Rubber and plastic	3.7	2.2	1.8
Metals	1.0	1.6	0.2
Printing and publishing	2.9	1.8	0.5
Paper	4.2	1.0	0.2
Food, drink, tobacco	1.6	1.2	0.1
Textiles	2.6	1.4	1.3
Clothing	1.3	0.5	0.5
Leather and footwear	2.3	1.4	2.3
Wood	1.8	1.4	0.2
Metal products	3.1	1.4	1.0
Mineral and nonmineral products	2.6	0.9	0.7
Other manufacturing	3.8	1.7	1.0
Oil	4.1	3.1	0.7
Total	3.6	3.8	1.2

Source: See table 1.

Note: Distribution includes the sales of noninnovating as well as innovating firms.

technological activities. For the Italian manufacturing sector as a whole, sales linked to the introduction of products *new in absolute terms* represent only 1.2 percent of total manufacturing sales in 1992, while products *new for the Italian market* or *new only for the firm* represent 3.8 and 3.6 percent of Italian manufacturing turnover. Again, the incremental nature of technological change seems to be a feature that characterizes not only traditional industries but also some of the most typical science-based sectors such as radio, TV, and telecommunications and chemicals.

6. Conclusions

The analysis of the results of the Italian survey has allowed us to empirically address three main issues of industrial innovation: the spread of innovation in the manufacturing industry, the nature of firms' technological activities, and the outcome of innovation. The most interesting results can be summarized as follows.

Firms rely on a variegated range of innovation sources.   Although R&D represents a crucial source for the generation of innovations and it is the single most important intangible source of innovation, it absorbs just over one-third of total innovation expenditures. The largest part of firms' innovative financial efforts is linked to the adoption and diffusion of technologies embodied in capital goods. The evidence presented also confirms that innovation patterns vary significantly across industries and firm size. This finding suggests that sector and firm-specific policy measures are highly advisable.

Only a fraction of small firms innovate.   We have shown that innovating small firms are just a minority, even though small firms that introduce innovations are no less innovative than their larger competitors. In order to foster the economic performance of small firms, it therefore seems important to *broaden* rather than *intensify* the innovating industrial base.

The leading sectors in innovation remain the same irrespective of the technological indicator used.   While the Italian survey has confirmed that there is much room to enlarge the understanding and measurement of technological change from a narrow R&D concept to a wider innovation concept, in this essay we have also shown that the *ranking* of industries according their innovativeness only to a limited extent depends upon the indicator used.

Technological change is very cumulative in nature.   Data on innovation output confirm the very cumulative nature of technical progress. Over a three-year period, the percentages of sales linked to the introduction of new products represent only a small portion of total turnover both at the level of all manufacturing industry and in many industries characterized by high technological opportunities.

APPENDIX

The Italian innovation survey covers innovative activities undertaken in the Italian manufacturing industry during the period 1990–92. Firms were asked whether they had introduced innovations during the three year period. With reference to the same period, firms were asked another set of qualitative questions on objectives of and obstacles to innovation and sources of information used. Some more quantitative data on firms' innovation inputs and outputs have been collected on a one-year basis. In particular, firms were asked to provide data on their innovation expenditures and innovative sales for the year 1992 only. Accordingly, the figures on innovation expenditures reported in tables 3, 4, and 5 refer to 1992 only. The data on firms' innovated sales reported in tables 6 and 7 also refer to 1992, although the definition of innovative sales includes product and process innovations introduced during the period 1990–92.

NOTES

1. This survey was carried out in 1993 by the National Statistical Institute of Italy and promoted and coordinated by the European Commission and Eurostat under the Community Innovation Survey (CIS) venture (cf. Istat 1995, Archibugi, Cohendet, Kristensen, and Schäffer, 1995, and Evangelista et al. 1996).

2. At the level of European industry as a whole, this percentage rises to 53 percent, though this value is likely to be somewhat overestimated (see Evangelista et al. 1996).

3. In the two logit equations estimated, the dependent variables are either equal to 1, if the firm has introduced innovation in the period 1990–92 (eq. 1) or performed R&D (eq. 2); or 0, if it has not.

4. As the dummy coefficients increase, the probability of the firm's introducing innovations or performing R&D increases. The value of the intercept refers to the firm with the reference characteristics, namely, nonmembership in a group, location in the islands, and belonging to the "other manufacturing industries" sector.

5. The value of the concordant test is similar to that of R^2 in a standard regression.

6. These figures partly reflect the peculiarity of the Italian productive structure. However, figures referring to the other main European countries are rather consistent with the Italian data. In particular, in all countries innovative investment emerges as the main component of innovation costs, followed by R&D and the other innovation items (see Evangelista et al. 1996).

7. In considering average values per size class, we obviously neglect the albeit significant specificities of sectors. For an analysis of the relationship between innovation intensity and firm size at the level of the main industrial sectors, see Archibugi, Evangelista, and Simonetti 1995.

REFERENCES

Acs, Z., and D. Audretsch. 1990. *Innovation and Small Firms.* Cambridge: MIT Press.

Archibugi, D., S. Cesaratto, and G. Sirilli. 1991. Sources of innovative activities and industrial organization in Italy. *Research Policy* 20:299–313.

Archibugi, D., P. Cohendet, A. Kristensen, and K. A. Schäffer. 1995. *Evaluation of the Community Innovation Survey.* Sprint/Eims Report, Project n. 93/94. Aalborg: IKE Group.

Archibugi, D., R. Evangelista, and R. Simonetti. 1995. Concentration, firm size, and innovation: evidence from innovation costs. *Technovation* 15, no. 3: 153–63.

Cohen, W. M. 1995. Empirical studies of innovative activities. In Stoneman 1995.

Evangelista, R. 1996. Embodied and disembodied innovative activities: evidence from the Italian innovation survey. In OECD 1996.

Evangelista, R., T. Sandven, G. Sirilli, and K. Smith. 1996. Measuring the cost of innovation in European industry. Paper presented at the international conference Innovation Measurement and Policies, Luxembourg, May 20–21.

Istat. 1995. *Indagine sull'innovazione tecnologica, anni 1990–92.* Rome: Istat.

Kline, S. J., and N. Rosenberg. 1986. An overview on innovation. In Landau and Rosenberg 1986.

Landau, R., and N. Rosenberg, eds. 1986. *The Positive Sum Strategy.* Washington, DC.: National Academy Press.

Levin, R., A. Klevorick, R. Nelson, and S. Winter. 1987. Appropriating the returns from industrial research and development. *Brooking Papers on Economic Activity* 3:783–831.

OECD. 1992. *Technology and the Economy: The Key Relationships.* Paris: OECD.

OECD. 1996. *Innovation, Patents, and Technological Strategies.* Paris: OECD.

Pavitt, K. 1984. Sectoral patterns of technological change: toward a taxonomy and a theory. *Research Policy* 13:343–73.

Pavitt, K., M. Robson, and J. Townsend. 1987. The size distribution of innovating firms in the UK, 1945–1983. *Journal of Industrial Economics* 35, no. 3 (March): 297–316.

Soete, L. G. 1979. Firm size and innovative activity. *European Economic Review* 12, no. 4 (Oct.): 319–40.

Stoneman, P., ed. 1995. *Handbook of the Economics of Innovation and Technical Change.* Oxford: Blackwell.

von Hippel, E. 1988. *The Sources of Innovation.* New York: Oxford University Press.

PART 4

From Microanalysis to Economic Growth

Human Capital, Technological Lock-in, and Evolutionary Dynamics

Gérard Ballot and Erol Taymaz

1. Introduction

We investigate the macroeconomic consequences of endogeneous changes of technological paradigms in an evolutionary micro-to-macro model. The changes we study are significant and pervasive. They affect the conditions of production in all sectors of the economy.[1] Firms can choose among many technological paradigms about which they have different, but limited, knowledge. We show that increasing returns and competition lead surviving firms to cluster in one or a small number of paradigms. We confirm and extend the results of Arthur (1988, 1989, 1994) on the existence of lock-in phenomena.[2] The economy can be locked into an inferior paradigm for a long time. Two paradigms may also coexist for long periods. However, we obtain as a new result that lock-out is possible, because among the many heterogeneous firms some are rich, competent, and lucky and under some circumstances they will be imitated. The most important novelty of the model is probably the introduction of these lock-in and lock-out phenomena in a complete evolutionary micro-to-macro model of an economy to clarify their macroeconomic systems effects.

Minor events, modeled as random events, are sufficient to generate completely different dynamic paths of the economy among the different possible paradigms and demonstrate the importance of history.[3]

The model emphasizes the interactions between human capital and technical progress and their effects on macroeconomic growth, inducing feedback on the growth of these factors.[4] This opens the way for the study and design of education and training policies as well as technology policies. We study the effects of various R&D subsidies and standardization policies. We find that the complexity of nonlinear interactions at the microeconomic as well as the macroeconomic level generates unexpected effects.

The essay is organized as follows. Section 2 exposes the methodological and theoretical framework embodied in the model. Section 3 presents the main specifications of the model. Section 4 reports on the results of the base experiments and five sets of technological policy experiments. Conclusions are drawn in section 5.

2. Methodological and Theoretical Framework

2.1. Methodology

Theoretical research on the endogenization of innovations and technical progress has advanced considerably over the past decade. Two schools of thought have followed completely different paths. The first school focuses on the strategic interactions of firms and uses game theory as its tool, emphasizing market equilibrium rather than growth and cycles (see Tirole 1988, chap. 10, for an introduction). The second school is based on evolutionary theory and emphasizes bounded rationality, learning, and dynamics, and hence disequilibrium and growth.

The game-theoretic race for patents (Reinganum 1989 shows R&D investment to have an ex-post return determined by a *tournament*. The winner takes all. Some models incorporate diffusion. This large literature shares common features that are far from reality. It builds on uncertainty, characterized by a probability law with known parameters. Firms are able to compute and maximize expected profits. The known distribution of mistakes has a zero mean, so that firms have nothing to learn. This literature is mainly concerned with the allocation of resources on R&D under different market structures. There are few attempts to incorporate this strategic behavior in an endogeneous growth framework, although various endogeneous growth models now include process or product innovation (Romer 1990, Aghion and Howitt 1992).

No model to our knowledge incorporates the training and hiring decisions of firms in a R&D model, decisions that may be crucial to win the race for the innovation and/or to obtain a successful implementation of the innovation. Even though mathematically and conceptually sophisticated, game-theoretic models have a very crude economic content; adding more elements increases the complexity and soon precludes analytical solutions. Yet to use these models for policy design, taking, for instance, the externalities caused by the diffusion of innovations into account, such enhancement of realism is necessary. One may also doubt the capacity of firms for complex strategic reasoning as backward induction in such an environment.

Finally, stochastic elements influence the innovation process: success in research, adoption, and implementation are highly stochastic. Probabilities are difficult to estimate. The result of the interaction of heterogeneous firms making many decisions in such a context is not an equilibrium even in the long run. Moreover, events are not repeated from unchanging sets but rather from an evolving set establishing difficult path dependance in the models.

Evolutionary theory starts from a different end, with Schumpeter's (1943) idea of competition as a dynamic process, with technical change the key factor. In the previous school, price competition constrains the decisions on innovations.[5] Evolutionary theory recognizes the highly stochastic nature of innovations and the difficulty of assigning probabilities (Saviotti and Metcalfe 1991b, Dosi and Nelson 1993). If this were not the case, it would mean that business uncertainty is assumed to be equal to insurable risks (Eliasson 1985). This theory, then, has to develop tools to deal with complexity in the form of boundedly rational decision processes.

This theory has also developed a detailed analysis of the different forms of innovations, which we will incorporate in our model. The distinction between incremental and radical innovations (Dosi 1984) is particularly relevant. Firms have only a local and very limited knowledge of existing technologies (Eliasson 1990). They do not have timeless and costless access to any technology other than the one they use. They may, however, improve the efficiency of their technology through experience, without changes in physical capital. This process has been known as learning by doing since Arrow (1962). There are additional processes of learning such as user-producer interaction (von Hippel 1988). Firms may even discover other technologies close to the present one through some R&D expenditures. This is incremental innovation, which requires investment in physical capital, exhibiting decreasing returns. A radical innovation, on the other hand, founded in basic science, in a major R&D effort, or as the result of chance, may create a completely new technology (or product), which can be improved upon later by learning and incremental innovation.

The evolutionary models that endogenize technical change at the microeconomic level, pioneered in the past 20 years by Nelson and Winter (1974, 1982), deal with incremental innovation, the purpose being to understand coordination at the market or aggregate level. More recent models detail specific real markets (Grabowski and Vernon 1987), with one industry but a differentiated product (Kwasnicki and Kwasnicka 1992), with one industry (Silverberg, Dosi, and Orsenigo 1988; Iosso 1993), with two sectors (capital goods and consumer goods) (Chiaramonte and Dosi 1992; Chiaramonte, Dosi, and Orsenigo 1993), with three industries composed of two capital goods and one consumption good (Smith 1991), with a complete model of an economy (Eliasson 1985), and with competence blocs (Carlsson, Eliasson, and Taymaz 1991). These complex models use microsimulation as a tool (Orcutt et al. 1961).

Evolutionary theorists often mention the importance of skills and competences in the process of innovation and in its diffusion through imitation. Human capital and skills, however, are not integrated in the models except in Silverberg, Dosi, and Orsenigo (1988), where it is an exogenous parameter randomly determined for each firm. Chiaramonte, Dosi, and Orsenigo (1993) have this parameter modified through learning by doing. Human capital is not treated as an endogeneous variable distinct from a technological or R&D stock. They are merged under the terms *competences, knowledge base,* and *absorptive capacity* (Cohen and Levinthal 1989, 1990). These concepts correspond to the accumulation of technological knowledge acquired through cumulated R&D and production with a technology. Unlike R&D, education, and (at least partly) training expenditures, they are difficult to measure. Moreover, competence or absorptive capacity is produced by R&D, human capital, learning by doing, and perhaps other factors, and it is therefore distinct.[6] Finally, human capital can be, like R&D, of different sorts, which are worth distinguishing and investigating.

There are other aspects that motivate our interest in a detailed treatment of human capital in relation to innovation and growth. First, the endogenous growth models of Lucas (1988) and Azariadis and Drazen (1990) have recognized the crucial role of human capital stock for the growth of an economy as a positive externality. There may exist a threshold in its level that determines which country will grow and which will stagnate, presenting a case for government intervention in educational matters (besides democracy and equity). The discussion should integrate the interactions with R&D. Second, the market failure problem in firm-sponsored training should be reexamined in the light of technological competition, since this market failure may be a source of stagnation in endogenous growth.

Modeling the interactions of heterogeneous firms with R&D and training policies in a complex environment requires numerical simulation, with many heterogeneous agents of the same type (firms), namely, microsimulation, also called microanalytic simulation (Orcutt 1961 et al., Harding 1996). We will improve on the standard methodology by using some tools (genetic algorithms) developed in artificial intelligence research by Holland (1975) in order to model firms' learning. Our model, then, is evolutionary, featuring variety (heterogeneity), learning, and selection in its core (Saviotti and Metcalfe 1991, 11–14). Moreover, changes in technical levels are determined by the innovation (rule) generating system and appear as discontinuities, both at the micro- and the macrolevel. Finally, the model is open ended: the economic system has a nonequilibrium nature, which means that it does not necessarily contain mechanisms that make it to converge to an equilibrium even in the long run. There are possibilities for bifurcations (à la Prigogine and Stengers 1984), determined by random events or minor decisions that lead to different macroeconomic states, new structures, and coordination mechanisms. This enhances irreversibility and path dependancy for the macrosystem. History matters.

We use the MOSES model, a complete micro-to-macro model, and add a detailed training-innovation module. We have already offered novel results exposed elsewhere. Ballot and Taymaz (1996) show that firm-sponsored training is very influential on the rate of growth through its effects on learning capacity and incremental innovation. Ballot and Taymaz (1994) show that such training is also influential for the timing of radical innovations and may accelerate a change of technological paradigm. Ballot and Taymaz (1997) analyzed the impact of the heterogeneity of firms and the role of diffusion by imitation and improvement. The essential result validated the intuition that the diffusion of radical innovations is important for growth, especially when feedbacks lead to a change in the global technological system of the economy, a change that our model is able to reproduce. These essays, however, used a version of the model in which only two paradigms existed, whereas the present version allows for a great number of potential paradigms in which the firms can try to go (or not), and this allows us to study lock-in and lock-out effects. We can then examine whether some technological policies can be effective enough to eliminate such lock-in effects.

2.2. Sponsoring General Training and Schumpeterian Competition: The Training for the Rent Hypothesis

No model recognizes that R&D may be a waste of resources if the firm does not have the adequate competences to profit from them. The bulk of R&D expenditures and internal training investments is conceived with building such receiver competence (Eliasson 1990). Let us consider three phases in this process: R&D, adoption, and implementation. Training researchers to the state of the art in science is necessary. Much of this training is general training. Once the technical discovery is made, the decision of adoption will be a better decision if top managers are highly endowed with human capital (Welch 1970). This is again general human capital, built from good initial education and experience and continued training. In the implementation phase, evidence is that a new technology (or the production of a new good) will be profitable only if the employees master the necessary skills. Demand for skills is higher than before the innovation. Employees must be able to cope with the unexpected problems associated with a little-known technology. This requires more general human capital (Nelson and Phelps 1966). Some specialized training is not always sufficient. Bartel and Lichtenberg (1987) have shown that the demand for general skills rises when an innovation is implemented and then declines.

Becker (1964) has argued, however, that firms should not sponsor general training since workers with general training have a higher market value. When they quit, a firm that has invested in their general training would incur a loss, and they are likely to leave because other firms, which have not paid for their training, can offer slightly higher wages. Hence, workers should pay themselves for general training. Firms in competitive equilibrium can pay for training only if they can recoup the cost through lower wages. Evidence is that firms do sponsor general training, and in many cases they do so without lowering the wage (Stern and Ritzen 1991). It is understandable that workers do not pay directly for the training expenditures, since they have strong budget constraints and difficulties in borrowing because human capital is not a guarantee. The minimum wage may also preclude the possibility for the firm to recoup the costs by lowering the wage. These factors, however, point to an underinvestment problem and do not explain how the firm could pay for general training.

We use a novel idea, which explains why firms might undertake an investment in general human capital (Ballot 1994). We label it the *training for the rent* hypothesis. The basic argument is straightforward: firms that innovate successfully obtain a quasi rent. We have shown that firms need trained workers in order to innovate successfully, that is, to earn profits. It should then be rational for them to pay for *general* training and not only specific training. They remain viable because they pay with the quasi rent both the general training and the higher wages necessary to keep the trained workers. Some pure profit may be left, since only a few firms have high enough human capital and technological knowledge to enter the race for competence, and this creates entry barriers. Then, if a given firm suffers for nonwage motives, the firm may still invest in general training.

The competition framework is Schumpeterian with repeated innovations, and therefore it allows for the existence of long-run rates of profit for innovators over the interest rate plus the risk premium. There is also a dispersion of these rates (in the short run), which is related partly to the stochastic nature of innovation and the tournament nature of competition, in which the winner gets all of the market (or a large share of it) until other firms successfully imitate it or find a better innovation. In the long run, the dispersion may remain because profits allow more investment in R&D and training and success feeds success.

The framework, then, allows for factors that influence the level of general investment and the rate of return, such as the rate of labor turnover and financial constraints. In pure competition, such factors have no influence, since the optimal investment in general training is zero and financial constraints do not exist, denying the interest of doing empirical work. Deficiencies in human capital will then occur and keep the firm inside the production possibility frontier in the short term, while they significantly slow down the outward shifting of this frontier in the long run. Preliminary tests of the effects of firm-sponsored training and R&D expenditures on profitability support the above hypothesis (Ballot and Taymaz 1993).

2.3. General Human Capital and Firms' Endogenous Learning

An economy characterized by continuous innovation and a process of creative destruction of heterogenous skills, jobs, and firms becomes very complex, but the model builder should not attempt to make excessive simplifications in order to write and solve optimization programs. Complex interactions fundamentally determine firms' decision processes and significantly affect the capacity of a macroeconomy to coordinate.

In the real world, the firms compensate the limitations of their information and capacity to process this information by learning continuously. They know they have not taken the best decision. They are constantly on the alert to identify, correct, and learn from mistakes, to improve next time. However, if they know *how* they have obtained a good result, they do not necessarily know *why* (by which mechanisms of the economy) because of complexity. A trial and error experimental process allows the agents to learn *how.* The training-innovation module uses a powerful tool offered by artificial intelligence: *genetic algorithms* (GAs), the principles of which are briefly recalled in subsection 3.3 (Holland 1975). We are not aware of applications to a micro-macroeconomic model of a complete economy so far, and if this is the case the present model is a substantial step forward in the use of genetic algorithms in macroeconomics.

In our model, a firm's general human capital is not an input in the production function, as opposed to specific human capital. It determines the efficiency of the search for new technologies and also influences the capacity to adopt the technologies of other firms. This has a fundamental methodological implication for the modeling of decision processes. *Since firms decide on their level of training, the learning capacity of a given firm is endogenous.*[7] Not only information but also learning capacity differs between firms, which is logical since it is bounded. The heterogeneity of firms has a more fundamental nature than their endowments (physical capital, financial assets . . .) which in the long run are endogenous to their behavior. This diversity generates a Schumpeterian creative destruction process with its macroeconomic implications (external competitiveness, unemployment . . .). In the process, innovation and technological progress are themselves explained.

3.   The Model

3.1.   General Features

We use the MOSES model, a complete Micro-to-macro model Of the Swedish Economic System, and add to it a training-innovation module.[8] It has been constructed initially to analyze industrial development and has been continuously improved and updated since the first version was published in Eliasson (1977). Manufacturing is modeled both at the level of individual firms and at the sectoral level, whereas the other sectors are aggregate. The manufacturing sector is divided into four industries (raw materials processing, intermediate goods, durable and capital goods, and consumer nondurables). Each industry produces a homogeneous product and consists of a number of firms (225 in total), *most of which are real Swedish firms.* Some are *synthetic,* the latter being designed so that firm accounts for each market/ sector sum up to the national accounts. The firms take decisions on all markets (products, labor, capital), and these decisions are based on adaptive expectations. Firms constantly climb ex-ante profit hills. Decisions are revised periodically, since firms' plans are likely not to be consistent. Markets are explicitly represented. On the goods markets, prices are set through the law of supply and demand, with a unique price per industry. The labor market is decentralized, each firm setting its wage rate. A firm may attract workers by offering a wage at least 10 percent higher than its present wage. Unemployment and vacant jobs coexist. There is a capital market in which firms compete for investment resources, and the interest rate is set endogenously. As a result of the competition, some firms are eliminated, but positive profits in an industry induce the birth of new firms.

The sectors interact through an 11-sector, Leontief-type, input-output structure, which evolves as the weight of the different firms changes and will also evolve when process innovation is introduced. There is an aggregate household sector with a Keynesian expenditure system, including saving. There is also a government, and the economy is open, with an exogenous outside world. Finally, the model is calibrated to reproduce the evolution of the main macroeconomic Swedish variables since 1982. The micro-to-macro coherence and the empirical content at both levels make the model unique among the evolutionary models, and allow us to undertake detailed extensions and experiments that are not totally academic but rooted in a fairly complete representation of a real economy. They also give more stability to the model, and it is this latter feature that is relevant in this essay, since its purpose is theoretical.

It is now time to describe briefly how the microdecisions of a population of firms interact to yield interesting aggregate relations. Firms operate inside their production possibility frontiers and can improve their efficiency. The original model also contains the possibility of failure and reorganization of the economy through exit and entry. This is a first level, where learning and selection take place. It makes the rate of technical progress endogenous at the *aggregate level,* under the upper limit set by the rate of scientific research, the state of which defines a technological paradigm.

The present training/innovation module goes further by making both training and technical progress endogenous at the *microlevel.* Interactions between firms through diffusion and competition/selection effects allow for more realistic modeling of the determinants of technical progress and of its effects at the aggregate level.

MOSES, as a micro-to-macro model with firms learning through genetic algorithms, appears as an *artificial world* (or economy) (Lane 1993a, 1993b). It might also be labeled a complex adaptive system, according to Holland and Miller (1991), since it has the three required characteristics: (1) it is a network of interacting agents, (2) it exhibits dynamic, aggregate behavior, and (3) its aggregate behavior can be described without detailed knowledge of the behavior of individual agents. The interesting property of these artificial worlds or complex adaptive systems is the emergence of coordination in the economy through self-organization. Such aggregate variables as the number of firms, the rate of growth, the rate of investment in training, and the rate of technical progress are endogenous. Relations between these variables are not built into the model but are observed after the simulation. They emerge.

In the following section, we first describe the production function and technology. Then we develop the new modules for learning technologies and the determinants of training and R&D expenditures.

3.2. The Production Function

The production function for each firm in MOSES is of the following form:

$$Q_t = \text{QTOP}_t \times [1 - \exp(-\text{TEC}_t \times L_t/\text{QTOP}_t)], \tag{1}$$

where Q_t is the potential output (in physical units) for a given employment level in number of hours (L_t); QTOP is the maximum level of output, which is approached asymptotically when infinite amounts of labor are used, given a certain level of capital stock; TEC is productivity of the first unit of labor (to be more precise, the slope of the production function at the origin); and exp (.) is the exponential function. Subscript t denotes time.

The maximum output, QTOP, depends on the (real) stock of physical capital, the stock of specific skills, and the efficiency of the stock of physical capital, as follows:

$$\text{QTOP}_t = \text{QTOPFR}_t \times (\text{MINRT} + \{(1 - \text{MINRT}) \times ST_1$$

$$\times [1 - \exp(-\text{SPECTR}_t/ST_2)]\}), \tag{2}$$

where QTOPFR is the level of productive capacity (the asymptotic limit of the QTOP variable) and SPECTR is the stock of specific skills. ST_1 and ST_2 are industry-specific parameters. MINRT is the minimum (percentage) level of output that can be produced with no stock of specific skills. It shows the productivity level of completely unskilled workers. Thus, if SPECTR = 0, QTOP = QTOPFR × MINRT. On the other hand, as SPECTR → ∞, QTOP → QTOPFR. The productive capacity, QTOPFR, is determined by the efficiency and amount of physical capital (QTOPFR = EFF × PK, where EFF is the output/capital ratio and PK the stock of physical capital).

As shown in the specification of production functions (eqs. 1 and 2), there are two critical *technology* variables that determine the performance of the firm: EFF and TEC. There are two methods to upgrade the EFF and TEC variables. In the case of *embodied* change, the technological level is upgraded by investment since new equipment embodies the stock of knowledge possessed by the firm. In the *disembodied* case, the EFF and TEC variables are increased by implementing what is known by the firm (organizational changes, rationalization, etc.).

Investment is the first mechanism to increase the EFF and TEC variables since newly installed capital embodies MEFF and MTEC levels of technology. The technological level of the capital stock is upgraded by investment as follows:

$$TEC_t^\tau = [(TEC_{t-1} \times QTOPFR_{t-1}) + (MTEC_t \times \Delta QTOPFR_{t-1})]/$$

$$(QTOPFR_{t-1} + \Delta QTOPFR_{t-1}) \tag{3}$$

$$EFF_t^\tau = [(EFF_{t-1} \times PK_{t-1}) + (MEFF_t \times INV_{t-1})]/(PK_{t-1} + INV_{t-1}), \tag{4}$$

where INV is the amount of investment and $\Delta QTOPFR$ is the additions to the productive capacity by investment ($\Delta QTOPFR_{t-1} = INV_{t-1} \times MEFF_{t-1}$). Superscript τ indicates that the TEC_t^τ and EFF_t^τ variables now have temporary values. Their final values for the period t are calculated in equations 5 and 6. MEFF is the efficiency of newly installed capital, and MTEC is the level of labor productivity associated with new capital. As is shown in equations 3 and 4, the TEC and EFF variables are calculated as weighted averages of technological levels of different vintages of capital. In a sense, the MEFF and MTEC variables reflect the stock of knowledge possessed by the firm. The technological level of the productive equipment actually used (measured by the TEC and EFF variables) is lower than the level known by the firm because of the vintage effect.

We assume that the firm can also gradually update its existing equipment without any investment in physical capital stock by applying what is learned, as follows:

$$TEC_t = TEC_t^\tau + (MTEC_t - TEC_t^\tau) \times ST_3 \times [1 - \exp(-SPECTR_t/ST_4)] \tag{5}$$

$$EFF_t = EFF_t^\tau + (MEFF_t - EFF_t^\tau) \times ST_5 \times [1 - \exp(-SPECTR_t/ST_6)], \tag{6}$$

where ST_3, ST_4, ST_5, and ST_6 are industry-specific parameters. Thus, as SPECTR $\to \infty$, the TEC and EFF variables are updated to the amount equal to ST_3 and ST_5 percent of the difference between known and applied knowledge. Thus, we assume that the stock of *specific* skills (those skills specific to the physical capital used in the firm) determines the pace of disembodied change for a *given* level of the MTEC and MEFF variables. The values of the MTEC and MEFF variables depend on the efficiency of learning, which is determined by the stock of *general* knowledge.

Equations 1 and 2 define the production function. Equations 3 through

6 show the way the technology variables are changed in the model. The capital accumulation equation

$$\text{QTOPFR}_t = [\text{QTOPFR}_{t-1} \times (1 - \delta_q)] + \Delta \text{QTOPFR}_{t-1} \tag{7}$$

closes the system of production. δ_q is the (constant) rate of depreciation,

3.3. Technology

The technological level of the firm is measured by the MTEC and MEFF variables. The values of those variables depend on the technology of the firm. The technology of a firm can be represented by a set of "techniques," as follows:

$$F^P = \{f^P_1, f^P_2, \ldots f^P_n\}, \tag{8}$$

where F^P is the technology used by the firm and f^P_i is the ith technique, $i = 1, 2, \ldots n$. Superscript P denotes the relevant technological paradigm. For simplicity (and without any lack of generality), a technique can be assumed to have only two values/alternatives, 0 and 1.

The best-practice technology of a technological paradigm (the "global technology"), which is defined similarly, describes the best *combination* of techniques. The firm that uses *all* techniques in the set of global technology reaches to highest technological "level" defined by that paradigm. A firm can know only a *part* of the global technology (or the opportunity set; see Eliasson 1990), and its technological level is determined by the correspondence between the global technology and the technology applied by the firm.

In our experiments, we use a 40-element vector for the global technology. The technological level of the firm depends on the degree of correspondence (DC^P) in the Pth paradigm between the global technology T and the technology F employed by the firm as follows:

$$DC^P = \sum_{i=1}^{n} a_i w_i, \tag{9}$$

with $a_i = 0$ if $t_i \neq f_i$ and 1 if $t_i = f_i$; w_i is the weight for the ith technique; and t_i and f_i denote the ith technique of T and F, respectively.

The technological level of the firm is computed by an exponential function of the DC value.

$$\text{MTEC}^P = \alpha^P \exp(\beta^P DC^P), \tag{10}$$

where α^P and β^P are industry- and paradigm-specific parameters ($\alpha > 0$, $\beta > 0$) and exp(.) is the exponential function. In our model, we use the same DC function for all global technologies. Differences in α and β values create a hierarchy between the different global technologies. Thus, the value of $\alpha^P \exp(\beta^P)$ defines the absolute limit for the Pth paradigm because $DC = 1$ if $F = T$. Although there may be many alternative specifications for the DC and MTEC functions, the one used in our model is quite flexible and sufficient for our purpose. The MEFF variable is defined in the same way.

3.4. Learning and Incremental Innovations

Firms use "genetic algorithms" to discover the global technology of a certain technological paradigm (Goldberg 1989). A firm has a memory to retain k number of alternative technology sets at a time (in our experiments, three sets) and uses the set that has the highest degree of correspondence. Firms "learn" about global technology by recombining their own technologies (*experimentation*), by recombining their sets with other firms' sets (*imitation*), or through *mutations*. One of the most important processes of evolutionary dynamics, *selection,* takes place at the sectoral level through the selection of firms. Badly performing firms (and the technologies used by them) will be nullified by the competition process in the market. This is the way learning takes place at the national economic system's level (see Eliasson 1994a, 36–37).

The learning process that takes place at the beginning of each year is executed in four steps for all technologies in each firm's memory. *First,* the firm decides whether it will try experimentation or imitation. The firm decides to try experimentation with INSEARCH/(INSEARCH + N) probability, where INSEARCH is a variable that depends negatively on the stock of general knowledge and N is the number of firms in the sector using the same type of technology.

Second, if the firm decides to try experimentation, it will select a technology *from its memory* for recombination. The probability of selection depends on the relative degree of correspondence with the global technology. If the firm decides to try imitation, then it will select a technology for recombination *from another firm* in the same market using the same type of technology. As may be expected, the probability of selection depends on the firms' technological levels (the MEFF or MTEC variables).

Third, the firm selects randomly NSEARCH number of elements of the technology to be used in recombination. Then, the values of those elements (i.e., techniques) are replaced with the corresponding elements from the selected technology vector. If the degree of correspondence improves, the firm keeps the modified technology in its memory. Otherwise, the existing technology remains in the memory. The main difference between experimentation and imitation is the source of the technology to be used in recombination. In the case of experimentation, the firm experiments by replacing NSEARCH number of techniques of one of its technologies with the corresponding techniques of another technology in its memory. Recall that a firm can keep three different technologies in its memory. In the case of imitation, the firm experiments by recombining the techniques of a certain technology in its memory with the corresponding techniques from another firm's technology.

Finally, the firm will try mutation with PMUTAT probability. In the case of mutation, a randomly selected NMUTAT number of elements of the technology vector are replaced with their opposites (0 1 and 1 0).

Our learning specification has four critical variables: INSEARCH, NSEARCH, PMUTAT and NMUTAT. A decrease in INSEARCH means that the firm will have a stronger tendency for outsearch (imitation). Intuitively, outsearch is usually better than insearch since the set of available technologies is broader in the case of outsearch (because the number of firms in the sector is higher than the number of technologies that reside in the firm's memory). Moreover, except for the most advanced firm, at least one firm's technological level is higher than that of the imitating firm. Our simulation experiments with the learning module support this intuition. When the INSEARCH variable is reduced, the learning process goes faster, that is, firms quickly discover the elements of the global technology.

The second variable, NSEARCH, is another critical variable for the performance of the learning process. A low value for NSEARCH means that the firm can change only a few elements (techniques) at a time. This implies a slow learning process. Experiments with the learning module show that increasing the NSEARCH variable improves the learning performance. The PMUTAT and NMUTAT variables, which determine the probability of mutation and the number of elements to be changed in mutation, have a positive impact on learning.

We assume that outsearch and mutation probabilities depend on firms' stocks of general knowledge (GENTRSTOCK). The firm with a larger stock of general knowledge will be able to experiment more with other firms' techniques so that it will achieve a higher rate of learning. The numbers of elements to be changed in experimentation, imitation (NSEARCH), and mutation (NMUTAT) are determined by real R&D expenditures. In a sense, the firm buys experiments for R&D activities, and the quality (the probability of success) of those activities depends on the stock of general knowledge.

A firm can improve its technological level by learning and incremental innovations only within the limits of its global technology (the technological paradigm). When the firm gets closer to the limit, it starts to allocate more funds for radical innovation because of difficulties in improving its technological level within the existing paradigm. Through radical innovation, the firm jumps into another technological trajectory.

3.5. Radical Innovations, User-Producer Interaction, and Changes in Techno-Economic Paradigms

Firms, especially those close to the technological frontier, may try to achieve a radical innovation (a new type of technology, a new paradigm) or imitate a radical innovation of other firms, as is shown in figure 1.

Radical innovations and imitations of different paradigms are determined in three steps. In the first step, we have a probabilistic draw for innovation/imitation. If the firm turns out to be an innovator/imitator, then we determine the paradigm PT to be innovated/imitated. If the new technology looks better according to the ensuing computations, the firm adopts it.

The probability of a radical innovation (PRINN) depends on real R&D expenditures aimed at radical innovation (RDRADICAL), the stock of general knowledge (GENTRSTOCK), and knowledge spillovers from other firms in the same sector (GENTRSPILL), which is also a positive function of GENTRSTOCK. Then the paradigm type to be innovated (PTN) is randomly drawn from an exponential distribution. Selection probability is inversely related to exp(PTN), which means that paradigms with high potential are less probable. Finally, the techniques of the new technology are determined randomly. The new technology should be seen first as a process prototype. Besides learning by doing, the firm improves

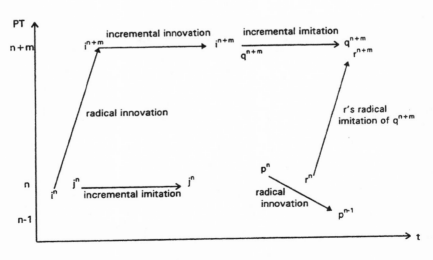

Fig. 1. Radical/incremental innovations/imitations

its technology by experimenting and/or imitating other firms. Even if no other firm is in the paradigm, it can learn by experimenting and from users. It estimates the rate of learning over five future years and compares the estimates of the technological efficiencies of the new and the old technology, MTEC old $(1 + \text{LEARN old})$ versus MTEC new $(1 + \text{LEARN new})$. The parameter LEARN depends on the number of users. The new paradigm is adopted if it looks better. The old technology is then forgotten, and the firm would have to reinnovate or imitate a technology to go back to the old paradigm, and this would be costly.

Radical imitations introduce an additional variable, the distance between the paradigm used by the firm and the paradigm to be imitated. The probability of imitation depends on the same variables, RDRADICAL, GENTRSTOCK, and GENTRSPILL. It also increases with the level of the firm's paradigm PTF, since a firm in a high paradigm has higher technological knowledge. Then the probability that the Mth paradigm will be imitated depends positively on the number of firms using PTM, the index number of PTM, and the distance between PTM and PTF. Finally, the techniques of the new technology are selected randomly since an imitator does not know all the techniques of the imitated firm (there is no patent licensing in the present version). The procedure is the same as that for radical innovations.

User-producer interaction plays a major role. In the case of the diffusion of radical innovations, we assume that capital goods producers and users can imitate each other's technologies. In other words, capital goods producer firms can imitate a radical innovation from *all* firms; other firms (users) can imitate from capital goods producers *and* those firms in their sector. Thus, we recognize that producers can "learn" from users. In that way, the capital goods sector becomes a "nodal" industry that facilitates the diffusion of radical innovations. Once a radical innovation is adopted by most of the firms in all sectors, the economy will move into a new technological trajectory defined by the new techno-economic paradigm.

3.6. Training and R&D Determinants

Training generates general knowledge and firm-specific skills. We also allow learning by doing. The stocks of specific skills and general knowledge per employee are accumulated as follows:

$$\text{SPECTR}_t = [\text{SPECTR}_{t-1} \times (1 - \rho_s)] + \text{LEARNEFF}_{t-1}$$
$$\times f(Q_{t-1}L_{t-1}, \text{INVST}_{t-1}) \tag{12}$$

$$\text{GENTRSTOCK}_t = [\text{GENTRSTOCK}_{t-1} \times (1 - \rho_g)] + \text{INVGT}_{t-1}, \tag{13}$$

where ρ_s and ρ_g are depreciation parameters; INVST and INVGT are (real) specific and general training expenditures per employee, respectively; $f(\cdot)$

is an exponential function; and LEARNEFF is the efficiency of learning, which depends on the stock of general knowledge. The depreciation rate (or the obsolescence rate) of the stock of specific skills, ρ_s, is a function of the rate of improvement in the case of incremental innovations. A different (and much higher) value is used for radical innovations.

General knowledge, once created, is applicable in all firms and therefore is transferable. If employees with a high level of general human capital move to another firm, they will increase the stock of general knowledge of the new firm. Firm-specific skills, as the name implies, cannot be transferred from one firm to another. Therefore, firms can increase the stock of specific skills only through specific training and learning by doing (Q_{t-1}/L_{t-1}), whereas the stock of general knowledge can be increased by general training *and* the hiring of highly trained workers from other firms.

The level of desired investment in training depends on three variables: existing stocks of knowledge and specific skills, (the inverse of) the rate of utilization of potential capacity (QTOP/QTOPFR), and sales revenue. Firms tend to increase stock at a certain rate and to spend a part of their sales revenue on training. If the QTOP/QTOPFR ratio is low, the firm will spend more on training since a low value of that ratio indicates that the firm is not able to use its productive capacity efficiently because of the lack of specific skills.

The desired level of investment in R&D depends on the stock of general knowledge, sales revenue, and the emphasis on radical innovations. If the firm spends a large part of its R&D funds to generate radical innovations, the level of R&D funds will be increased.

In addition to training and R&D, the firm calculates its desired level of investment in physical capital and liquid assets. Then, given the level of net cash flow, the firm decides on the level of desired borrowing (desired total investment *minus* net cash flow). The actual level of borrowing depends on the resources of the bank and total demand for borrowing. Finally, after the level of borrowing has been set in the credit market, the firm allocates its resources (net cash flow *plus* net borrowing) among four different assets (training, R&D, physical capital, and liquid assets) in proportion to its desired levels.

Total investment in training, INVTR, is allocated to general and specific training, according to a distribution parameter and the QTOP/QTOPFR ratio. Similarly, total investment in R&D, INVRD, is also allocated to two different types of R&D investments: RDRADICAL (for radical innovations) and RDINC (for incremental innovations). If the firm is able to improve the MTEC and MEFF variables, it will spend more on incremental innovations. On the other hand, if many firms are using a new global technology, the firm will spend more on radical innovations to adopt the new technology.

4. Experiments

We first present the reference experiment. We have run 80 simulations, differing only by the initial sequence of random numbers.[9] This allows us to design a typology of the patterns of evolution of the economy from paradigm to paradigm and uncover the lock-in phenomena. Then we compare the macroeconomic outcomes of the different patterns of technological evolution. The differences in these outcomes suggest that we study various technological policies in order to enhance growth and avoid lock-in. Five sets of experiments are described.

4.1. Paradigm Switching Patterns, Lock-in, and Lock-Out

In each of the 80 runs, all incumbent firms are in the paradigm 1.0 at year 0 (100 paradigms rank from 1.0 to 10.0). Figures 2 through 4 display the diffusion curves of the paradigms that are used by at least 10 firms in a

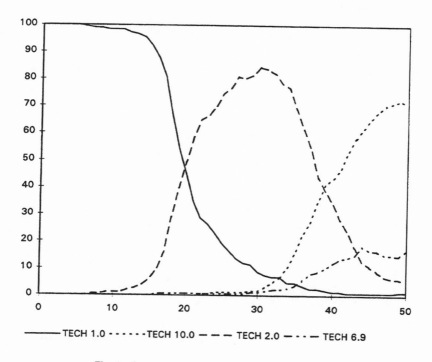

———— TECH 1.0 ······ TECH 10.0 — — — TECH 2.0 — · · — TECH 6.9

Fig. 2. Smooth transition pattern (BASE 16 run)

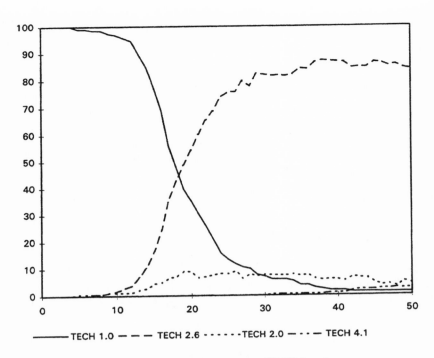

Fig. 3. Single lock-in pattern (BASE 1 run)

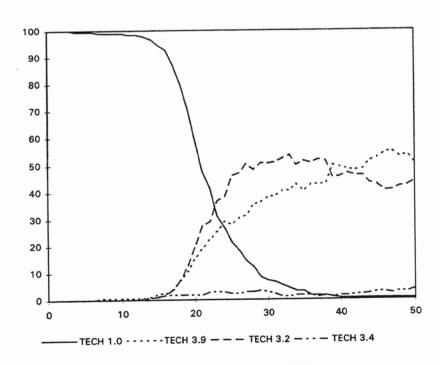

Fig. 4. Multiple lock-in pattern (BASE 8 run)

given year, for three runs, which are representative of the three main switching patterns.

A *first* general result is that only a few paradigms are significantly active at any one time, namely, four or five among 100. Firms cluster in certain paradigms because of increasing returns to adoption. Arthur (1988) has given five explanations of such a phenomenon: learning by using, network externalities, scale economies in production, informational increasing returns, and technological interrelatedness. In the present model, learning by using, in Arthur's terminology, is modeled in several ways. First, firms learn through experience (we call it learning by doing). Second, the technology is improved through user-producer interaction. Third, the quality of the technology is also improved through experiments and imitation of other firms. Scale economies of production appear also since R&D expenditures are a fixed cost.

The *second* major result is that three different switching patterns appear.

1. *Smooth transition* (see, e.g., fig. 2). A paradigm becomes dominant, then gives way to another dominant paradigm, and so on. Of course, during fairly long periods there is a transition, but no lock-in appears. This is the most frequent pattern (38 percent of runs).

2. *Single lock-in* (fig. 3). A paradigm becomes dominant and blocks the emergence of a better paradigm for a long time. Here the dominant paradigm is 2.6, and the better paradigm is 4.1. This pattern is found in 24 percent of the runs.

3. *Multiple lock-in* (fig. 4). Several new paradigms emerge and coexist. None is able to drive out the other(s). One may have a larger diffusion rate, but it is not necessarily the best. Even if it is the best, it blocks the emergence of higher paradigms. This pattern is also very frequent (29 percent of cases).

As these results make clear, the model allows for the possibility of lock-out since firms are very heterogeneous and some may take very bold decisions, that is, enter an untried paradigm alone. This is a novel feature not modeled by Arthur (1988).

We have also studied another minor pattern, "*Lock-in to transition.*" From paradigm 1.0, the economy locks into a single or multiple paradigms but eventually locks out to a higher paradigm. This patterns represents only 5 percent of the runs. Finally, we have noted the reverse pattern: an evolution starts with smooth transitions and then locks in. We call this "*transition to lock-in.*" It corresponds to 5 percent of the runs.

A *third* major result is that different patterns are generated through differences in minor events, on the basis of the same system (initial conditions, parameters, exogenous variables, etc.), though they are different exogenous systems in Arthur (1988). History matters. A very troublesome result for forecasters is that minor events can tilt a system into very different evolution patterns.[10] We will later examine whether certain policies can gear the economy to some of the best paths with (almost complete) certainty.

4.2. Comparing Macroeconomic Performances

Table 1 displays the mean outcomes for the BASE experiments for each switching pattern. The smooth transition pattern yields the highest paradigm and the highest manufacturing output at the end of the simulation

TABLE 1.   Mean Outcomes of the Six Sets of Experiments

Cases	BASE	SUB	ALL	DOM	INT	COM
Single lock-in						
% cases	0.24	0.21	0.13	0.35	0.24	0.25
Manufacturing output	465,884	663,384	484,380	500,611	605,738	392,976
Learning	3.56	4.15	4.14	3.70	3.87	3.67
Technology	3.90	4.53	4.58	3.97	5.60	3.85
Multiple lock-in						
% cases	0.29	0.21	0.20	0.04	0.20	0.03
Manufacturing output	602,392	708,771	699,992	459,349	465,535	929,033
Learning	3.80	4.33	4.35	3.15	3.53	4.81
Technology	3.95	4.00	4.11	3.00	4.35	4.98
Smooth transition						
% cases	0.38	0.43	0.56	0.56	0.50	0.69
Manufacturing output	764,660	809,627	834,391	824,425	790,646	820,377
Learning	4.17	4.60	4.66	4.33	4.50	4.72
Technology	4.85	5.17	5.09	4.24	5.17	4.77
Transition to lock-in						
% cases	0.05	0.10	0.09	0.04	0.01	0.04
Manufacturing output	788,934	696,590	733,684	919,222	242,442	878,892
Learning	4.15	4.14	4.44	4.38	2.56	4.41
Technology	5.03	5.06	4.88	3.59	3.39	4.62
Lock-in to transition						
% cases	0.05	0.05	0.03	0.01	0.05	—
Manufacturing output	865,578	699,645	989,625	845,692	724,203	—
Learning	4.91	4.45	4.76	5.23	3.88	—
Technology	4.85	5.19	4.69	3.39	5.29	—
All						
Number of cases	80.00	80.00	80.00	80.00	80.00	80.00
Manufacturing output	653,308	740,316	758,829	701,221	671,533	718,438
Learning	3.96	4.39	4.52	4.08	4.10	4.45
Technology	4.38	4.77	4.81	4.06	5.09	4.54

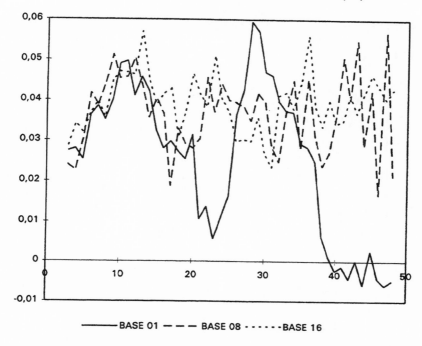

——— BASE 01 — — — BASE 08 · · · · · ·BASE 16

Fig. 5. Manufacturing output growth rates (five-year moving averages)

period. The multiple-lock-in case yields lower outcomes and the single-lock-in pattern the lowest outcomes. We will not comment on the *transition to lock-in* and *lock-in to transition* cases because the small number of runs (four) does not allow the computation of reliable mean statistics.

Figure 5 displays the evolution of manufacturing output growth rates for the three runs selected in figures 2 through 4. The multiple-lock-in run has a more unstable growth rate than does the smooth transition run. The single-lock-in case has a very striking feature. The economy slows down to zero growth as it locks into a mediocre paradigm. Why is multiple lock-in preferable?

Figure 6 provides an answer. It displays the rate of learning for each of the runs. The rate of learning is the average of the rates of increase of labor and capital productivity. It becomes very low in the single-lock-in case because the firms have improved the technology fairly close to the global technology through incremental innovation and imitation, while with several paradigms at the same time firms are slower to benefit from the increasing returns. They may also switch between the two paradigms, down as well as up, and higher levels of human capital investment and learning result. The particular case of the difference between single lock-in and multiple lock-in is confirmed by the difference in the average rates of learning in table 2.

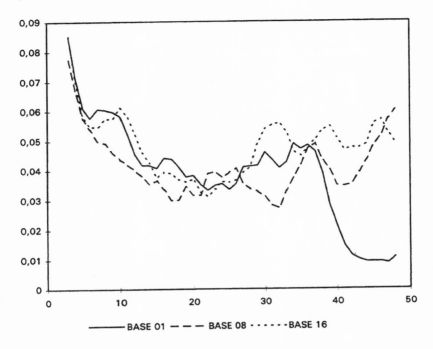

Fig. 6. Learning rates (five-year moving averages)

4.3. Technology Policy Experiments

We have tried five sets of experiments, SUB, ALL, DOM, INT, and COM, to be described subsequently. A technology policy may not only enhance the expected growth rate, as in endogenous growth theory. It may also lower the probability of lock-in, with the risk of zero growth.

In SUB, the firm decides on its R&D radical expenditures as in BASE. The government then adds a subsidy as a percentage of these expenditures. It subsidizes at 70 percent when a paradigm has a market share of 70 percent or more, at 50 percent when its market share is 50 to 70 percent, 30 percent when its market share is 30 to 50 percent, and 0 percent below. The purpose is to improve variety, and consequently the emergence of higher paradigms, since no firm knows whether a new paradigm is better than the present paradigms and can recommend it with certainty.

The smooth transition case rises to 43 percent, while the single- and multiple-lock-in cases have an equal share of 21 percent. In each of these three patterns, the manufacturing output is higher than in BASE as a result of the higher R&D investments and so are the learning rate and the technologies used. Overall, the economy is much better off.

In ALL, the government subsidizes any kind of R&D at 30 percent, so that the average subsidy is similar to the case of SUB. It has a significant

TABLE 2.   Regression Results

	Manufacturing Output		Technology Level		Learning Rate	
Constant	489.99	653.31	4.30	4.38	3.61	3.96
	(−15.84)	(23.25)	(24.21)	(29.99)	(−36.38)	−46.43
Policy variables						
SUB	69.21	87.01	0.33	0.40	0.40	0.44
	(1.98)	(2.19)	(1.62)	(1.93)	(3.58)	(3.63)
ALL	58.70	105.52	3.30	0.43	0.45	0.56
	(1.67)	(2.66)	(1.48)	(2.08)	(4.03)	(4.65)
DOM	31.99	47.91	−0.50	−0.31	0.06	0.12
	(0.90)	(1.21)	(−2.45)	(−1.51)	(0.56)	(1.01)
INT	−1.12	18.23	0.62	0.71	0.09	0.15
	(−0.03)	(0.46)	(3.10)	(3.46)	(0.79)	(1.23)
COM	17.59	65.13	−0.09	0.16	0.36	0.49
	(0.49)	(1.64)	(−0.41)	(0.80)	(3.15)	(4.09)
Evolution patterns						
Multiple lock-in	101.69		−0.48		0.15	
	(3.03)		(−2.51)		(1.40)	
Smooth transition	291.15		0.46		0.67	
	(11.58)		(3.21)		(8.29)	
STR to MLI	217.27		0.28		0.31	
	(4.48)		(0.99)		(2.01)	
MLI to STR	280.74		0.37		0.71	
	(4.61)		(1.06)		(3.62)	
R^2	0.257	0.021	0.125	0.061	0.212	0.072
N	480	480	480	480	480	480

Note: t-statistics are in parentheses.

effect on the frequency patterns. There are fewer single lock-ins (13 percent) and more frequent smooth transition runs (56 percent) than in SUB. A possible explanation would be that more firms come close to the global technology and then try to go into new paradigms. Manufacturing output reaches its highest value in these experiments.

In DOM, the government selects as a standard for 15 years the paradigm that has more than 20 percent of the market share. The purpose is to favor the increasing returns that are expected from the imitation processes by a large number of firms. This results in a very low incidence of multiple lock-in (4 percent) and a large incidence of single lock-in (35 percent), as would be expected. Smooth transitions remain numerous (56 percent). As there are no subsidies, manufacturing output lies between the level of BASE and the levels of SUB and ALL. The standard looks like an inexpensive technology policy instrument.

In the INT set of experiments, government experts evaluate the potentials of the incumbent paradigms, just as firms do when they find a radical innovation, and select as a standard the paradigm that has the highest potential. This evaluation was already done by each firm in the BASE experiments. However, the existence of a standard induces the entry of many firms in the same paradigm and generates increasing returns to adoption. INT has more numerous smooth transition cases than BASE does but fewer than DOM (50 percent). The mean outcome of these cases is good, although somewhat less good than in DOM. It has less single lock-in than in DOM. Firms may prefer to remain in their paradigms rather than adopting the standard, which may not be the best paradigm in use at the moment it is selected by the experts. However, the result of the multiple lock-in is very bad, as in DOM, since firms stick to a paradigm. Overall, the mean outcome of INT is inferior to the mean outcome of DOM. It is better for the government to select the standard out of the market than through experts. Yet some standard is better than no standard.

Finally, the COM set of experiments differs from DOM only in that the government subsidizes all firms' R&D at 30 percent. The frequency of smooth transition runs rises to become the highest of all the experiments (69 percent), and single lock-in is reduced but remains significant (25 percent). As in DOM, multiple lock-in is avoided. Overall, the mean outcome for manufacturing output is only slightly better than in DOM and not as good as in ALL.

The two policies, subsidizing and setting standards, appear as substitutes rather than complementary. This is logical since subsidizing favors the emergence of variety and some outstanding paradigms, while setting a standard yields the benefits of increasing returns in a current paradigm.

Table 2 provides a macroeconometric evaluation of the effects of policies and patterns on the three aggregate outcomes. The first regression controls for the switching pattern, assuming independence between these two variables (which is not strictly true). The second regression does not control for the patterns. The results already presented are confirmed. *Subsidizing appears to be more effective on manufacturing output than standards are.* The learning rate regression says why. Standards delay learning new paradigms, and learning is incremental and slower. If the technology level is considered, the hierarchy is different. The experts do better than the market, because more paradigms are evaluated than when firms cannot use their services, and this should protect us, as model builders, from the criticism of having set a bias against the experts.

5. Conclusions

The model has proved to be able to reproduce endogenously the changes in paradigms that occur in the long run, and this view of technological change as discontinuous corresponds much better to the history of the last two centuries than do Solow's steady-state growth models. As such, it also offers a challenging alternative to the real business cycle school that invokes exogenous technological shocks to explain the dynamics of the macroeconomy (Nelson and Plosser 1982).

The first essential and novel result is that minor events can tilt an economy into different patterns of paradigm evolution. It can get locked for long periods into one or more paradigms. The consequences in terms of growth, manufacturing output, and productivity appear to be considerable. There is a lock-in both when several paradigms coexist, so that increasing returns are not fully used, and when the economy is trapped in an aging, dominant paradigm where the bounds on increasing returns have already been reached. The economy can then regress, because learning, the essential engine for growth, stops. General and specific human capital, as well as R&D stock, decrease in interaction with learning.

General human capital, as the capacity to learn and innovate, and R&D, as the innovation activity, appear clearly as the fundamental mechanisms that generate growth differentials in interaction with stochastic events. The training for the rent hypothesis gives to the firms a central rationale for investing in general training: the desire to win the technological competition. It fits in a Schumpeterian framework. For Europe, where firms often sponsor more training than in the United States and where students pay low tuition fees, this may appear to be a more realistic story of human capital and technological change interactions than one based on standard human capital theory and workers' investment, as in Eicher (1996).

The second important result is that technology policies may improve the aggregate outcomes somewhat, notably by lowering the probability of lock-in in a mediocre technological paradigm or several such paradigms. However, the policies we have examined are unable to lower the probability of lock-in under 32 percent (COM experiments).

A third result is that among the technology policies, R&D subsidies appear as more efficient than the setting of a technological paradigm as a standard, although the results may be sensitive to the parameter values. Moreover, these two types of policies rely on opposite mechanisms and cannot be used in a complementary way.

Beyond the parameters, various assumptions on important variables should be studied. More detailed analysis of technology policies, for instance, with patent laws, and of training and education policies as in order, as well as more systematic evidence on the impossibility of avoiding lock-in.[11]

NOTES

We are very grateful to Gunnar Eliasson for stimulating discussions and a careful reading of the manuscript, which has greatly improved it. We nevertheless remain responsible for all remaining errors. Erol Taymaz thanks the University of Paris II for several stays as a guest professor during which time much of the research was done.

1. Freeman and Perez (1988) coined the term *techno-economic paradigm.* For the sake of elegance, we use the term *technological paradigm* coined by Dosi (1982), even though the former discusses the organizational changes that accompany technological changes. A supplementary reason is that our model, like any model, does not take into account all the qualitative changes that take place with a change of the techno-economic paradigm.

2. See also David (1985), Semmler (1993), and Greiner and Semmler (1994).

3. See the pleas of Freeman (1991) and Foray (1991) on the modeling of history.

4. Such a model offers novel results at the aggregate level that are not always easy to understand due to the complexity of the numerous and nonlinear interactions. A good understanding of the mechanisms at work and of the results implies studies at the microeconomic as well as the macroeconomic level (see Ballot and Taymaz 1995 for some results using microeconometrics).

5. The reference to Bertrand competition is standard.

6. Eliasson (1990) and Carlsson and Eliasson (1995) argue for an even wider concept, "business or economic competence," because innovation is determined by different capabilities that promote success through other mechanisms as well. Some aspects of economic competence, notably those reflected in X-efficiency are modeled in the model we use.

7. See Lane (1993b, 178–80) for a plea for modeling rationality as an endogenous variable. Learning capacity is a form of rationality, close to Eliasson's (1990, 1994b) concept of economic competence.

8. A short description is given in Eliasson (1991). A set of books gives a full description of MOSES and the data base: Albrecht et al. 1989, 1992 and Taymaz (1991).

9. Different random numbers create a different microenvironment and different decisions. Hence, aggregate outcomes can differ in this path-dependant process. The choice of the number of the runs is based on the computation of a manufacturing output cumulative mean, run after run. It shows no significant variation after 40 runs. To be sure, we have run twice as many experiments.

10. In figure 5, this happens after some 15 years.

11. Some preliminary and encouraging work on patents has been done by J.-D. Roebben at ERMES.

REFERENCES

Aghion, P., and P. Howitt. 1992. A Model of Growth through Creative Destruction. *Econometrica* 60:323–51.
Albrecht, J. W., et al. 1989. *MOSES Code.* Stockholm: IUI.
——. 1992. *MOSES Database.* Stockholm: IUI.
Arrow, K. 1962. The Economic Implications of Learning-by-Doing. *Review of Economic Studies* 29 (2): 155–73.
Arthur, W. B. 1988. Competing Technologies: An Overview. In *Technical Change and Economic Theory,* edited by G. Dosi et al. London: Pinter.

——. 1989. Competing Technologies, Increasing Returns, and Lock-in by Small Historical Events. *Economic Journal* (March): 99, no. 394: 116–31.

——. 1994. *Increasing Returns and Path Dependance in the Economy*. Chicago: University of Chicago Press.

Azariadis, C., and A. Drazen. 1990. Threshold Externalities in Economic Development. *Quarterly Journal of Economics* 105, no. 2 (May): 501–26.

Ballot, G. 1994. Continuing Education and Schumpeterian Competition: Elements for a Theoretical Framework. In *Human Capital Creation in an Economic Perspective*, edited by R. Asplund. Berlin: Physica Verlag.

Ballot, G., and E. Taymaz. 1993. *Firms Sponsored Training and Performance: A Comparison between France and Sweden Based on Firms Data*. 5th EALE Conference, Maastricht, Netherlands, October 1–3. ERMES Working Paper 93–09.

——. 1994. Training, Learning, and Innovation: A Micro-to-Macro Model of Evolutionary Growth. Paper presented at the J. A. Schumpeter Society conference, Economic Dynamism: Analysis and Policy, Münster, Germany, August 17–20.

——. 1997. The Dynamics of Firms in a Micro-to-Macro Model with Training, Learning, and Innovation. Paper presented at the Eunetic conference, Evolutionary Economics of Technical Change, Strasbourg, October 6–8. ERMES Working Papers, no. 94–09. Forthcoming in the *Journal of Evolutionary Economics* 7, no. 4.

——. 1995. Human Capital and Endogeneous Change in the Technological Paradigm: Dynamics of the Firms and the Economy in a Schumpeterian Growth Model. Paper presented at the EARIE Conference, Juan les Pins, France, September 3–6. ERMES Working Papers, no. 95–03.

——. 1996. Firm Sponsored Training, Technical Change, and Aggregate Performance in a Micro-Macro Model. In *Microsimulation and Public Policy*, edited by A. Harding. Amsterdam: North-Holland.

Bartel, A. P., and F. R. Lichtenberg. 1989. The Comparative Advantage of Educated Workers in Implementing New Technology. *Review of Economics and Statistics* 69 (1): 1–11.

Becker, G. S. 1964. *Human Capital*. New York: National Bureau of Economic Research.

Carlsson, B., and G. Eliasson. 1995. "The Nature and Importance of Economic Competence." In B. Carlsson, ed., *Technological Systems and Economic Performance: The Case of Factory Automation*. Dordrecht: Kluwer.

Carlsson, B., G. Eliasson, and E. Taymaz. 1991. The Macroeconomic Effects of Technological Systems: Micro-Macro Simulations. Paper presented at the EARIE Conference, Tel-Aviv, September 4–7.

Chiaramonte, F., and G. Dosi. 1992. The Microfoundations of Competitiveness and Their Macroeconomic Consequences. In *Technology and the Wealth of Nations*, edited by D. Foray and C. Freeman.

Chiaramonte, F., G. Dosi, and L. Orsenigo. 1993. Innovative Learning and Institutions in the Process of Development: On the Microfoundation of Growth Regimes. In *Learning and Technological Change*, edited by R. Thomson. New York: St. Martin's.

Cohen, W. M., and D. A. Levinthal. 1989. Innovation and Learning: The Two Faces of R&D. *Economic Journal* 99:569–96.

——. 1990. Absorptive Capacity: A New Perspective on Learning and Innovation. *Administrative Science Quarterly* 3:128–52.

David, P. 1985. Clio and the Economics of QWERTY. *American Economic Review Proceedings* 75:332–37.

Dosi, G. 1982. Technological Paradigms and Technological Trajectories: A Suggested Interpretation of the Determinants and Directions of Technical Change. *Research Policy* 11:147–62.

——. 1984. *Technical Change and Industrial Transformation.* London: Macmillan.

Dosi, G., and R. R. Nelson. 1993. Evolutionary Theories in Economics: Assessment and Prospects. Mimeo.

Eicher, T. S. 1996. Interaction between Endogeneous Human Capital and Technological Change. *Review of Economic Studies* 63:127–44.

Eliasson, G. 1977. Competition and Market Processes in a Simulation Model of the Swedish Economy. *American Economic Review* 67:277–81.

——. 1985. *The Firm and Financial Markets in the Swedish Micro-to-Macro Model.* Stockholm: IUI and Amquist & Wicksell.

——. 1989. The Dynamics of Supply and Economy Growth: How Industrial Knowledge Accumulation Drives a Path-Dependant Economic Process. In *Industrial Dynamics: Technological, Organizational, and Structural Changes in Industries and in Firms,* edited by B. Carlsson. Boston: Kluwer Academic.

——. 1990. The Firm as a Competent Team. *Journal of Economic Behavior and Organization.* 13 (3): 273–98.

——. 1991. Modelling the Experimentally Organized Economy. *Journal of Economic Behavior and Organization* 16:163–82.

——. 1994a. The Markets for Learning and Educational Services: A Micro Explanation of the Role of Education and Competence Development in Macro Economic Growth. Paper presented at the OECD Directorate for Social Affairs conference Manpower and Education, DEELSA/ED, CERI, CD(94)9. Paris.

——. 1994b. "Technology, Economic Competence and the Theory of the Firm: Discussing the Economic Forces Behind Long-Term Economic Growth." In *Economics of Technology,* edited by O. Granstand. Amsterdam: Elsevier Science.

——. 1996. Spillovers, Integrated Production, and the Theory of the Firm. *Journal of Evolutionary Economics* 6 (2): 125–40.

Foray, D. 1991. Dynamique Economique et Nouvelles Exigences de l'Investigation Historique. *Revue Économique* 2:301–11.

Freeman, C. 1991. Innovation, Changes of Techno-Economic Paradigm, and Biological Analogies in Economics. *Revue Économique* 2:211–32.

Freeman, C., and C. Perez. 1988. Structural Crises of Adjustment: Business Cycles and Investment Behavior. In *Technical Change and Economic Theory,* edited by G. Dosi et al. London: Pinter.

Goldberg, D. E. 1989. *Genetic Algorithms in Search, Optimization, and Machine Learning.* Reading, MA: Addison-Wesley.

Grabowski, H. G., and J. M. Vernon. 1987. Pioneers, Imitators, and Generics: A Simulation Model of Schumpeterian Competition. *Quarterly Journal of Economics* 102, no. 3: 491–525.

Greiner, A., and W. Semmler. 1994. *Endogenous Change through Learning.* Proceeding of the Eunetic conference Evolutionary Economics of Technological Change, Strasbourg, October 6–8. 1:545–69.

Harding, A., ed. 1996. *Microsimulation and Public Policy.* Amsterdam: North-Holland.

Holland, J. 1975. *Adaptation in Natural and Artificial Systems.* Ann Arbor: University of Michigan Press.

Holland, J., and J. H. Miller. 1991. Artificial Adaptive Agents in Economic Theory. *American Economic Review,* papers and proceedings, 81 (May): 365–70.

Iosso, T. R. 1993. Industry Evolution with a Sequence of Technologies and Heterogeneous Ability: A Model of Creative Destruction. *Journal of Economic Behavior and Organization* 21:109–29.

Kwasnicki, W., and H. Kwasnicka. 1982. Market, Innovation, Competition: An Evolutionary Model of Industrial Dynamics. *Journal of Economic Behavior and Organization* 19:343–68.

Lane, D. A. 1993a. Artificial Worlds and Economics, Part I. *Journal of Evolutionary Economics* 3 (2): 89–107.

———. 1993b. Artificial Worlds and Economics, Part II. *Journal of Evolutionary Economics* 3 (3): 177–97.

Lucas, R. E. 1988. On the Mechanism of Economic Development. *Journal of Monetary Economics* 21:3–42.

Nelson, R. R., and E. S. Phelps. 1966. Investment in Humans, Technological Diffusion, and Economic Growth. *American Economic Review* 56 (2):69–82.

Nelson, C., and C. Plosser. 1982. Trend and Random Walks in Macroeconomic Time Series. *Journal of Monetary Economics* 10, no. 2 (Sept.): 139–62.

Nelson, R. R., and S. Winter. 1974. Neoclassical vs. Evolutionary Theories of Economic Growth: Critique and Prospectus. *Economic Journal* 84:886–905.

———. 1982. *An Evolutionary Theory of Economic Change.* Cambridge: Belknap Press of Harvard University Press.

Orcutt, G. H., et al. 1961. *Microanalysis of Socioeconomic Systems: A Simulation Study.* New York: Harper and Row.

Prigogine, I., and I. Stengers. 1984. *Order Out of Chaos.* London: Fontana.

Reinganum, J. 1989. The Timing of Innovation: Research, Development, and Diffusion. In *Handbook of Industrial Organization,* edited by R. Schmalensee and R. Willig. Vol. 1. Amsterdam: North-Holland.

Romer, P. 1990. Endogenous Technical Change. *Journal of Political Economy* 98, no. 5, part 2 (Oct.): S71–102.

Saviotti, P. P., and J. S. Metcalfe, eds. 1991a. *Evolutionary Theories of Economic and Technological Change.* Chur, Switzerland: Harwood Academic.

———. 1991b. Present Development and Trends in Evolutionary Economics. In Saviotti and Metcalfe 1991a.

Schumpeter, J. 1943. *Capitalism, Socialism, and Democracy.* London: Allen and Unwin.

Semmler, W. 1993. The Dynamics of Innovation and Diffusion with Competing Techniques. In *Learning and Technological Change,* edited by R. Thomson. New York: St. Martin's.

Silverberg, G., G. Dosi, and L. Orsenigo. 1988. Innovation, Diversity, and Diffusion: A Self-Organization Model. *Economic Journal* 98:212–21.

Smith, S. 1991. A Computer Simulation of Economic Growth and Technical Progress in a Multisectoral Economy. In Saviotti and Metcalf 1991a.

Stern, D., and J. M. M. Ritzen, eds. 1991. *Market Failure in Training?* New York: Springer Verlag.

Taymaz, E. 1991. *MOSES on PC: Manual, Initialization, and Calibration.* Stockholm: IUI.

Tirole, J. 1988. *The Theory of Industrial Organization.* Cambridge: MIT Press.

von Hippel, E. 1988. *The Sources of Innovation.* New York: Oxford University Press.

Welch, F. 1970. Education in Production. *Journal of Political Economy* 78:35–59.

Specialization in Areas of Strong Technological Opportunity and Economic Growth

Valentina Meliciani and Roberto Simonetti

1. Introduction

Since Solow's empirical study of the process of economic growth in the United States the importance of technical change in economic growth has been widely recognized (Solow 1957). Recently, the "new growth theories" have developed models of long-run growth sustained by the endogenous rate of innovation (Romer 1986, 1990; Grossman and Helpman 1991; Aghion and Howitt 1992). Evolutionary theories of economic growth have also emphasized the role played by technical change in affecting the disequilibrium path along which countries grow or decline as a consequence of the successful or unsuccessful innovative activities of their firms. Within these frameworks, a number of empirical analyses, both of a quantitative and qualitative nature, have investigated the processes by which the production of new knowledge affects the performance of economic systems (for a review, see Fagerberg 1994). An important result of these new approaches is the role that specialization can play in affecting the long-run rate of growth of a country.

Long before the development of this literature, post-Keynesian theories of economic growth (Kaldor 1966, Thirlwall 1979) identified differences in the income elasticity of demand of different products as a channel through which specialization could affect the performance of countries. In this framework, growth can be hampered by a lack of sufficient demand, thus the emphasis on the crucial role played by international competitiveness in the theories of "export-led" and "balance of payments constrained" growth. These models, however, keep an aggregate structure that does not allow further exploration of the link between the composition of national activities and the rate of growth. In the Ricardian tradition, Pasinetti (1981) also identifies a link between specialization and performance through the income elasticity of demand: considering that there is a saturation level for each consumption good, as income increases there is a shift in demand toward more sophisticated goods, and it becomes important for countries to specialize in the production of those goods for which there is sufficient international demand.

The new neoclassical theory of trade and growth follows the traditional neoclassical approach in describing growth as being determined only by supply-side factors. In these models, however, the structure of countries' activities can play a role in affecting their performance through differences in the rate of endogenous technical change and technological externalities. For example, Grossman and Helpman (1991) have shown that, when technological spillovers are higher at a national rather than international level, a country that specializes in high-tech products can experience higher rates of growth than a country that is specialized in the production of traditional products because its opportunities of innovation are higher.

In the evolutionary approach, technical change plays a crucial role for economic development, but demand side factors are also important (for a survey of evolutionary theorizing on economic growth, see Silverberg and Verspagen 1995). In this framework, different patterns of specialization can have different impacts on country performance both through differences in technological opportunities and through differences in income elasticities of demand.

Most of the studies in the evolutionary tradition find their inspiration in the work of Joseph Schumpeter. In the *Theory of Economic Development* (1926), Schumpeter identified innovation, entrepreneurship, and credit as the essential elements that drive economic growth. This emphasis on innovation was also present in his later work. In *Business Cycles* (1939), Schumpeter argued that changes in population and savings occur slowly and generate a smooth growth of the system, in contrast to development caused by innovations, which assume a cyclical nature.

In the Schumpeterian framework, every cycle receives impulses from specifically determined innovating industries, and other industries are subject to the impulses generated by the innovating ones. The innovating industries are generally newly emerging sectors in the economy and experience very high rates of growth stemming from the exploitation of clusters of related innovations. The introduction of innovations in the emerging industries, together with new purchasing power created by the banks, generates an increase in the demand for capital goods and, in turn, in their prices and output, and another period of growth begins as the rest of the economy is stimulated to expand production through intersectoral links. In the Schumpeterian tradition, Freeman and Perez (1988) have stressed the importance of new pervasive technologies that can lead to technological revolutions affecting directly or indirectly every branch of the economy.

Despite the differences that characterize these approaches, they all point to the importance of the composition of countries' activities for their aggregate economic performance. The aim of this essay is to explore whether differences in the patterns of technological specialization across countries play an important role in the process of uneven growth. Using data on patents registered at the U.S. Patent Office (USPO) at different levels of disaggregation, this essay examines how the distribution of technological competencies influenced economic growth across a sample of OECD and medium-income countries over the period 1970–94. The next section describes the indicator used to identify areas of strong technological opportunities and carries out a preliminary qualitative analysis of these classes. After the exploration of the patenting data, the essay investigates the link between specialization in these areas of high technological opportunity and countries' rates of growth in total output. Some final considerations conclude.

2. Information and Communications Technologies and the Fastest-Growing Patent Classes

2.1. Two Indicators of the Direction of Technological Activities

Nowadays, there is widespread consensus that technological change is a primary engine of economic growth. It is also acknowledged that the rate and the nature of innovation vary across economic activities. Pavitt's sectoral taxonomy of innovation is a well-known example of how scholars have been trying to identify some regularities in the way in which technological change unfolds and affects economic activity (1984). Other recent studies have stressed the importance of information and communications technologies (ICTs) as agents of major structural change (Freeman and Perez 1988, Piore and Sabel 1984, Audretsch 1995). Freeman and Perez, in particular, have mentioned the emergence of a new long wave associated with the emergence of ICTs and the growth of other science-based technologies such as biotechnology and advanced materials.

In his recent work with Soete, Freeman has also shown that the East Asian countries that have specialized in the new technologies have achieved very high rates of growth of exports and output (Freeman and Soete 1994). The work of Alfred Chandler (1990) on the history of the largest industrial corporations in this century has also supported the view that the mastering of new radical technologies was a key element in the achievement of high economic performance. Rosenberg (1976), in addition, has pointed out that technological change in capital goods industries has a decisive importance for advances in downstream sectors.

Although the evidence from historical and case studies is generally in agreement, the quantitative study of the effects of the rate and the direction of innovative activity on economic growth is more problematic. It is important to keep in mind that technological change is a primarily qualitative phenomenon, and therefore it is difficult to quantify by its nature. The knowledge required to introduce innovations is very different across sectors and in some industries reaches a high level of complexity, as knowledge from many different disciplines is required in order to achieve economically successful technological change.

In spite of the obvious limitations of the quantitative analysis of technology, a number of studies have shown that the statistical analysis of technological indicators can provide useful insights into the relationships between technological and economic variables. In most of the studies that have analyzed the effect of innovative activities at the aggregate level, however, technological indicators have been used in an aggregate fashion and have represented a proxy for the overall level of technological activities rather than their direction.

This study is an attempt to use an indicator of the direction of technological activities (rather than the rate of growth) in order to analyze the effect of the direction of innovative activities on the economic performance of countries. Two different indicators of technological specialization will be employed: in ICTs and in the fastest-growing patent classes. The first indicator is more appropriate for analyzing the aggregate impact of the emergence of a new technological paradigm; the second one does not rely on any a priori hypotheses regarding the most promising technological fields, and is particularly well suited to measure technological opportunity. Both indicators should measure the economic benefits that accrue to countries from being specialized in areas with a high rate of technical change and growing international demand. Countries' specialization is measured as the share of patents (in the ICTs or fastest-growing patent classes) granted in the United States to residents in a country at two different levels of disaggregation (91 and 367 patent classes).

The data classified at the Science Policy Research Unit (SPRU) of the University of Sussex in 91 classes are available from 1970 to 1994, while the data disaggregated into 367 USPO patent classes are available from 1975 to 1988. In order to exploit the longer time series, the former classification has been used more extensively, and the eight fastest-growing patent classes have been identified in two periods, 1970–74 to 1980–84 and 1980–84 to 1990–94. The more detailed classification has been used to analyze in greater detail the fast-growing technologies in the second period, and the top 30 classes in the period 1978–81 to 1985–88 have been examined.

Patel and Soete (1988) and Breschi and Mancusi (1996) have also used the rate of growth of patents in order to identify areas of strong technological opportunity; this study differs from the others, as it tries to link technological opportunity to economic growth.

2.2. The Fastest-growing and ICT Patent Classes:
An Overview
Before starting the statistical analysis of the relationship between the specialization in fast-growing patent classes and economic growth, it is interesting to examine the nature of the fast-growing technologies in various periods. From the evidence that comes from historical and case studies, we would expect to find that a substantial proportion of the fastest growing patent classes is related to the emerging technologies mentioned previously. This analysis is carried out at two levels of disaggregation: the 367

patent classes for the period 1978–88 and the 91 classes for the period 1970–94. Only the second classification will then be used in the regression analysis. Moreover, it is important to stress that, although we select dynamic classes only on the basis of rates of growth, the values of the indicators of specialization are mainly determined by the classes with the highest number of patents. Table 1 lists the 30 fastest growing USPO patent classes from 1978–81 to 1985–88.

TABLE 1.   Fast-Growing Patent Classes

USPO Code	Subclass	Rate of Growth (%)	Rank of Growth	Patents 1978–81	Patents 1985–88
800	Multicellular organisms	900.0	1	4	40
291	Track sanders	200.0	2	2	6
267	Spring devices	196.5	3	173	513
371	Error det/corr, fault det/rec	165.1	4	318	843
382	Image analysis	160.9	5	230	600
375	Pulse/digital communications	149.3	6	375	935
474	Endless belt power transmission	148.2	7	274	680
440	Marine propulsion	146.7	8	167	412
281	Books, strips, and leaves	146.4	9	56	138
370	Multiplex communications	145.7	10	534	1,312
300	Brush, broom, and mop making	138.5	11	13	31
346	Recorders	135.8	12	676	1,594
604	Surgery, infusion/removal	134.9	13	974	2,288
360	Dynamic magnetic info stor/ret	127.7	14	1,150	2,619
364	Elec computers and data processing systems	124.3	15	2,898	6,500
358	Facsimile or television picture recording and communication	119.8	16	1,983	4,359
503	Rec rec w/plural leaves	115.2	17	145	312
372	Coherent light generators	113.0	18	477	1,016
283	Printed matter	112.2	19	98	208
329	Demodulators, detectors	111.3	20	97	205
87	Textiles: braid, net, lace	109.5	21	21	44
369	Dynamic info stor, retr	103.8	22	533	1,086
110	Furnaces	102.8	23	286	580
270	Sheet-mat. associating, folding	102.7	24	112	227
409	Gearcutting, milling, planing	100.5	25	216	433
332	Modulators	100.0	26	82	164
341	Coded data/conversion	94.4	27	337	655
441	Buoys, rafts, aquatic devices	93.4	28	137	265
623	Artificial body members	90.7	29	386	736
419	Powder metallurgy	88.8	30	134	253
Total top 30		125.4		12,888	29,054
Total all classes		25.1		242,485	303,346
Share of top 30 (%)		80.2		5	10

Source: Elaborations on the SPRU-OTAF data base.

The growing importance of ICTs is well supported by table 1, although very different economic activities are included in the list. The eleventh place of "brush, broom, and mop making," for instance, was hardly foreseeable. However, considering that the classes with the highest numbers of patents are those that determine the behavior of the indicators of specialization, countries with a high share of activities in large classes such as "computing and data processing systems" (about 3,000 patents) and "facsimile or television picture recording and communication" (about 2,000 patents) will show higher specialization indices.

Another interesting feature that appears from table 1 is the importance of scientific and professional instruments; "surgery, infusion/removal" (about 1,000 patents) is very sizable in the group. The importance of instrumentation suggests that the indicator could be particularly well suited for analyzing the influence of technological change on economic performance. The work of Rosenberg (1994) suggests that technology is very complex and systemic and that important scientific and technological breakthroughs have been linked historically to developments in the instrumentation available. The quality of the instruments, thus, should influence the quality of the research and development carried out in a country and, therefore, should be related to its economic performance.

Similar patterns are apparent in table 2, which reports the fastest-growing technologies in two different periods at a higher level of aggregation (91 technology classes).

The importance of ICTs in the 1980s is apparent: five out of the eight fast-growing classes are ICT technologies; the other three are "dentistry and surgery," related to instrumentation technology; "superconductors"; new materials; and "bioengineering." The picture is completely different in the 1970s, when the fast-growing patent classes did not include any ICTs but did include some classes related to capital-intensive technologies such as "internal combustion engines" and "mineral oil apparatus."

2.3. The Fastest-Growing Patent Classes: Distribution by Country

Table 3 shows the specialization of each country in the fast-growing classes (30 USPO classes in 1985–88, eight SPRU classes in 1970–84 and 1980–94) and ICTs.

Specialization is measured using the index of Revealed Technological Advantage (RTA), which assumes a value greater than 1 when the specialization is positive and between 0 and 1 when the country has a comparative disadvantage in the technologies considered. Table 4 reports the correlation coefficients between the various indices of specialization.

All the profiles of the indices are very significantly positively correlated in the 1980s (the correlation coefficient is always greater than 0.8). It is particularly interesting to note the very high correlation between the

TABLE 2.   Rate of Growth of Fast-Growing and ICT Patent Classes (91 subclasses)

Code	Technological Class	Period 1, 1970–74 to 1980–84			
		Rank of Growth Period 1	Rate of Growth Period 1 (%)	Patents 1970–74 (average)	Patents 1980– 84 (average)
24	Drugs	1	142	780	1,887
54	Internal combustion engines	2	101	498	1,001
25	Bioengineering	3	68	390	655
6	Agricultural chemicals	4	56	175	273
87	Typewriters	5	52	124	189
18	Mineral oil apparatus	6	20	5	6
99	Dentistry and surgery	7	26	1,229	1,554
19	Heating, combustion, nonelectric furnaces	8	25	1,069	1,336
Total top 8			62	4,269	6,900
Total all classes			−16	72,983	61,401
Share top 8 (%)			92	6	11

Code	Technological Class	Period 2, 1980–84 to 1990–94			
		Rank of Growth Period 2	Rate of Growth Period 2 (%)	Patents 1980–84 (average)	Patents 1990–94 (average)
27	Superconductors	1	n.a.[a]	0	231
82	Semiconductors	2	216	734	2,318
72	Laser technology	3	215	143	451
85	Calculators, computers, data processing systems	4	184	1,958	5,566
99	Dentistry and surgery	5	157	1,554	3,993
25	Bioengineering	6	142	655	1,586
77	Television, facsimile	7	132	1,308	3,034
73	Telecommunications equipment	8	130	1,063	2,450
Total top 8			165	7,415	19,629
Total all classes			57	61,401	96,588
Share top 8 (%)			68	12	20

Source: Elaborations on the SPRU-OTAF data base.
[a]Nonapplicable.

RTAs of the 8 fast-growing technologies and of the ICTs in the 1980s. The correlation coefficient of 0.97 suggests that the two indices are almost identical. Also, the correlation coefficient between specialization in the fast-growing classes computed using the 367 classes and the 91 is very high (0.87), despite some differences in the period for which it has been calculated. On the other hand, we find insignificant correlation coefficients between the fast-growing classes and the ICTs in the 1970s. Finally, there is

TABLE 3. Country Specialization Profiles (RTAs) in Fast-Growing and ICT Classes

Country	Top 30 1978–88 (367)	Top 8 1970–84 (91)	Top 8 1980–94 (91)	ICT 1970–84 (91)	ICT 1980–94 (91)
Australia	0.56	1.13	0.65	0.55	0.51
Austria	0.57	0.91	0.49	0.59	0.43
Belgium	0.87	0.84	0.52	0.50	0.48
Canada	0.65	0.80	0.66	0.80	0.70
Denmark	0.34	1.61	0.83	0.58	0.43
Finland	0.39	0.61	0.52	0.46	0.63
France	0.87	1.17	0.90	1.09	0.97
Germany	0.59	1.13	0.57	0.74	0.61
Greece	0.70	0.86	0.71	0.65	0.57
Eire	1.17	1.12	1.14	0.68	0.96
Italy	0.56	1.26	0.65	0.69	0.58
Japan	1.64	1.13	1.38	1.51	1.61
Netherlands	1.34	0.74	1.25	1.61	1.43
New Zealand	—	1.08	0.48	0.44	0.28
Norway	0.72	0.74	0.49	0.43	0.48
Portugal	0.00	2.19	0.35	0.25	0.08
Spain	0.36	1.38	0.42	0.27	0.33
Sweden	0.70	1.00	0.67	0.64	0.56
Switzerland	—	1.20	0.51	0.73	0.56
United Kingdom	0.85	1.12	0.84	0.94	0.91
United States	0.93	0.94	1.00	0.99	0.90
South Korea	—	1.74	2.46	0.68	2.56
Mexico	—	1.49	0.47	0.37	0.26

Source: Elaboration on the SPRU-OTAF data base.

TABLE 4. Selected Correlation Coefficients of Countries' Specialization Profiles in ICTs and Fast-Growing Classes

Correlation Coefficients	Fast 1978–88 (367)	Fast 1980–94 (91)	ICT 1980–94 (91)	Fast 1970–84 (91)
Fast 1978–88 (367)	1	0.87	0.92	
Fast 1980–94 (91)		1	0.97	0.17
ICT 1970–84 (91)			0.62	−0.31

Source: Elaborations on the SPRU-OTAF data base.

no correlation between specialization in the fast-growing classes over the 1970s and the 1980s (the classes are not the same), while there is a significant correlation between specialization in the ICTs over the 1970s and the 1980s, confirming the evidence of stickiness in specialization patterns. Considering the high correlation between the indices computed at different levels of disaggregation, we used only the 91 classes in the regression analysis; however, we kept the distinction between fast-growing classes and ICTs because of the different behavior of the indicators over the 1970s.

An examination of table 3 shows interesting patterns. Besides Japan and South Korea, which were economically very successful in the period considered, the Netherlands is the only country with a positive specialization in the ICTs patent classes. The very high value of the indicator for the Netherlands is accounted for by the presence of Philips, which is responsible for the very high specialization of the country in electronics-related technologies. It is worth pointing out, however, that many of the economic benefits that arise from the production of high-quality technology from Philips are bound to be appropriated by other countries since the Netherlands is a small country and Philips' economic activities are very internationalized (von Tunzelmann 1992). In the case of fast-growing technologies, Ireland also shows a positive specialization.

Another interesting feature highlighted by table 3 is the low level of patenting in the top 30 by countries that have started the process of industrialization relatively recently, such as Portugal, Spain, and Mexico.[1] This finding is hardly surprising since it is widely accepted that in the early phases of industrialization the main channel of technological change is the acquisition of foreign technology, especially through the activity of investment. Only when countries have at least partially caught up with the most advanced countries and are nearer to the technological frontier do their innovative activities that are reflected in patent statistics become more relevant for economic performance.

In this light, the positive specialization of South Korea in the fast-growing and ICT technologies offers even more support to Freeman and Soete's argument that the economic success experienced by East Asian countries is strongly linked to their success in emerging pervasive technologies. Moreover, among the countries with a positive specialization index in ICTs only South Korea managed to shift from a nonspecialized to a specialized country from the period 1970–84 to the period 1980–94. On the contrary, the Netherlands and Japan already had a revealed technological advantage at the beginning of the 1970s. This evidence is interesting, as, on one hand, it seems to support the view of strong path dependence in specialization patterns, but, on the other, it does not exclude the possibility of a powerful role played by the effort of entering the most promising technological fields. If there is a relationship between a high rate of activity in fast-growing technologies and aggregate performance, the analysis of the

mechanisms that shape the pattern and the evolution of countries' specialization becomes crucial to understanding the causes of the long-run surge
and decline of nations. This issue, which is not explored here, deserves
further investigation.

3. Specialization in New Technologies and Economic Performance

3.1. The Model Estimated

In the last 20 years, theoretical developments in the field of economic
growth have inspired numerous empirical investigations. As the theoretical
debate has mostly dealt with the issues of convergence and the role played
by endogenous technical change, the empirical investigations have also
focused on these two main issues (Fagerberg 1994). Two main results can
be drawn from these studies: (1) convergence is a time- and country-
specific phenomenon; and (2) differences in the rate of knowledge accumulation across countries (proxied either by measures of human capital, R&D
expenditures, or patent statistics) are related to differences in national
economic performance.

These two propositions will be our point of departure for the analysis
of the role played by technological opportunity in countries' rates of
growth. In particular, we aim to capture the effect of the direction of
technical change on economic growth, taking into account, at the same
time, the effect of convergence and embodied and disembodied knowledge
accumulation. In our view, the long-run rate of growth of a country depends on the rate of technical change and its direction:

$$\dot{y}/y = f(\dot{i}/t, q)$$

where $\dot{y}/y$ is the rate of growth of per capita income, $\dot{i}/t$ the rate of technical
change, and q a measure of the direction of technical change. Which countries are successful over a long period of time depends not only on their rate
of innovation but also on the nature of their innovative activity, since different patterns of technological specialization can have more or less pervasive
effects on the economy. Moreover, the nature of technical change should
also affect the rate of innovation: if some technologies are more productive
than others, countries that are specialized in those technologies may innovate at a faster rate. This interaction between technological opportunity and
the rate of innovation is not taken explicitly into account here.

Having already discussed our proxies for the rate of technical change,
in order to specify the equation to be estimated we have to identify some
indicators that capture differences in the rate of knowledge accumulation
across countries. The quantitative character of our study constrains us to

choose few proxies that do not do justice to the complexity of the phenomenon: these are the share of investment in gross domestic product (GDP) (a measure of embodied knowledge accumulation) and the rate of growth in the number of scientists and engineers (an indicator of the rate of disembodied knowledge accumulation). Moreover, we use the initial level of per capita GDP in order to allow for technological catching up or economic convergence. Finally, as we are interested in growth of per capita income and we do not want to make any assumption on the value of the coefficient of population, we also include the rate of growth of population in the estimation. The proxies for the "quality" of countries' specialization are the share of technological activities in fast-growing areas and ICTs.[2]

The general specification we test is therefore the following:

$$GRGDP_{it} = f(GDPH_{it}, GRPOP_{it}, INV_{it}, GRRS_{it}, SPE_{it}),$$

where $GRGDP_{it}$ is the growth of gross domestic product in country i and time t; GDPH is the initial level of per capita GDP; GRPOP is the rate of growth of population; INV is the share of gross fixed capital formation in GDP; GRRS is the rate of growth of researchers; and SPE is the share of a country's patents on its total patents, either in the ICT (SPEICT) or in the fast-growing patent classes (SPEFAST). All variables are in logarithms.

In this approach, as in most empirical studies of economic growth, there can be problems of simultaneity between the explanatory and the dependent variables. Technical change and economic growth are interdependent nonlinear phenomena; nevertheless, we think that simple analyses of this type can help to shed some light on the different impact of various sources of the rate and direction of technical change on growth.

Moreover, the specification of our equation, with the exception of the indicators of the direction of technical change, is very similar to growth equations tested in the framework of the new growth theory, in which a measure of knowledge is added to capital and labor as an input of the production function. Indeed, we are convinced that the estimation of a growth equation does not allow discrimination between technology gaps, evolutionary approaches, and new neoclassical models of growth since their main differences rest on the microeconomic behaviors of the economic agents rather than on the final determinants of growth.

The model is tested on two different samples. The first one includes 21 OECD countries plus Mexico and Korea; the second one includes only OECD countries. The data are pooled over the two periods: 1970–74 to 1980–84 and 1980–84 to 1990–94.[3] In order to explore the changing effects of our indicators of the direction of technical change over the 1970s and the 1980s, we allowed these coefficients to vary. Also, the intercepts (T1 and T2) and the coefficient on convergence (only for the enlarged sample) were allowed to vary. With this specification, all the F-tests on the stability of the regression coefficients of the remaining variables over the two subperiods did not reject the hypotheses of stability at 5 percent.

3.2. The Results of the Estimation

The results of the estimation are reported in table 5. In the regressions run on the largest sample, investment has a highly significant effect on economic growth. Convergence is highly significant only in the 1970s, while specialization in fast-growing technologies and specialization in ICTs are highly significant only in the 1980s. Overall, the model has high explanatory power.

It is interesting to note that, although specialization in ICTs and fast-

TABLE 5.   Regression Results

Explanatory Variables	Large Sample	Large Sample	OECD Sample	OECD Sample
T1	1.168**	0.941***	0.229	0.115
	(3.104)	(2.928)	(0.830)	(0.455)
T2	0.0232	0.260	0.066	0.053
	(0.084)	(0.897)	(0.260)	(0.209)
INV	1.494***	1.403***	1.146***	1.018***
	(3.244)	(2.868)	(2.906)	(2.490)
GRPOP	0.401	0.370	0.551**	0.502*
	(1.474)	(1.284)	(2.178)	(1.912)
GDPHt1	−0.129***	−0.118***		
	−(3.683)	−(3.523)		
GDPHt2	−0.029	−0.048*		
	−(1.054)	−(1.686)		
GDPH			−0.025	−0.018
			−(1.023)	−(0.733)
SPEFASTt1	−1.151		−0.757	
	−(1.446)		−(1.274)	
SPEFASTt2	1.500***		0.873***	
	(5.168)		(2.594)	
SPEICTt1		0.569		0.077
		(1.174)		(0.214)
SPEICTt2		1.131***		0.584**
		(4.630)		(2.235)
GRRS			0.110**	0.136***
			(2.152)	(2.640)
Adjusted R^2	0.68	0.65	0.42	0.38
F-value	14.554	12.715	5.160	4.444
Signif. F	(0.000)	(0.000)	(0.000)	(0.001)

Note: t-statistics are in parentheses.
*Significant at the .10 level.
**Significant at the .05 level.
***Significant at the .01 level.

growing technologies are not significant in the 1970s, the coefficient of SPEICT is always positive, while SPEFAST is negative. This suggests that it is not the fact that technologies are growing fast that is related to a country's growth, but rather it is the nature of the technology that matters. As table 2 shows, the fast-growing technologies in the 1970s were related to the old capital-intensive paradigm that was confronted with economic crises, not the least of which were the two oil shocks. In the 1980s, by contrast, countries that were specialized in the new fast-growing ICTs enjoyed substantial advantages.

The regression on the sample including only OECD countries has a lower explanatory power when compared with the enlarged sample, suggesting difficulties in explaining growth differentials among countries with a closer level of development. For this sample, the rate of growth of researchers was also included as a proxy for the rate of technical change.[4] Investment generally proves to be a highly significant factor for economic growth; also, the rate of growth of population is significant, while the convergence variable is negative but insignificant and is stable between the two periods. The rate of growth of researchers is significant at 5 percent in the regression, including specialization in fast-growing technologies, while it is significant at 1 percent in the regression including specialization in ICTs. Looking at the indicator of the direction of technical change, it is significant also in this sample over the 1980s, and the t-ratio on specialization in fast-growing technologies is higher than that on ICTs.

The good overall performance of our explanatory variables suggests that investment and technological growth all have an impact on countries' economic performance; the instability of the catching-up variable over time and across different samples shows that catching up, falling behind, and forging ahead are all possible outcomes of the process of economic development.

The positive and significant effect of the specialization variable seems to give support to those theories that point to the role played by the composition of technological activities on countries' rates of growth. Those countries that are specialized in ICTs have exploited the new opportunities offered by ICTs in the economic system, thus experiencing above average rates of growth. The lack of significance and the negative sign of our indicator of specialization in fast-growing technologies in the 1970s also suggests that the link between the composition of countries' technological activities and their aggregate performance is not a mechanical one. On the contrary, the nature of the technologies that are growing and their ability to perform as agents of major structural change seem to matter. Moreover, the effect of the direction of technical change on economic growth has to be investigated over the long run and changes across different historical periods. In the case of ICTs, it seems that the potential benefits of these technologies for economic growth already existed in the 1970s but have been fully exploited only in the 1980s. Finally, the higher level of significance of specialization in fast-growing technologies in explaining differences in countries' rates of growth over the 1980s, compared with specialization in ICTs, suggests that other new technologies (e.g., new materials, instrumentation, and biotechnology) also played a significant role in the 1980s, although the very high correlation between the two indicators suggests that specialization in the ICTs has been the most significant factor in the economic growth of countries in the last decade.[5]

4. Conclusions

The main aim of this essay was to analyze the influence of fields with high technological opportunity on the process of economic growth over a sample of OECD and medium-income countries. A qualitative analysis of the fastest-growing patent classes in the United States showed that, over the 1980s, they can be used as proxies for emerging technologies that have pervasive effects on the economy (mainly ICTs but also instruments, new materials, and biotechnology). The essay, thus, investigated whether countries that are specialized in the fast-growing technological areas or in ICTs experience above-average rates of growth.

The main finding of the study is that there is a positive association between the quality of technological specialization of countries and their rates of growth, which holds for both the enlarged sample and the sample including only OECD countries. These considerations lead us to conclude that the distribution of technological competencies across countries has to be taken into account in the investigation of the microeconomic foundations of economic growth, as it plays an important role in understanding the process of growth and decline of national economies.

The empirical analysis, therefore, supports the theoretical models in which specialization influences aggregate performance. However, we cannot either discriminate between competing models or identify the channels through which the composition of technological activities affects countries' growth. Future research could try to shed some light on the possible mechanisms, distinguishing between demand-side and supply-side factors.

Our results also point to the emergence of a new technological paradigm represented by the rapid rate of growth, over the 1980s, of information and communications technologies. Together with these technologies, new materials, instruments, and bioengineering also appear to be areas of growing technological opportunity. Unfortunately, our indicators can measure the development of software only very imperfectly and cannot capture its specific role, which is likely to be substantial, in the new technological revolution (Pavitt 1996). The possibility for countries to grow through the exploitation of clusters of related innovations gives support to the Schumpeterian view of long waves of development driven by the introduction and diffusion of new technologies.

The positive results obtained for the specialization variable do not have to obscure the other important finding of the regression analysis, namely, that investment activity and the rate of technical change are powerful engines of growth (Pianta 1995). On the other hand, the unstable results for the convergence variable indicate that convergence is far from being a mechanical process, as suggested by the traditional neoclassical theory of growth. On the contrary, catching up, forging ahead, and falling behind are all possible outcomes of the process of economic development.

Policy recommendations from this exercise on its own are not reliable, but the results are in line with other empirical and historical work that stresses the importance of technology in the process of economic growth. Therefore, it appears that attention should be devoted to the accumulation of technological capabilities in areas of strong technological opportunities. Nonetheless, this is more easily said than done. A necessary precondition is that it is possible to identify the most promising technologies, and this is not easy given the inherent uncertainty that surrounds the innovation process. Technological forecasting and close monitoring of developments in new technologies are possible areas in which government intervention could be useful.

In addition, the systemic nature of technology should be recognized, and governments should improve the support to industry innovative activities by providing a good educational infrastructure and supporting advanced scientific research. The importance of good instrumentation in the advancement of knowledge has been documented by a number of previous studies of important innovations (see, e.g., the cases of the steam engine described by Scherer [1984] and Nelson's account of the introduction of the transistor [1962]).

This essay represents only the first stage in a research project that aims to study the relationship between technological change, specialization, and economic growth. The analysis will aim at improving the specification and estimation of the dynamics of economic growth using panel data. Another related issue that will be addressed in the future is the link between fast-growing patent classes and the extent of technological specialization. The number of countries included in the sample will also be increased, and more disaggregated data will be collected to analyze the relationship considered here in greater detail.

It is important, however, to keep in mind that econometric exercises only provide at best a partial explanation of the phenomenon studied, and they must be considered, in truly Schumpeterian fashion, only in conjunction with theoretical developments and qualitative investigations.

NOTES

This essay is the result of the joint work of the authors; however, sections 1, 2.3, and 3.1 can be attributed to V. Meliciani and sections 2.1, 2.2, and 3.2 to R. Simonetti. We would like to thank D. Archibugi, R. Baldebros, P. Patel, K. Pavitt, N. von Tunzelmann, B. Verspagen, and the participants at the conferences organized by the University of Rome Tor Vergata (1996), the Schumpeterian Society (1996), and MERIT, University of Linburg (1996). V. Meliciani is also grateful to the European Union for a grant under the scheme Training and Mobility of Researchers.

1. This does not apply over the 1970s, when many of the fast-growing technologies were still linked to older technological paradigms.

2. In the regression analysis, we prefer to use national shares rather than RTAs because the RTA has a skewed distribution.

3. Rates of growth are computed on averages in order to reduce problems due to the oscillation of patent data and to attenuate the effects of the business cycle.

4. This variable was not available for the enlarged sample.

5. The regressions have also been run excluding Japan, but the results are substantially the same, with SPEFAST still significant at 5 percent level.

REFERENCES

Aghion, P., and P. Howitt. 1992. "A Model of Growth through Creative Destruction." *Econometrica* 60:323–51.

Archibugi, D., and M. Pianta. 1991. *The Technological Specialization of Advanced Countries: A Report to the EEC on International Science and Technology Activities.* Dordrecht: Kluwer Academic.

Audretsch, D. B. 1995. *Innovation and Industry Evolution.* Cambridge: MIT Press.

Breschi, S., and M. L. Mancusi. 1996. "Il modello di specializzazione tecnologica dell'Italia: un'analisi basata sui brevetti europei." Paper presented at the conference Technological Innovation, Internationalization, and Corporate Finance, Mediocredito Centrale, Rome, May.

Chandler, A. D. 1990. *Scale and Scope: The Dynamics of Industrial Capitalism.* Cambridge, MA: Belknap.

Dosi, G., C. Freeman, R. R. Nelson, L. Soete, and G. Silverberg. 1988. *Technical Change and Economic Theory.* London: Pinter.

Fagerberg, J. 1994. "Technology and International Differences in Growth Rates." *Journal of Economic Literature* 32:1147–75.

Freeman, C., and C. Perez. 1988. "Structural Crises of Adjustment, Business Cycles, and Investment Behaviour." In Dosi et al. 1988.

Freeman, C., and L. Soete. 1994. *Work for All or Mass Unemployment.* London: Pinter.

Grossman, G. M., and E. Helpman. 1991. *Innovation and Growth in the Global Economy.* Cambridge: MIT Press.

Kaldor, M. 1966. *Causes of the Slow Rate of Economic Growth in the United Kingdom.* Cambridge: Cambridge University Press.

NBER. 1962. *The Rate and Direction of Inventive Activity.* Princeton: Princeton University Press.

Nelson, R. R. 1962. "The Link between Science and Invention: The Case of the Transistor." In NBER 1962.

Pasinetti, L. 1981. *Structural Change and Economic Growth.* Cambridge: Cambridge University Press.

Patel, P., and L. Soete. 1988. "International Comparisons of Activity in Fast-Growing Patent Fields." SPRU. Mimeo.

Pavitt, K. 1984. "Sectoral Patterns of Technical Change: Towards a Taxonomy and a Theory." *Research Policy* 13 (6): 343–73.

———. 1996. "Innovation, Internationalisation, and Revolutionary Technologies." Summary of presentation made at the conference Technological Innovation, Internationalization, and Corporate Finance, Mediocredito Centrale, Rome, May.

Pianta, M. 1995. "Technology and Growth in OECD countries." *Cambridge Journal of Economics* 19 (1): 175–88.

Piore, M. J., and C. F. Sabel. 1984. *The Second Industrial Divide: Possibilities for Prosperity.* New York: Basic Books.

Romer, P. M. 1986. "Increasing Returns and Long-Run Growth." *Journal of Political Economy* 94:1002–37.

———. 1990. "Endogenous Technological Change." *Journal of Political Economy* 98: S71–102.

Rosenberg, N. 1976. *Perspective on Technology.* Cambridge: Cambridge University Press.

———. 1994. *Exploring the Black Box: Technology, Economics, and History.* Cambridge: Cambridge University Press.

Scherer, F. M. 1984. *Innovation and Growth: Schumpeterian Perspectives.* Cambridge: MIT Press.

Schumpeter, J. A. 1926. *Theory of Economic Development.* Cambridge: Harvard University Press.

———. 1939. *Business Cycles.* New York: McGraw-Hill.

Silverberg, G., and B. Verspagen. 1995. "Evolutionary Theorizing on Economic Growth." Forthcoming in *The Evolutionary Principles of Economics,* edited by K. Dopfer. Norwell, MA: Kluwer Academic.

Solow, R. 1957. "Technical Change and the Aggregate Production Function." *Review of Economics and Statistics* 39:312–20.

Thirlwall, A. P. 1979. "The Balance of Payments Constraint as an Explanation of International Growth Rate Differences." *Banca Nazionale del Lavoro Quarterly Review* 32 (128): 45–53.

Verspagen, B. 1993. *Uneven Growth between Interdependent Economies.* Aldershot: Avebury.

von Tunzelmann, G. N. 1992. "Evolution of Corporate Technology Profiles in IT&T: A Test Study of the Patent Approach." SPRU report for the Commission of European Communities, no. DGXIII. Mimeo.

Technology Regimes and the Distribution of Real Wages

George Johnson and Frank Stafford

1. Introduction

In the United States, the early postwar period marked the end of an era when jobs involving less skill gained in importance.[1] In our interpretation, the resulting wage compression was the outcome of an era when a broad spectrum of market organizations, ranging from manufacturing to retailing and service, increasingly applied scientific management (SM). Under this organizational structure, or "technology," the main thrust was to simplify work tasks through extensive division of labor in the workplace. We hypothesize that from approximately the mid-1960s to today there was a rise in the importance of information technologies in economic life, both in market and nonmarket activity. Suppose this new technology regime augmented the capacity of skilled workers to carry out a wide array of tasks while being of much less advantage to less-skilled workers. How would this skill-biased technical change (Bound and Johnson 1992) shape the distribution of wages between skilled and nonskilled workers?

In this essay, we offer an explanation of some stylized facts about changing technology, wages, and unemployment (particularly for Europe more recently) over the period 1965–95. Our main goal is to set out a model of skill-biased technical change, which has strong similarities to our earlier work (Johnson and Stafford 1992, 1993) and other recent work on the effect of technology changes in a general equilibrium, open-economy context (Gomory 1994, Gomory and Baumol 1996, Johnson and Stafford 1996b). That work studies the effect of industry-specific technology improvement by one of two trading partners when both countries are active in the industry. A central and robust finding is that technology improvement by the one country can raise the real wage there, partly at the expense of the laggard country, which experiences a declining real wage.

In this essay, the approach is expanded and redirected to a closed-economy setting where we address the following circumstance: skilled individuals and less-skilled individuals are potentially in the same type of technological competition as are the countries in the trade models. If one group avails itself of a new technology that improves its productivity in market sectors in which both are active, results similar to those in the open-economy model obtain. To illustrate, skilled workers, via the computer

348

and, more broadly, information technology (IT), have improved their ability to produce (more) products previously produced by less-skilled workers. This will act to lower the real wage of the less skilled. On the other hand, if IT had as its primary effect improvement of the ability of skilled workers to produce products that have been in their traditional niche (such as the output of professional service occupations of education, law, medicine, and business services), both skilled and unskilled workers would benefit.

In an environment in which skill-biased technical change allows skilled workers to carry out tasks previously performed by the less educated (as illustrated by the large increase in the number of college graduates in manufacturing), the apparent demand for skilled workers, as indicated by a rising real wage, will not be as readily subject to downward pressure via an increased supply. We show that, under certain rather plausible conditions in a general equilibrium model, the relative wages are independent of relative supply, a result that can obtain in a partial equilibrium approach only when the substitution elasticity between skilled and unskilled labor is infinite in each industry.

A second theme centers on governmental efforts to intercede as technology evolves. First, we examine attempts to help less-skilled workers by supporting the relative value of their wage. We then examine what we call the Lindbeck government expansion model or the policy of promoting expansion of the output of sectors employing skilled labor (such as medicine). This is often done because these sectors are seen as producing output to which citizens are entitled, as in the case of high-quality medical care or education.[2] We conclude with preliminary evidence on the shift toward more skilled workers in the manufacturing sector of the United States and illustrative facts about the extent of subsidies to medical care and education in the United States.

2. A Simple Macroeconomic Framework

We first set out a parsimonious model of the equilibrium of the labor market in a closed economy with which to analyze some of the factors just discussed. The aggregate production function for the economy is represented by

$$Y = F[G(E_1, E_2, E_3), K], \tag{1}$$

where Y is aggregate output, G is the flow of aggregate labor services, each E_i represents efficiency units of the three jobs in the economy, and K is the stock of capital. F and G are both linear homogeneous, so an increase in each of the E_is and K by x percent causes Y to increase by x percent.

Our concern is with issues dealing with the long-run growth of the economy. Assuming a constant saving rate (which, in particular, is unaffected by the distribution of income among different labor skill groups), the long-run value of K is proportional to Y. Arbitrarily specifying that $F_G = 1$ at all points in growth equilibrium, the real price of a unit of labor services is one and the aggregate wage bill is equal to G.

We next posit that at each moment in time there are two types of labor in the economy, "skilled" labor (the aggregate quantity of which is S) and unskilled labor (U). Both skilled and unskilled workers can, in principle, perform any one of the three jobs. The level of efficiency units of each job is

$$E_i = \lambda_{si}S_i + \lambda_{ui}U_i, \tag{2}$$

where S_i and U_i are the (nonnegative) quantities of the two types of labor employed in job i. λ_{si} and λ_{ui} are the productivities of the two types of labor in each job, and these are exogenous, reflecting technology. The relative efficiency of skilled labor in each job is $\lambda_{si}/\lambda_{ui}$. This is presumably greater than one, but it is assumed to be largest in job 1 and smallest in job 3.

It is in fact assumed that $\lambda_{s1}/\lambda_{u1}$ is so large that no Us are ever employed in job 1 and that $\lambda_{s3}/\lambda_{u3}$ is so small that no Ss are ever hired in job 3. At issue is whether job 2 is staffed (1) only by Us (Zone I), (2) by both Us and Ss (Zone II), or (3) only by Ss (Zone III). The marginal conditions with respect to the three types of labor imply that the real wage rates of the two types of labor satisfy

$$\begin{aligned}
W_s &= \lambda_{s1}G_1 \geq \lambda_{s2}G_2 \\
W_u &= \lambda_{u3}G_3 \geq \lambda_{u2}G_2,
\end{aligned} \tag{3}$$

where $G_i = \partial G/\partial E_i$. At most, one of the inequalities in equation 3 can hold. If it applies for skilled labor, the economy is in Zone I (i.e., all the Ss are in job 1. If it applies to unskilled labor, the economy is in Zone III. And, if it applies to neither type of labor, the economy is in Zone II.

To make matters more explicit, we will assume that the functional form of G is Cobb-Douglas,[3] that is,

$$G = E_1^{\alpha_1} E_2^{\alpha_2} E_3^{\alpha}, \tag{4}$$

where $\alpha_1 + \alpha_2 + \alpha_3 = 1$. In this case each marginal product is given by $G_i = \alpha_i G/E_i$. Assuming that the aggregate supplies of each type of labor are fixed at U and S and that the real wage levels of both types of labor are free to adjust so that there is full employment, equations 2 and 3 can be used to obtain the condition for the economy to be in Zone II:

$$\frac{(1 - \alpha_3)}{\alpha_3} \frac{U}{S} > \frac{\lambda_{s2}}{\lambda_{u2}} > \frac{\alpha_1}{(1 - \alpha_1)} \frac{U}{S}. \tag{5}$$

If the right-hand inequality is not satisfied, the economy is in Zone I, and if the left-hand inequality is not satisfied the economy is in Zone III.

The aggregate wage bill in the three zones depends on the value of the technology parameters (the values of the relevant λs) and the aggregate supplies of the two types of labor. The values of the aggregate real wage bill in each of the three zones are given by

$$G = \alpha_2^{\alpha_2}\alpha_3^{\alpha_3}(1 - \alpha_1)^{-(1-\alpha_1)}\lambda_{s1}^{\alpha_1}\lambda_{u2}^{\alpha_2}\lambda_{u3}^{\alpha_3}S^{\alpha_1}U^{\alpha_2+\alpha_3}, \quad \text{Zone I}$$

$$G = \alpha_1^{\alpha_1}\alpha_2^{\alpha_2}\alpha_3^{\alpha_3}\lambda_{s1}^{\alpha_1}\lambda_{u3}^{\alpha_3}\lambda_{u2}^{-\alpha_3}\lambda_{s2}^{-\alpha_1}[\lambda_{s2}S + \lambda_{u2}U] \quad \text{Zone II} \tag{6}$$

$$G = \alpha_1^{\alpha_1}\alpha_2^{\alpha_2}(1 - \alpha_3)^{-(1-\alpha_3)}\lambda_{s1}^{\alpha_1}\lambda_{s2}^{\alpha_2}\lambda_{u3}^{\alpha_3}S^{\alpha_1+\alpha_2}U^{\alpha_3}, \quad \text{Zone III.}$$

G is homogeneous of degree one in both U and S and the three λs in all three zones. However, changes in the individual technology parameters have very different implications concerning the distribution of labor earnings in the three zones.

3. The Distribution of Earnings

The long-run values of the real wage rates of skilled and unskilled workers in the relevant zone are given by the values of $\partial G/\partial S$ and $\partial G/\partial U$ from equation 6. If skilled and unskilled workers do not compete with each other for job 2 (Zones I and III), their wage rates are proportional to G divided by, respectively, S and U. In Zone I, for example, changes in the relevant technology parameters have the same proportional effect on W_s and W_u, for

$$\hat{W}_s = \hat{W}_u = \alpha_1\hat{\lambda}_{s1} + \alpha_2\hat{\lambda}_{u2} + \alpha_3\hat{\lambda}_{u3}, \tag{7}$$

where $\hat{W}_s = d(\log W_s)$, etc. Thus, if the aggregate wage bill rises by ΔG due to increases in any combination of increases in λ_{s1}, λ_{u2}, and λ_{u3}, skilled workers' total earnings rise by $\alpha_1\Delta G$ and unskilled workers' earnings rise by $(\alpha_2 + \alpha_3)\Delta G$. Further, the skilled/unskilled relative wage differential, $R = W_s/W_u$, is unaffected by changes in the any of the λs. An analogous result applies to the effects of changes in λ_{s1}, λ_{s2}, and λ_{u3} in Zone III.

In Zone II, in which skilled and unskilled workers both compete for job 2, changes in λ_{s1} and λ_{u3} have the same effect on both wage rates as in equation 7. Change in λ_{s2} and λ_{u2}, however, have very different effects. Holding λ_{s1} and λ_{u3} (as well as U and S) constant, the proportional change in the aggregate wage bill is

$$\hat{G} = (v - \alpha_1)\hat{\lambda}_{s2} + (1 - v - \alpha_3)\hat{\lambda}_{u2}, \tag{8}$$

where $v = W_s S/G$ is skilled labor's share of the total wage bill. In Zone II, both of the coefficients in equation 8 are positive, for $v > \alpha_1$ (there are some skilled workers in job 2) and $1 - v > \alpha_3$ (there are also some unskilled workers in job 2). The proportional changes in the skilled and unskilled wage rates in Zone II are

$$\hat{W}_s = (1 - \alpha_1)\hat{\lambda}_{s2} - \alpha_3\hat{\lambda}_{u2} \tag{9}$$

and

$$\hat{W}_u = -\alpha_1\hat{\lambda}_{s2} + (1 - \alpha_3)\hat{\lambda}_{u2}. \tag{10}$$

An exogenous increase in the productivity of skilled workers in job 2 causes the skilled wage to rise and the unskilled wage to fall. By equation 8, the total wage bill rises in Zone II in response to an increase in λ_{s2} (as long as $v > \alpha_1$), but the increase in the earnings of skilled workers is greater than ΔG. An analogous set of conclusions apply to the effects of an increase in λ_{u2}.

The distributional effects of changes in technology that, ceteris paribus, increase the productivity of skilled workers in job 2 are shown geometrically in figure 1. For low values of λ_{s2}, it is not profitable for firms to hire Ss in job 2 $(\lambda_{sw}/W_s < \lambda_{u2}/W_u)$, and increases in their latent productivity in that job have no effect on aggregate output or either wage rate. At a certain point (the

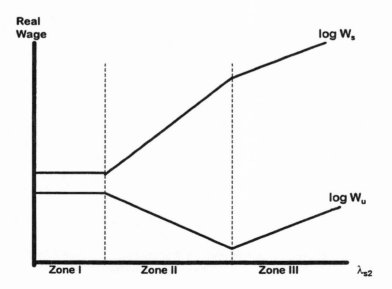

Fig. 1. Effect of the technology parameter for skilled workers in job 2 on the real wage rates of skilled and unskilled labor

boundary between Zones I and II), λ_{s2} reaches the value at which the Ss can compete with the Us for job 2, and further increases in the parameter cause the Ss to move from job 1 to 2 and the Us to be "crowded into" job 3 from job 2. This raises the marginal product of skilled workers and lowers that of unskilled workers. Finally, when the size of λ_{s2} gets sufficiently large, all the Us have been pushed out of job 2, and (in Zone III) further increases in λ_{s2} increase both W_s and W_u in the same proportion.

To some extent, the result that the skilled/unskilled relative wage is affected only by λ_{s2} and λ_{u2} only in Zone II and never by λ_{s1} and λ_{u3} is a result of the Cobb-Douglas assumption for equation 4.[4] However, the point of the preceding exposition, that the demand for labor by skill is very different when the skills are competitive for a particular job, is quite robust with respect to the specification of equation 4.

4. The Model with Long-Run Unemployment

The results in sections 2 and 3 are very dependent on the assumption that the real wage rates of both types of labor are free to adjust, so that the economy, net of cyclical disturbances, is characterized by full employment. This assumption is quite defensible for the United States and a few other industrialized countries (Japan, perhaps Britain), but for several industrialized countries — principally in Western Europe — the full employment assumption would be at best questionable. In this section, we explore the implications of skill-biased technological change in the context of two alternative models of labor market equilibrium. The first of these focuses on relative wage rigidities and the second on the effect of unemployment benefits.[5]

First, suppose that the skilled labor market is characterized by full employment (in the sense that $S_1 + S_2$ are equal to the effective supply of that type of labor) and that W_s is free to adjust to the appropriate market-clearing level. Government policy, however, successfully keeps the unskilled wage rate at too high a value relative to the skilled wage[6] rate, such that $U_1 + U_2$ is less than the effective supply of unskilled labor. Whatever the source of this "distortion," the unskilled wage rate is assumed to be a constant multiple $1/R_*$ of the skilled wage rate, and this causes *structural unemployment* of the unskilled.

In Zone I of the long-run equilibrium of such an economy, job 2 is completely filled by unskilled workers. The skilled real wage is $W_s = \alpha_1 G/S$, and the marginal conditions for jobs 2 and 3 are $W_u = W_s/R = \alpha_2 G/U_2 = \alpha_3 G/U_3$. Letting (for notational simplicity — they make little difference in the story) $\lambda_{s1} = \lambda_{u3} = 1$, the aggregate wage bill in Zone I is

$$G = \alpha_1^{-(1-\alpha_1)}\alpha_2^{\alpha_2}\alpha_3^{\alpha_3}\lambda_{u2}^{\alpha_2}R_*^{1-\alpha_1}S. \tag{11}$$

R_* is institutionally set below the value consistent with full employment of the Us,[7] and the aggregate wage level is lower than its full employment value as a result.

In Zone I, it is not profitable for employers to hire skilled workers in job 2, for $\lambda_{s2}/W_x > \lambda_{u2}/W_u$. However, if λ_{s2} rises to and then slightly above a critical value, in this case λ_{u2}/R_*, employers will replace all their unskilled Us with Ss. Because R is fixed, there is no Zone II in which both Us and Ss are employed in job 2; it is, instead, a knife-edge situation. In Zone III, the marginal conditions for skilled labor are $W_s = \alpha_1 G/S_1 = \alpha_2 G/S_2$, where $S = S_1 + S_2$, and the marginal condition for unskilled labor in job 3 is $W_u = W_s/R_* = \alpha_3 G/U_3$. It then follows that the aggregate real wage bill is

$$G = \alpha_1^{\alpha_1}\alpha_2^{\alpha_2}\alpha_3^{\alpha_3}(1 - \alpha_3)^{-1}\lambda_{s2}^{\alpha_2}R^{\alpha_3}S. \tag{12}$$

This is, as in Zone I, below the value associated with full employment.

It is interesting to note that a rise in the value of λ_{s2} from just below to just above its critical value for the entry of skilled labor into job 1, λ_{u2}/R_*, causes a sharp fall in G. This is seen by dividing equation 12 by equation 11, which yields

$$\frac{G(\text{Zone I})}{G(\text{Zone III})} = \left(\frac{\alpha_1}{\alpha_1 + \alpha_2} \right) \left(\frac{\lambda_{s2}}{R\lambda_{u2}} \right)^{\alpha_2}. \tag{13}$$

At the boundary between Zones I and III, the second term in brackets in equation 13 is equal to one, so, since the first term is less than one, G falls as soon as λ_{s2} rises to the point at which the Ss enter job 2 (en masse).[8] The reason for this fall in G is that at the critical value of λ_{s2} the aggregate level of unskilled employment falls from $(1 - \alpha_1)RS/\alpha_1$ to $\alpha_3 RS/(1 - \alpha_3)$. The value of W_s (and hence of W_u) is unaffected by the shift from Zone I to Zone III, but as λ_{s2} rises further both real wage rates rise.

An alternative approach to the explanation of the phenomenon of recent European unemployment focuses on the effect of high social benefits to nonemployed adults, which can be called the *induced unemployment* model. Each unskilled worker has the option of receiving W_u when employed or a real benefit level B when not employed. The result of this social policy is to shift the effective supply function for unskilled workers and, if B is not adjusted as W_u changes, to make the effective labor supply function very wage elastic. This is illustrated in figure 2, in which the effective supply of unskilled labor is given by the upward-sloping curve, which is

$$U = \varphi \left(\frac{W_u}{B} \right) L_u, \tag{14}$$

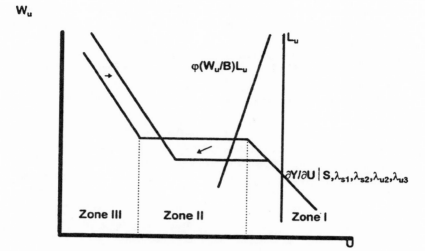

Fig. 2. Equilibrium of the unskilled labor market with induced unemployment

where L_{ui} is the supply of unskilled workers in the absence of the availability of a transfer payment to the nonemployed. The transfer payment is assumed to have no effect on the labor supply behavior of skilled workers, and S is independent of W_s as in the full employment model discussed in sections 2 and 3 and the structural unemployment model presented earlier.

The solution of the induced unemployment model proceeds exactly as in the full employment version, except that equation 13 is added in order to determine the value of $U = U_2 + U_3$. Of particular interest is the effect of changes in the technological parameters λ_{s2} and λ_{u2} in Zone II in which the two types of labor are directly competitive with each other. The changes in W_{s1} and W_{u1} are the same as in equations 9 and 10—because the relative demand curve is at this point horizontal so that the effects on wages are not altered by an upward-sloping supply schedule for the Us. The change in the aggregate real wage bill, however, is

$$\hat{G} = \{(v - \alpha_1)[1 + (1 - v)\epsilon]\}\hat{\lambda}_{s2} + \{(1 - v)[1 + (1 - \alpha_3)\epsilon] - \alpha_3\}\hat{\lambda}_{u2}, \quad (15)$$

where $\epsilon = (W_u/B)\varphi'/\varphi$ is the wage elasticity of the supply of unskilled labor. Comparing equation 14 with equation 10, the equivalent result in the full employment model, the coefficient on the change in λ_{s2} is smaller in the induced model, possibly negative, and the coefficient on the change in λ_{u2} is larger.

The effect of an increase in λ_{u2} in the induced unemployment model is shown geometrically in figure 2. The demand for U is downward sloping in

W_u in Zones I and III, but $\partial Y/\partial U$ is constant in Zone II. An exogenous increase in λ_{s2} shifts the demand curve down in Zone II and up in Zone III. The effects of the increase in λ_{s2} on the unskilled labor market thus depend critically on where the initial equilibrium is.

5.   Subsidizing Skilled Labor

Another important phenomenon that may be relevant in the determination of the distribution of earnings in an economy is the tendency to subsidize certain services (e.g., medicine, education, and, in the United States, law). We will specify that there are two such subsidies — one on the services of skilled labor in job 1 and the other on the services of unskilled labor in job 2.[9] Both skilled and unskilled workers in job 2 are not subject to the subsidy.[10]

If the subsidy rates for jobs 1 and 3 are, respectively, x_1 and x_3, the long-run marginal conditions for the equilibrium of the labor market are

$$
\begin{aligned}
W_s &= \lambda_{s1} G_1 \frac{1}{1 - x_1} \geq \lambda_{s2} G_2 \\
W_u &= \lambda_{u3} G_3 \frac{1}{1 - x_3} \geq \lambda_{u2} G_2.
\end{aligned}
\tag{16}
$$

Assuming, again, that G is generated by a Cobb-Douglas function and the economy is at full employment, the skilled/unskilled relative wage in Zone I (in which there are no skilled workers in job 2) is

$$
R = \frac{W_s}{W_u} = \frac{\alpha_1}{1 - \alpha_2} \left(\frac{S}{U} \frac{1 - x_1}{1 - x_3} \right)^{-1}.
\tag{17}
$$

An increase in the subsidy rate for skilled workers in job 1 raises R. Equal subsidy rates for jobs 1 and 2 would obviously have no effect on R.[11]

In Zone II, however, subsidies on the employment of S_1 or U_3 have no effect on the skilled/unskilled relative wage, for, given that neither inequality in equation 15 is satisfied, $R = \lambda_{s2}/\lambda_{u2}$. An increase in x_1 causes S_1 to rise above its optimal value (and thus causes U_2 to be too high and U_3 to be too low), but it does not change the proportions of the total wage bill going to each type of labor.

6.   A More General Specification of the Basic Model

The simple model set out in section 2 is based on the assumption that there are only three "jobs" in the economy. An alternative to this is to assume that there is a continuum of jobs. In this section, we make this modification and see how the major implications of the simple specification are altered.

Instead of $G(E_1, E_2, E_3)$ in equation 1, it is assumed instead that there are θ jobs. The aggregate flow of labor services is generated by

$$\log G = \log \theta + \frac{1}{\theta} \int_0^\theta \log E(j)dj. \tag{18}$$

$E(j)$ is the effective flow of labor services in job j, and this is given by

$$E(j) = \eta(j)S(j) + U(j). \tag{19}$$

$\eta(j)$ is the relative productivity of skilled workers in job j, and it is assumed that its value is η_0 at $j = 0$ and that it declines monotonically with j until $j = \omega\theta < \theta$, after which η is uniformly equal to one (skilled and unskilled workers are equally productive).[12]

A parametric assumption that is consistent with this story is

$$\eta(j) = \eta_0^{1-\frac{j}{\omega\theta}}, \; j < \omega\theta$$
$$\eta(j) = 1, \qquad j > \omega\theta. \tag{20}$$

The parameters η_0 and ω represent the distribution of comparative advantage parameters across jobs. The distribution is represented geometrically in figure 3. An increase in η_0 causes the $\eta(j)$ distribution to rotate up from

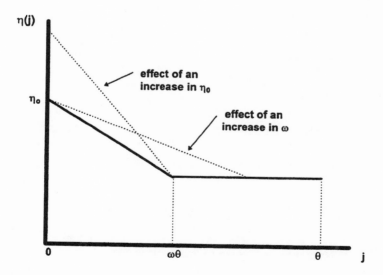

Fig. 3. The distribution of relative productivity across the θ jobs in the economy

its value at $j = 1$. An increase in ω causes the distribution to rotate up from its initial value at $j = 0$. The increase in η_0 is analogous to an increase in λ_{s1} in the three-job model—skilled workers getting better at what they normally do. The increase in ω is analogous to an increase in λ_{s2}—skilled workers getting better at jobs they formally did not hold. We refer to an increase in η_0 as *skill-intensive technological change* and an increase in ω as *skill-extensive technological change.*

It is assumed that the aggregate supplies of skilled and unskilled labor (S and U, respectively) are such that the equilibrium skilled/unskilled relative wage, $R = W_s/W_u$, is greater than one. The first $a\theta$ jobs are filled by skilled workers, and the remaining $(1 - a)\theta$ jobs are filled by the unskilled. The assumption that there is an internal solution means that $a\theta < 1$. (If this were not so, R would equal to one.) Since $j = a\theta$ is the dividing line between the use of skilled and unskilled labor, $R = \eta(a\theta)$. The marginal condition for each skilled job is $W_s = (1/\theta)G/S(j)$, and for each unskilled job $W_u = (1/\theta)G/U(j)$. Since $S(j) = S/a\theta$ and $U(j) = U/(1 - a)\theta$, the skilled and unskilled wage rates are given by

$$W_s = a \frac{G}{S}$$

(21)

$$W_u = (1 - a) \frac{G}{U}.$$

The skilled/unskilled relative wage satisfies

$$R = \frac{a}{1 - a} \left(\frac{S}{U} \right)^{-1} = \eta_0^{1 - a/\omega}.$$

(22)

The values of the endogenous variables, a and R, are determined by the two parts of equation 20 as functions of the exogenous variables S/U, η_0, and ω. In proportional change terms, these are

$$\hat{a} = \frac{1}{\Delta} \left[\hat{S} - \hat{U} + \left(1 - \frac{a}{\omega} \right) \hat{\eta}_0 + \frac{a}{\omega} \log \eta_0 \hat{\omega} \right]$$

(23)

and

$$\hat{R} = \frac{1}{(1 - a)\Delta} \left[-\frac{a(1 - a)}{\omega} \log \eta_0 (\hat{S} - \hat{U}) + \left(1 - \frac{a}{\omega} \right) \hat{\eta}_0 + \frac{a}{\omega} \log \eta_0 \hat{\omega} \right],$$

(24)

where

$$\Delta = \frac{1}{1-a} + \frac{a}{\omega}\log\eta_0 > 0.$$

These results imply that skilled labor's share of total labor earning, a, rises with S/U, η_0, and ω and that the skilled/unskilled relative wage, R, falls with S/U and rises with the two technology parameters.

It is interesting to note that the absolute elasticity of substitution between skilled and unskilled labor is

$$\sigma = -\frac{\partial \log\left(\frac{S}{U}\right)}{\partial \log R} = 1 + \frac{\omega}{a(1-a)\log \eta_0}. \tag{25}$$

This is, despite the Cobb-Douglas form of equation 17, greater than one. The reason for this is that an increase in S/U shifts the relative supply function to the right, but it also increases the share parameter, a, such that the relative demand function also shifts to the right (although by a smaller amount). This is distinct from a specification in which the share parameters are technological constants (say, α instead of a), in which case σ would be equal to one.

7. Implications of the More General Specification

What happens to the average level and the distribution of labor earnings in response to the two types of technological change involving skilled labor, the intensive (an increase in η_0) and the extensive (an increase in ω) varieties?

It is first necessary to discern the effects of changes in S, U, η_0, and ω on the aggregate level of earnings. Substituting equations 18 and 19 and the solution values of $S(j)$ and $U(j)$ into equation 17, the solution value of G is seen to equal

$$\log G = \frac{1}{\theta}\int_0^{a\theta}\left(1 - \frac{j}{\omega}\right)\log \eta_0 dj + a \log S$$

$$+(1-a)\log U - a\log a - (1-a)\log(1-a). \tag{26}$$

The solution value of the proportional change in a depends on changes in S/U, η_0, and ω according to equation 22. It then follows that the proportional change in G is

$$\hat{G} = a\hat{S} + (1-a)\hat{U} + a\left(1 - \frac{a}{2\omega}\right)\hat{\eta}_0 + \frac{a^2}{2\omega}\log \eta_0\hat{\omega}. \tag{27}$$

This implies that (not surprisingly) increases in both types of labor as well as both types of technical change increase aggregate labor earnings and output.

Now consider the effect on the skilled/unskilled relative wage of an increase in η_0 or ω per unit increase in total labor earnings. This is found by dividing the relevant coefficient in equation 23 by its equivalent in equation 26. For intensive technical change, this is

$$\frac{\dfrac{\partial(\log R)}{\partial(\log \eta_0)}}{\dfrac{\partial(\log G)}{\partial(\log \eta_0)}} = \frac{1 - \dfrac{a}{\omega}}{a(1 - a)\Delta\left(1 - \dfrac{a}{2\omega}\right)}, \tag{28}$$

and for extensive technical change it is

$$\frac{\dfrac{\partial(\log R)}{\partial(\log \omega)}}{\dfrac{\partial(\log G)}{\partial(\log \omega)}} = \frac{2}{a(1 - a)\Delta}. \tag{29}$$

The value of equation 28 is greater than the value of equation 27, which means that R is more sensitive to extensive than to intensive technical change.

The real wage rate of unskilled workers is $W_u = (1 - a)G/U$. Changes in both types of technology cause G to increase and $1 - a$ to decrease, and the specific effects are

$$\hat{W}_u = \frac{a^2}{(1 - a)\Delta}\left[\frac{1}{2\omega} + \left(1 - \frac{a}{2\omega}\right)\frac{1 - a}{2\omega}\log \eta_0\right]\hat{\eta}_0$$

$$+ \frac{a^2 \log \eta_0}{2(1 - a)\Delta\omega}\left[\frac{a(1 - a)}{\omega}\log \eta_0 - 1\right]\hat{\omega}. \tag{30}$$

The coefficient on the proportional change in η_0 is positive, which means that intensive technical change benefits unskilled as well as skilled workers (although the latter more than the former). The coefficient on the proportional change in ω, however, is of ambiguous sign. Indeed, $\partial W_u/\partial\omega$ is negative unless $\log R > (\omega - a)/a(1 - a)$. For example, if $\omega = 0.5$ and $a = .25$ (skilled workers have a comparative advantage in half of the jobs economy but full only a quarter of them), $\log R$ would have to equal at least 1.33 in order for an increase in ω not to lower W_u. This corresponds to a skilled/unskilled relative wage of almost four.

8. Evidence of Shifting Technology Regimes and Subsidies

In this section, we offer some evidence for the hypothesis of a technology shift favoring more skilled workers in sectors that previously were a primary domain of less-skilled workers. That this can shift toward more skilled workers can be seen in manufacturing in the United States. To illustrate a case in point, in 1978, the year before the second oil shock, there was a strong automobile market in the United States. The Dodge Main plant in Detroit, Michigan, admittedly a plant due for replacement, had total employment of about 18,000. As the oil shock and the ensuing recession played themselves out, the plant was closed. The site remained idle until the mid-1980s, when in its place the new General Motors (GM) Poletown Assembly Plant was put into operation. The new plant had a capacity fairly close to that of the old Dodge Main, but it had total employment of about 3,000, and this smaller employment had a higher percentage of highly trained workers.

Another feature of manufacturing in the United States and the other advanced industrial economies has been the trend toward smaller firms. These smaller firms are dependent on a set of suppliers external to the firm. To illustrate, GM remains a large manufacturing firm, but it relies on external engineering services in an amount in the range of $1 billion per year. This indirect dependence on skilled workers to produce manufacturing output (the Bill Gates effect) is the type of skill-biased technical change we have in mind.

What about direct employment in manufacturing? Utilizing data from the Current Population Surveys, 1973–88, table 1 shows the percentage employment shares in durable manufacturing by education and years of experience. For men, over the period there was a clear reduction in the share of less educated (high school and less than high school) at the different levels of potential work experience. For college and more, there was a modest rise in the share employed in manufacturing (except for those with 10 to 19 years of potential work experience). That is, despite the declining share of employment directly in manufacturing, there was a rise in the percentage of workers with college and more in manufacturing. (A similar pattern holds for nondurable manufacturing; see table 2.) We suspect that this understates the growing role of skilled workers in manufacturing, since they would also show up as a large portion of the labor force of business service providers outside the direct manufacturing sector.[13]

We regard the rising employment of women in manufacturing as part of the shift toward skilled workers in sectors far more heavily dependent on less-skilled workers in the past. As demonstrated in tables 1 and 2, the employment of women with college or more education in manufacturing has risen strongly over the period 1973–88, particularly for those with less

TABLE 1. Percentage of Employment Shares in Durable Manufacturing by Education and Years of Potential Work Experience, 1973 and 1988

	Less Than High School				High School Graduates				Some College				College or More			
	0–9	10–19	20–29	30+	0–9	10–19	20–29	30+	0–9	10–19	20–29	30+	0–9	10–19	20–29	30+
Men																
1973	26.3	29.1	30.8	30.1	27.7	27.7	25.2	24.2	19.5	24.2	21.1	23.4	12.2	15.7	16.1	14.6
1988	15.7	23.9	25.5	25.6	16.8	22.2	23.6	23.6	12.4	18.7	19.9	21.1	14.0	15.5	16.4	18.4
Women																
1973	14.9	21.0	16.3	14.6	12.2	12.7	11.2	9.6	7.5	8.8	6.1	6.4	2.7	1.0	1.8	1.7
1988	8.4	14.6	14.7	14.1	7.8	10.6	10.3	9.2	6.2	6.9	7.3	5.2	5.7	4.3	4.2	2.4

Source: Current Population Surveys, 1973 and 1988.

TABLE 2. Percentage of Employment Shares in Nondurable Manufacturing by Education and Years of Potential Work Experience, 1973 and 1988

	Less Than High School				High School Graduates				Some College				College or More			
	0–9	10–19	20–29	30+	0–9	10–19	20–29	30+	0–9	10–19	20–29	30+	0–9	10–19	20–29	30+
Men																
1973	14.2	13.4	13.6	13.9	12.1	12.5	12.8	13.2	8.7	10.6	10.0	10.4	7.7	9.4	7.8	9.3
1988	10.9	12.0	12.5	12.3	9.4	10.7	12.1	12.3	6.6	8.5	8.5	9.0	7.2	7.1	7.6	8.1
Women																
1973	26.7	24.7	25.5	24.1	11.7	11.8	9.7	9.0	6.0	6.2	5.0	6.3	3.1	2.0	0.8	1.1
1988	14.3	20.4	20.7	18.7	7.6	10.1	9.2	8.8	4.8	4.5	5.4	5.4	5.9	3.6	2.6	2.0

Source: Current Population Surveys, 1973 and 1988.

than 30 years of potential work experience. This pattern is consistent with the recent study on closing the gender gap in Swedish manufacturing, 1913–90 (Svensson 1995). As the technology has shifted to favor skill, the relative productivity of women should grow, thereby improving their relative wages. As he points out, over the longer run the ratio of female to male hourly wages in Swedish manufacturing rose from .58 in 1913 to .89 in 1990. From the perspective of our hypothesis, it was during the IT era, the mid-1960's to 1990, that the ratio rose from approximately .70 to .90 (Svensson 1995, 9).

The other factor shaping labor markets, subsidized production of output in the skill-intensive sectors, can be seen as a type of collective frustration with the slow productivity in those service sectors. In the United States, there has been a dramatic change in the share of GDP devoted to medicine, rising from just over 5 percent in 1960 to nearly 15 percent today. At the same time, the percentage of health expenditures paid directly by recipients has fallen from over half in 1960 to about 20 percent in 1990 (Fuchs 1993). The real per pupil expenditure for K–12 schooling relative to the earning of a 40-year-old male high school graduate has risen steadily, from .060 in 1960 to .189 in 1990 (Johnson and Stafford 1996a). Because of these subsidies to the low-productivity sector, we can expect that an economic slowdown (declining average real wages) may occur even though the economy is otherwise subject to a form of technical progress: skill-biased technical change. A closer empirical assessment is called for, examining evidence from various industrialized economies.

NOTES

We thank William Baumol, Gunnar Eliasson, and Sidney Winter for comments on an earlier draft. Research support from the Alfred P. Sloan Foundation is gratefully acknowledged.

1. During the period 1939–59, the wage distribution in the United States was compressed substantially (Goldin and Margo 1992).

2. The rationale for this is found in the unbalanced growth literature (Baumol 1967, Keynes 1933). Here economic growth provides income effects toward the service sector, but the slow productivity there creates political pressure to subsidize the output. This may be done either by creating employment there or, as in the United States, by introducing consumption subsidies.

3. The Cobb-Douglas assumption is adopted for expositional convenience. The principal results that follow also apply to a more general functional form such as that of a constant elasticity of substitution (CES).

4. If, instead, it had been assumed that G is generated by a CES, that is,

$$G = \left[\sum_i \delta_i E_i^{\frac{\sigma-1}{\sigma}} \right]^{\frac{\sigma}{\sigma-1}},$$

where σ is the elasticity of intrafactor substitution. The skilled/unskilled relative wage in Zone I is

$$R = \frac{W_s}{W_u} = \frac{\delta_1 \lambda_{s1}^{1-1/\sigma}}{\delta_3 \lambda_{u3}^{1-1/\sigma} + \delta_2 \lambda_{u2}^{1-1/\sigma}} \left(\frac{S}{U}\right)^{-1/\sigma}$$

If $\sigma > 1$, an increase in λ_{s1} increases R, and increases in λ_{u2} and λ_{u3} decrease R. In Zone II, however, R is equal to $\lambda_{s2}/\lambda_{u2}$, as in the Cobb-Douglas case.

5. In his very useful summary of research on European unemployment, Bean (1994) suggests that both of these are sources of the *perpetuation* of the effects of previous shocks on unemployment rather than the initiating factors.

6. This social policy could be accomplished with direct government control over wages through legislation, by permitting and encouraging trade unions, or some combination of both.

7. This value is

$$R = \frac{\alpha_1}{1 - \alpha_1} \left(\frac{S}{U}\right)^{-1}.$$

If R_* were equal to this, equation 11 would equal the value of G in equation 6.

8. In reality, of course, it would take some time for such an adjustment to occur—especially given the nature of protective labor regulations in most European countries. Further, most of the adjustment would be experienced by young, unskilled labor.

9. An alternative way of considering this is to think of the three Es as being individual goods produced by Ricardian production functions, $E_i = \lambda_{si} S_i + \lambda_{ui} U_i$. The subsidies are in this case on the goods rather than directly on the factors producing them, but the effect of the subsidies is strictly analogous to a subsidization of S_i and/or U_3.

10. It is assumed that the subsidy is financed by a proportional tax on labor earnings in all three jobs and that this has no effect on labor supply.

11. However, a positive subsidy rate would be inefficient in the sense that G is less than it would be without the subsidy if it affects the allocation of U and/or S among the three jobs. In Zone I, $x_3 > 0$ is inefficient because it causes a shift of Us from job 2 to job 3, but x_1 is not inefficient because it affects the *distribution* of G but not its level.

12. The model could easily be developed with productivity distributions for the Us as well as the Ss in the θ jobs, but this does not add very much to the analysis.

13. These and similar phenomena have been termed "upskilling" and the substitution of knowledge for data and goods workers by, respectively, Collechia and Papaconstantinou (1996) and Wolff (1996). The empirical analysis of the first of these papers refers to a wide range of OECD countries.

REFERENCES

Aoki, Masahiko. 1988. *Information, Incentives, and Bargaining in the Japanese Economy.* Cambridge: Cambridge University Press.

Baumol, William J. 1967. "Macroeconomics of Unbalanced Growth: The Anatomy of Urban Crisis." *American Economic Review* 57 (June): 415–26.

Bean, Charles R. 1994. "European Unemployment: A Survey." *Journal of Economic Literature* 32 (June): 573–619.

Berman, Eli, John Bound, and Zvi Grilliches. 1994. "Changes in the Demand for Skilled Labor within U.S. Manufacturing: Evidence from the Annual Survey of Manufacturers." *Quarterly Journal of Economics* 109, no. 2 (May): 367–97.

Bernstein, Jeffrey I., and M. Ishaq Nadiri. 1989. "Research and Development and Intra-Industry Spillovers: An Empirical Application of Dynamic Duality." *Review of Economic Studies* 56; 249–69.

Bound, John, and George Johnson. 1992. "Changes in the Structure of Wages during the 1980's: An Evaluation of Alternative Explanations." *American Economic Review* 82, (June): 371–92.

Brezis, Elise S., Paul R. Krugman, and Daniel Tsiddon. 1993. "Leapfrogging in International Competition: A Theory of Cycles in National Technological Leadership." *American Economic Review* 83 (Dec.): 1211–19.

Carlsson, Bo. 1983. "Industrial Subsidies in Sweden: Macro-Economic Effects and an International Comparison." *Journal of Industrial Economics* 32 (Sept.): 9–14.

Collechia, A., and G. Papaconstantinou. 1996. "The Evolution of Skills in OECD Countries and the Evolution of Skill." Economic Analysis and Statistics Division, OECD, June. Mimeo.

Davis, Steven J. 1992. "Cross-Country Patterns of Change in Relative Wages." In *1992 Macroeconomics Annual,* edited by Olivier Blanchard and Stanley Fischer. National Bureau of Economic Research. Cambridge, MA: MIT Press.

Dollar, David, and Edward N. Wolff. 1988. "Convergence of Industry Labor Productivity Among Advanced Economics, 1963–1982." *Review of Economics and Statistics* 70, no. 4 (Nov.): 549–58.

Eklund, Klas, et al. 1993. "Sweden's Economic Crisis: Diagnosis and Cure." Occasional Papers, no. 42. SNS Economic Policy Group, February. Mimeo.

Eliasson, Gunnar. 1989. *Technological Competition and Trade in the Experimentally Organized Economy.* Stockholm: Industrial Institute for Economic and Social Research.

Fuchs, Victor. 1993. "Health Care Cost Containment: No Pain, No Gain." *Economic Times* 4 (Mar.): 4–7.

Goldin, Claudia, and Robert A. Margo. 1992. "The Great Compression: The Wage Structure in the United States at Mid-Century." *Quarterly Journal of Economics* 107 (Feb.): 1–34.

Gomory, Ralph E. 1994. "A Ricardo Model with Economies of Scale." *Journal of Economic Theory* 62 (Apr.): 394–419.

Gomory, Ralph E., and William J. Baumol. 1997. "Productivity Differences, World Market Shares, and Conflicting National Interests in Linear Trade Models." *Japan and the World Economy* 9, no. 2 (May): 123–50.

Griliches, Zvi. 1988. "Productivity Puzzles and R and D: Another Nonexplanation." *Journal of Economic Perspectives* 4 (Fall): 9–21.

Hicks, J. R. 1953. "An Inaugural Lecture, 2: The Dollar Problem." *Oxford Economic Papers* 5, no. 2 (June): 117–35.

Johnson, George E., and Frank P. Stafford. 1992. "Models of International Competition and Real Wages." Department of Economics, University of Michigan, July. Mimeo.

———. 1993. "International Competition and Real Wages." *American Economic Review Papers and Proceedings* 83, no. 2 (May): 127–30.

———. 1996a. "On the Rate of Return to Schooling Quality." *Review of Economics and Statistics* 78, no. 4 (Nov.): 686–91.

———. 1996b. "Productivity Differences, World Market Shares and Conflicting National Interests in Linear Trade Models: Comments." *Japan and the World Economy* 9:151–58.

Jones, Ronald W., and J. Peter Neary. 1984. "The Positive Theory of International Trade." In *Handbook of International Trade,* edited by R. W. Jones and P. B. Kenen. Vol. 1. Amsterdam: Elsevier.

Keynes, John Maynard. 1933. "National Self-Sufficiency." *Yale Review* 22, no. 4 (June): 755–69.

Klodt, Henning. 1992. "Technology Based Trade and Multinational Investment in Europe: Structural Change and Competition in Schumpeterian Goods." In *Multinationals in the New Europe and Global Trade,* edited by Michael W. Klein and Paul J. J. Welfens. Berlin and Heidelberg: Springer-Verlag.

Kravis, Irving B., and Robert E. Lipsey. 1992. "Sources of Competitiveness of the United States and of Its Multinational Firms." *Review of Economics and Statistics* 74, no. 2 (May): 193–201.

Krueger, Alan B., 1993. "How Computers Have Changed the Wage Structure: Evidence from Microdata, 1984–1989." *Quarterly Journal of Economics* 108:33–60.

Krugman, Paul. 1979. "A Model of Innovation, Technology Transfer, and the World Distribution of Income." *Journal of Political Economy* 87 (Apr.): 253–66.

Lawrence, Robert Z., and Barry P. Bosworth. 1987. "Adjusting to Slower Economic Growth: The External Sector." In *The Swedish Economy,* edited by Barry P. Bosworth and Alice M. Rivlin. Washington, DC: Brookings Institution.

Lindbeck, Assar, et al. 1993. "Options for Economic and Political Reform in Sweden." *Economic Policy* 8, no. 17 (Oct.): 220–63.

Lundberg, Erik. 1985. "The Rise and Fall of the Swedish Model." *Journal of Economic Literature* 23 (Mar.): 1–36.

Pencavel, John, and Bertil Holmlund. 1988. "The Determination of Wages, Employment, and Work Hours in an Open Economy with Centralized Wage Setting: Sweden, 1950–1988." *Economic Journal* 98 (Dec.): 1105–26.

Stafford, Frank P. 1988. "Erosion of Advanced Country Rents, Insurance, and System Solvency." *Carnegie-Rochester Conference Series on Public Policy, Stabilization Policy and Labor Markets* 28 (Spring): 221–30.

Svensson, Lars. 1995. *Closing the Gender Gap: Determinants of Change in the Female-Male Blue Collar Wage Ration in Swedish Manufacturing.* Lund: Lund University Dept. of Economic History.

Topel Robert, and Dae-Il Kim. 1992. "Labor Markets and Economic Growth: Lessons from Korea's Industrialization, 1970–1990." University of Chicago, April. Mimeo.

Vernon, Raymond. 1966. "International Trade and International Trade in the Product Cycle, No. 2." *Quarterly Journal of Economics* 80, no. 2 (May): 190–207.

———. 1979. "The Product Cycle Hypothesis in a New International Environment." *Oxford Bulletin of Economics and Statistics* 41 (Nov.): 255–67.

Wolff, Edward N. 1996. "The Growth of Information Workers in the U.S. Economy, 1950–1990: The Role of Technological Change, Computerization, and Structural Change." New York University, June. Mimeo.

Wright, Gavin. 1990. "The Origins of American Industrial Success, 1879–1940." *American Economic Review* 80, no. 4 (Sept.): 651–68.

Corporate Restructuring, Technological Change, and the Distribution of Labor Income

Dagobert L. Brito, Michael D. Intriligator, and Erica R. Worth

1. Introduction: The Puzzle of Corporate Restructuring

Corporate restructuring is a recent phenomenon in many major firms. Many major corporations have either already undergone restructuring or will be doing so soon. This phenomenon, while it is largely ignored by economists, does raise some interesting questions and important issues. The purpose of this essay is to identify these issues and propose a formal model for analyzing them.

There is a puzzle in corporate restructuring. When a corporation undergoes restructuring, it will reduce its work force considerably, often letting go thousands of workers. Typically, however, there is little if any change in the output or sales of the firm. In some cases, output has actually increased. The result has been an increase in profits and productivity. If, however, workers are let go with little if any change in output, then these workers must have a minimal marginal product, since usually there are few if any changes in the other inputs to the production process. There then arises the puzzle as to why the firm employed them at all. By all standard economic theories, a firm would never hire a worker with a zero marginal product. This puzzle is addressed by relating it to another puzzle, that of the productivity slowdown.

2. The Puzzle of the Productivity Slowdown

The puzzle of apparent zero marginal product of labor in corporate restructuring can be related to another puzzle, that of the productivity slowdown of the 1970s and 1980s. These two puzzles are juxtaposed since each can be used to help solve the other. The productivity puzzle involves the slowdown in the growth of productivity in the United States and other countries in this period despite the introduction of many innovations in technology, any one of which should have increased productivity. Productivity had been rising consistently in the earlier decades.[1] The technological innovations that

369

were introduced should have increased the growth of productivity, but instead the rate of growth slowed considerably.[2] The technological innovations of this period included the introduction of computers in general use throughout the economy, which should have had, by itself, significant effects on productivity. This period also included the introduction of robots and automated systems, the development of new managerial techniques such as just-in-time inventory systems, and many other new management science or operations research developments. Any of these developments should have increased productivity, yet productivity was stagnant in this period, the result being what has come to be known as the "productivity puzzle."

3. Implicit Contracts

There is an interpretation of the productivity slowdown that helps to explain it and also helps to explain the later corporate restructuring. This interpretation involves implicit contracts between employers and their employees.[3] Under this theory, firms had an implicit contract with their workers as to the profile of their lifetime earnings. Initially, in the first stage of their employment life cycle, workers were paid more than their marginal product, as this is the time when they acquire human capital. In the second stage of their employment life cycle, workers were paid less than their marginal product. Finally, in the third stage of their employment life cycle, workers age and their marginal product drops; however, the firm did not decrease the wages of workers. This implicit contract was based on the expectation that the time of retirement of workers was determined. It had properties that created incentives that were both beneficial to the firm and attractive to the worker.

Initially, the new technology created quasi rents and firms were able to honor their existing implicit contracts. In the later 1980s and 1990s, however, there were two developments that led to the breakdown of this institution. First, as would be expected, quasi rents began to be eliminated and marginal firms were forced to reduce employment. Second, in the United States the 1988 Age Discrimination in Employment Act created ambiguities as to the terms of the implicit contract as firms became uncertain as to their liability in the third stage of the employment life cycle.[4] The General Accounting Office has reported that 80 percent of the Fortune 500 companies had some form of early retirement plan by 1989.

Eventually, these implicit contracts between employers and their employees were broken under the pressure of competition. The initial corporations to break these implicit contracts were the weak ones, which found that they could only stay in business if they restructured their labor force to eliminate nonproductive workers. The idea caught on among other weak firms, which did the same. The breaking of the implicit contracts of lifetime employment by the weak firms provided a type of signal to all firms, whether weak or strong and whether large or small, that these implicit contracts could be broken. The result was that productivity began to rise. Implicit contracts can thus be used to explain both the puzzle of restructuring and the puzzle of the productivity slowdown.

As a result of this corporate restructuring, major corporations have eliminated nonproductive workers, resulting in increases in output, productivity, and profits. Offsetting these positive developments are some negative ones, however. Jobs are being created either at the bottom of the corporate pyramid for unskilled workers in occupations where automation is difficult or at the very top of this pyramid where automation is again difficult and very few jobs are available. Thus, technology is changing in a fashion that has led to a distribution of income that is becoming more unequal.

4. Changes in the Distribution of Labor Income

Technology is changing in such a way that information has become relatively more important as a factor of production. Given the public-good nature of information, goods where information is an important component will have a cost structure characterized by high fixed costs and very low marginal costs. The fixed cost of production is the cost of producing the information necessary for the production process, while the marginal cost is the cost of the raw materials and necessary labor. This type of technology creates policy problems for the distribution of income in both developed and less developed countries.

Recent evidence in the United States suggests that technological change is leading to a less equal distribution of income. In the last decade, only the top 20 percent of the U.S. labor force has had an increase in their share of real pretax income, and, even within that group, most of the increase has been in the top 5 percent.[5] There is the growing gap in the United States between the earnings of college graduates and high school graduates. An increasing number of jobs once filled by high school graduates, for example, now require some college training or even a college degree.

The fundamental problem is not productivity. In real terms, GNP per capita is greater that it has ever been. At the end of World War II, the United States was the only country whose industrial infrastructure was undamaged by war. For the two decades that followed the end of the war, the United States was the dominant economic and technological power in the world. American workers enjoyed the fruits of that dominance. They shared in the economic rents that were the result of postwar conditions. The resulting distribution of income supported a prosperous blue-collar middle class. As Robert Reich, former U.S. Secretary of Labor, has observed:

> By the mid-1950s, almost half of all American families fell comfortably within this middle-class group. . . . Notably, most of these middle-class families were headed not by professionals or business executives but by skilled and semiskilled factory workers and clerks, who managed the flow of products and paperwork through the great corporations.
>
> The prosperity and growth of America's middle class was one of American capitalism's great triumphs for which the core American corporation could claim significant credit.[6]

In more recent years, the American economy has been viewed as declining, with increased inequality. Europe and Japan have rebuilt their economies and now compete with American workers on an even footing. Furthermore, the technology that was once the exclusive property of a few developed nations has spread to the rest of the world. The workers in these countries can now compete with American workers in many markets that once were the source of well-paid employment for Americans exclusively. In spite of these changes in the global economy, Americans are richer now than in the halcyon days of the 1950s. Census data suggest that over 80 percent of American families in 1992 have access to more goods and services than did the fortunate middle class of 1950. Furthermore, the increase in the goods and services available to consumers relative to 1950 is understated in that the Consumer Price Index (CPI) does not capture improvements in quality.

Is there more inequality, however? The income distribution in 1970 was relatively more equal, but the income distribution in 1950 and 1992 was essentially the same.[7] The argument could be made that the income distribution of the late 1960s was the result of government policy that could not be sustained. The reason for the increase in inequality in the period from 1970 to 1990 is a subject of some dispute among economists, with four, not mutually exclusive, candidates for the change in the distribution of income. They are: (1) the decline of the manufacturing sector, partly due to foreign trade; (2) the decline in the power of unions; (3) changes in the demographic composition of the population following the baby boom; and (4) technological change. Bound and Johnson (1992) have analyzed these changes and concluded that the major cause was an increase in the demand for high-skilled labor brought about by biased technological change. Thus, the econometric evidence is consistent with both the anecdotal evidence and various case studies that suggest that technological change has not only been eliminating good jobs but has also led to increased income inequality that is not yet reflected in the census data.

This technological change may in time result in a distribution of income that is very different from what is politically desirable. Explicit redistribution of income is in many ways foreign to the American ethos, but implicit redistribution through education and training is not only acceptable but desirable. The idea that investing in human capital can be used to change the distribution of income is an attractive one that has been embraced on both sides of the political spectrum. In the American culture, it is hard to be against education. However, the resulting redistribution of income may not be acceptable. Evidence on this point is at best mixed. There is a high return to education, with the college graduate earning more than twice as much as a person who does not finish high school and one and one-half as much as a high school graduate.[8] However, efforts to measure the value of a college education have problems with what is known as a "self-selection" bias. One would expect that individuals who are more able are more likely to go to college, so it is difficult, if not impossible, to separate that portion of the higher earnings of college graduates that is due to their education from the portion that is attributable to their higher ability. Inasmuch as there is a substantial ability component in the higher income, the rate of return to human capital in the form of education must be corrected. If, in addition, there is an interaction between native ability and efficiency in acquiring human capital, then this rate of return must be further corrected. It may not be economically feasible to use investment in human capital as a means of correcting the distribution of income. There may be no level of educational expenditure that would be sufficient to endow a substantial fraction of the population with the ability to perform the tasks necessary to earn the level of income that was once earned in manufacturing.

When the question of the displacement of labor by new technology is discussed, there is a natural predilection to find comfort in the Industrial Revolution. Contemporary fears notwithstanding, labor was not displaced by the introduction of the new technology in the long run. However, Rome in the second century B.C. may be a better historical comparison. Slavery became an important factor in the Roman economy after the Punic Wars. Free labor was not able to compete with slave labor. Although it may seem strange in the context of the twentieth century to think of the introduction of the institution of slavery as technological change, slaves did compete with free workers and displaced them. Functionally, this was no different than replacing workers today. The introduction of the institution of slavery created a class of economically redundant workers with political power. This is a class that the historian R. E. Smith describes as "the *plebs urbana* [which] was allowed to continue its aimless existence as the pampered drone of the Rome world."[9] The Roman solution was later known as "bread and circuses." The machines that were introduced in the nineteenth century required labor and thus were a complementary factor of production, while slave labor was a substitute for free labor. A similar observation was made by Norbert Wiener: "The automatic machine is the precise economic equivalent of slave labor. Any labor that competes with slave labor must accept the economic consequences of slave labor."[10]

Technological change does not occur in a vacuum. Companies introduce new technology to make money. They are most likely to look at those portions of their production processes where costs are high, so it is not an accident that high-paying jobs are being replaced by low-paying jobs. The first priority of a company trying to become more competitive is unlikely to be the elimination of low-paying jobs. If workers at McDonald's and other fast food restaurants were well paid, it is likely that someone would automate the making of hamburgers. Even if technological changes were to result in the substitution of skilled high-paying jobs for unskilled low-paying jobs, the employment effects may not be beneficial. Substituting skilled labor for unskilled labor is efficient only if it reduces costs. Holding output constant, creating a 15-dollar-per-hour job is economical only if it eliminates at least three five-dollar-per-hour jobs. An optimist might argue that output will not remain constant, and one of the benefits of increased efficiency is an increase in output. This may be true, but a threefold increase is very optimistic.

Likely candidates for elimination are jobs that require highly skilled and highly paid workers, but only where the job can be reduced to a series of well-defined steps. In other words, the best candidates for elimination are those jobs that can be reduced to algorithms. These jobs can be eliminated or modified so that high-skilled workers can be replaced by less-skilled and less well paid workers or by machines. Reich's dichotomy of the work force between symbolic analysts and others is misleading. It is easy to forget that one of the first skills that was eliminated by electronic computers was that of human computation.[11] Elaborate numerical computations that once challenged Richard Feynman or Hans Bethe can now be done by a student on a throwaway calculator. What is important is that the process by which these calculations are done can be reduced to an algorithm that can be implemented by a machine. Many of the tasks in inventory management and scheduling that formerly required high-skilled individuals can now be performed by computers. Many of the middle-management jobs involving complicated tasks that could be reduced to algorithms have already been eliminated.

5.   Microeconomics of Technical Change

We develop a very simple model of an economy with two types of workers that can be used to analyze technological change and restructuring. We interpret the two types of workers as "skilled" and "unskilled," but we use these terms in a very specific way. Skilled workers are those whose jobs cannot be programmed, that is, replaced by a computer or a robot, while unskilled workers are those whose jobs can be so programmed. Thus, for example, a nurse would be skilled, while a master machine operator, who can be replaced by a computer-controlled machine, would, in our terminology, be unskilled, even though operating a machine tool may require a considerable amount of human capital.

Many tasks that can be reduced to algorithms can be performed by machines, and it is possible to derive the relationship between the wage of workers that perform those tasks in the old technology and the cost of producing the new technology. This expression is essentially a variation of the Samuelson rule for the provision of public goods, which states that the marginal cost of the public good should equal the sum of the marginal benefits across individuals.

The upper bound of the wage for the labor that can be reduced to an algorithm is less than or equal to the cost of developing the new technology divided by the amount of labor it replaces times the interest rate. The constant depends on the relative capital cost of the two technologies, and, a priori, there is no reason to expect that one technology will be more capital intensive than the other.

Consider an activity that can be performed by two technologies. The first technology involves skilled labor $L_{\alpha 1}$, unskilled labor, $L_{\beta 1}$, and capital K_1, where the subscripts denote the type of labor and the technology. An output q_1 is produced by the process, where the subscript denotes the technology

$$q_1 = G_1(L_{\alpha 1}, L_{\beta 1}, K_1). \tag{5.1}$$

The second technology involves skilled labor, $L_{\alpha 2}$, capital K_2, and the public good Z,

$$q_2 = G_2(L_{\alpha 2}, K_2, Z), \tag{5.2}$$

where we assume for simplicity that the function, $G_2(L_{\alpha 2}, K_2, Z)$ is homogeneous of degree 1 in $L_{\alpha 2}$ and K_2.[12] The cost for the economy of providing a level of activity Q using the first technology is given by

$$V_1(Q) = \min N(w_\alpha L_{\alpha 1} + w_\beta L_{\beta 1} + rK_1) \tag{5.3}$$

subject to

$$Q = NG_1(L_{\alpha 1}, L_{\beta 1}, K_1), \tag{5.4}$$

where r is the interest rate, w is the wage rate, and N is the number of firms. The cost of providing the activity using the second technology is given by

$$V_2(Q) = \min N(w_\alpha L_{\alpha 2} + rK_2) + C(Z), \tag{5.5}$$

subject to

$$Q = NG_2(L_{\alpha 2}, K_2, Z), \tag{5.6}$$

where $C(Z)$ is the cost of providing the public good. Denoting the optimal value by $*$, if both activities are operated at the same level, then the difference in their cost is given by

$$\Delta V = w_\alpha N(L_{\alpha 2}^* - L_{\alpha 1}^*) - w_\beta NL_{\beta 1}^* + rN(K_2^* - K_1^*) + C(Z^*). \tag{5.7}$$

Solving for w_β^e, the highest β wage rate that is sustainable in equilibrium yields

$$w_\beta^e = \frac{w_\alpha N(L_{\alpha 2}^* - L_{\alpha 1}^*) + rN(K_2^* - K_1^*) + C(Z^*)}{NL_{\beta 1}^*}. \tag{5.8}$$

If the two technologies use the same amount of physical capital and skilled labor (since there is no reason to presume that one process is more intensive in these factors than the other), it is then optimal to change technologies at the point where the unskilled wage bill is greater than the cost of the new technology. This expression is essentially a variation of the Samuelson rule for the provision of public goods.

The decision faced by an individual firm is similar and differs only in that the firm is only concerned with its own inputs. The level of the public good is given to the firm. The cost function for the firm associated with the old technology is

$$v_1(q) = \min(w_\alpha L_{\alpha 1} + w_\beta L_{\beta 1} + rK_1), \tag{5.9}$$

subject to

$$q = G_1(L_{\alpha 1}, L_{\beta 1}, K_1), \tag{5.10}$$

while the cost function associated with the new technology is

$$v_2(q) = \min(w_\alpha L_{\alpha 2} + rK_2) + S(Z), \tag{5.11}$$

subject to

$$q = G_2(L_{\alpha 2}, K_2, Z), \tag{5.12}$$

where $S(Z)$ is the licensing fee to the firm of the new technology. The wage rate that will cause the firm to switch technologies is given by

$$w_\beta^s = \frac{w_\alpha(L_{\alpha 2}^* - L_{\alpha 1}^*) + r(K_2^* - K_1^*) + S(Z)}{L_{\beta 1}^*}. \tag{5.13}$$

This static formulation of the problem, however, masks two important factors. If the problem is formulated in an intertemporal framework, then the social cost is that associated with developing the public good, so the cost charged to individual producers should be zero. If the technology is developed privately and the users are homogeneous, the producer will charge them so as to appropriate all the rents. If there are limits to the duration of the rights to a patent, then there will be some additional complications. It may be that this limit will make the development of the new technology infeasible because the developer may not be able to recover the fixed costs. However, if it is feasible to develop the new technology with limited patent life, then the lower bound on the wage w_β will be the differential in other factor costs of the two processes since everyone will have free access to the public good after the patent expires.

6. Corporate Restructuring and Technological Change

A firm facing the choice of technology when it is a party to an implicit labor contract has to solve a nonconcave programming problem. The firm's cost function if it can use either technology is

$$v^*(q) = \min[w_\alpha(L_{\alpha 1} + L_{\alpha 2}) + w_\beta L_{\beta 1} + r(K_1 + K_2) + S(Z) + \delta(L_{\beta 1}, \bar{L}_{\beta 1}, \pi)], \tag{6.1}$$

subject to

$$q = G_1(L_{\alpha 1}, L_{\beta 1}, K_1) + G_2(L_{\alpha 2}, K_2, Z), \tag{6.2}$$

where $\delta(L_{\beta 1}, \bar{L}_{\beta 1}, \pi)$ is the cost to the firm of lowering employment in the old technology below the level $\bar{L}_{\beta 1}$. The cost to the firm depends on the behavior of all other firms in the industry. This is reflected by the parameter π. The implicit contract is reflected in the reduced productivity of unskilled labor. If π changes such that $\delta(L_{\beta 1}, \bar{L}_{\beta 1}, \pi) < w_\beta \bar{L}_{\beta 1}$, then the firm will change and use only the new technology. Given the public-good nature of Z, we would expect to see a large decrease in employment of unskilled workers with little change in output.

The implicit contract is viable in equilibrium only if it is subgame perfect. Before the introduction of the new technology, the implicit contract was subgame perfect because of two factors. First, it creates the correct initiatives for workers who have already invested in firm-specific human capital, and, second, it allows the firm to recruit new entrants into the work force. Technological change weakens the first factor directly in that it lowers the value of firm-specific human capital, as workers can be replaced by the second technology. Technological change weakens the second factor directly in that it lowers the value of unskilled workers. As more firms breach the implicit contract or stop offering implicit contracts to their work force, the reputational cost of breaching the implicit contract declines, creating a chain reaction leading to more and more breaches of the implicit contract.

7. A Two-Sector Model

In this section, we use a two-sector model to analyze the impacts of the introduction of the new technology on the distribution of income and the role of government in redistributing income. Among our results, we show that, if the wage of skilled labor in the new technology sector is sufficiently high, it is socially optimal to eliminate the old technology sector altogether. A historical example of such a change is modern agriculture. In the year 1920, some 27 percent of the U.S. labor force was employed directly in agriculture. The mechanization of agriculture led to the elimination of most unskilled workers from farming, with a migration of former farm workers to the cities, so now only 2 percent of the labor force is employed in agriculture. In many cases, this has resulted in high societal costs in terms of unemployment and the instability of families.

We address four questions here. First, what is the impact of the new technology on the distribution of income if there is no government intervention? Second, what is the impact of this new technology on output and aggregate welfare if there is no government intervention? Third, what is the impact of government intervention if government is restricted to an optimal income tax? Fourth, is it possible that the unskilled workers might become economically unemployable?

To analyze these questions, we develop a two-sector model that captures the stylized facts that we want to explore. As before, we assume that there are two types of workers, "skilled" and "unskilled," furnishing different types of labor and deriving utility from consumption and leisure. Skilled workers can furnish either skilled or unskilled labor, while unskilled workers can furnish only unskilled labor. In the initial technology, only labor is used in the production of the good and both types of workers enter the production process in a symmetric way. Assuming perfect competition, all individuals will consume identical bundles, yielding a first-best solution with no need for redistribution. We then introduce a new, information-based technology for which the skilled workers can produce the good without using any of the unskilled workers. In the new economy, there are two sectors using different technologies to produce the same good. The old technology uses both types of workers, while the new technology uses only skilled workers. Thus, both sectors produce a single good, but the sector using the new technology is specialized in that it employs only skilled workers. Skilled workers are free to move between the two sectors, while unskilled workers are not mobile. The two types of workers, α and β, are indexed by i, where $i = \alpha$ refers to skilled workers and $i = \beta$ refers to unskilled workers.[13] The two types of workers have identical utility functions, defined on a single good and leisure, but they furnish different types of labor. This assumption is very different from the usual one about ability, such as that in Mirrlees (1971), in which individuals are assumed to provide the same quality or type of labor but differ in their productivity per unit of time. In that alternative framework, a low-skilled worker could perform any task if he or she devoted sufficient time to it. A low-skilled sign painter could paint a Vermeer with sufficient patience. By contrast, in our model, a Vermeer can paint a sign, but a low-skilled sign painter can never paint a Vermeer, no matter how much time he or she devotes to it.

Letting C_i be the consumption and L_i be the labor supplied by a type i worker, the utility function of a worker of type i is given by the concave function

$$U(C_i, L_i), \tag{7.1}$$

where $(1 - L_i)$ is the amount of leisure available to a type i worker, $i = \alpha, \beta$. We assume that leisure is a normal good and that there are A workers of each type, where, without loss of generality, $A = 1$. The social welfare function, to be maximized by government redistribution, is given as the total utility obtained by the two types of workers:

$$W = U(C_\alpha, L_\alpha) + U(C_\beta, L_\beta), \tag{7.2}$$

where the government cannot distinguish between skilled and unskilled workers. Thus, there is nothing to prevent a skilled worker from pretending to be an unskilled worker for the purpose of income distribution.

We assume that two sectors are using different technologies to produce the same good, where Y_j is the output of sector j for $j = 1, 2$. For simplicity, we will ignore capital.[14] The technology in the first sector is given by the aggregate linearly homogeneous production function with two factors of production:

$$Y_1 = F(L_{\alpha 1}, L_\beta), \tag{7.3}$$

where L_{i1} is the total labor supply of type i workers. We assume that the production function is symmetric in both types of labor, and, without loss of generality, we assume that if $L_{\alpha 1} = L_{\beta 1}$, then both marginal products of labor are equal and can be set equal to one.

$$\frac{\partial F(L_{\alpha 1}, L_{\beta 1})}{\partial L_{\alpha 1}} = \frac{\partial F(L_{\alpha 1}, L_{\beta 1})}{\partial L_{\beta 1}} = 1. \tag{7.4}$$

If only the first technology is feasible, then, assuming perfect competition, symmetry implies that the solution is a first-best solution, with no need for redistribution, since all levels of consumption and leisure are equal.

Now consider the introduction into this "Garden of Eden" of a "serpent" in the form of a new technology. This new technology replaces unskilled labor by a public good, Z, which allows the skilled workers to produce the good without using any of the unskilled workers. We assume that the technology is linear in skilled labor, so

$$Y_2 = M(Z)L_{\alpha 2}. \tag{7.5}$$

The new economy can then described by the following system of equations.

$$Y_1 = F(L_{\alpha 1}, L_\beta) \tag{7.6}$$

$$Y_2 = M(Z)L_{\alpha 2} \tag{7.7}$$

$$Y_1 + Y_2 = C_\alpha + C_\beta \tag{7.8}$$

$$L_\alpha = L_{\alpha 1} + L_{\alpha 2}. \tag{7.9}$$

$L_{\alpha 1}$ in equation 7.6 is the labor supply of skilled workers in sector 1, which uses the joint linearly homogeneous technology; L_β in equation 7.6 is, as before, the labor supply of unskilled workers, which is employed only in sector 1; and $L_{\alpha 2}$ in equation 7.7 is the labor supply of skilled workers in sector 2. In equation 7.8, the total product is allocated as consumption between the two types of labor. In equation 7.9, the total supply of labor of skilled workers, L_α, is the sum of the supply of skilled workers allocated to the two sectors.

If the marginal product of labor of skilled workers in sector 2 is large enough, then some fraction of the skilled workers will shift to the new technology. Since skilled workers and unskilled workers are complements, this shift will lower the marginal productivity of unskilled workers.

8. Market Allocation

We first address the free-market case and prove three propositions based on the model of two types of workers in an initial technology that, following the technological change, includes both the initial technology that uses both types of labor and a new linear technology that uses only skilled workers.

Proposition 1. An increase in the level of the public good, Z, will change the market equilibrium in such a way that the marginal product of the unskilled workers will fall.

Proof. Let w_α be the wage of the skilled workers and w_β be the wage of the unskilled workers. An efficient allocation requires that the marginal product of the skilled workers must equal the wage in both sectors, so, from the assumption that the production function is linearly homogenous,

$$\frac{\partial}{\partial L_{\alpha 1}} F\left(\frac{L_{\alpha 1}}{L_\beta}, 1\right) = w_\alpha = M(Z). \tag{8.1}$$

Since the marginal product of the unskilled workers must equal their wage,

$$\frac{\partial}{\partial L_\beta} F\left(1, \frac{L_\beta}{L_{\alpha 1}}\right) = w_\beta. \tag{8.2}$$

Since $\partial^2/\partial L_{\alpha 1}^2 F(L_{\alpha 1}/L_\beta, 1) < 0$ and $\partial^2/\partial L_\beta^2 F(1, L_\beta/L_{\alpha 1}) < 0$, it follows that $(\partial w_\beta/\partial M)(dM/dZ) < 0$.

Proposition 2. If the supply of both types of labor is fixed, the level of output at the competitive equilibrium will increase as a result of the introduction of the new technology.

Proposition 3. In the competitive equilibrium, the utility of the skilled workers will increase and the utility of the unskilled workers will decrease as a result of the introduction of the new technology.   □

The second proposition follows from the fact that one factor is more productive and there is no change in the level of employment of the factors. The third proposition is almost as simple. The budget set of the skilled workers after an increase in their productivity contains the previous budget set, while the budget set of the unskilled workers after an increase in the productivity of the skilled workers is contained in their previous budget set.

In proposition 2, if we drop the assumption that the supply of labor is fixed, then the change in output depends on the changes in the supply of labor. It is then possible that the change in the demand for leisure as a result of the wage change can lead to lower output.

9. Nonmarket Allocation

An alternative way of addressing the problem of technological change is to consider the implications of government intervention with respect to the allocation of income so as to maximize social welfare. One possible case is that in which the government can intervene in such a way that it can directly allocate all factors.[15] This case is unrealistic, however, in that it requires the government to have complete information and control. Nevertheless, it provides a comparison with the allocation by optimal taxation, since in the latter case the government is bound by the individual's optimizing behavior. Since we are trying to provide an intuitive baseline, we will assume that the individual's utility function is of the logarithmic form $U(C_i, L_i) = [\ln(C_i) + \ln(1 - L_i)]$ and the production function in the first technology is Cobb-Douglas with exponents 1/2 for both types of labor. The Lagrangian can be written

$$\mathcal{L} = [\ln(C_\alpha) + \ln(1 - L_\alpha)] + [\ln(C_\beta) + \ln(1 - L_\beta)]$$

$$+ \lambda_1[2L_{\alpha 1}^{1/2}L_\beta^{1/2} + M(Z)L_{\alpha 2} - C_\alpha - C_\beta] + \lambda_2(L_\alpha - L_{\alpha 1} - L_{\alpha 2}), \qquad (9.1)$$

where λ_1 and λ_2 are the Lagrange multipliers associated with the goods and α-labor constraints respectively. The solution is characterized by the following first-order conditions with respect to C_α, C_β, L_α, $L_{\alpha 1}$, $L_{\alpha 2}$, and L_β, respectively:

$$\frac{1}{C_\alpha} = \lambda_1 \qquad (9.2a)$$

$$\frac{1}{C_\beta} = \lambda_1 \qquad (9.2b)$$

$$\frac{1}{1 - L_\alpha} = \lambda_2 \qquad (9.2c)$$

$$\lambda_2 = \lambda_1 \left(\frac{L_\beta}{L_{\alpha 1}} \right)^{\frac{1}{2}} \qquad (9.2d)$$

$$\lambda_2 = \lambda_1 M(Z) \tag{9.2e}$$

$$\frac{1}{1 - L_\beta} = \lambda_1 \left(\frac{L_{\alpha 1}}{L_\beta} \right)^{\frac{1}{2}} \tag{9.2f}$$

Conditions 9.2c, 9.2d, 9.2e, and 9.2f imply that

$$\frac{1}{1 - L_\alpha} = \lambda_1 M(Z), \tag{9.3}$$

$$\frac{1}{1 - L_\beta} = \frac{\lambda_1}{M(Z)}. \tag{9.4}$$

Since it is assumed that $M(Z) > 1$, it follows that $L_\alpha > L_\beta$. Note that equations 9.3 and 9.4 imply that

$$\lambda_1 M(Z)(1 - L_\alpha) = \frac{\lambda_1}{M(Z)} (1 - L_\beta), \tag{9.5}$$

so, using equations 9.2a and 9.2b, it follows that

$$C_\alpha + M(Z)(1 - L_\alpha) = C_\beta + \frac{1}{M(Z)} (1 - L_\beta). \tag{9.6}$$

Equation 9.6 states that if leisure $(1 - L_i)$ is valued at the marginal product of the workers then the implicit values of the consumption bundle of both groups are equal. The utility of the α workers, however, is less than the utility of the β workers.[16]

The production functions are linearly homogeneous, so Euler's theorem implies that

$$Y = \frac{1}{M(Z)} L_\beta + M(Z)(L_{\alpha 1} + L_{\alpha 2}). \tag{9.7}$$

If follows that

$$C_i = \frac{1}{2} \left[\frac{1}{M(Z)} L_\beta + M(Z)L_\alpha \right].$$

10.   Optimal Taxation

In the full information case, an α worker always has less utility than a β worker. If, however, the government cannot distinguish between α workers and β workers, then, since a worker can always pretend to be a β worker, the government faces the constraint that the utility of an α worker must be at least as great as that of a β worker. This "self-selection constraint" requires that

$$U(C_\alpha, L_\alpha) - U(C_\beta, L_\beta) \geq 0. \tag{10.1}$$

The Lagrangian is

$$\mathcal{L} = U(C_\alpha, L_\alpha) + U(C_\beta, L_\beta) + \lambda_1[F(L_{\alpha 1}, L_\beta) + M(Z)L_{\alpha 2} - C_\alpha - C_\beta]$$
$$+ \lambda_2(L_\alpha - L_{\alpha 1} - L_{\alpha 2}) + \lambda_3[U(C_\alpha, L_\alpha) - U(C_\beta, L_\beta)], \tag{10.2}$$

where λ_3 is the Lagrange multiplier associated with the self-selection constraint. The Kuhn-Tucker conditions are

$$(1 + \lambda_3) \frac{\partial U(C_\alpha, L_\alpha)}{\partial C_\alpha} = \lambda_1 \tag{10.3a}$$

$$(1 - \lambda_3) \frac{\partial U(C_\beta, L_\beta)}{\partial C_\beta} = \lambda_1 \tag{10.3b}$$

$$(1 + \lambda_3) \frac{\partial U(C_\alpha, L_\alpha)}{\partial L_\alpha} = \lambda_2 \tag{10.3c}$$

$$(1 - \lambda_3) \frac{\partial U(C_\beta, L_\beta)}{\partial L_\beta} + \lambda_1 \frac{\partial F(L_{\alpha 1}, L_\beta)}{\partial L_\beta} \leq 0 \tag{10.3d}$$

$$L_\beta \left[(1 - \lambda_3) \frac{\partial U(C_\beta, L_\beta)}{\partial L_\beta} + \lambda_1 \frac{\partial F(L_{\alpha 1}, L_\beta)}{\partial L_\beta} \right] = 0 \tag{10.3e}$$

$$-\lambda_2 + \lambda_1 \frac{\partial F(L_{\alpha 1}, L_\beta)}{\partial L_{\alpha 1}} \leq 0; \quad L_{\alpha 1} \left[-\lambda_2 + \lambda_1 \frac{\partial F(L_{\alpha 1}, L_\beta)}{\partial L_{\alpha 1}} \right] = 0 \tag{10.3f}$$

$$-\lambda_2 + \lambda_1 M(Z) \leq 0; \quad L_{\alpha 2}[-\lambda_2 + \lambda_1 M(Z)] = 0. \tag{10.3g}$$

Equations 10.3a, 10.3c, and 10.3e imply that

$$\frac{\dfrac{\partial U(C_\alpha, L_\alpha)}{\partial L_\alpha}}{\dfrac{\partial U(C_\alpha, L_\alpha)}{\partial C_\alpha}} = \frac{\partial C_\alpha}{\partial L_\alpha} = \frac{\lambda_2}{\lambda_1} = M(Z). \tag{10.3}$$

Furthermore, if $L_\beta > 0$ then equations 10.3b, 10.3d, and 10.3e imply that

$$\frac{\dfrac{\partial U(C_\beta, L_\beta)}{\partial L_\beta}}{\dfrac{\partial U(C_\beta, L_\beta)}{\partial C_\beta}} = \frac{\partial C_\beta}{\partial L_\beta} = \frac{\partial F(L_{\alpha 1}, L_\beta)}{\partial L_\beta}. \tag{10.4}$$

If both types of workers are employed, then their marginal rate of substitution is equal to their marginal rate of transformation and the marginal tax on both types of workers is zero. If $\lambda_3 > 0$, it follows that $C_\alpha > C_\beta$ and $L_\alpha < L_\beta$. Thus, the optimal tax consists of a lump-sum transfer from the α workers to the β workers. Letting T be the amount of the transfer, the tax schedules can be written

$$C_\alpha = M(Z)L_\alpha - T \tag{10.5}$$

$$C_\beta = \frac{\partial F(L_{\alpha 1}, L_\beta)}{\partial L_\beta} L_\beta + T. \tag{10.6}$$

This result is general, and it does not depend on any particular form for the utility function. However, it *does* depend on the assumptions that an α worker is no more productive in β tasks than a β worker is and that both types of workers have identical preferences.

The conditions imply that individuals face a feasible set characterized by a zero marginal tax and a lump-sum tax or transfer. If we assume that consumption is a normal good, then we can describe the effects of an increase in the marginal product of labor in the new technology on employment. An increase in the marginal product of labor in the new technology implies that for skilled workers the marginal rate of transformation is greater than the marginal rate of substitution. This will result in an increase in the supply of skilled labor. Since skilled workers must be indifferent between working in either sector, this implies that there must be a shift in the allocation of skilled workers from the old technology to the new technology. This, in turn, implies that the wage rate of unskilled workers in the new technology will decline, as the marginal product of unskilled workers depends on the ratio of the unskilled to skilled workers, which has now declined. This implies that there is a decrease in the amount of unskilled labor employed.

Proposition 4. An optimal income tax implies that employment of unskilled workers decreases as the marginal product of the skilled workers in the new technology increases. □

11. Conclusions

We have used some simple models to study an economy characterized by the following three stylized facts. First, labor is heterogeneous, and there are two types of labor, skilled and unskilled. Second, the demand for skilled labor is growing as a result of technical change. Third, the supply of labor is determined by an implicit life-cycle employment contract. We have addressed four issues. First, what is the impact of the new technology on corporate restructuring and the distribution of income if there is no government intervention? Second, what is the impact of the new technology on output and aggregate welfare if there is no government intervention? Third, what is the impact of government intervention if government is restricted to an optimal income tax? Fourth, is it possible that the unskilled workers might become economically unemployable?

We have found that under competitive market conditions an increase in the marginal product of labor of the skilled workers in the new technology will change the market equilibrium in such a way that all skilled workers benefit at the expense of the unskilled workers and the implicit contract is breached. The driving force for this breach of the implicit contract and the resulting corporate restructuring is the elimination of the quasi rents associated with the increased productivity that resulted from the technical change. Social welfare declines even though output increases. These effects of the introduction of new technology could be mitigated if the government introduces an optimal income tax. If government redistribution is introduced, then, under the special assumption of identical preferences, the government can achieve a first-best allocation. The optimal tax is a lump-sum tax (and subsidy) with a zero marginal tax on wages for both types of workers. The utility of both groups is equal, however. As the productivity of the skilled workers in the new technology increases, unskilled workers become redundant as the sector that uses them declines in favor of the sector using skilled workers. It may be socially optimal, then, to eliminate the industry employing the unskilled workers, who will not be employed.

Our models are very simple, but their results highlight the implications of some stylized facts. Inasmuch as these stylized facts reflect reality, these implications should be explored using more complex models, which will probably not permit analytical solutions but could be solved numerically.

NOTES

1. See Intriligator (1965, 1992).
2. See Bailey (1982), Berndt and Wood (1986), Griliches (1988, 1994), and Jorgenson (1988).
3. See Lazear (1979).
4. See Worth (1996).
5. See *Statistical Abstract of the United States, 1994,* 470.
6. Reich (1991).
7. The Gini index is a measure of inequality, where the larger the coefficient, the more the inequality. Its value for the United States in 1950 was .38, while its value for 1990 was .37. Census data in the *Statistical Abstract of the United States* (various years) suggest that the least inequality was attained in 1968, with a Gini coefficient of .32.
8. See *Statistical Abstract of the United States, 1995,* 465.
9. Smith (1955).
10. Wiener (1954).
11. See Gleick (1992) for an account of the value of the ability to do computation before the electronic computer was introduced during the Manhattan Project.
12. See Romer (1986).
13. For related models, involving skilled (α) and unskilled (β) workers in the context of Pareto-efficient taxation, see Sadka (1976a, 1976b); Stiglitz (1982); and Brito, Hamilton, Slutsky, and Stiglitz (1990).
14. Since we are using a static model, this is not a restrictive assumption and it simplifies the algebra.
15. See Sadka (1976b).
16. This result was also obtained by Sadka (1976a, 1976b).

REFERENCES

Bailey, M. N. 1982. "The Productivity Growth Slowdown by Industry." *Brookings Papers on Economic Activity* 2:423–54.
Berndt, E. R., and D. O. Wood. 1986. "Energy Price Shocks and Productivity Growth in U.S. and U.K. Manufacturing." *Oxford Review of Economic Policy* 2:1–31.
Brito, D. L., J. Hamilton, S. Slutsky, and J. E. Stiglitz. 1990. "Pareto Efficient Tax Structures." *Oxford Economic Papers* 42:61–77.
Gleick, J. 1992. *Genius: The Life and Times of Richard Feynman.* New York: Pantheon.
Griliches, Z. 1988. "Productivity Puzzles and R&D: Another Nonexplanation." *Journal of Economic Perspectives* 2:9–21.
———. 1994. "Productivity, R&D, and the Data Constraint." *American Economic Review* 84:1–23.
Intriligator, M. D. 1965. "Embodied Technical Change and Productivity in the United States, 1929–1958." *Review of Economics and Statistics* 47:65–70.

——. 1992. "Productivity and the Embodiment of Technical Progress." *Scandinavian Journal of Economics* 94:75–87.

Jorgenson, D. W. 1988. "Productivity and Postwar U.S. Economic Growth." *Journal of Economic Perspectives* 2:23–41.

Lazear, E. P. 1979. "Why Is There Mandatory Retirement?" *Journal of Political Economy* 87:1262–63.

Mirrlees, J. A. 1971. "An Exploration of the Theory of Optimal Taxation." *Review of Economic Studies* 38:175–208.

Reich, R. 1991. *The Work of Nations.* New York: Knopf.

Romer, P. M. 1986. "Increasing Returns and Long-Run Growth." *Journal of Political Economy* 94:1002–37.

Sadka, E. 1976a. "On Income Redistribution: Incentive Effects and the Optimal Income Taxation." *Review of Economic Studies* 43:261–68.

——. 1976b. "Social Welfare and Income Distribution." *Econometrica* 44:1239–52.

Smith, R. E. 1955. *The Failure of the Roman Republic.* Cambridge: Cambridge University Press.

Statistical Abstract of the United States. 1994. Washington, DC: Government Printing Office.

Stiglitz, J. E. 1982. "Self Selection and Pareto Efficient Taxation." *Journal of Public Economics* 17:213–40.

Wiener, N. 1954. *The Human Use of Human Beings: Cybernetics and Human Beings.* Rev. ed. Boston: Houghton Mifflin.

Worth, E. R. 1996. "In Defense of Targeted ERIPs: Understanding the Interaction of Life Cycle Employment and Early Retirement Incentive Plans." *Texas Law Review* 74:411–45.

Intangible, Human-Embodied Capital and Firm Performance

Gunnar Eliasson and Pontus Braunerhjelm

Technological advance, resting in new knowledge and
occurring accidentally or mechanically, seems to be
the only possible offset to this "natural" tendency to
diminishing returns.
—*Frank H. Knight, "Diminishing Returns
from Investment"*

1. Introduction

Human-embodied competence capital dominates other forms of capital in
production. Many will, however, probably add that such intangible capital,
as distinct from tangible capital, cannot be properly measured and therefore should not be activated in the capital accounts of the firm.

This essay (1) disputes that view and discusses the measurement of
capital in general. It (2) proposes a method of measuring intangible,
human-embodied educational, marketing, and R&D capital. And (3) it
relates those capital items to firm performance.

It is found that human-embodied competence capital significantly increases productivity and profitability in Swedish manufacturing firms. We
also investigate to what extent a particular balance between intangible and
hardware capital improves the contribution to performance among a sample
of Swedish manufacturing firms.

Human-embodied competence capital leverages up productivity of
other factor inputs like machines and labor hours. Hence, coming to grips
with capital means to somehow quantify it in terms of the hierarchies and
markets through which it has been allocated. To get coherence in the
discussion to follow, we begin by defining the purpose of our capital measurement, namely, *to define the scale by which all capital that plays a role in
physical production becomes visible.*

2. The Capital Problem

The evasiveness of the concept of aggregate capital partly has to do with
the differences in the purpose of measuring it but also with static aggregation. In static equilibrium, the transaction costs associated with allocating

capital are zero and there is no difference between capital as a wealth object and its role as a factor of production. Few economic concepts are as incompatible as aggregate capital and a dynamic growth process.

It has long been observed that the diminishing returns postulated by theory have not been borne out by empirical research. To account for that anomaly, Frank Knight (1944) suggested that some unmeasured capital was contributing to production, which had increased and more than compensated for the diminishing returns on measured capital inputs. He called that unmeasured capital "knowledge."

McKenzie (1959) made the same observation when noting that the failure of factor payments to exhaust total product value must depend on the presence of some unmeasured capital that generated measured excess production value and profits. Again, it was natural for him to call that capital "knowledge."

Such general observations are, however, not very operational. The residual income is attributed to every conceivable capital item that contributes to production. Above all, it contains capital items not measured in official statistics or activated in firms' balance sheets. The academic "solution" has been to ignore what you cannot see, a procedure that became dominant with the birth of empirical production (function) analysis.

The old literature, on the other hand, very much recognized industrial knowledge as a source of industrial wealth. The king of Sweden, for instance, provided generous incentives in the seventeenth century for skilled workers in the Netherlands to immigrate to Sweden to set up factories. Westerman (1768) went to Holland and England to "learn" about the new production techniques that made possible the production of ships at half the measured inputs (of labor) in Swedish shipyards. He observed the use of "these new machines" but concluded that without the skills to operate them and the art of organizing production around them, there was no productivity gain to be captured. Even so, it was not easy to return home and simply tell the people how to do it better. The capacity to receive and implement the know-how (the *receiver competence* [Eliasson 1986, 57ff.; Eliasson 1990a]) was lacking. To introduce the competence to build ships efficiently in Sweden, you had to invite the competent people to come. To build receiver competence for physical capital production certainly is a resource-using activity.

The analysis of economic growth in the postwar period very much focused on the empirical estimation of macroproduction functions. In its simplest form, the macroproduction function includes measures of capital and labor inputs weighted together by a power function and quite often a shift factor, representing what has come (after Solow 1957) to be called disembodied technical change. Solow (1959) developed this earlier model into the equally well known vintage representation, wherein each vintage was a constant-returns-to-scale production function, which shifted upward for each vintage of best-practice introductions of new capital. Each vintage embodies a new superior technology. However, while some technical progress may be embodied in capital and labor to be captured by adjusting labor hours and capital stocks for quality change, other improvements occur through "outside" disembodied influence. The well-known Horndal effect observed by Lundberg (1961) was christened "learning by doing" by Arrow (1962). Intriligator (1965) brought the two approaches together. Jorgenson and Griliches (1967) almost managed to remove the shift factor through quality corrections of aggregate factor inputs using assumed equilibrium, residual income, and price data to adjust capital and labor inputs for quality. This procedure comes very close to being tautological, and in all these approaches production growth is exogenously determined (for a critical overview, see Eliasson 1989).

The upgrading of quality of products through R&D spending was introduced as a separate factor of production by Nadiri, who also coined the term *spillover* (see Nadiri 1978) to denote the fact that innovations in firms tend to diffuse to other firms. But, if R&D capital is important, how about marketing capital, educational capital, and general organizing, innovative, and entrepreneurial know-how embodied in the people of the organization and making the firm appear to be a *competent team* (Eliasson 1990a, 1996a).

Romer (1986) suggested that knowledge was the reason for observed economies of scale. Such scale economies, however, posed well-known mathematical problems in the neoclassical model, which were cleared in Romer's analysis by the assumption of strongly diminishing returns to knowledge accumulation, that is, to economic learning. In these models, however, economic growth is still exogenous. Attempting to explain it explicitly, we break up the assumptions necessary for (static) aggregation.

Our ambition is to take this one step further and make the allocation of competence capital in, or organizational learning of, the firm (Eliasson 1992a) the source of its competitiveness in markets and hence the mover—through dynamic competition—of macroeconomic growth. But organizational learning also occurs at higher levels of aggregation (between firms) through selection and resource reallocation in markets (Eliasson 1990a, 1992a, 1992b), and at each level the allocation of tacit, human-embodied competence requires superior human-embodied competence (Pelikan 1989). Macroproduction functions are not stable when capital productivity becomes dependent, not only on the dynamics of the allocation of production capital but also on the allocation of a dominant human-embodied competence. The explanation has to be taken down to the micromarket level and into the firms. The theoretical problem of this essay, therefore, is to explain how competence allocation moves economic growth. The empirical problem of this essay is to formulate a "reduced" form of this model on a testable format. We thus conceptualize (following Eliasson 1989, 1992a, 1997) a microbased (within and between firms) allocation of tacit, dominant, human-embodied competence capital that confers increasing returns to scale on other factors of production and thus endogenizes economic growth through these allocation mechanisms. Under this a priori hypothesis, firm data would appear as if reflected by a firm production function exhibiting constant returns to scale in physical capital and labor, holding human-embodied competence constant, but increasing returns in competence, figuring as "infrastructure capital" (Eliasson 1989). Under our prior assumptions as to the nature of the competence capital, the "corresponding" neoclassical production function is, however, unstable. Hence, *we interpret the results in terms of our original microallocation-based growth explanation.*

3. Capital: Content and Delimitations

Making organizational learning through the allocation of competence capital within and between firms the source of macroeconomic growth by definition makes tacit knowledge the source of economic growth. This is not a pleasant analytical situation. For one thing, with tacit knowledge, tradability in markets is reduced. Since the values set on firm assets in capital markets influence real decision making, information allocation in markets becomes imperfect and the circumstances of a market for lemons will be at hand, superior knowledge assets being undervalued and their price level being lowered to the value the market traders can understand (Eliasson 1990a).

Second, attributing ultimate value creation to tacit, unmeasurable, knowledge capital that generates residual rents leaves the analyst in the uncomfortable situation of having to explain the increase in productivity measured by the increase in income from the same production: the original Cambridge-Cambridge controversy over capital.

The way capital is represented in mainstream empirical production analysis, hence, is unsatisfactory. There are intangible capital items that can be measured in a satisfactory way using the same methods of measurement as those applied for visible, tangible, hardware capital. The residual capital income gains problem, furthermore, causes principal problems of interpretation in standard, macroproduction function analysis, even when complemented with new intangible capital items.

Among intangible capital items that should be accounted for explicitly are:

Soft capital like marketing know-how and R&D capital
Infrastructure capital (spillovers; see Eliasson 1997a)
Competence at all levels embodied in human beings or teams of human beings
Entrepreneurial talent, often associated with unique individuals

Table 1 gives a principal breakdown of a balance sheet that also accounts for these items. A particularly tricky capital problem (Eliasson 1990a) is how to distinguish human-embodied competence from disembodied *information* in the sense of coded knowledge that can be traded "freely" in the market. Human-embodied competence cannot easily be moved and reallocated. There are two important exceptions to the general lack of secondary markets for trading in capital, namely, the market for secondary trading in human-embodied competence, the labor market or (better) the *market for competence,* and (second) the mergers and acquisitions (M&A) markets trading in all capital associated with entire firms or large chunks of firms (Eliasson 1991).

We will use valuations in the M&A market in particular to bracket the measures of intangible capital that we need. This amounts to making the same assumptions on the markets for M&A as is done on human capital in labor market theory. Two aspects should therefore be borne in mind. First, such measures become dependent on the competence to assess (to value) capital that market agents possess (see sec. 4). Second, actors in the M&A markets, through their valuation, also affect the investment decisions and thus the allocation of tangible and intangible capital. At a more aggregate

TABLE 1. Capital Balances of the 10 Largest Swedish Manufacturing Corporations, 1985 (SEK billion, percentages)

	Replacement Value	Book Value
Visible capital		
Machines, buildings, and		
inventories	35	43
Financial assets	35	57
Total visible assets	70	100
Intangible assets		
Software	0	0
Technical knowledge (R&D)	11	0
Marketing knowledge	13	0
Educational capital	6	0
Total intangible capital made		
visible	30	0
Total visible capital	100 (%)	100 (%)
Entrepreneurial competence		
capital	0	0
Total debt, including hidden		
tax debt	46	74
Net worth	54	26
Market valuation of net worth	37 (%)	130 (%)
Market valuation of total		
visible assets	66 (%)	108 (%)

Source: Eliasson 1990a, 1990b.

level, the traders, hence, influence the nature and composition of capital. This important competence allocation role, first pointed out by Pelikan (1989), makes the whole matter of aggregate capital analysis and valuation impossible in principle but perhaps possible in practice.

4.   Capital: Its Value and Measurement

In Eliasson (1990a; 1992, 49ff.; 1996a, 80ff.; 1997b), these considerations were brought together into a principal design to measure total capital, attempting to bracket capital values using different methods. Each of these valuation principles embodies different purposes, information, and assumptions. We are using the following four methods (see table 2).

1. *Present value of insider profit forecasts.* The origin of capital value is current and expected future profits. Those who best understand the fundamentals, or the future earnings capacity of the firm (top management, dominant owners, insiders), are best informed about the value of capital invested in the firm. All other agents have to base their assessments on less information, even though they may occasionally be more competent in making the assessment.

2. *Present value of outside proxies of fundamentals.* Outsiders, including stock market experts, rely on partial information (compared to insiders) or on proxies. They can assess the market situation, the general business cycle, competitors of the firm, and so on, which they may in fact do better than the insiders. What they typically lack is information on what is going on within the firm, an imminent technical breakthrough, and—above all—the possibilities of a hands-on evaluation of the competence of management and other high-level staff. As a rule, external assessments are based on much fewer resources than the business itself devotes to the same assessment.

The difference between the first and the second method is that the first

TABLE 2.   Capital Valuation Principles

1. Present value of insider profit forecasts (fundamentals)
2. Present value of outsider proxies of fundamentals
3. Accounting methods
   —Historic purchase costs
   —Investment cumulation (static neoclassical method)
4. Market valuation
   —Stock market of all assets
   —Secondary market of tradable capital
5. Benchmark valuations

Source: Eliasson 1992, 87.

is based on insider knowledge about the fundamentals while the second is based on projections of proxies of the same fundamentals by external analysts.

3. *Accounting methods* are entirely different. We have the traditional accounting method of using historic, depreciated investments valued at purchase prices. This method is entirely unreliable in external analyses. Such capital measures are distorted by inflation, arbitrary depreciation methods, and technological change. The accountant/analyst may also take stock of the replacement value of the invested stock of resources. The appropriate neoclassical valuation principle (assuming perfect markets and known future capital costs) then is to cumulate inflation-adjusted investments net of estimated depreciation.

The neoclassical investment cumulation principle is as clear as book valuation, but the data can be interpreted. Distortions enter through the arbitrary, externally determined, depreciation principle. If not exogenously set, depreciation would have to relate to the profit prospects of the firm, and we are back at valuation principle 1.

4. *Market valuation* can be done in two ways. The entire stock of assets net of debt (net worth) is constantly measured (for public firms) in the stock market or when firms are sold or acquired in the market. Capital items can also be valued separately in secondary markets for investment goods. Both these market valuations depend critically on the efficiency of the market actors to evaluate the earnings capacity of the capital and on the purpose of the particular market valuation.

An open stock market valuation will be influenced by information based on all three valuation principles and the subjective "competence" weight every trader in the market attaches to his or her respective sources of information. The secondary market valuation of individual capital items is standard for inventories, but it is normally ruled out for used equipment because of the absence of secondary markets or because most investment goods are dedicated in the sense that they have been designed, produced, and installed for special purpose use. Large transaction costs for secondary trading, hence, normally rule out such a market valuation. The stock market, however, is the secondary market for trading in the entire capital stock of the firm. As a consequence, we will (in this study) compute capital measures of the firm using—for some firms—as many as four methods.

Theoretical considerations suggest that the proper accounting method (based on replacement values) will exaggerate capital, while the stock market valuation will underestimate capital even in well-functioning markets. First of all, (stock) market valuations are normally heavily discounted due to uncertainty about technical change and competitors and overly cautious investors. This is not the case with ex-post investment cumulation. Second, knowledge is the most difficult of capital items to assess for trade (see Eliasson 1996, 69ff.). Excellence will always be tacit and embodied in human beings. Proper assessment requires ex-post examination in use, and excellence will be generally undervalued. The neoclassical accounting method, on the other hand, computes capital values as if all investments have carried the average rate of return. There is no precautionary excess discounting or depreciation. We expect our own (external) evaluations based on profit projections or dividends mostly to fall in between the neoclassical investment cumulation and the stock market methods. When a true autonomous insider valuation can be identified, however, we expect this to be the best valuation, provided it can be assumed that the insider valuation does not incorporate any expected synergy effects from a takeover.

There is a *fifth* method, which is often resorted to in firms in which management does not believe in abstract capital measurements. Instead, they use various forms of benchmarks or proxies assumed to reflect performance, like partial productivity indicators or profit margins for profitability (Eliasson 1976).

The estimates on intangible capital for the 10 largest Swedish manufacturing firms in table 1 is half insider, half neoclassical, and partly based on such benchmarks. When collecting this statistical material, the managers helped us (see Bergholm and Jagrén 1985) to reclassify the internal cost accounts of these firms on investment and current expenditure categories, indicating their long run importance for output and competitiveness. Another example of the use of proxies is the educational capital variable. The internal accounts of firms (see Eliasson 1986) typically include only external expenditures (sending people to courses, hiring external lecturers) on a format readily available at corporate headquarters and thus significantly underestimate internal firm investment in training and education. As a substitute, we have also (in the regressions to follow) used a quality classification of employees by educational level. This variable, in addition to reflecting internal investments in education (the more education you have, the more firm education you receive; see Eliasson 1986), captures external acquisitions of knowledge through the hiring of competent people

Capital data used in the regression analysis to follow, furthermore, are based on internal appreciations by firm managers (insider valuations). For some of the firms, we have stock market valuations and cumulative investment as well as book values. We can thus, for these firms, compare the different measures.

Unfortunately, we have to use two data sets to illustrate the measurement problem. Eliasson (1990a, 1990b) includes data on book, replacement, and market values for entire firms during a year of business upswing, 1985, and Braunerhjelm (1994) data for another year (1989) and another set of firms on insider and market values. Table 1 presents these data. The differences between replacement, book, and market values 1985 for the 10 largest Swedish manufacturing corporations are striking and as expected theoretically. The market valuation of total assets amounts to 66 percent of neoclassically cumulated replacement values. The book value amounts to 58 percent of the replacement value. Hence, the market only overvalues the book value by some 8 percent. This amounts to saying that the market places practically no value on the knowledge and competence capital residing in these 10, very high performance Swedish firms for a year characterized by brisk business.

5. A Simple Model of a Competence-Based Production Technology

Consider the following basic structure of production of a representative firm. Profit-maximizing firms employ regular production technologies using three factors of production; homogeneous labor (L) and capital (K) and a composite factor, H, that consists of accumulated investments in R&D, marketing, education, and software. For the moment, we will treat it as an aggregate competence stock.

Firms encounter perfect competition in the markets for capital and labor, while H is firm-specific, heterogeneous, and embodied within the firms' organization. Production is organized such that upstream, firm-specific, knowledge capital (H) adds value to downstream production by differentiating it from other close varieties, thus exercising a positive leverage or scale factor[1] on K and L. Assuming identical Cobb-Douglas technologies,

$$Q_1 = AK_i^{1-\alpha}L_i^{\alpha}H_i^{\gamma} \tag{1}$$

subject to

$$0 < \alpha, \gamma < 1.$$

The restriction on γ recognizes that firms cannot handle unlimited amounts of H, that is, decreasing returns to H are postulated. Hence, the production function (eq. 1) is linearly homogenous in capital and labor but exhibits limited increasing returns to H. Next we decompose H on four different items (R&D, marketing, education, and software), where H_{ij} denotes firm i's stock of competence capital j. The production function then takes the following form:

$$Q_i = AK_i^{1-\alpha}L_i^{\alpha}(H_{i1}^{\beta1}H_{i2}^{\beta2}H_{i3}^{\beta3}H_{i4}^{1-\beta1-\beta2-\beta3})^{\gamma}, \tag{2}$$

where $0 < \alpha, \beta, \gamma < 1$. By decomposing competence capital on its different categories, we attempt to identify their individual contributions to firm output. By imposing the restriction that $\in \beta = 1$, we assume H to be a weighted geometric average of the different items that constitute total H. We may, however, want to keep the sum of the β-coefficients open for the time being.

The firm's gross profit is:

$$\pi_i = P(AK_i^{1-\alpha}L_i^{\alpha}H_i^{\gamma}) - W_i(V_i), \tag{3}$$

where V refers to capital and labor inputs, while W represents competitive rewards to those inputs. If profits are not exhausted by factor rewards to capital and labor, the residual can be viewed as an excess return to the firm's "invisible" competence stock H (McKenzie 1959, Eliasson 1990a). Hence,

$$\pi_i = f(H_i), \quad \partial \Pi_i / \partial H_i > 0. \tag{4}$$

6. Data and Hypotheses

Data have been collected directly from Swedish firms through surveys and interviews for the year 1990, representing approximately 45 percent of employment in the Swedish engineering industry. The data set contains detailed information on sales, costs, skill-structures, assets, and so on. Altogether, the data base covers 137 firms.

Most empirical work on knowledge variables has used aggregate R&D expenditures only. At times, simply approximated R&D stocks have been used as explanatory variables. Different studies use different techniques and apply different depreciation and deflating principles, introducing a considerable element of a priori arbitrariness into the results. The competence capital applied here is derived from a broader definition, including separate data on R&D, marketing, software, and educational capital.[2] This should give a more accurate estimate, since R&D is just one component of firms' total competence capital. Total knowledge capital has been operationalized by activating current cost charges where such costs could be considered an investment. All values are net of depreciation and at reproduction costs.[3]

This method has some obvious advantages. First, assuming that insiders are correctly informed, we can disregard the lag problem. At present, there is no consensus concerning the lag structure. For instance, in capitalizing R&D expenditures Terleckyj (1982) used a three-year lag, while Pakes and Schankerman (1984) and Griliches and Lichtenberg (1984) implemented a two-year lag. Several other lag structures have also been used (see, e.g., Ravenscraft and Scherer 1982). The depreciation rate to use on R&D is another tricky matter. Griliches (1973, 1979), Terleckyj (1982), and von Weizsäcker (1986) argue that it is most reasonable to assume no depreciation at all, while others claim that yearly depreciation is more likely to be around 20 to 30 percent (Pakes and Schankerman 1984). We partly avoid this problem by asking firms directly. The problem of deflating the R&D stock has been subjected to even more diverse opinions.[4] Using cross-sectional data, however, this is no problem.

7. The Econometric Models

The econometric analysis is done in three steps. *First,* we want to establish the existence of a competence leverage, as in equation 1. Hence, we regress both equations 1 and 3 on a composite, unweighted average of the different components of competence capital. The dependent variable in equation 1 is production (value added). In equation 3, the dependent variable profitability is defined as the rate of return on total capital over the interest rate ($= \xi = \Pi$/total capital; see eq. 4). Our *second* hypothesis tested, however, is that the components of H do not have the same elasticities vis à vis Q, that is, that the weights should differ. The limited number of data, however, makes such regressions quite shaky and subject to all kinds of spurious correlations. After having established the dominant increasing returns effect of H, we therefore (*third*) experimented with the data set on the expectation that some reasonable prior weighting together of the components of H would produce a better fit than the other two did. If so, we would have a more precise hypothesis to test later on new data.

The K variable is defined as the repurchase value of fixed assets after depreciation. L is defined as total wage cost.

First, standard OLS is applied on the aggregate model. Then we proceed to estimate the effects of the separate components of H. Nonlinearities introduced through the multiplicative coefficients of the H-variables (in eq. 2) force us to use nonlinear regression techniques. In both cases, the error terms are assumed to exhibit standard properties. The results are shown in tables 3 and 4. Since a positive relationship exists between ξ and total factor productivity growth (Eliasson 1992a), the coefficients should have the same signs in both equations 1 and 3. We expect knowledge capital, notably marketing capital, to exercise a stronger influence on profitability than on output, since it embodies the consequences of economic choices of markets and products on the value of output.

For estimated profitability functions, we have the following form:

$$\xi_i = c_i + \lambda h_i + \boldsymbol{\theta} z_i + \eta_{1i} \tag{5}$$

$$\xi_i = c_i + \phi \lambda_1 h_{i1} + \phi \lambda_2 h_{i2} + \phi \lambda_3 h_{i3} + \phi(1 - \lambda_1 - \lambda_2 - \lambda_3)h_{i4} + \boldsymbol{\theta} z_i + \eta_{2i}, \tag{6}$$

where z is a vector of control variables and $\boldsymbol{\theta}$ the corresponding vector of parameters. We assume the same standard properties as above for the error terms.

TABLE 3.   The Determinants of Firms' Output and Profitability, 1990

| | Dependent Variable = Value Added (logarithmic) | | | Dependent Variable = Profitability (levels) | | |
| | Method | | | | | |
	OLS	NLS		OLS		
Constant	.28***	.20***	.21***	.02***	.02***	.08***
	(11.80)	(6.02)	(6.55)	(4.51)	(4.28)	(4.49)
Labor	.96***	.95***	.95***	−.0004	−.0004	−.00005
	(40.32)	(40.99)	(40.80)	(1.21)	(.66)	(1.21)
Fixed capital	.04	.05**				
	(1.59)	(1.96)				
Competence capital		.03***	.03***	.0006	.0005	
		(3.11)	(2.83)	(1.25)	(1.20)	
R&D capital						.00009
						(1.29)
Marketing capital						.00003
						(.29)
Skill				.03***	.03***	.09***
				(3.63)	(3.32)	(3.61)
Software capital						−.00005
						(.26)
Marketing and educa-			.05			
tion capital			(0.04)			
R&D and software			.95			
capital			(1.03)			
Size					−.006	
					(.66)	
DF	136	134	133	133	133	132
Adjusted R^2	.975	.976	.976	.11	.10	.09

Note: OLS = ordinary least squares, NLS = nonlinear least squares. *T*-ratios are in parentheses.
*Significant at the .10 level.
**Significant at the .05 level.
***Significant at the .01 level.

The control variable contained in the vector **z** (in addition to the labor costs defined earlier) includes the size of the firm. Size captures the market position, and the firm's price-setting power is expected to increase with size. Hence, size, measured as number of employees, is expected to be positively related to profitability.

8.   Econometric Results

The econometric results are shown in tables 3 and 4. Starting with the production functions, the overall explanatory power of the regressions are well above 90 percent. The parameter value of the labor coefficient is

TABLE 4.   The Determinants of Firms' Profitability, 1990

	Dependent Variable = Profitability				
	Method = OLS			Method = NLS	
Labor costs	−.44***		.14		−.57***
	(12.59)		(1.02)		(4.46)
Competence capital	.54***			.36***	.44***
	(8.53)			(16.9)	(16.75)
R&D capital		.14***	.14***	−.20	−.22
		(1.99)	(1.91)	(.71)	(1.01)
Marketing capital		.27***	.24***	.13	.41*
		(3.36)	(2.93)	(.43)	(1.71)
Software capital		.23***	.22***	.31	.49
		(3.36)	(5.36)	(.73)	(1.51)
Skill	.70***	−.20***	−.23***	.76***	.32
	(4.51)	(8.56)	(6.45)	(2.30)	(1.25)
DF	134	133	132	132	131
R^2	.26	.71	.63	.75	.72

Note: OLS = ordinary least squares, NLS = nonlinear least squares. For calculation of R-values, see Haessel (1978). T-ratios are in parentheses.

*Significant at the .10 level.

**Significant at the .05 level.

***Significant at the .01 level.

surprisingly high (around .95 in all three cases), leaving a mere .05 of production to be explained by physical capital. Although all individual components of competence capital were not significant (not shown), aggregate competence capital H was positive and statistically significant. Hence, an increase in the firm's competence stock by 1 percent would lead to an increase in value added of 0.03 percent. The level of this scale effect seems reasonable, and it remained roughly the same in the different estimations.

The strong correlation between the different competence variables poses a problem. After the influence of aggregate H on output had been established by the testing of the original hypothesis, we therefore experimented with a number of combinations of the different categories of competence capital, as well as regressions with only some of the individual components, to see if a more precise hypothesis could be formulated to be tested on a new data set. The most successful estimates of the disaggregated competence stock are shown in table 3 (col. 3). R&D and software capital appear to play a separate role, but marketing and education capital do not. Furthermore, as expected, the parameter estimate of the R&D-intensive component of competence capital is dominant, although it fails to reach significance. We should also observe that, even though some parameter estimates appear a bit off expectations, this is not unusual in microeconometrics. Such instabilities are often explained by uneven data quality, notably of capital stock data. It should also be observed that the explained variation (R^2) is very high for microbased models.

The main conclusions to be drawn from the regressions is that we can measure competence capital and that a statistically significant increasing returns' effect on firms' value added has been established.

The results for the profitability model are less conclusive (tables 3 and 4). The overall explanatory power is, of course, lower since we are explaining a ratio. Table 4 also shows the results of a restricted version, wherein the intercept has been forced through the origin. The justification is that without any competence capital, firms should not be able to generate a rate of return that exceeds the interest rate. In the unrestricted model (table 3), significance was obtained only when absolute values (levels) were employed in the regressions. The sign of the variables are as hypothesized, even though the only statistically significant variable is the skill structure of firms' employees, assumed to reflect "educational capital." In table 4, the explanatory variables are the same as in the previous regression, except that they have been expressed in relation to firms' fixed assets. Furthermore, all variables are in logarithms, and linear as well as nonlinear estimation techniques have been applied. As can be seen from table 4, significance increases substantially, and the explained residual variation is surprisingly high for a micro(firm)-based model.

The third method was to search the data for a better configuration of soft capital. The a priori hypothesis was that if an unweighted average turned out to be significant there should exist a weighted average that represented the relative contributions better, a more exact hypothesis to be tested on new data. We thus added R&D and marketing capital as a proxy for innovative product quality performance and tried different assumed weights on this aggregate and the sum of educational and software capital that minimized residual variance with no restrictions on K and L. We then did the same for R&D and software capital against educational and marketing capital. The first "manipulation" is the theoretically most reasonable one and also turned out to have the lowest unexplained variation when the two soft capital measures were assigned elasticities of 1 percent each.

9. Economic Interpretations

We have hypothesized that economic growth is the result of the allocation of human-embodied tacit competencies between firms in markets and within firms' administrative systems. This allocation of dominant human-embodied competencies endogenizes the driving forces behind economic growth, and is largely intermediated in labor and financial markets. We argued that aggregate firm data would reflect that process at a superficial level as if they were generated by a firm's aggregate production function, exhibiting constant returns to scale in physical capital and labor, and holding human-embodied knowledge constant, but increasing returns in human-embodied knowledge (Eliasson 1989). Our firm data did not reject that hypothesis. We can thus keep both our main organizational learning (competence allocation) hypothesis of growth and a proximate, neoclassical, new growth production function. The new growth theory version we reject, however, on a priori grounds as a biased special case of our model and, in fact, no growth theory but a statistical way of measuring the observed components of growth (Eliasson 1992). More important, however, is that, if labor and financial markets are instrumental in allocating scarce industrial competence capital, then ill-conceived manipulation of these markets by policymakers can significantly lower macroeconomic performance. Examples of such negative influences on competence capital allocation would be the attempts, common in European welfare economics, to reallocate the control of financial resource flows away from private capitalists to government investment accounts.

NOTES

We are very grateful to Erik Mellander for valuable comments on an earlier version of this essay.

1. Already Knight (1921) objected to the idea that increasing returns to scale were external in all respects to firms.

2. For a survey of the role of intangibles in firm performance, see Braunerhjelm (1994).

3. The data are based on estimates coming directly from the firms, that is, those who should be best at evaluating these values. Each value has been thoroughly checked in interviews with each of the 137 firms. The request was formulated in the following way: "Please quantify the firms' accumulated assets in R&D, marketing, software, and education, either by giving the value directly in Swedish kronor or as percentage of fixed assets. Values should be calculated as accumulated investments in each category, after depreciation and in repurchase prices" (Braunerhjelm 1992).

4. For a survey of these problems, see the study by the U.S. Department of Labor (1989).

REFERENCES

Albrecht, James W., et al. 1992. *MOSES Database.* Research Reports, no. 40. Stockholm: IUI.

Arrow, Kenneth J. 1962. "The Economic Implications of Learning by Doing." *Review of Economic Studies* 29, no. 3: 155–73.

Bergholm, Fredrik, and Lars Jagrén. 1985. "De utlandsinvesterande företagen—en empirisk studie" [Firms investing abroad: An empirical study]. In Eliasson et al. 1985.

Braunerhjelm, Pontus. 1992. "Competence, Capacity, and Capital: A Description of a Complementary IUI Firm Survey of Small and Large Firms and of Subcontractors." In Albrecht et al. 1992.

――――. 1994. *Regional Integration and the Location of Multinational Corporations: Implications for Comparative Advantage and Welfare between Insiders and Outsiders.* Ph.D. diss., IUI.

Carlsson, Bo, ed. 1997. *Technological Systems: Cases, Analyses, Comparisons.* Boston, Dordrecht, and London: Kluwer Academic.

Eliasson, Gunnar. 1976. *Business Economic Planning: Theory, Practice, and Comparison.* London: Wiley.

――――. 1985. *Hur styrs företagen* [How are large firms run?]. Stockholm: IUI.

――――. 1986. *Kunskad, Information och Tjanster* [Knowledge, information and services]. Stockholm: IUI.

――――. 1989. "The Dynamics of Supply and Economic Growth: How Industrial Knowledge Accumulation Drives a Path-Dependent Economic Process." In *Industrial Dynamics: Technological, Organizational, and Structural Changes in Industries and Firms,* edited by B. Carlsson. Boston, Dordrecht, and London: Kluwer Academic.

――――. 1990a. "The Firm as a Component Team." *Journal of Economic Behavior and Organization* 13, no. 3: 275–98.

――――. 1990b. "The Knowledge-Based Information Economy." In *The Knowledge Based Information Economy,* edited by G. Eliasson et al. Stockholm: IUI.

――――. 1991. "Financial Institutions in a European Market for Executive Competence." In *Financial Regulation and Monetary Arrangements after 1992,* edited by C. Wihlborg, M. Fratianni, and T. D. Willet. Amsterdam: Elsevier.

――――. 1992a. "Business Competence, Organizational Learning, and Economic Growth: Establishing the Smith-Schumpeter-Wicksell Connection." In *Entrepreneurship, Technological Innovation, and Economic Growth: Studies in the Schumpeterian Tradition,* edited by F. M. Scherer and M. Perlman. Ann Arbor: University of Michigan Press.

――――. 1992b. "The MOSES MODEL: Database and Applications." In Albrecht et al. 1992.

――――. 1996. *Firm Objectives, Controls, and Organization: The Use of Information and the Transfer of Knowledge within the Firm.* Boston, Dordrecht, and London: Kluwer Academic.

――――. 1997. "General Purpose Technologies, Industrial Competence Blocs, and Economic Growth." In Carlsson 1997.

Eliasson, Gunnar, et al. 1985. *De svenska storföretagen—en studie av internationaliseringens konsekvenser för den svenska ekonomin* [The giant Swedish groups: a study of the consequences of internationalization for the Swedish economy]. Stockholm: IUI.

Griliches, Zwi. 1973. "Research Expenditure and Growth Accounting." In *Science and Technology in Economic Growth,* edited by B. Williams. New York: Wiley.

――――. 1979. "Issues in Assessing the Contribution of Research and Development to Productivity Growth." *Bell Journal of Economics* 10:92–116.

Griliches, Zwi, and F. Lichtenberg. 1984. "R&D and Productivity and the Industry Level: Is There Still a Relationship?" In *R&D, Patents, and Productivity,* edited by Z. Griliches. Chicago: University of Chicago Press.

Haessel, W. 1978. "Measuring Goodness of Fit in Linear and Non-Linear Models." *Southern Economic Journal* 44:648–52.

Hayek, J. 1945. "The Use of Knowledge in Society." *American Economic Review* 35:520–30.

Jorgenson, Dale W., and Zwi Griliches. 1967. "The Explanation of Productivity Change." *Review of Economic Studies* 34, no. 3: 249–82.

Knight, Frank. 1921. *Risk, Uncertainty, and Profit.* Boston: Houghton Mifflin.

———. 1944. "Diminishing Returns from Investment." *Journal of Political Economy* 52 (Mar.):26–47.

Lundberg, E. 1961. *Produktivitet och räntabilitet.* Stockholm: Studieförbundet Näringsliv och Samhälle.

McKenzie, L. W. 1959. "On the Existence of General Equilibrium for a Competitive Market." *Econometrica* 27, no. 1: 30–53.

Nadiri, I. 1978. "A Dynamic Model of Research and Development Expenditure." In *The Importance of Technology and the Permanence of Structure in Industrial Growth,* edited by B. Carlsson, G. Eliasson, and I. Nadiri. Conference Reports, 1978, no. 2. Stockholm: IUI.

Pakes, A., and M. Schankerman. 1984. "The Rate of Obsolescence of Patents, Research Gestation Lags, and the Private Rate of Return to Research Resources." In *Patents and Productivity,* edited by Z. Griliches. Chicago: University of Chicago Press.

Pelikan, Pavel. 1989. "Evolution, Economic Competence, and the Market for Corporate Control." *Journal of Economic Behavior and Organization* 12, no. 3: 279–303.

Ravenscraft, D. 1983. "Structure-Profit Relationship at the Line of Business and Industry Level." *Review of Economics and Statistics* 65:22–31.

Ravenscraft, D., and F. Scherer. 1982. "The Lag Structure of Returns to Research and Development." *Applied Economics* 14, no. 6 (Dec.): 603–20.

Romer, P. M. 1986. "Increasing Returns and Long-Run Growth." *Journal of Political Economy* 94, no. 5: 1002–37.

Solow, R. M. 1957. "Technical Change and the Aggregate Production Function." *Review of Economics and Statistics* 39, no. 3: 312–20.

———. 1959. "Investment and Technical Progress." In *Mathematical Methods in the Social Sciences,* edited by K. Arrow, S. Karlin, and P. Suppes. Stanford: Stanford University Press.

Terleckyj, N. 1982. "R&D and US Industrial Productivity in the 1970's." In *The Transfer and Utilization of Technical Knowledge,* edited by D. Sahel. Lexington: Lexington Books.

U.S. Department of Labor. 1989. "The Impact of Research and Development on Productivity Growth." Bureau of Labor Statistics, Bulletin 2001. Washington, DC.

von Weizsäcker, C. 1986. "Rights and Relations in Modern Economic Theory." In *The Markets for Innovation, Ownership, and Control,* edited by R. H. Day, G. Eliasson, and C. Wihlborg. Stockholm and Amsterdam: IUI and North-Holland.

Westerman, J. 1768. *Om Svenska Näringarnes Undervigt emot de Utländske, förmedelst en trögare Arbets-drift* [On the inferiority of the Swedish compared to foreign manufacturers because of a slower work organization]. Stockholm: Lars Salvius.

PART 5

Bringing the Pieces Together
Do We Need a New Theory?

New Microfoundations for the Theory of Economic Growth?

Robert W. Clower

A theory is a cluster of conclusions in search of a
premise
        —N. R. Hanson, Patterns of Discovery

In honor of our intellectual founder, I start with a sentence from the concluding paragraph of Joseph Schumpeter's (1954) *Economic Doctrine and Method:* "[B]ecause an economist rarely has other assenting economists for his public . . . everybody has to fight for his position [by furnishing] his contribution with a long polemical introduction." In keeping with Schumpeter's dictum, I propose to furnish requisite polemics—but in the body of the essay rather than the introduction.

When I was first asked to talk about the foundations of growth theory, I knew nothing about my probable audience nor other speakers; now that I am better informed, I recognize that I'm not among fanatic fabricators of rigorous rubbish—that is to say, among devotees of Arrow-Debreu-style theory—but have to deal instead with people, most of whom are *real* economists. In my present remarks, therefore, I focus not on formalistic ritual but on common sense growth theory.

My designated topic is "The Microeconomic Foundations of Economic Growth: The Need for New Theory?" so my talk is just an introduction to the subsequent panel discussion of "How Should We Theorize about This?" Let me start by stating candidly my impression that the present literature of growth theory contains nothing sufficiently coherent to be called "foundations," unless one can regard a particular *style* of theorizing as relevant. The closest approach to a style of theory that could be considered a foundation for growth theory is the body of doctrine sometimes referred to as "neoclassical," which is more accurately called "neo-Walrasian" because its adherents believe themselves (rightly or wrongly) to be continuing a tradition of mathematical economics inaugurated by Walras.

The essential feature of neo-Walrasian theory is its obsession with "fully articulated model economies," "rational" behavior, and rigor to the exclusion of historical, institutional, and even mathematical considerations (e.g., nonconvexities) that might complicate the statement of tractable formal models (see Montgomery 1993). Most early modern growth theories—even Harrod's 1939 "Essay in Dynamic Theory"—were of this ilk,[1] but the *locus classicus* of stylish theory is the axiomatically based analysis of Arrow and Debreu (1954) and Debreu (1959) that serves as a standard of "good theory" in all modern teaching, not only in microeconomics but in macroeconomics, growth theory, money and banking, finance, and econometrics—in short, the style of theory that fills contemporary textbooks and dominates contemporary journals.

Now, there is no reason to sneer at standard microtheory as a potential foundation for restarting the engines of modern growth theory; after all, the only unquestioned classic of existing growth theory is Adam Smith's *Wealth of Nations*—not stylish by modern standards but superb microtheory all the same. Judging from recent work (see, particularly, Romer's review [1994] of theories of endogenous growth), growth theory could benefit from extension in a variety of directions that would bring it into closer relation to formal theorizing in standard (modern) microtheory. I have no doubt this would be fruitful *if it could be shown that standard microtheory offered useful insights*—as Smith's classic treatment surely did—into the organization, adaptation, and development of real world economies. To claim that standard microtheory offers any such insights, however, would be to assert a most doubtful proposition.

An acceptable microeconomic theory should provide a foundation for all economic inquiry. To date, however, modern microtheorists have never seriously addressed, much less resolved, the question a persuasive answer to which is a required ingredient of good theory: how are the activities of the millions of independent transactors in market economies coordinated? It is correct, of course, to assert that coordination is performed by an "invisible hand" or "the price system" (Coase 1937, 387–89), correct, to be sure, but just as surely inane, because such a response is no better than an appeal to Jupiter or Providence (Ahmed 1990, 144). An intellectually respectable answer should consist of something more than tired clichés; observable economic events derive ultimately not from unspecified coordinating mechanisms, whether invisible hands, price systems, or neo-Walrasian "auctioneers," but, as James Tobin has argued, from definable actions of real people (1980, 796). What we economists have yet to explain is the working of the *fingers* of the invisible hand (on this, see Clower 1994 and Clower and Howitt 1996). Until we do so, we will do well to look elsewhere for new foundations of growth theory.

With respect to the unresolved coordination problem, it seems that the *style* considered essential for "good theory" is not compatible with statement of a theory that is compatible with "good sense." Let me elaborate. It is widely believed that a great achievement of post-Marshallian (neo-Walrasian) economics was the "discovery" of exact conditions under which perfect coordination of individual economic activities will be achieved automatically (Samuelson 1972 469–703). The truth is different. The neo-Walrasian version of general equilibrium theory provides a mathematically rigorous statement of conditions under which a competitive equilibrium "exists,"[2] but the statement is interpretable only for a hypothetical world where coordination uses no resources, where no agent ever imagines that a failure of coordination might prevent trading plans from being completed, and where institutions such as business firms and markets through which agents routinely interact in real world economies are not just absent but otiose. In any case, neo-Walrasian theory makes no mention of any mechanism or agent that undertakes the task of coordination.[3] The closest it comes is in the theory of *"tâtonnement,"* where it is postulated that prices adjust to eliminate discrepancies between demand and supply. But if we ask, Who changes prices? Who pays whom, and with what? Who matches buyers with sellers? Who pays the costs of arranging and executing transactions? Who goes long or short when demands don't match supplies? and What incentives motivate any agent to perform coordinating tasks? then the theory is silent.

How might we resolve these and similar questions? Einstein wrote (1950, 98):

> Science is the attempt to make the chaotic diversity of our sense-experience correspond to a logically uniform system of thought. . . . The sense experiences are the given subject matter, but the theory that shall interpret them is man-made. It is the result of an extremely laborious process of adaptation: hypothetical, never completely final, always subject to question and doubt.

Of course, Einstein's reference is to physics and astronomy; but, from a nonnormative point of view, economics is just social astronomy. Its aim, one would hope, is to enhance understanding of the economic universe. If we are ever to be taken seriously as practitioners (Keynes 1936, 33), we would be well advised to proceed with this task as practitioners of other inductive sciences have proceeded—by studying the world around us in a serious effort to lend intellectual order to whatever "chaos" strikes our eyes at first sight.

What information is appropriate as empirical background for economic theory, supposing we wish to portray salient aspects of real world economic behavior during, say, the past three centuries? More shortly, what are we to regard as relevant stylized facts? I propose the following (Clower 1977, 206–7).

    1. Trading occurs in decentralized, geographically disconnected, privately owned and operated retail, wholesale, and auction markets. Centralized direction occurs only as an incidental aspect of law enforcement.

    2. In virtually all exchanges, sellers routinely insist on receiving cash or its equivalent for every sale: all market economies are "monetary."

3. No transactor has direct knowledge about the state of the economy at any point in time, about the supposed laws that govern its behavior, or about the trading plans of any other transactor: what is known must first be learned.

4. All market economies have evolved without central direction, through self-organization (Kauffman 1993). Markets are created and operated as income-earning institutions (firms) by self-interested individuals, who, in exchange for implicit or explicit fees, provide physical facilities (location, office equipment, transport, telephones, and other communications devices) that make trading a routine aspect of everyday life.

5. Prices "asked," "bid," and "realized" are "made" by agents, not by ineffable "market forces" (Osborne 1970, 1:76–83).

6. Transactors are able routinely to execute pairwise (commodity for "money") trades at such times, and in such size lots, as they desire, generally without previous communication with any market maker.

7. Because the probability is zero that sales of any commodity will equal purchases over any specified time interval, as a practical matter actual markets may be regarded always as "nonclearing."

How does the preceding sketch compare with the conception of economic life implicit in neo-Walrasian theory? To save time, let me state the situation baldly. In neo-Walrasian theory:

1. Although demands, supplies, and excess demands are well defined, there are no markets.

2. There is no communication between prospective trading agents. Prospective trades are signaled only to a central "demon."

3. Agents generate no observable data. "Trading plans" are stored, as it were, in the random access memory of a mediating "demon."

4. There are no endogenous institutions. All behavioral logistics are imposed from outside the theory (contrived by theorists).

5. No agent announces bid or asked prices. Rates of exchange are proposed and changed only by a demon mediator.

6. There is no competition among agents because agents never interact directly.

7. No agent voluntarily holds inventories or buffer stocks.

8. There is no money or other medium of exchange (Coase 1937, 28).

9. There is no trading. The theory does not define much less deal with commodity transfers from one agent to another (Starr 1971, 49).

This list should be sufficient to condemn neo-Walrasian theory as material for anything but a future episode of "Star Wars." But the list is merely indicative of deeper inadequacies deriving from the fact that the theory does not deal with real-time processes; it is concerned exclusively with hypothetical mental states (Walras called them "trading dispositions") of "agents" whose "actions" are described in terms of concepts (e.g., production, consumption, and choice) that strongly, but misleadingly, suggest observability. Because "actions" in neo-Walrasian theory refer to "plans" (Debreu 1959, 37–38, 43) that are purely mental or metaphysical, the implications of so-called actions could be confronted "empirically" only by a demonic being (e.g., the neo-Walrasian "auctioneer") capable of collecting data by reading minds and performing other feats that would put even most mythical wizards to shame.

The scientific vacuousness of neo-Walrasian theory appears to be recognized by few of its leading practitioners. How else can we account for Frank Hahn's assertion, in connection with the postulated "existence" of a large number of "contingent futures markets," that we have here "an empirical confrontation since we know that these markets are in fact very scarce" (1973, 15). Arrow-Debreu theory deals with an indefinitely great number of "commodities" and excess demand functions, but it does not define much less deal with anything that remotely resembles a market in the ordinary sense of that word (but compare Debreu 1959, 76, 80); how, then, can the scarcity of actual spot or futures markets be brought into empirical confrontation with neo-Walrasian theory? A more remarkable example of similar confusion is Koopmans's discussion (1957, 62–63) of "Survival of Consumers in a Competitive Equilibrium"! Finally, in the same vein, a distinguished colleague, referring obliquely to the "stylized facts" 1 through 7, above, wrote in a recent letter;

> [Y]ou know as well as I do that all the Walrasians are perfectly aware of the basic facts about organized markets. . . . I presume that they must be taking it for granted that, with enough competition, the general-equilibrium model will give broad steady-state results that approximate [the basic facts]. They have not proved that, but neither have you disproved it.

Apart from the fatuousness of the phrase "with enough competition," this passage reflects not only an apparent unawareness of the vacuousness of neo-Walrasian analysis but an unawareness also of the impossibility of proof or disproof of any assertion about real-time processes (Hanson 1969, 270).

It should be obvious from all this that neo-Walrasian theory offers nothing of either style or substance that could prove useful in growth theory. Those who know my other writings will recognize that, despite long-harbored doubts about the merit of standard microtheory, I have for the most part adhered to a neo-Walrasian style of analysis throughout my 50 years of professional life (the exceptional case sets the stage for the next section of this essay). So my objection to neo-Walrasian analysis derives not from its failure to capitalize on the easy opportunities for publication inherent in the faddish formalism of neo-Walrasian theory or even from its lack of "realism" (whatever that might mean); my objection derives entirely from its scientific vacuousness. I object to neo-Walrasian theory for the same kind of reasons that led Galileo and Newton to disown Aristotelian physics: because it effectively precludes coherent analysis of observable events.[4]

If we eschew conventional approaches to growth theory, what remains? The answer seems plain. We do as applied economists have always done: apply common sense rather than standard theory to the study of available facts. As Will Rogers once remarked in a similar context: "Our problems come not from the things we don't know, but from the things we know that *just ain't so!*" Personally, I believe common sense applied to known facts can carry us further in the study of economic growth than is commonly supposed. By "common sense," however, I mean not what is commonly referred to as "informed intuition" or "casual empirical knowledge"; on the contrary, I mean the species of inspired data inspection (Hanson 1958, 72–85) that led Kepler to state his laws of motion and induced Milton Friedman to enunciate his "permanent income" theory of consumption (1957b).

On a past occasion, when I used such data extensively, I developed a paper (Clower and Johnson 1968), which, for the first time in more than 20 years of professional work, persuaded me that fact-based theory could elicit genuinely new insights—knowledge not previously used to formulate the theory. It was my first experience with the "Eureka" phenomenon that must have been common among leading mathematical physicists (notably Rutherford, Poincaré, Planck, and Einstein) around the turn of the Twentieth Century.[5] That paper, incidentally, cost me six years of intense effort during which time I was unable to concentrate on any other project. Fact-based theory (unlike data-mining econometrics) is not conducive to frequent or easy publication. My pleasure and relief at concluding that six-year effort must have made the gods angry, because the published paper attracted little professional attention. I was particularly disappointed that it failed to elicit a note from Milton Friedman, whose permanent income theory of consumption was shown in it to be a special case of the Clower and Johnson model.

Because even now I recall feeling that while working on that paper my mind was controlled by ineffable "forces" over which I had little personal control, I can with genuine modesty assert that the economics profession suffered a severe loss as a result of its untimely neglect of that seminal contribution![6] All the same, I do not propose to carry that work further today. First, despite the passage of some 30 years, no person or institution has so far attempted a systematic sample survey of consolidated income, expenditure, and balance sheet accounts that provided the data for my work in the 1960s.[7] Second, it now seems more purposeful to present a heuristic account of the anatomy of growth theory as a prolegomena to a systematic statement on some future occasion of a microstochastic model of growth along lines adumbrated in my 1968 paper (see also Johnson 1971, 121–32).

Let me first outline an idealized description of the technical and institutional framework of economic growth—a description sufficiently devoid of empirical content to apply to almost any society yet sufficiently "realistic" to help us think more clearly about some central issues in growth theory. Imagine a world with just two generic commodities: "goods," such as food, clothing, automobiles, roads, raw materials, and buildings that can be either consumed to meet immediate human needs and desires or used to facilitate future production; and "labor services" (skilled, unskilled, administrative, and managerial) available for organizing and carrying out production, distribution, and exchange activities. To assign unambiguous measures to quantities of these two "commodities," we must in strict logic suppose that the proportional composition of each is fixed. Whether or not this condition is exactly satisfied, however, we may think of the annual (per capita) output of goods of any society as a function of its accumulated stock of unconsumed goods, its current labor force, and its present technology. This relation may be represented graphically by a curve such as YY' in figure 1, which I shall refer to henceforth as the *wealth-income locus*. The intercept of the wealth-income locus with the vertical axis represents the annual per capita flow of output that can be achieved by labor without depleting previously accumulated capital goods. The curve is shown sloping upward from left to right to reflect the conjecture that larger per capita rates of (net) output (Y) are obtainable the greater is the quantity of accumulated wealth (W) available for current use. The slope of the wealth-income locus at any point thus represents the marginal rate of return on wealth, the real rate of interest, so to speak, on previously accumulated capital.

The form and position of the wealth-income locus will depend on the

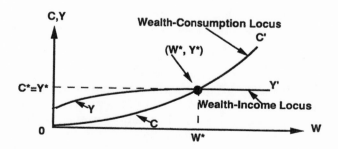

Fig. 1. Wealth-income and wealth consumption loci

technology of the society, the term *technology* being interpreted in the broadest possible sense to include the skill and energy of the labor force, the intelligence and ingenuity of managers, and the flexibility of social and legal arrangements, as well as the state of engineering knowledge in a narrow sense.[8] The wealth-income locus effectively summarizes a list of *environmental obstacles* to economic progress, obstacles that can and might be altered gradually with the passage of time but only by measures that fundamentally alter existing technical and institutional arrangements.

Granted that every society confronts a wealth-income locus; economic well-being can be increased in the short run only by abstaining from current consumption, thereby increasing the quantity of productive wealth available to facilitate future production. At this point, we have to consider "obstacles to growth" of quite another kind: *volitional* (behavioral) *obstacles*. In practice, the distinction between environmental and volitional obstacles will almost certainly be one of degree rather than kind because many of the social constraints that affect the form and position of the wealth-income locus will also influence individual attitudes toward the accumulation of wealth. For our present purposes, however, it is useful to think of a society as exhibiting a certain propensity to consume current wealth, a propensity that is largely independent of its current resources, technology, and level of output. We may express this graphically by supposing that there exists a functional relation between current (per capita) consumption and current (per capita) wealth, as illustrated by the *wealth-consumption locus*, CC′ in figure 1. The wealth-consumption locus may be described in more operational terms by saying that it indicates for alternative levels of per capita wealth what the level of per capita income must be in order for the society to be willing to consume no more than its net output and so maintain its existing stock of capital intact. According to this conception, a "thrifty" society, whether rich or poor, is characterized by a relatively flat wealth-consumption locus—a relatively low marginal propensity to consume wealth. Correspondingly, a "prodigal" society is characterized by a relatively steep wealth-consumption locus, indicating that small increases in current wealth tend to generate proportionately larger increases in per capita rates of consumption.

The point of intersection of the wealth-income locus with the wealth-consumption locus (W*,Y*) in figure 1 defines a stationary state—a level of wealth such that per capita income is just equal to per capita consumption, hence a situation in which existing wealth is neither rising nor falling over time. Provided the slope of the wealth-consumption locus is everywhere greater than the slope for the income locus, it is apparent that the economy will tend over time to approach such a stationary state, regardless of the initial level of its accumulated wealth. For, if wealth is initially below the stationary level, income will exceed consumption, saving will be positive, and wealth will rise more rapidly than income; hence, saving will gradually

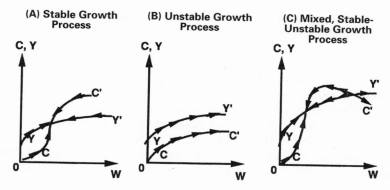

**Fig. 2. Stable, unstable, and mixed stable-unstable growth pro-
cesses. (A) Stable growth process, (B) unstable growth process,
(C) mixed, stable-unstable growth process.**

converge to zero (i.e., wealth will eventually cease to grow). A similar
analysis applies to the contrary situation in which the initial level of wealth is
such that consumption exceeds income. Provided the slope of the wealth-
consumption locus is greater than the slope of the wealth-income locus,
consumption will fall more rapidly than income as wealth is depleted, and so
a point will eventually be reached at which dissaving is zero (i.e., wealth will
cease to decline).

As indicated by the alternative possibilities illustrated in figure 2,
capital accumulation may be a permanent phenomenon even with given
wealth-income and wealth-consumption loci. This will be true if the slope
of the wealth-consumption locus is less than the slope of the wealth-income
locus in the neighborhood of a stationary level of wealth, as is illustrated in
figures 2b and 2c. Except as theoretical curiosities, however, these two and
similar possibilities are of little interest. Studies of household spending and
saving indicate that the behavior of the vast majority of households, even in
advanced societies, conforms to the pattern illustrated in figure 2a: that is
to say, most families tend, with the passage of time, to consume virtually
the whole of any *given* level of income. Saving thus appears as a *transitory*
rather than *permanent* phenomenon, a consequence of autonomous change
in realized income (or in household attitudes toward consumption) rather
than a result of purposive efforts to save and accumulate wealth (cf. Clower
1928, 274).

In every society, to be sure, there exist some individuals, misers and
others, who tend to save and accumulate wealth regardless of income level.
By and large, however, household saving and dissaving appear to represent
merely a lagged adjustment of consumption to changes in real income and
wealth. When income rises, wealth, and thus consumption, also tend to rise
but not so rapidly as income. When income is increasing, therefore, saving

will tend to be positive and wealth will increase over time. Conversely, when income falls, consumption will also tend to fall but not so rapidly as income. When income is declining, therefore, saving will tend to be negative and wealth will decrease over time. Accordingly, if we wish to account for the rapid growth of productive capital that has characterized advanced societies during the past century or two, we must look not to misers and other lovers of wealth but rather to impersonal economic forces of invention and innovation and to institutional and policy considerations that have acted to produce autonomous increases in real per capita income.

The assertion that the forces generating income growth are impersonal is subject to certain qualifications. Invention and innovation would be of little practical consequence were it not for the existence in some societies of a substantial number of entrepreneurs—individuals whose marginal propensity to consume wealth is so weak that relatively small increases in income induce them to add relatively large increments to previously accumulated wealth. Such individuals are important, not so much because of their direct effect on current levels of production—though this may be considerable in some cases—but rather because their improvements in technology typically are embodied in newly produced capital goods. If increases in real income generated little or no saving (as would be the case if wealth-consumption loci were relatively steep), there would be little scope for the introduction of new technology. Human beings no doubt are capable of improved productive performance through education and training, but improvements of that kind would be of little importance were they not accompanied by simultaneous increases in the efficiency of nonhuman factors of production.

To suggest that the connection between capital accumulation and technological progress is either straightforward or clearly understood would be misleading. The truth is that we know very little about causal interrelations between entrepreneurial saving and related processes of invention and innovation. What does seem clear, however, is that significant technological advances are possible only in societies in which increases in current income tend to produce relatively large increases in holdings of productive wealth. One can imagine a society of misers in which the accumulation of wealth has little if any impact on technology, but it is difficult to conceive of a society in which significant technological advances occur even though all households tend to consume the whole of such increases in wealth as occur. To put the point more directly, *the existence of a substantial group of households whose marginal propensities to consume wealth are low relative to prevailing rates of return on wealth appears to be a necessary if not a sufficient condition for sustained economic growth.*

My discussion of the anatomy of growth contains three main links. The first link connects capital accumulation with autonomous changes in real income. The second connects innovation with capital accumulation. The third connects real income growth with innovation. The three links together form a closed chain that is capable of explaining how development, once initiated, may be sustained. If we try to assign priorities to the various links, we run into trouble because no one link is in any sense more fundamental than another. Supposing, however, that certain entrepreneurial individuals initiate a development process in a certain area, there is little mystery about the conditions that must exist if the process is to gather momentum. The initiation of development will tend to increase the real incomes not only of innovating entrepreneurs but also of their employees, suppliers, and customers. These induced increases in real income will bear fruit in further development only if they accrue in important measure to individuals who themselves have entrepreneurial leanings—that is to say, to individuals whose marginal propensity to consume wealth is relatively low. This is likely to be true only if the initial development process serves to attract to the area in which it occurs a substantial number of people who are dedicated to improving not only their income but their wealth position.

We know historically that such attractive forces have operated; the effects are discernible in the high degree of geographical concentration of industry and wealth that characterizes advanced economies. A common-sense explanation of this phenomenon is provided by noting that it is typically easier to obtain the initial wherewithal to establish one's own enterprise in an already developed and developing area (where real incomes are relatively high and rising) than to perform the same feat in a backward and underdeveloped area (where real incomes are relatively low and stagnant). In effect, the superior income prospects associated with developed areas serve to strengthen the first link in the development chain—the link connecting capital accumulation with real income growth. The concentration of development activities in particular areas then follows almost as a matter of course.

Concluding Observations

The central thesis of the preceding discussion is that economic progress in advanced and backward economies is a function not so much of its resources and technology as its "willingness" to abstain from consuming increases in productive wealth. I can think of no way to test this contention directly (cf. Olson 1996, 5–7). As mentioned earlier, consolidated data on wealth, income and expenditure[9] are not available for advanced much less for backward economies. Under these circumstances, it would be pure presumption to say that the preceding discussion does more than phrase the problems of economic development in a fresh manner, but that is perhaps enough for it to merit consideration.

Possibly the greatest puzzle of growth economics is the apparent inability of presently underdeveloped countries effectively to exploit known techniques for increasing output from existing resources. Unlike advanced countries whose further economic progress depends on the discovery of new techniques, underdeveloped countries have only to apply existing knowledge to achieve vast increases in agricultural and manufacturing output. Granted that no underdeveloped country can hope to do as well as an already developed country, even if it somehow managed to introduce all *feasible* technical improvements, the fact remains that no underdeveloped country has so far exploited even a minor fraction of such possibilities, despite substantial technical and material assistance from the developed nations of the world. If my discussion of growth processes makes sense, the puzzle is solved by supposing that virtually all households in underdeveloped countries tend quickly to consume rather than hold increments in wealth. This would account for the poor showing of technical assistance programs. To be effective, such programs must not only raise output from existing resources but also be accompanied by sustained increases in holdings of productive wealth. But the latter condition cannot be satisfied in a society in which households tend to consume virtually the whole of any increment in wealth produced by rises in income—unless households are not left to themselves but instead are forced by government action to save and accumulate as productive wealth a significant portion of increases in output.

Another problem that has bemused development economists is the failure of indigenous entrepreneurial talent to emerge and successfully exploit development opportunities that expatriate firms would gladly seize upon if they were permitted to do so. The usual explanation of this phenomenon runs in terms of the inexperience, lack of education, scarcity of funds, or administrative shortcomings of indigenous businessmen. It seems never to have been noted—except by Karl Marx—that an essential characteristic of the successful entrepreneur is a passion to accumulate income-producing wealth. Vast numbers of people in advanced countries have the education, know-how, organizing talent, and so on to function brilliantly as managers of large enterprises. But few such persons have sufficient itch for wealth to undertake the short-run sacrifices of consumption that are necessary to establish and develop their own businesses. Academics and other professional men are classic examples; possessing the talent but lacking the will to accumulate and hold wealth, most of them will be found in the ranks of the moderately comfortable, few of them in the ranks of the rich. Entrepreneurs are known as managers of assets; professors are noted more for managing debts. The lack among underdeveloped countries of "educated" people is no doubt regrettable, but I doubt this contributes to the lack of entrepreneurs.

A study of income distributions within and across nations would show, I believe, that the distribution within any advanced society is similar to the distribution among countries. The sad truth is that most individuals in every society—and so also most societies—are better at dissipating than acquiring or maintaining income-earning assets. We often hear of "self-made" men, by which we ordinarily mean men of considerable means. In a very real sense, however, men of little means are also self-made, for few individuals—and fewer societies—are compelled by nature or external circumstances to be as poor as they actually are! Economic growth and development, for nations as for individuals, seem to be a matter more of temperament than of resource endowment or technical skill. If that is the case, then presently underdeveloped countries (including Eastern European nations) have little hope of improving their lot through external assistance, material or otherwise. Development assistance from outsiders can never be significant relative to resources available domestically. Neither can anything useful be expected to come from indigenous efforts to improve communications for cities, educate citizens, eliminate disease, and generally enhance economic and social environments. Where increased consumption is the primary goal of the great bulk of people, economic development is simply not attainable by means that merely increase income. What is required are programs that aim at increased abstinence—programs that diminish the marginal propensity to consume wealth through induced effects of capital formation and, more importantly, set the stage for rapid and sustained improvements in technology. The difficulty is that we have no idea how to promote abstinence, no reliable knowledge that might help us design programs to promote frugality.

NOTES

1. For a fairly complete collection, see Stiglitz and Uzawa (1969).

2. To show that a competitive equilibrium "exists" does not show that such an equilibrium can be calculated. We know from the fundamental theorem of algebra that every algebraic equation has solutions in the field of complex numbers; but the theorem does not tell us how solutions known to exist may be located. So, in the final analysis, the "important" achievements of neo-Walrasian theory lose much of their apparent luster, which should in any case adhere to the mathematical geniuses Gauss and Brouwer, whose work underlies all "economic" existence proofs. I do not in any way mean to denigrate the intellectual excellence of neo-Walrasian proofs of competitive equilibrium; I intend only to suggest that such work is better categorized as set-theoretic logic than economics.

3. For an extensive critical discussion of this and related issues by a doctoral student working under the supervision of Kenneth Arrow in the late 1960s, see Starr (1971, 3).

4. The difficulty, as described by Born (1962, 226) in his explanation of Einstein's theory of relativity, is that when one becomes habituated to conventional habits of thought (e.g., to the idea that the earth is the center of the physical

universe or the idea that absolute space and time are inherent features of "reality"), supposedly "true" theoretical results become problematic" due to a confusion of habits of thought with logical consistency, a tendency we all recognize to be an obstacle to progress."

5. I have in mind the excitement many persons must have experienced when, by adopting new perspectives, physicists were able to make sense of facts that had puzzled H. Poincaré in the 1890s (described in his account [1913, 303–12] of "The Present Crisis in Mathematical Physics").

6. Apologies to Walras, who said something similar about his earlier (neglected) work in the preface to the definitive (1900) edition of his *Éléments*.

7. I refer especially to Goldsmith (1956), Lydall and Lansing (1959), Friend (1957), Klein and Liviatan (1957), Fisher (1957), and Friedman (1957a).

8. On this and related issues, see Mancur Olson's inspired lecture (1996) concerning "why some nations are rich, and others poor."

9. The Panel Study of Income Dynamics data used by Hurst, et al. (1996) and other researchers at the University of Michigan are useful for limited purposes. But, because they are do not involve consolidated income, expenditure, *and* wealth accounts, they are worthless for studying household development processes.

REFERENCES

Ahmed, Syed. 1990. "Adam Smith's Four Invisible Hands." *History of Political Economy* 22, no. 1 (Spring): 137–44.

Arrow, Kenneth J., and Gerard Debreu. 1954. "Existence of an Equilibrium for a Competitive Economy." *Econometrica* 22 (July): 265–90.

Born, Max. 1962. *Einstein's Theory of Relativity.* Rev. ed. New York: Dover.

Clower, F. W. 1928. "Note on Supply Curve for Capital." *American Economic Review* 18, no. 2: 272–74.

Clower, Robert W. 1977. "The Anatomy of Monetary Theory." *American Economic Review* 67, no. 1 (Feb.): 206–12.

———. 1994. "The Fingers of the Invisible Hand." *Brock University Review* 3, no. 1: 3–13.

Clower, Robert, and P. W. Howitt. 1996. "Taking Markets Seriously: Groundwork for a Post Walrasian Macroeconomics." In *Beyond Microfoundations,* edited by David Colander. Cambridge: Cambridge University Press.

Clower, Robert, and M. B. Johnson. 1968. "Income, Wealth, and the Theory of Consumption." In *Value, Capital, and Growth: Essays in Honour of Sir John Hicks,* edited by J. N. Wolfe. Edinburgh: Edinburgh University Press.

Coase, Ronald H. 1937. "The Nature of the Firm." *Economica* 4 (Nov.): 386–405.

Debreu, Gerard. 1959. *Theory of Value: An Axiomatic Analysis of Economic Equilibrium.* New Haven: Yale University Press.

Einstein, A. 1950. *Out of My Later Years.* New York: Philosophical Library.

Fisher, M. R. 1957. "A Reply to Critics." *Bulletin of the Oxford University Institute of Statistics* 19:179–99.

Friedman, M. 1957a. "Savings and the Balance Sheet." *Bulletin of the Oxford University Institute of Statistics* 19:125–36.

———. 1957b. *A Theory of the Consumption Function.* Princeton: Princeton University Press.

Friend, I. 1957. "Some Conditions for Progress in the Study of Savings." *Bulletin of the Oxford University Institute of Statistics* 19:165–70.

Goldsmith, R. W. 1956. *A Study of Saving in the United States.* Princeton: Princeton University Press.

Hahn, F. H. 1973. *On the Notion of Equilibrium in Economics. An Inaugural Lecture.* Cambridge: Cambridge University Press.

Hanson, Norwood R. 1958. *Patterns of Discovery.* Cambridge: Cambridge University Press.

———. 1969. *Perception and Discovery.* San Francisco: Freeman, Cooper.

Harrod, R. F. 1939. "An Essay in Dynamic Theory." *Economic Journal* 49, no. 193 (March): 14–33.

Hurst, et al. 1996. *Wealth Dynamics of American Families, 1984–1994.* Discussion Papers. Ann Arbor: University of Michigan, Department of Economics and Institute for Social Research.

Johnson, M. B. 1971. *Household Behavior.* Harmondsworth: Penguin.

Kauffman, S. A. 1993. *The Origins of Order.* New York: Oxford University Press.

Klein, L. R., and N. Liviatan. 1957. "The Significance of Income Variability on Savings Behavior." *Bulletin of the Oxford University Institute of Statistics* 19:151–60.

Koopmans, Tjalling C. 1957. *Three Essays on the State of Economic Science.* New York: McGraw-Hill.

Lydall, H. F. and J. B. Lansing. 1959. "A Comparison of the Distribution of Personal Income and Wealth in the United States and Great Britain." *American Economic Review* 49:43–67.

Montgomery, M. R. 1993. "Rethinking Rigor." Paper presented at the 1993 conference of the Southern Economic Association, New Orleans.

Olson, M. 1996. "Distinguished Lecture on Economics in Government." *Journal of Economic Perspectives* 10 (Spring): 3–24.

Osborne, M. F. M. 1970. *The Stock Market from a Physicist's Viewpoint.* Temple Hills, MD: M. F. M. Osborne.

Poincaré, H. 1913. *The Foundations of Science.* Lancaster, PA: Science Press.

Romer, P. M. 1994. "The Origins of Endogenous Growth." *Journal of Economic Perspectives* 8, no. 1: 3–22.

Samuelson, P. A. 1972. *Collected Scientific Papers.* Vol. 3. Cambridge: MIT Press.

Schumpeter, J. A. 1954. *Economic Doctrine and Method.* London: George Allen and Unwin.

Smith, Adam. 1976. *An Inquiry into the Nature and Causes of the Wealth of Nations.* Edited by R. H. Campbell and A. S. Skinner. Oxford: Clarendon.

Starr, R. 1971. "Notes on Microeconomic Monetary Theory." Ph.D. diss., Stanford University.

Stiglitz, Joseph, and Hirofumi Uzawa, eds. 1969. *Readings in the Modern Theory of Economic Growth.* Cambridge: MIT Press.

Tobin, James. 1980. "Are New Classical Models Plausible Enough to Guide Policy?" *Journal of Money, Credit, and Banking* 12, no. 4, pt. 2 (Nov.): 788–99.

Walras, Léon. 1900. *Éléments d'économie politique pure ou Theéorie de la richesse sociale.* 4th ed. Lausanne, Switzerland: F. Rouge.

Contributors

Daniele Archibugi, National Research Council of Italy, Rome, Italy.

Spyros Arvanitis, Eidgenössische Technische Hochschule (ETH Zentrum), Zurich, Switzerland.

David B. Audretsch, Wissenshaftszentrum Berlin für Socialforschung, Berlin, Germany, and Policy Research Program, Georgia State University, Atlanta, Georgia.

John R. Baldwin, Micro-Economic Studies and Analysis Division, Statistics Canada, Ottawa, Canada.

Gérard Ballot, Université Pantheon-Assas and ERMES-CNRS, Université Paris II, Paris, France.

Pontus Braunerhjelm, Industriens Utredningsinstitut (IUI), Stockholm, Sweden.

Dagobert L. Brito, Department of Economics, Rice University, Houston, Texas.

Uwe Cantner, Department of Economics, University of Augsburg, Augsburg, Germany.

Bo Carlsson, Weatherhead School of Management, Case-Western Reserve University, Cleveland, Ohio.

Robert W. Clower, Professor of Economics, University of South Carolina, Columbia, South Carolina.

Richard H. Day, Department of Economics, University of Southern California, Los Angeles, California.

Gunnar Eliasson, Royal Institute of Technology (KTH), Stockholm, Sweden.

Rinaldo Evangelista, National Research Council of Italy, Rome, Italy.

Jan Glete, Historiska Institutonen, Stockholms Universität, Stockholm, Sweden.

Christopher Green, Department of Economics, McGill University, Montreal, Quebec, Canada.

Horst Hanusch, Department of Economics, University of Augsburg, Augsburg, Germany.

Heinz Hollenstein, Eidgenössische Technische Hochschule (ETH Zentrum), Zurich, Switzerland.

Michael D. Intriligator, Department of Economics, University of California-Los Angeles (UCLA), Los Angeles, California.

George Johnson, Department of Economics, University of Michigan, Ann Arbor, Michigan.

Joanne Johnson, Micro-Economic Studies and Analysis Division, Statistics Canada, Ottawa, Canada.

Staffan Laestadius, Department of Industrial Economics and Management, Royal Institute of Technology (KTH), Stockholm, Sweden.

Richard N. Langlois, Department of Economics, University of Connecticut, Storrs, Connecticut.

Aija Leiponen, Research Institute of the Finnish Economy (ETLA), Helsinki, Finland.

Frank M. Machovec, Wofford College, Spartanburg, South Carolina.

Charles R. McCann Jr., University of Pittsburgh, Pittsburgh, Pennsylvania.

Maureen McKelvey, Department of Technology and Social Change, Linköping University, Linköping, Sweden.

Valentina Meliciani, Science Policy Unit, University of Sussex, Falmer, Brighton, United Kingdom.

Douglass C. North, Department of Economics, Washington University, St. Louis, Missouri.

Giulio Perani, National Research Council of Italy, Rome, Italy.

Andreas Pyka, Department of Economics, University of Augsburg, Augsburg, Germany.

Fabio Rapiti, National Research Council of Italy, Rome, Italy.

Roberto Simonetti, The Open University, Walton Hall, Milton Keynes, United Kingdom.

Frank Stafford, Department of Economics, University of Michigan, Ann Arbor, Michigan.

Paula E. Stephan, Policy Research Program, Georgia State University, Atlanta, Georgia.

Erol Taymaz, Department of Economics, Middle East Technical University, Ankara, Turkey.

Clas Wihlborg, School of Economics and Commercial Law, Göteborg University, Göteborg, Sweden.

Erica R. Worth, University of Texas Law School, Austin, Texas.

S. Y. Wu, Department of Economics, University of Iowa, Iowa City, Iowa.

Index